World Histories of Crime, Culture and Violence

Series Editors

Marianna Muravyeva
Faculty of Law
University of Helsinki
Helsinki, Finland

Raisa Maria Toivo
University of Tampere
Tampere, Finland

Palgrave's World Histories of Crime, Culture and Violence seeks to publish research monographs, collections of scholarly essays, multi-authored books, and Palgrave Pivots addressing themes and issues of interdisciplinary histories of crime, criminal justice, criminal policy, culture and violence globally and on a wide chronological scale (from the ancient to the modern period). It focuses on interdisciplinary studies, historically contextualized, across various cultures and spaces employing a wide range of methodologies and conceptual frameworks.

More information about this series at
http://www.springer.com/series/14383

Kerstin von Lingen
Editor

War Crimes Trials in the Wake of Decolonization and Cold War in Asia, 1945–1956

Justice in Time of Turmoil

palgrave
macmillan

Editor
Kerstin von Lingen
Heidelberg University
Heidelberg, Germany

World Histories of Crime, Culture and Violence
ISBN 978-3-319-82710-0   ISBN 978-3-319-42987-8 (eBook)
DOI 10.1007/978-3-319-42987-8

© The Editor(s) (if applicable) and The Author(s) 2016, corrected publication 2018
Softcover reprint of the hardcover 1st edition 2016
This work is subject to copyright. All rights are solely and exclusively licensed by the Publisher, whether the whole or part of the material is concerned, specifically the rights of translation, reprinting, reuse of illustrations, recitation, broadcasting, reproduction on microfilms or in any other physical way, and transmission or information storage and retrieval, electronic adaptation, computer software, or by similar or dissimilar methodology now known or hereafter developed.
The use of general descriptive names, registered names, trademarks, service marks, etc. in this publication does not imply, even in the absence of a specific statement, that such names are exempt from the relevant protective laws and regulations and therefore free for general use.
The publisher, the authors and the editors are safe to assume that the advice and information in this book are believed to be true and accurate at the date of publication. Neither the publisher nor the authors or the editors give a warranty, express or implied, with respect to the material contained herein or for any errors or omissions that may have been made.

Cover image Morotai Island, Halmahera Islands, Netherlands East Indies, c. 1945-11-28. Courtesy of Australian War Memorial

Printed on acid-free paper

This Palgrave Macmillan imprint is published by Springer Nature
The registered company is Springer International Publishing AG
The registered company address is: Gewerbestrasse 11, 6330 Cham, Switzerland

Contents

1 Justice in Time of Turmoil: War Crimes Trials in Asia
  in the Context of Decolonization and Cold War   1
  Kerstin von Lingen and Robert Cribb

2 Colonialism, Anti-Colonialism and Neo-Colonialism in
  China: The Opium Question at the Tokyo War Crimes
  Tribunal   25
  Neil Boister

3 The French Prosecution at the IMTFE: Robert Oneto,
  Indochina and the Rehabilitation of French Prestige   51
  Beatrice Trefalt

4 Decolonization and Subaltern Sovereignty: India and the
  Tokyo Trial   69
  Milinda Banerjee

5 The Legacy of Extraterritoriality and the Trial of Japanese
  War Criminals in the Republic of China   93
  Anja Bihler

6 The Burma Trials of Japanese War Criminals, 1946–1947   117
   Robert Cribb

7 Colonization and Postcolonial Justice: US and Philippine
   War Crimes Trials in Manila After the Second World War   143
   Wolfgang Form

8 Justice and Decolonization: War Crimes on Trial in
   Saigon, 1946–1950   167
   Ann-Sophie Schoepfel

9 Netherlands East Indies' War Crimes Trials in the Face
   of Decolonization   195
   Lisette Schouten

10 Australia's Pursuit of the Taiwanese and Korean 'Japanese'
   War Criminals   221
   Dean Aszkielowicz

11 From Tokyo to Khabarovsk: Soviet War Crimes Trials
   in Asia as Cold War Battlefields   239
   Valentyna Polunina

12 Resurrecting Defeat: International Propaganda
   and the Shenyang Trials of 1956   261
   Adam Cathcart

Erratum to: From Tokyo to Khabarovsk: Soviet War Crimes
Trials in Asia as Cold War Battlefields   E1

Index   279

Contributors

Dean Aszkielowicz teaches at Murdoch University and is the author of *The Australian pursuit of Japanese war criminals, 1943–1957: from foe to friend* (2017). He is also one of the four authors of *Japanese war criminals: the politics of justice after the Second World War* (2017).

Milinda Banerjee is Assistant Professor, Department of History, at Presidency University, Kolkata (India). His doctoral dissertation (from Heidelberg University) was titled '"The Mortal God": Debating Rulership and Genealogies of Sovereignty in Colonial India, 1858–1947' (with a primary focus on Bengal); it is now forthcoming as a book. He is also a Research Fellow in the Junior Research Group 'Transcultural Justice: Legal Flows and the Emergence of International Justice within the East Asian War Crimes Trials, 1946–1954', Cluster of Excellence Asia and Europe in a Global Context, Heidelberg University, Germany; the working title of the project is 'An Intellectual History of the Tokyo Trial: Judge Radhabinod Pal and Debates on International Justice.' Banerjee specializes in intellectual history (eighteenth to twentieth centuries), with a particular focus on ideas of sovereignty and justice. He is also the author of two books and a number of articles in peer-reviewed journals and volumes on the intellectual history of Bengal.

Anja Bihler is a doctoral candidate in Chinese Studies at the Cluster of Excellence Asia and Europe in a Global Context at Heidelberg University. She is currently completing her dissertation on the history of war crimes trials in the Republic of China between 1946 and 1948. She holds an MA degree in Chinese Studies, Economics and Law from Ludwig-Maximilians-University Munich.

Neil Boister is Professor at Te Pringa Faculty of Law, University of Waikato. In 2012, he was a Visiting Fellow at the Institute for Criminal Law Sciences, Faculty of Law, University of Hamburg and a Visiting Fellow at the Law Department, European

University Institute, Florence. In 2014, he served as an invited expert to a Transnational Institute (TNI)/ International Drug Policy Consortium (IDPC) Expert Seminar on the Future of the UN Drug Control Treaties. He was also an invited participant in Open Society Initiative for Southern Africa (OSISA)/and Open Society Foundation's Program Without Borders Grand Corruption Roundtable held in Victoria Falls 27–28 November 2011. He serves as a member of the editorial board of the *International Journal on Human Rights and Drug Policy* and as a member of the advisory board of the *New Zealand Yearbook of International Law*. He has published extensively in the areas of international criminal law and transnational criminal law.

Adam Cathcart is Lecturer in Chinese history at the University of Leeds (UK). Under the supervision of Donald Jordan, he wrote his dissertation on the subject of early postwar Chinese responses to Japan, and subsequently researched in the People's Republic of China (PRC) Foreign Ministry Archive, publishing articles on investigations and trials of Japanese war crimes in the early PRC. He also maintains an active research program in Sino–North Korean relations and transnational aspects of the Korean War, with a focus on eastern Manchuria.

Robert Cribb is Professor of Asian History at the Australian National University. His research focuses on Indonesian history, with special attention to violence, national identity and environmental politics. His recent publications include *Wild Man from Borneo: a cultural history of the orangutan* (with Helen Gilbert and Helen Tiffin, 2014) and *Historical Atlas of Northeast Asia 1590–2010* (with Li Narangoa, 2014). With Sandra Wilson, Beatrice Trefalt and Dean Aszkielowicz, he is author of *Japanese war criminals: the politics of justice after the Second World War* (2017).

Wolfgang Form co-founded the International Research and Documentation Center for War Crimes Trials, Marburg, in 2003 and has been its scientific manager since. He studied political science, sociology, social- and economic history, and public law in Marburg, and received his doctoral degree on political criminal justice during National Socialism in Germany from the University of Marburg. Since 1992, he has been Lecturer in Political Science and Peace and Conflict Studies at the University of Marburg, and Member of the Austrian Research Center for Post-War Trials Advisory Board. His main fields of research are political criminal and military justice, history of international criminal law, peace and conflict studies, and local and regional history of National Socialism. Among his publications are *Politische NS-Justiz in Hessen*, 2 vols (2005); 'Justice 30 Years Later? The Cambodian Special Tribunal for the Punishment of Crimes against Humanity by the Khmer Rouge,' *Nationalities Papers*, Vol. 37, Issue 6 (2009), pp. 889–923; and *National Socialism, Holocaust, Resistance and Exile 1933–145 Online* (2006) (co-editor).

Valentyna Polunina is a PhD candidate at the Cluster of Excellence at Heidelberg University where she is finalizing her PhD project on the Soviet war crimes trial at Khabarovsk and the question of prosecuting bacteriological warfare. She holds an MA in International Relations from Kiev State University and in Peace and Conflict Studies from Marburg University.

Ann Sophie Schoepfel is a PhD candidate at the Graduate Programme for Transcultural Studies at the Cluster of Excellence, Heidelberg University, and member of the Transcultural Justice Research Group. Her PhD focuses on the French case at the International Military Tribunal in the Far East in Tokyo and at the French domestic court in Saigon (Indochina). She graduated in History and Art History (Tübingen University and Aix-en-Provence University) and in Anthropology (Strasbourg University). She wrote two Master's theses dealing with aspects of memory of the Second World War in East Asia.

Lisette Schouten is a PhD candidate at the Graduate Programme for Transcultural Studies at the Cluster of Excellence, Heidelberg University, and member of the Transcultural Justice Research Group. Her research focuses on Dutch war crimes trial policy in the Netherland East Indies and Japan between 1945 and 1955. She holds an MA in History (2009) from Leiden University where she participated in the MA Europaeum Programme in European History and Civilization (Leiden, Paris, Oxford).

Beatrice Trefalt is a Senior Lecturer in Japanese Studies in the School of Languages, Literatures, Cultures and Linguistics at Monash University. Her research area is early postwar Japanese history, focusing especially on war legacies, dislocation and repatriation. She has recently published articles on the aftermath of war crimes trials in the Philippines and Indochina, and has co-authored a book with Sandra Wilson, Robert Cribb and Dean Aszkielowicz on the arrest, conviction, incarceration and release of Japanese war criminals, entitled *Japanese War Criminals: the Pursuit of Justice after the Second World War* (2017). She has also written on the experience of Japanese soldiers and civilians in the Pacific and on the evolution of memories of the war in the first 30 years of Japan's postwar period.

Kerstin von Lingen is a historian and teaches history at Heidelberg University in the Cluster of Excellence Asia and Europe in a Global Context. Since 2013, she has led an independent research project entitled 'Transcultural Justice: Legal Flows and the Emergence of International Justice within the East Asian War Crimes Trials, 1946–1954,' supervising four doctoral dissertations on the Soviet, Chinese, Dutch and French war crimes trial policies in Asia, respectively. Her many publications include two monographs in English, *Kesselring's Last Battle: War Crimes Trials and Cold War Politics, 1945–1960* (2009) and *Allen Dulles, the OSS and*

Nazi War Criminals: The Dynamics of Selective Prosecution (2013), as well as the (co)edited volumes *Kriegserfahrung und nationale Identität in Europa* [War experience and national identity in Europe after 1945] (2009) and *Zwangsarbeit als Kriegsressource in Europa und Asien* [Forced labor as a resource of War: European and Asian perspectives] (with Klaus Gestwa, 2014).

List of Figures

Map 6.1	Allied military command areas in Asia and the Pacific, 15 August 1945	123
Map 6.2	First SEAC suspect list. September 1945: location of reported offenses (Constructed from data in WO 208/3899; some unidentified locations omitted)	125
Map 6.3	Location of atrocities prosecuted or planned for prosecution in war crimes trials in Burma (Compiled from TNA LONDON, WO sources. All trials took place in Rangoon or Maymyo)	137
Fig. 9.1	Number of convictions given by sentence (Numbers compiled by author)	205
Fig. 9.2	Korean defendants by sentence (Numbers compiled by author)	206
Fig. 9.3	Kempeitai and Tokkeitai defendants by sentence (Numbers compiled by author)	207
Fig. 9.4	Accused by rank and sentence (Numbers compiled by author, not included are those with unknown ranks, civilians or militarized civilians)	208

List of Tables

Table 6.1	Span and intensity of the British trial program in Burma	139
Table 6.2	Verdicts and sentences by month, 1946–1947	140
Table 7.1	US war crimes trials in the Philippines, September 1945–April 1947	157
Table 7.2	American trials in Yokohama – crime scene: the Philippines – victims: POWs	158
Table 7.3	Sentences Philippines MC	165
Table 8.1	Allied class B and C trials in Asia	180
Table 8.2	Number of convictions, death sentences and acquittals	183
Table 8.3	Locations of Japanese war crimes in Indochina	184
Table 8.4	Charges against class B and C war criminals	187
Table 8.5	Overview of the Japanese defendants	189
Table 8.6	Defendants by rank	190
Table 8.7	Number of convictions given by sentence	192

CHAPTER 1

Justice in Time of Turmoil: War Crimes Trials in Asia in the Context of Decolonization and Cold War

Kerstin von Lingen and Robert Cribb

During the half-decade following the end of the Second World War, Allied military tribunals in Asia and the Pacific tried Japanese military personnel for war crimes committed during the hostilities. The trials commenced on the Pacific island of Guam in September 1945 and encompassed over 2,300 proceedings in more than 50 locations in Asia and the Pacific. Australia,

---

For this chapter, we draw also on results of intensive discussions with 2014's visiting fellows to the Research Group 'Transcultural Justice' on Asian War Crimes trials at the Asia and Europe in a Global Context Cluster of Excellence at Heidelberg University, Sandra Wilson and Kirsten Sellars, whom we would like to thank for their valuable input. Additionally, we thank Beatrice Trefalt and Neil Boister, as well as members of the Heidelberg Research Group Milinda Banerjee, Lisette Schouten, Anja Bihler, Ann-Sophie Schoepfel and Valentyna Polunina, who commented on an earlier draft of the chapter.

K. von Lingen (✉)
Heidelberg University, Heidelberg, Germany

R. Cribb
Australian National University, Canberra, Australia

© The Author(s) 2016
K. von Lingen (ed.), *War Crimes Trials in the Wake of Decolonization and Cold War in Asia, 1945–1956*,
DOI 10.1007/978-3-319-42987-8_1

(Nationalist) China, France, the Netherlands Indies, the Philippines, the Soviet Union, the United Kingdom and the USA all convened trials in the period to April 1951. The Communist government of the People's Republic of China, although not one of the wartime Allies, held its own trials in 1956. Around 5,700 people working for the Imperial Japanese armed forces were prosecuted. Approximately 4,500 were found guilty and in the end just over 900 were executed.[1] The remainder of those found guilty were sentenced to prison terms. Alongside the national tribunals that undertook the vast bulk of the trial work, the International Military Tribunal for the Far East (IMTFE, also known as the Tokyo Trial) convened between April 1946 and November 1948 to prosecute 28 senior Japanese political and military figures. None of the accused in this trial was acquitted, but one was found unfit for trial and two died during the proceedings.

These trials occupied a pivotal place in three major historical phenomena of the twentieth century: in the development of international humanitarian law, in the Cold War confrontation between capitalism and communism (and, on a geopolitical scale, between the USA and the Soviet Union) and in the decolonization process that led to the retreat of Western colonial empires and the emergence of new states in Asia. Yet in all three processes, the place of the war crimes trials is ambiguous, even contradictory. The trials were both a dramatic advance in international humanitarian law and an unsatisfactory dead end. They both served and confounded the Cold War interests of the prosecuting powers. And they reinforced the decolonization process in Asia while at the same time they were used to resist the end of colonialism.

These contradictions have been a major obstacle to understanding the historical significance of the trials, but this volume brings together recent research that begins to sort out this complexity.[2] The central conclusion of the book is that the trials cannot be understood simply as confirming or amplifying known historical trends. Rather, on key issues—the development

---

[1] Philip R. Piccigallo, *The Japanese on trial: Allied war crimes operations in the East, 1945–1951* (Austin, TX: University of Texas Press, 1979), 264–265. For a more recent analysis of the trials, see Sandra Wilson, Robert Cribb, Beatrice Trefalt and Dean Aszkielowicz, *Japanese War Criminals: The Politics of Justice After the Second World War* (New York, NY: Columbia University Press, 2017).

[2] This volume draws on papers presented at the conference 'Rethinking Justice? Decolonization, Cold War and Asian War Crimes Trials,' at Heidelberg University, 26–29 October 2014.

of international law, the resolution of wartime and Cold War rivalries, and the process of decolonization—the trials operated on both sides of the historical ledger.

Drawing on new research, this book demonstrates and debates the ways in which political and ideological considerations emanating from decolonization and the Cold War shaped, and were shaped by, the structure and outcome of the trials as a new post-imperial world gradually began to emerge. It juxtaposes their political and juridical roles in order to show the connections between the two. The war crimes trials in Asia were a watershed moment, coinciding with the demise of an old political-legal international order defined by European hegemony and the advent of a new, putatively anti-imperial one, based on contestations between the American and Soviet blocs and the rise of postcolonial nation-states.

INTERNATIONAL HUMANITARIAN LAW

Although there had been incidental efforts in earlier centuries to limit cruelty in the context of war, the modern construction of international humanitarian law in relation to war began in the mid-nineteenth century.[3] It took serious form in the successive Hague and Geneva conventions. The Geneva Conventions, commencing in 1864, defined the rights of prisoners in wartime. The Hague conventions from 1899 and 1907 set standards which restricted the use of what were seen as barbarous weapons such as expanding bullets and poison gas and set out rules for the treatment of surrendered combatants. There was also some impulse to establish rules that would protect civilians from unnecessary harm in times of war, notably the 1910 convention against the bombardment of civilian settlements from the sea.[4] Although the experience of war atrocities in the First World War in Europe had led to a codification of rules and a clearer definition about the nature of war crimes (the so-called 'Versailles list'), no agreements had been made on setting up an international court to punish these offences. Trials in Leipzig and Constantinople, which dealt

---

[3] Martti Koskenniemi, *The Gentle Civilizer of Nations: the Rise and Fall of International Law, 1870–1960* (Cambridge: Cambridge University Press, 2002); Mark Lewis: *The Birth of the New Justice: the Internationalization of Crime and Punishment, 1919–1950* (New York: Oxford University Press, 2014); Geoffrey Best, *Humanity in Warfare* (New York: Columbia University Press, 1980).

[4] Antonio Cassese, Guido Acquaviva, Mary Fan and Alex Whiting, *International Criminal Law: Cases and Commentary* (Oxford: Oxford University Press, 2011), 134.

with German and Ottoman war crimes respectively, were deemed a failure because they relied on the courts of the offending nation to prosecute perpetrators.[5] The interwar period was characterized by diplomatic efforts to ban all war, rather than framing legal rules for the next one.[6]

Thus, by the time of the outbreak of the Second World War, the formal legal protections for civilians were meager and there had still been no systemic prosecution of war crimes. The sequence of policy decisions which led to the postwar war crimes trial program began in London in January 1942, when a group of representatives of governments-in-exile from Nazi-occupied countries in Europe met at St James's Palace and declared a principal aim of the war to be 'the punishment, through the channel of organised justice, of those guilty of or responsible for [war] crimes, whether they have ordered them, perpetrated them or participated in them.'[7] Japan had not yet launched its attack on Malaya and Pearl Harbor, but it was at war in China and the representatives of the Chinese Republic declared that China would 'apply the same principles to the Japanese occupying authorities in China when the time comes.'[8] This resolution led in 1943 to the founding of the United Nations War Crimes Commission (UNWCC) with its headquarters in London, which undertook the fundamental work of determining the legal basis for war crimes trials and which also began the task of collecting evidence for postwar tribunals.[9]

---

[5] James F. Willis: *Prologue to Nuremberg. The politics and diplomacy of punishing war criminals of the First World War* (Contributions in legal studies no. 20, Westport, CN: Greenwood, 1982); Gerd Hankel, *Die Leipziger Prozesse: Deutsche Kriegsverbrechen und ihre strafrechtliche Verfolgung nach dem Ersten Weltkrieg* (Hamburg: Hamburger Edition, 2003); Vahakn N. Dadrian and Taner Akçam, *Judgment at Istanbul: the Armenian Genocide Trials* (New York: Berghahn, 2011); Michelle Tusan, '"Crimes against Humanity": Human Rights, the British Empire and the Origins of the Response to the Armenian Genocide,' in: *American Historical Review* 119, (1), (2014), 47–77.

[6] M. Cherif Bassiouni, '"Crimes against Humanity": The need for a specialized convention', in: *Columbia Journal of Transnational Law* 31 (1993–1994), 457–494, here 466. Bassiouni underlines that the leading powers allowed the period after the First World War to become a 'bypassed occasion to establish definitive law.'

[7] *Punishment for war crimes: the Inter-Allied Declaration signed at St James's Palace London on 13 January 1942, and relevant documents* (London: HMSO, 1942), 6; Madoka Futamura, *War crimes tribunals and transitional justice: the Tokyo Trial and the Nuremburg legacy* (London: Routledge, 2008), 166.

[8] *Punishment for war crimes*, 16.

[9] Arieh J. Kochavi, *Prelude to Nuremberg. Allied War Crimes Policy and the Question of Punishment* (Chapel Hill: University of North Carolina Press, 1998); Dan Plesch and Shanti Sattler (eds.), 'Symposium: The United Nations War Crimes Commission and the Origins of International Criminal Justice,' *Criminal Law Forum* 25, 1 (June 2014).

These changes in global legal-political norms and institutions were debated in international forums, the most prominent being the Legal Committee of the United Nations War Crimes Commission, also formed in 1943. Although China also took active part in all meetings and pushed for a global rhetoric in UNWCC recommendations, the debate initially was focussed on crimes of Nazi occupation forces in Europe, on the problem of violence among states prior to a state of war, and on the issue of a state's violence against its own nationals, as the murder of European Jewry had shown this was a pressing issue.[10] The Western Allies, or United Nations as they called themselves during wartime, responded to the horrors of the Second World War in two ways: by encouraging states to commit themselves to international law, with the aim of liberating the world from war itself, and second, with the Holocaust crimes in mind, by banning crimes against civilians and developing a system of what we today call international humanitarian law.[11]

The postwar trials represented a dramatic advance both because they involved large numbers of prosecutions for war crimes under the Geneva Conventions and because, in a leap of legal imagination based on the never-ratified third Hague Peace Conference provisions as well as discussions at Versailles in 1919, they interpreted as war crimes a range of actions against civilians that had previously been regarded only as morally reprehensible.[12] The prosecution process confirmed that the provisions of the Geneva Conventions protecting prisoners of war could be enforced in a court of law and it consolidated an expanded definition of war crimes that provided new protection to the inhabitants of occupied territories from

---

[10] Kerstin von Lingen, 'Setting the Path for the UNWCC: The Representation of European Exile Governments on The London International Assembly and The Commission For Penal Reconstruction and Development, 1941-1944,' in: *International Criminal Law Forum*, 25, 1 (2014), 45–76, here 69; Kerstin von Lingen, 'Defining Crimes against Humanity: The Contribution of the United Nations War Crimes Commission to International Criminal Law, 1944–1947,' in: Morten Bergsmo, Wui Ling CHEAH, Ping YI (eds.), *Historical Origins of International Criminal Law*, (Brussels: Torkel Opsahl, 2014), 475–506, here 481.

[11] Daniel Thürer, *International Humanitarian Law: Theory, Practice, Context*, (The Hague: The Hague Academy of International Law, 2011), 32, quoting preamble of UN Charter 1945.

[12] Arthur Eyffinger, 'A Highly Critical Moment: Role and Record of the 1907 Hague Peace Conference,' in: *Netherlands International Law Review* Vol. 54, 2 (2007), 197–228, refers on pp. 234–235 on the US-led plans for a third Hague conference, envisioned for 1915, as well as on the draft program. On the debates at Versailles, see Beth van Schaack, 'The Definition of Crimes against Humanity: Resolving the Incoherence,' in: *Columbia J Transnational Law*, Vol. 37 (1998–1999), 787–850, here 796.

cruel and arbitrary treatment by those acting on behalf of the occupying power. Piccigallo's 1979 survey of Allied war crimes trials in the Asia-Pacific region pioneered this interpretation of the trials as a major legal advance, albeit one that was subsequently overshadowed by the attention given to trials in Europe.

As well as identifying an expanded range of actions as criminal under international law, the proceedings also consolidated an extended conception of guilt. They affirmed the principle of command responsibility, under which officers bore legal responsibility for the actions of their subordinates, even if they had done no more than shape the circumstances in which atrocities were committed. The proceedings also asserted the inadmissibility of a defense of superior orders, a claim which had still been possible in the trials after the First World War: the accused could not escape culpability by showing that they had merely followed the orders of their commanders. New research continues to draw attention to the hitherto little-recognized legal innovation of the postwar trials. Neil Boister's chapter in this volume, for instance, reveals the role of the IMTFE in extending the scope of international law to regulate the trade in addictive drugs.

As Wolfgang Form and Robert Cribb argue for the Philippines and Burma respectively, and as Lisette Schouten's chapter shows in the case of the Netherlands Indies, the trial process was driven above all by a determination to do justice, rather than out of overt political considerations. The investigators and prosecutors believed that terrible crimes had been committed and they wanted to see the perpetrators—or at least the worst of them—appropriately punished. Their determination reflected the mood expressed by Allied leaders in the Potsdam Declaration of 26 July 1945: 'Stern justice shall be meted out to all war criminals, including those who have visited cruelties upon our prisoners.'[13] Indeed, there was competition among the prosecuting powers, not only to indict high profile suspects but also for a general record of prosecution.[14] Each of the prosecuting powers in the Asia-Pacific region conducted its trials under national legislation or regulations, but to varying degrees they cooperated first in the pooling of

---

[13] 'Proclamation by the heads of governments, United States, China and the United Kingdom,' 26 July 1945, United States Department of State, *Foreign Relations of the United States: Diplomatic Papers: the Conference of Berlin (the Potsdam Conference), 1945*, Vol. II (Washington DC: US Government Printing Office, 1945), 1476.

[14] This argument is raised and discussed in Barak Kushner, *'Men to Devils, Devils to Men': Japanese War Crimes and Chinese Justice*, (Cambridge MA: Harvard University Press, 2015), 39–40 and 155.

evidence and later in the exchange of suspects and witnesses. Judges and prosecutors sometimes sat in other jurisdictions. The prosecuting powers in Asia and Europe moreover watched each other closely, to identify the techniques that might work best in the process of investigation and prosecution, and to test new principles against the practicalities of prosecution. They sought to avoid approaches that might have undesired side-effects and they often tried to remain in step with each other in determining the pace and the scope of the trials. The records of the United Nations War Crimes Commission and of Allied Military Command bodies such as SCAP (Supreme Commander for the Allied Powers) or SEAC (South East Asia Command) thus reveal a transcultural dimension in which the war crimes trials in Europe as in Asia constituted a 'learning system.'

Nonetheless, since the 1970s, there has been growing scholarly attention to procedural shortcomings in the trial process. In particular, inconsistencies in the selection of defendants and inadequacies in the treatment of evidence began to cast a shadow over the quality of the trials. Minear's *Victors' Justice* (1971) focused on the Tokyo trial alone, arguing that the USA's determination to achieve convictions led to serious unfairness.[15] The subsequent work of Totani and of Boister and Cryer on the IMTFE has revealed a legal process that fell short of the expectation of fairness on many fronts, while nonetheless boldly upholding new and higher standards of legal accountability for wartime actions.[16] As several chapters in this book demonstrate, this critique can be applied also to the national trials of Japanese after the war. The prosecuting powers saw the trials as important business that needed to be finished quickly so that the world could move on. Changing political circumstances in many parts of the region strengthened the imperative to wrap up the trials. There was little appetite for making the trial process any longer or more comprehensive than it was; on the contrary, most dissenting voices on the prosecuting side argued for a more expeditious process, closer to summary justice. Lisette Schouten's chapter in this volume shows both the determination of the Dutch colonial authorities to follow a justifiable procedure and

---

[15] Richard H. Minear, *Victors' Justice: the Tokyo War Crimes Trial* (Princeton, NJ, Princeton University Press, 1971). See also Richard L. Lael, *The Yamashita precedent* (Wilmington, DE.: Scholarly Resources, 1982).
[16] Neil Boister and Robert Cryer, *The Tokyo International Military Tribunal: a reappraisal* (New York: Oxford University Press, 2008); Yuma Totani, *The Tokyo war crimes trial: the pursuit of justice in the wake of World War Two* (Cambridge, MA: Harvard University Asia Center, 2008).

their tolerance of irregularities that inevitably arose in the difficult circumstances of the trials.[17]

Decolonization

A powerful nexus also existed between the war crimes trials and the process of decolonization in Asia. Over the period from 1930 to 1960, most of Southeast Asia moved from an unambiguously colonial status to at least formal independence. This transition, defined by Duara as 'the process whereby colonial powers transferred institutional and legal control over their territories and dependencies to indigenously based, formally sovereign, nation states,'[18] profoundly transformed the international order in Asia and prefigured the decolonization of Africa. Japan's imperial expansion in Asia was intimately connected with the decolonization process in several respects. First, Japan's success in modernizing, industrializing and developing serious military capacity after 1868 was a source of inspiration to colonized peoples throughout Asia. Japan's achievement was a potent refutation of racist assumptions of Asian inferiority, offering vivid proof that the West was not all-powerful. Japan's rapid expansion in 1941–42 humiliated the Western powers in Southeast Asia and parts of the Pacific, making it impossible that they could return to the comfortable pre-war assumptions of superiority. Second, the Japanese victories and the destruction and disruption that accompanied the war seriously weakened the military capacity of the Western powers and the direct economic value of the Southeast Asian colonies. The ferocious fighting over Manila, the Allied bombing of cities such as Rangoon and Surabaya, catastrophic famines in northern Vietnam and Java, and the running down and repurposing of colonial infrastructure for the war effort meant that the elaborate apparatus of colonial profit that had been developed in the colonies over several decades could not simply be switched on again after the surrender.

Japan's imperial venture had also had an ideological impact on the people of the region. Japanese imperial expansion after 1931 was embedded

---

[17] A similar picture emerges in Yuma Totani, *Justice in Asia and the Pacific region, 1945–1952: Allied war crimes prosecutions* (New York, NY: Cambridge University Press, 2015).

[18] Prasenjit Duara, 'Introduction: the Decolonization of Asia and Africa in the 20th century,' in: Prasenjit Duara (ed.), *Decolonization: Perspectives from now and then* (London: Routledge 2004), 1–18, here 2.

in a discourse that blended Pan-Asianism and nationalist specificity.[19] Japan's Pan-Asian propaganda in effect invited all Asian peoples to be part of the Japanese success story on the basis of their shared Asian culture. At the same time, a strong exclusionary strand in Japanese thinking led them to celebrate national difference within Asia and to encourage nationalisms in Mongolia, China, Southeast Asia and India. In the course of their wartime expansion, the Japanese authorities presided over the creation of quasi-independent states in Manchuria, Mongolia, China, the Philippines, Burma, Vietnam, Laos and Cambodia. They created a Provisional Government of Free India in anticipation of conquering the subcontinent, and they were prevented from conferring independence on Indonesia only by the sudden end of the war. Within the territories they occupied, moreover, Japanese forces adopted a very different political style from that of the Western colonial powers. Whereas the West had generally made much use of indirect rule, recruiting the traditional authority of indigenous rulers to mask and to underpin colonial hegemony, the Japanese imperialists preferred to rule directly, recruiting ambitious young men who shared the Japanese sense of mission and urgency. Furthermore, unlike the colonial powers, Japanese authorities spoke directly to the mass of the people, launching sustained propaganda campaigns to win public support. Three quarters of a century later, these propaganda materials look crude and unconvincing, but their effect was electrifying on peoples whose approval for their rulers had never previously been sought.

On the other hand, Japan was itself an imperial power. Prominent Japanese thinkers such as Fukuzawa Yukichi described Japan as 'leaving Asia' and entering the modern world inhabited by the Western powers.[20] Japan's economic vision for its empire, encapsulated in the idea of a Greater East Asia Co-Prosperity Sphere, envisaged a subordinate role for the other parts of Asia as suppliers of raw materials for Japanese industry. When Japan's interests were at stake, Japanese officials could be ruthless in dealing with their fellow Asians. Far more Asian labourers (*rōmusha*) than Western prisoners of war perished on the Thailand–Burma Railway, and

---

[19] Li Narangoa and Robert Cribb, 'Japan and the transformation of national identities in Asia in the Imperial era,' in: Li Narangoa and Robert Cribb, eds, *Imperial Japan and national identities in Asia, 1895–1945* (London: RoutledgeCurzon, 2003), 1–22.
[20] Urs Matthias Zachmann, 'Blowing up a Double Portrait in Black and White: The Concept of Asia in the Writings of Fukuzawa Yukichi and Okakura Tenshin,' in: *Positions: East Asia Cultures Critique* 15, 2 (Fall 2007), 345–368.

the public rhetoric of Pan-Asian solidarity was qualified by private expressions of deep prejudice.[21]

This ambivalence in Japanese imperialism persisted after the end of the war. On the one hand, Allied officers sometimes recognized in their Japanese counterparts a shared military-imperial culture that facilitated cooperation between the two. In both Vietnam and Indonesia, Japanese troops accepted orders from the Allied commanders to take military action against the local nationalist uprisings. On the other hand, some Japanese officers assisted nationalists in Indonesia by handing over weapons for the future anti-colonial struggle while hundreds of ordinary Japanese soldiers deserted after the surrender and offered their services to the nationalist struggles in the lands they had once occupied. The Dutch colonial authorities were sufficiently concerned by this development to include such actions within their definition of war crimes and they tried at least one Japanese corporal on such charges, as Lisette Schouten's chapter shows.

Korea's decolonization raised a different set of issues. Japan had forcibly annexed the previously independent country in 1910, but Allied planners limited the war crimes investigation process after the Second World War to the period from 1928. In the eyes of the prosecutors, Koreans were thus Japanese subjects and had none of the protections enjoyed under international law by the inhabitants of occupied territories. Japan's efforts to erase Korean culture,[22] therefore, as well as the brutal treatment of Korean labourers and the recruitment of Korean women for enforced prostitution were not addressed by Allied courts, even though they would have constituted war crimes had the status of Koreans been considered to be different in international law. Koreans might have been protected by the new concept of crimes against humanity, which paid no attention to the national status of the victims, but that concept was barely formed and was initially of limited use, as it was bound to the so-called 'war nexus' and could be applied only jointly with other charges, such as war crimes or crimes against peace.[23] Only with time did the concept become tied to Holocaust crimes and is today seen as a tool against genocidal violence. Neither the

---

[21] See for instance Haruko Taya Cook, 'Japan's war in living memory and beyond,' in: Remco Raben, ed., *Representing the Japanese Occupation of Indonesia: personal testimonies and public images in Indonesia, Japan and the Netherlands* (Zwolle: Waanders, 1999), 53.

[22] Mark Caprio, *Japanese Assimilation Policies in Colonial Korea, 1910–1945* (Seattle, WA: University of Washington Press, 2009).

[23] Beth van Schaack, 'The Definition of Crimes against Humanity: Resolving the Incoherence,' in: *Columbia Journal of Transnational Law* 37 (1998–1999), 787–850, here 791.

USA nor the Soviet Union in their respective occupation zones in postwar Korea saw any political value in prosecuting Japanese for their actions in Korea or against Koreans outside the country.

Under these circumstances, it is hardly surprising that the program of war crimes trials in Western colonies in Southeast Asia had the same ambivalence in relation to the decolonization process as it had to the Cold War and to the development of international humanitarian law.

Incidental comments by Western officials involved in the investigation and prosecution of war crimes make it clear that they believed the trials would contribute to upholding colonial prestige. Public occasions that reaffirmed the restoration of colonial authority—formal local ceremonies to accept the Japanese surrender, for instance—were important symbolic repudiations of Japan's wartime claims to superiority and hegemony. The right to establish courts and to prosecute alleged criminals was central to state authority, in the colonies as much as anywhere else. This authority was especially important in French Indochina, as the chapter by Ann-Sophie Schoepfel explains. French colonial authority was fragile because until March 1945 the colony had been governed by Vichy French authorities, allied with Nazi Germany and thus with Japan. France's status as one of the victorious Allies in Asia was by no means secure. Moreover, responsibility for accepting the Japanese surrender in northern Indochina was allocated to the Nationalist Chinese government. France had wrested hegemony over Vietnam from the Qing rulers of China barely half a century earlier, and it was by no means clear that the Nationalists would willingly restore French authority. In southern Indochina, the British-led South East Asia Command (SEAC) had responsibility for accepting the surrender. The British military authorities were more accommodating to French interests than the Nationalist Chinese forces, but Britain had other, higher priorities in the region than helping the French to regain their colony. In this context, placing Japanese on trial was an important element in French strategy.[24] Beatrice Trefalt's chapter in this volume, too, shows how important it was for France, for the purposes of the IMTFE, to be recognized as a victim of Japanese aggression, rather than as a wartime ally of Japan. To have been held to account for the Vichy administration's collaboration with Japan might have been catastrophic for the French

---

[24] Beatrice Trefalt, 'Japanese War Criminals in Indochina and the French Pursuit of Justice: Local and International Constraints,' *Journal of Contemporary History* 49, 4 (Oct. 2014), 727–742.

effort to restore colonial authority in Indochina. Yet there is no sign that the Tokyo proceedings delivered France any positive benefits.

In many jurisdictions, moreover, military planners chose as the first trial to be conducted a case involving non-Western victims. British, Dutch and Australian trials, as well as American trials in the Philippines, all regularly prosecuted Japanese for crimes against local people. China and the Philippines prosecuted only crimes against their own nationals. Although the archives do not record any political rationale for the choice of cases to be pursued, it is likely that all the Western powers were conscious that it might be politically damaging if the only prosecutions were for crimes against Westerners. The propaganda value of the trials, however, was limited by the fact they generally did not begin until months after Western authority had been restored.

Amongst all the colonial powers except France, legal responsibility for investigating and prosecuting war crimes lay with the military as part of the effort to defeat Japan. Authorities with responsibility for the long-term future of the colonies were generally not part of the planning or implementation of the trials process. The Netherlands Indies had opted for a hybrid system: although investigation was carried out by military personnel, the courts made wide use of militarized civilians as judges and prosecutors, and the head of the body for the investigation of war crimes was the civil government's attorney general. The language used by military planners, to the extent that it offered any rationale for the trials, often stressed retribution, rather than local political motives.

In important respects, the Japanese occupation had simply accelerated changes that were already under way in the rest of Asia. In 1935, the USA had transferred most internal administrative functions in the Philippines to a commonwealth under a Filipino president, Manuel Quezon. The Act creating the commonwealth foreshadowed the Philippine independence that would come ten years later. The British government granted Burma a high degree of self-rule in 1937 under its own prime minister, Ba Maw. Even the French and Dutch colonial powers, which were much more hesitant to imagine future independence, had made some moves towards popular representation in government in the pre-war period. In the immediate aftermath of the war, all the colonial powers in Southeast Asia, with the insignificant exception of Portugal in East Timor, realized that they would need to shift to a new political format involving much greater participation in government by local leaders. By making this shift, they calculated, they would be able to retain their most important economic interests in the region. In other words, they aimed to hand as much power as was necessary to modern and friendly local elites who would see their interest as being tied to the continuing economic presence of the West. Karl Hack argues that decolonization 'was, in a sense, a way of maximizing British world power,' because it had the aim of maximizing benefits and minimizing the costs of a continued administration of these territories.[25]

This strategy rested on two pillars. First was the restoration of public order. In the months that followed the Japanese surrender, much of Southeast Asia slipped into chaos or revolution or both. In Burma, Malaya and much of Indonesia, public order disappeared. Nationalist gangs emerged to defend local interests and to take revenge for wartime wrongs. In the Philippines, Vietnam and Malaya, indigenous armies that had emerged to fight the Japanese occupiers (often with some support from the Allies) revealed strong communist inclinations. With military experience and established influence in the countryside, these forces were a serious challenge to the returning colonial authorities and made economic recovery impossible.

The second pillar was the identification of an appropriate 'moderate' local elite which could partner with the colonial power in the decolonization process. The challenge for each colonial power was to decide how accommodating they needed to be in the new political circumstances. The Americans in the Philippines and the British in Burma were willing both to make extensive political concessions to the nationalists—independence in the short term—and to deal in good faith with leaders who had collaborated with the Japanese forces. In doing so, they hoped to marginalize what they regarded as the extreme forces of the left. The British in Malaya as well as the Dutch in Indonesia made fewer concessions but they, too, tried to work with groups they regarded as moderate. The aim, for example, of British forces in Malaya was to create quickly a successor state, in order to end the costly aspects of engagement in the region,[26] and not leave a power vacuum behind, where communist forces or others could take over. Even the French in Indochina tried to find common ground with conservative Vietnamese, though their efforts in the end proved fruitless.[27]

---

[25] Karl Hack, 'Screwing Down the People: the Malayan Emergency, Decolonization and Ethnicity,' in: Hans Antlöv and Stein Tønneson (ed.), *Imperial Policy and Southeast Asian Nationalism, 1930–1957* (Richmond: Curzon Press, 1995), 83–109, here 104.

[26] Hack, 'Screwing Down the People,' 100.

[27] Hugues Tertrais: 'France and the Associated States of Indochina,' in Marc Frey, Ronald W. Pruessen and Tan Tai Yong, *The Transformation of Southeast Asia* (Armonk, NY: M. E. Sharpe, 2003), 83–104.

In this postwar colonial strategy, the trials seem to have played an important declarative function by tainting those who had collaborated with Japan. As we have seen, the idea of Japanese national or collective guilt was as central to the Pacific War dimension of the war crimes trials as it was antithetical to their Cold War dimension. In the tangled politics of Southeast Asia, nationalist leaders who had worked most closely with Japanese authorities were often those who most strongly opposed continuing Western influence in the region. Nationalist leaders such as José P. Laurel and Ba Maw, who headed the client states in the Philippines and Burma respectively, as well as Aung San in Burma and Sukarno in Indonesia, were potential candidates for prosecution under treason laws. They represented relatively radical nationalist opposition to continuing colonial influence and were potentially highly vulnerable to prosecution. Aung San had been involved in the murder of a pro-British village headman; Sukarno had used his authority to recruit laborers for Japanese wartime projects, including the Thailand–Burma Railway on which tens of thousands had died. Direct trials of those leaders for collaboration, however, were difficult or impossible, if only because any trial would have provided the nationalist leaders with a public platform for repudiating the colonial claim on their loyalty. But the trial of Japanese personnel for atrocities against local people had at least some potential to undermine the political standing of those who had worked with Japan. Only in China, where such issues did not arise, did treason trials take place on a large scale.

And it was not just those who worked with Japan who were to be tainted. Soiling the reputation of Japan as a whole was a small but significant element in Allied efforts to limit the extent that postwar Japan might recover its influence in Southeast Asia by peaceful means. Japan's economic penetration of the region had been a source of concern to the Western colonial powers well before the outbreak of the Second World War. Japanese shipping and other enterprises had been powerful competitors for Western firms before the war, and the retreating colonial powers worried that military Japan might simply build on its pre-war and wartime links to recreate an informal empire in the region. In this context, the economic interests of the retreating colonial powers meant that affirming the brutality of Japanese rule had an importance that increased, rather than diminished, as the postwar settlement took shape.

A greater problem for the colonial powers, however, was not the difficulty of calibrating the war crimes trials to specific political needs but rather the underlying contradiction between the insistent universalism of international humanitarian law and the deep-seated legal inequalities of the colonial system. International humanitarian law, of which the laws governing war crimes were a part, involved a partial surrender of the once sacrosanct principle of national sovereignty for the sake of human rights. The colonial territories in which most of the war crimes trials took place were under the sovereignty of Western powers, but they were not part of the system of rule of law that applied in the metropoles. Instead, the colonies existed under separate laws which, as a rule, were more punitive than metropolitan law (more inclined to resort to the death penalty and more inclined to punish minor infractions harshly). Colonial law was also more likely to endorse expedited legal procedures that diminished the protections available to defendants. Colonial law, furthermore, was more inclined than metropolitan law to criminalize political action. In practice, and sometimes in theory, colonial law tended to be plural, applying different laws to different ethnic groups (especially distinguishing Westerners from the rest). The public justification for this pluralism, moreover, tended to be rooted in a notion of decisive cultural difference; in other words, 'natives' could be subject to different laws because those laws were consistent with some construction of traditional culture. This argument presented an obstacle to legal reform because it allowed for no democratic means of achieving legal change. By contrast, war crimes law was vigorously universal. Even if individual judges were inclined at times to blame undesirable characteristics of Japanese culture for Japanese war crimes, that culture was never permitted as a moral excuse or legal defense. The principles of international humanitarian law trumped cultural particularism. Inconveniently for the colonial powers, they thereby trumped also the intellectual basis for colonial legal pluralism. Even with colonialism in formal retreat as the war crimes trials took place, this refutation of an underlying principle of colonial rule was an additional embarrassment.

China, as in other respects, was something of an exception here. Although not formally colonized by western powers, the extraterritoriality enjoyed by Western residents in China and the concession areas in some Chinese ports created a semi-colonial environment. Additionally, the north-eastern provinces had been invaded by Japan in 1931 and ruled as the nominally independent state of Manchukuo. Extraterritoriality had been justified publicly by the claim that China's own legal system was not up to international standards. As Anja Bihler's chapter shows, extraterritoriality was the form that the legal pluralism of the colonial era took in China, allowing Westerners (and those with Western protection) to be tried in separate courts, immune from the procedural problems of Chinese domestic courts. Participation in war crimes trials therefore helped the Chinese government to establish the validity of its own judicial system in the wake of decades of extraterritoriality, and to establish its ability to follow Western standards in the punishment of wartime atrocities. In this strategy, they followed the earlier approach of Japan in the late nineteenth century, when it had worked hard to align its legal system with Western models in order to remove any pretext for extraterritoriality. For China, the trial of 871 Japanese defendants in Chinese courts represented a triumphant ending of extraterritoriality, though that triumph was qualified by the fact that the USA also held trials in Shanghai.

Milinda Banerjee points out in this volume that the universalist claims of international criminal law remained embedded in an overall Western legal-intellectual hegemony that perturbed Radhabinod Pal, Indian judge in the IMTFE. Pal was deeply uneasy at what he saw as the uncritical imposition of Western assumptions in the Tokyo Trial. For him and for other Indian intellectuals, the Tokyo Trial demanded debate about the implications of decolonization for the transformation of structures and discourses relating to sovereignty and rule of law.

In the colonial context, too, the list of war crimes charges brought against Japanese personnel could make for uncomfortable comparisons with colonial practice. In all the colonial realms in Southeast Asia, the principal charges brought against Japanese defendants—ill-treatment of labourers, summary execution of prisoners, torture of suspected spies and rebels—were part of recent historical memory. Writing in 1949, Alan Gledhill, a British legal official in Burma, considered the charges against the Japanese military personnel in Burma and concluded that Japanese behaviour had remained within the broad limits set by British military law for British forces under normal circumstances. He added that it was unreasonable to expect the Japanese commanders to be milder than their British counterparts.[28]

PACIFIC WAR VERSUS COLD WAR

Western popular culture is inclined to portray the Japanese attack on Pearl Harbor as a bolt from the blue, an unexpected and unprovoked act of war. In reality, the attack was the culmination of years of rivalry between the

---

[28] A. Gledhill, 'Some aspects of the operation of international and military law in Burma, 1941–1945,' *Modern Law Review* 12 (1939), 191–204, here 197.

USA and Japan for hegemony in East Asia.[29] From early in the twentieth century, successive Japanese governments had aimed to create a Japanese sphere of influence in the region. This aim had been challenged by the USA, which, having the larger economy, was more likely to succeed in an open economic environment. The competition between the two had sharpened in 1932 when the Japanese Kwantung Army created the client state of Manchukuo in Manchuria in the teeth of US diplomatic opposition. It became still more acute when war broke out between China and Japan in 1937 and Japanese forces seized large areas of China. The Japanese attack on Pearl Harbor came in the context of tightening US economic sanctions against Japan, intended to force it to give up its position in China.

In these circumstances, the war crimes trials of Japanese were a conclusion of the business of war by judicial means. Japan had already been defeated, of course, but the trials were meant to confirm that the victory of the West was not just a matter of superior force but also a moral victory of good over evil. This intention built on the savage racialist propaganda of the USA during the war, in which the Japanese enemy was constructed as bestial and brutal.[30] Despite the formal character of the trials as prosecutions of individual perpetrators, they were also a judgment against Japanese culture. Prosecutors and judges, along with journalists and members of the public in the West used the opportunity of the trials to present an interpretation of the war as a cultural clash. The message was that the core of Japanese culture, usually identified as *bushido*, was primitive, violent and irreconcilable with civilized modernity. In this view, the war crimes trials underpinned the demilitarization of Japan—meaning that it would never again be able to threaten US hegemony—and its democratisation, meaning that it would never again have the will to do so.

This conclusive erasure of Japan's strategic identity, however, was irreconcilable with the increasing urgent imperatives created for the USA by the Cold War. American leaders were in no doubt that the future struggle would be with the Soviet Union and with communism, rather than with Japan. In this global struggle, Japan's role was as a pliant but potent ally,

---

[29] W. G. Beasley, *Japanese imperialism, 1894–1945* (Oxford: Clarendon Press, 1987); Robyn Lim, *The geopolitics of East Asia: search for equilibrium* (London: RoutledgeCurzon, 2003); Paul R. Schratz, 'The Orient and US Naval Strategy' in Joe C. Dixon, ed., *The American Military in the Far East: Proceedings of the Ninth Military History Symposium* (Washington, DC: Superintendent of Documents, 1980), 127–138.

[30] John W. Dower, *War without Mercy: Race and Power in the Pacific War* (New York: Pantheon Books, 1986).

not as an empty space on the map. The Cold War required that Japan be allowed to reconstruct its economy as a bulwark for US power in East Asia and that it be rehabilitated as a respectable member of the global community.[31] This imperative required that Japanese civilization not be destroyed and that Japan not be loaded with eternal responsibility for the war. The most dramatic manifestation of this strategic calculation was the decision of the US occupation authorities not to place the Japanese emperor on trial, nor even to demand his abdication, despite his position as head of state throughout the hostilities. It was also manifest in the 1948 decision of the occupation authorities not to proceed with a second round of IMTFE trials, even though the potential defendants were conveniently available in detention in Tokyo's Sugamo Prison. In the late 1940s and early 1950s, the British and other prosecuting authorities made similar decisions to wind up their trial processes for the sake of facilitating Japan's rehabilitation. This effort to clear the moral ground for a new postwar order in East Asia influenced the position of the Japanese already convicted of war crimes. The formal position that they were individual perpetrators bearing responsibility for the specific crimes that they had committed increasingly gave way to a perception, especially in Japan, that they were scapegoats unreasonably being punished for a nation whose guilt was now being forgiven by the prosecuting powers in the interest of Cold War realities.

A key feature of the strategic reconfiguration of East Asia was a change in the status of Japan's most important colonies, Taiwan (Formosa) and Korea. In the immediate postwar plans, Taiwan, which had been held by Japan since 1895, was 'restored' to the Chinese Republic, even thought it had been a Japanese possession since well before the Republic's foundation in 1911. Korea, seized and colonized by Japan during the half-decade to 1910, was to recover independence, though perhaps not at once. During the immediate postwar years, however, Taiwan became increasingly important to the Chinese Republic's leaders as a secure offshore haven in their battle against the Chinese Communist Party; in 1949 they were to withdraw there entirely. Korea quickly divided into rival camps, the Americans sponsoring anti-communist forces in the south and the Soviets supporting communists in the north. International and ideological tension over the Korean peninsula and in the Taiwan Strait was one of

---

[31] John W. Dower, *Embracing Defeat: Japan in the wake of World War II* (New York: Norton, 1999);
Herbert Bix, *Hirohito and the making of modern Japan* (New York: HarperCollins, 2000).

the most important elements pushing the memory of the Pacific War into the background. Dean Askielowicz shows in his chapter nonetheless how ragged this shift from Pacific War to Cold War was in practice. Australian authorities were dogged in their insistence that the changed postwar circumstances of Korea and Taiwan would not influence the war guilt of Korean and Taiwanese perpetrators. He also shows that convicted Korean and Taiwanese war criminals benefited equally with Japanese war criminals from Australia's later shift to offering clemency.

Not only the USA but also the Soviet Union and the competing authorities in China—Nationalist and Communist—faced similarly conflicting Cold War imperatives. The Soviet Union had entered the Pacific War very late. Soviet forces attacked Japanese-controlled Manchukuo only on 9 August 1945, but Russia's history of competition with Japan for hegemony in Northeast Asia went back to the Russo-Japanese War of 1904–1905 and Japan's intervention in Siberia in 1918–1922 to oppose the Bolshevik Revolution. Soviet and Japanese forces had also clashed on the Manchukuo–Siberia border several times since 1932. The Soviet authorities, moreover, were strongly aware of the wartime Japanese government's demonization of communism. As Valentyna Polunina argues in her chapter in this book, the Soviet Union was unhappy with the limited number of defendants brought before the IMTFE and frustrated with its meager influence in Tokyo in comparison with the strong role it had played in the International Military Tribunal (IMT) in Nuremberg. In order to strengthen the public case for further rounds of prosecution after the completion of what they saw as only the first of a series of Tokyo trials— the IMT in Nuremberg which tried the Nazi leaders had been followed by a series of other Nuremberg trials in which, for instance, industrialists were indicted—the Soviet Union held its own trial of Japanese personnel in Khabarovsk in December 1949. The court heard charges of crimes against humanity against staff of the notorious Unit 731, which had conducted medical experiments on thousands of live human subjects.[32] This prosecution appeared to gain moral high ground for the Soviet Union because the USA had failed to prosecute the commander of Unit 731, Ishii Shirō. The trial also allowed the Soviet Union to assert its friendship for the new People's Republic of China, on whose territory the crimes had been committed and with which a Treaty of Friendship was signed only weeks

---

[32] See Sheldon H. Harris, *Factories of Death: Japanese Biological Warfare, 1932–45, and the American Cover-up* (New York: Routledge, 1994).

later. This advantage diminished when the court imposed only light sentences on the defendants, as the Soviet Union had temporarily abolished the death sentence. The timing of this lenience, however, may have been beneficial for the Soviet Union, because it was apparently able to obtain information on the outcome of the experiments in exchange. The Soviet Union could thus underline how it was exerting firm justice while at the same time benefitting from its own (temporal) lenient war crimes policy.

The terrible Japanese violence in the newly captured Chinese capital, Nanjing, in 1937 had attracted global attention and the embattled Nationalist government in China had urged the prosecution of Japanese war crimes from the moment that the idea of a systematic prosecution of Axis war crimes had been put forward in 1942. Moreover, the Nationalist authorities had hosted the Far Eastern and Pacific Sub-Commission of the UNWCC in its provisional capital, Chongqing, since November 1944. By the end of the war, China had suffered for longer and on a larger scale than any other region in Asia. Nonetheless, China did not dominate the postwar trials process. As in some other parts of Asia, most notably Korea, the postwar thirst for retributive justice focussed on collaborators much more than on Japanese. In the developing conflict between communists and anti-communists it was more important to show the consequences of disloyalty than to punish a defeated foreign enemy. Moreover, in this conflict Japanese troops had great potential for assisting Nationalist forces against their communist enemies. As time passed, the recovering economic significance of Japan also encouraged the Chinese government to be restrained in its prosecution of alleged Japanese war criminals. Nor was the insurgent Chinese Communist Party (CCP) any less ambiguous. In its rhetoric, the party portrayed Chiang Kai-shek and his party, the Guomindang, as more deserving of war crimes trials than Japanese troops. The communists also benefited from the services of some Japanese troops after the war.[33] Even following the communist victory in 1949, as Adam Cathcart argues in this volume, the party saw value in lenient treatment of the ordinary soldiers whom it eventually tried in Shenyang and Taiyuan. Leniency was a way of expressing solidarity with the Japanese masses whom the CCP still hoped might have revolutionary potential.

---

[33] Barak Kushner, 'Ghosts of the Japanese Imperial Army: the "White Group" (*Baituan*) and early post-war Sino-Japanese relations,' *Past and Present*, Supplement 8 (2013), 117–150.

No attempt has been made to estimate the overall cost of the postwar trials effort. Accounting principles of the time referred only to direct costs, such as accommodation and transport costs for witnesses, and largely ignored the actual commitment of human and material resources to the trials themselves, let alone the huge investment in the investigation and detention of suspects prior to trial. Nonetheless, it seems likely that the 2,300-odd trials conducted in Asia and the Pacific were a bargain in comparison with later international trials for war crimes and crimes against humanity conducted in the International Criminal Tribunals for the former Yugoslavia and for Rwanda (ICTY and ICTR), and in the International Criminal Court (ICC). During its first 23 years of existence, the ICTY indicted 161 persons and achieved 80 sentences at a total cost of around US$2 billion. In its first decade, the ICC delivered one verdict for a budget cost of US$900 million.[34] In light of this, the view that the postwar trials of Japanese achieved much under difficult circumstances remains widespread.[35]

CONCLUSION

This volume offers a globally oriented overview of postwar justice in Asia in a time of transition. It examines the application of new international laws to the specific context of Asia, the conflicting priorities of the main colonial powers—Great Britain, France, the Netherlands and the USA—and the contradictions that arose from the Cold War rivalry of the USA and the Soviet Union as former wartime allies. The volume reveals new dimensions of the Tokyo Trial, while also drawing attention to the scale and importance of the national trials.

Conducted by ten different authorities and prosecuting thousands of defendants of different ranks and ethnicities over more than a decade, the

---

[34] David Wippman, 'The Costs of International Justice,' *American Journal of International Law*, 100, 4 (Oct., 2006), 861–881; David Akerson, 'The Comparative Cost of Justice at the ICC,' *Denver Journal of International Law and Policy*, 26 March 2012, http://djilp.org/1877/the-comparative-cost-of-justice-at-the-icc/. See also the ICTY's own presentation: 'The Cost of Justice,' http://www.icty.org/en/about/tribunal/the-cost-of-justice

[35] Dean Michael Aszkielowicz, 'After the surrender: Australia and the Japanese Class B and C war criminals, 1945–1958' (Ph. D. dissertation, Murdoch University, 2012); Georgina Fitzpatrick, 'War crimes trials, 'victor's justice' and Australian military justice in the aftermath of the Second World War,' in Kevin Jon Heller and Gerry Simpson, eds, *The hidden histories of war crimes trials* (Oxford: Oxford University Press, 2013), 327–347.

war crimes trials of Japanese after the Second World War are an immensely complex phenomenon in their own right. The authorities which carried out these trials were united by their focus on atrocities and aggression committed by Japanese forces in Asia and the Pacific from 1928 to 1945. The trials were underpinned by a common conviction that formal legal proceedings were the most appropriate means of achieving what would now be called transitional justice. They grappled, as later attempts at transitional justice have grappled, with the twin problems of scale and time: how could any justice system cope with crimes of such enormity? And how could justice fairly take into account the specific circumstances of crimes carried out in often vastly difficult circumstances? They struggled over the purpose of punishment and over the broader question of what might be necessary to achieve satisfactory justice. They contributed to the emergence of a transcultural legal discourse which engaged with the tensions between legal universalism and Western legal hegemony in Asia.

The ten distinct authorities who conducted the trials faced very different political circumstances. It is not surprising that the trials defy straightforward incorporation into the grand historical narratives of the era in which they took place. They were a major advance in international humanitarian law, but that advance was qualified by their one-sided character as the policy of victorious powers in the Pacific War. The trials contributed to winding up the business of the Pacific War by affirming the defeat of Japan and consolidating a discourse claiming that the Allies were morally superior to their defeated enemy. This discourse, however, was often at odds with the emerging imperatives of the Cold War, which on one hand demanded that Japan return to the community of nations as an important Asian ally of the USA and on the other saw the Japanese masses as a potential revolutionary force. In turn, the demands of international humanitarian law, of ending the Pacific War and of waging the Cold War sat uneasily with the complexities of decolonization in Southeast Asia and Korea. Holding war crimes trials of Japanese perpetrators enabled former colonial powers to reassert their authority in the colonies that they had temporarily lost and in which they were challenged by newly invigorated nationalist movements. It enabled them to show their concern to deliver justice on behalf of peoples who had suffered under Japanese occupation. But Japanese military personnel were sometimes too useful to be put on trial and the trials often came too late to deliver any noticeable political benefit to the prosecuting authorities. Trials which prosecuted Japanese or Korean guards for cruelty towards Asian labourers or arraigned members of the Kenpeitai for the torture and murder of suspected enemy sympathizers, moreover, drew uncomfortable attention to the West's own history of exploitation and repression in the region. The contradictory status of Koreans as Japanese subjects who were both victims of Japanese colonialism and perpetrators of war crimes added to the complexity of the situation.

In the end, these multiple contradictions define the trial process as an arena for moral and political conflict. We can only understand the international legal norms which took shape in these trials in the broader context of decolonization and the Cold War.

CHAPTER 2

Colonialism, Anti-Colonialism and Neo-Colonialism in China: The Opium Question at the Tokyo War Crimes Tribunal

Neil Boister

INTRODUCTION

One of the overlooked aspects of the Tokyo War Crimes Tribunal is that it was the first and perhaps only international military tribunal to take jurisdiction over the illicit traffic in drugs. The drug in question was opium. The foundations of modern international drug control arise from China's opium problem of the nineteenth and twentieth centuries. The opium trade into China by Euro-American traffickers was the mode through which China encountered the West.[1] That trade was characterized by the export of opium grown in Western colonies (small scale licensed cultivators were obliged to sell to monopolies) for consumption in China. The very

---

[1] Carl A. Trocki, *Opium, Empire, and the Global Political Economy* (London: Routledge, 1999), 88.

N. Boister (✉)
Waikato University, Hamilton, New Zealand

© The Author(s) 2016
K. von Lingen (ed.), *War Crimes Trials in the Wake of Decolonization and Cold War in Asia, 1945–1956*,
DOI 10.1007/978-3-319-42987-8_2

high profits were used to address the trade deficits generated by Western purchase of luxury goods from China including tea, as well as generating healthy customs revenues for the exporting authority.[2] Although the trade was initially controlled by private interests, official involvement grew steadily. The Indian trade, for example, was initially under the monopoly control of private companies like the British East India Company (from 1773), until control was assumed by the British Government. Although the drug was prohibited in China from 1729, the market for it steadily expanded, with the corruption of Chinese officials facilitating the trade. After 1838, the cultivation and production of opium in China began to increase steadily. The victory of the Western powers in the 'opium wars'[3] forced China to accept legalization of the trade in 1858 but in the early part of the twentieth century,[4] the moral suasion of missionaries persuaded the USA to try to bring the trade to an end. Britain was economically involved and so initially resisted.[5] This encounter provided both a justification for later Japanese intervention and a model for Japan's exploitation of opium in China. Japan, a relative late-comer to colonialism in Asia, adopted monopoly policies that were late variations of similar European colonial policies.[6]

Yet as opium is a product with a value both economic and in terms of state power, so too does the solution to the opium question, the policy of global prohibition of opium, also have value. Intent on controlling Japan's security threat to their interests in East Asia,[7] the USA and Britain used the League of Nations Advisory Committee on the Trafficking of Opium and Other Drugs (the Opium Advisory Committee or OAC) to engage in

---

[2] Hunt Janin, *The India–China Opium Trade in the nineteenth century* (Jefferson, NC, McFarland, 1999), 31 et seq; Peter War Fay, *The Opium War: 1840–42* (Chapel Hill, NC: University of North Carolina Press, revised edition 1997), 41 et seq.
[3] See Edgar Holt, *The Opium Wars in China* (London: Putnam, 1964).
[4] The Treaty of Tientsin, signed at the end of the Second Opium War.
[5] William O. Walker III, *Opium and Foreign Policy: The Anglo American Search for Order in Asia 1912–1954* (Chapel Hill, NC: The University of North Carolina Press, 1991), 44–46.
[6] See Kathryn Meyer, 'Japan and the World Narcotics Trade' in Jordan Goodman, Paul E. Lovejoy and Andrew Sherratt, eds, *Consuming Habits: Drugs in History and Anthropology* (London: Routledge, 1995), 186; John M. Jennings, *The Opium Empire: Japanese Imperialism and Drug Trafficking in Asia, 1895–1945* (Westport, CN: Praeger, 1997); William B. McAllister, *Drug Diplomacy in the twentieth century: An International History* (London: Routledge, 2000).
[7] Walker, *Opium and Foreign Policy*, 21.

trenchant condemnation of Japanese drug policy in its colonies in China. This chapter examines the hypothesis that these debates, cut short by Japan's withdrawal from the League and then war, played out in a final act at the International Military Tribunal for the Far East (IMTFE) held in Tokyo from 1946 to 1948.[8] It argues that the Tokyo Tribunal's condemnation of Japanese policy played a role in ending one kind of imperial exploitation (opium supply) and in introducing a form of moral imperialism (the US-buttressed prohibition of opium).

Part 2 sketches the legal framework within which the debate about drug control in China occurred. Parts 3–7 trace the perspectives of the main players—the erstwhile colonizer, Britain, the *nouveau* colonizer, Japan, the neo-imperialist, the USA, and the colony, China—as revealed at the Tokyo Trial. Part 8 contrasts this version with the more nuanced version of historians. Part 9 concludes that the Tokyo Trial provided a venue to the USA for achieving hegemony over the global drug control system.

THE INTERNATIONAL LEGAL FRAMEWORK ON DRUG CONTROL

At the Shanghai International Opium Commission held in 1909 the USA and Japan resolved together with other participating states to limit the use of opium to medical purposes and to control its supply as well as that of its harmful derivatives.[9] As parties to the International Opium Convention signed at The Hague on 23 January 1912[10] (the 1912 Hague Convention) both states (along with inter alia China and Britain) promised to control its production and distribution[11] and limit its export.[12] Colonial states agreed to 'restrict and control' opium use in their Chinese territories[13] and to gradually reduce the number of retail outlets.[14] The convention also limited the manufacture, sale, use[15] and traffic in morphine.[16] Compliance

---

[8] See generally Neil Boister and Robert Cryer, *The Tokyo International Military Tribunal: A Reappraisal* (Oxford: OUP, 2008).
[9] Hamilton Wright, 'The International Opium Commission', *American Journal of International Law* 3 (1909): 648, 827.
[10] League of Nations Treaty Series, Vol. 8 (hereinafter 8 L.N.T.S.), 187; in force 1920.
[11] 8 L.N.T.S. 187 Article 1.
[12] 8 L.N.T.S. 187 Articles 2, 3, and 5.
[13] 8 L.N.T.S. 187 Article 17.
[14] 8 L.N.T.S. 187 Article 18.
[15] 8 L.N.T.S. 187 Article 9.
[16] 8 L.N.T.S. 187 Article 11.

monitoring was initiated when the League of Nations assumed supervision of drug control and in 1920 established the OAC.[17]

Steady progress towards prohibition was halted in a 1924 Geneva Conference, participation in which was limited to states with Far Eastern interests that still permitted personal use of opium. Led by Britain, the participating states, which included Japan, opted for government monopolies on production and supply, and this approach was formalized in a 'closed' agreement made in 1925.[18] The merits of prohibition versus monopolistic supply and use were debated at an 'open' conference held in 1924–25 in Geneva. The International Opium Convention signed on 19 February 1925[19] (the 1925 Geneva Convention) which stiffened control of 'raw opium'[20] and set out an export/import authorization scheme for international trade supervised by a permanent central board,[21] failed, however, to adopt limits on the production of raw opium. Frustrated, the USA and China withdrew from the conference and neither acceded to the convention. Japan, however, ratified the 1925 Convention[22] and the Convention for Limiting the Manufacture and Regulating the Distribution of Narcotic Drugs, signed at Geneva on 13 July 1931 (the 1931 Geneva Convention) which limited licit production of narcotic drugs (morphine, heroin, cocaine, etc.) based on estimated need so as to prevent diversion into the illicit traffic.[23]

Prosecution's Theory

The theory that Japan had breached its international drug control obligations in China was revealed in the indictment laid by the prosecution at the Tokyo Trial in 1946. The 'Group One' counts of 'Crimes Against Peace' charged 'wars of aggression' and 'wars in violation of international

---

[17] Japan along with the China, The Netherlands, Britain, France, India, Siam and Portugal were original members (1921). The USA, a non-League member, was invited on to the OAC in 1922.

[18] The Agreement Concerning the Suppression of the Manufacture of, Internal Trade in and Use of, Prepared Opium, signed at Geneva on 11 February, 1925; 51 LNTS 337, in force 26 July 1926, to which Japan was a signatory and party.

[19] 81 L.N.T.S. 317; in force September 1923.

[20] 81 L.N.T.S. 317, Article 2.

[21] Provision was made for these measures in Chaps. 5 and 6 of the convention, respectively.

[22] On 10 October 1928.

[23] 139 L.N.T.S. 301; in force 9 July 1933. Japan ratified it on 3 June 1935.

law, treaties, agreements and assurances.'[24] Appendix A, which expanded on the count of aggression in China, made a number of allegations crucial to the prosecution's argument about opium control.[25] First, the Japanese had 'pursued a systematic policy of weakening the native inhabitants will to resist ... by directly and indirectly encouraging increased production and importation of opium and other narcotics and by promoting the sale and consumption of such drugs among such people.' Second, 'revenue from the above mentioned traffic in opium and other narcotics was used to finance the preparation for and waging of the wars of aggression ... and to establish and finance the puppet governments set up by the Japanese Government in the various occupied territories.' Third, the Japanese Government 'was actively participating in the proceedings of the League of Nations Committee on Traffic in Opium and other Dangerous Drugs and profess[ing] ... to the world to be co-operating fully with other member nations in the enforcement of treaties governing traffic in opium and other narcotics to which she was a party.' Opening this part of the prosecution's case, China's associate prosecutor, Judge Hsiang put it to the court that:

> The evidence will show the opium and narcotics traffic was sponsored by Japan for two purposes: (1) To weaken the stamina and undermine the will to resist of the Chinese people; (2) To provide substantial revenue to finance Japanese military and economic aggression.[26]

It later reiterated the US view expressed in the OAC that although Japan had used a 'technically permissible' argument to justify non-prohibition, this had created a 'serious menace to the rest of the world.'[27] Three factual theses are revealed: the Japanese were (1) deliberately pursuing a policy of narcotization of the Chinese in order to (2) exploit the profits to finance a war of aggression in China, all the while (3) professing otherwise at the League of Nations.

---

[24] See, for example, Count One, the indictment is reproduced in Boister and Cryer, *Documents on the Tokyo War Crimes Tribunal. Charter, Indictment and Judgments* (Oxford: OUP, 2008), 16.
[25] Section 4, see Boister and Cryer, *Documents on the Tokyo War Crimes Tribunal*, 37.
[26] See *United States v Araki, Sadao, et al*, Transcripts of Proceedings (IMTFE Transcript), vol. 11, 3892.
[27] IMTFE Transcript, vol. 14, 4668.

Prosecution Evidence

Introduction

Although certain suspects had revealed Japan's role in the supply and sale of drugs in occupied China,[28] the prosecution relied chiefly on two sources of evidence to support its theory:

(i) US Treasury and State Department Reports investigating drug control conditions in the Far East, compiled from reports made by US consular officials distributed across the region 'as part of the US Government's program to combat the smuggling of opium and narcotics in the United States.'[29]
(ii) Reports of the meetings of the League of Nations OAC where Japanese conduct in China in regard to opium and narcotics was subject to criticism by the USA and Chinese representatives.

The prosecution then led evidence of Japanese practise in three phases, Manchuria, North China and Central China, in order to illustrate that Japan had breached its international promises.

Manchuria

After leading evidence of trafficking from Japan's concessions in Manchuria into China,[30] the first piece of key documentary evidence was the US Treasury Attaché in Shanghai M. R. Nicholson's 1934 report on the opium position in Manchukuo[31] which had been requested in December 1933 by a Conference of the Treasury, State, Labour, and Customs Departments and the Federal Bureau of Narcotics (FBN).[32] Excerpts from the report gave details of levels of addiction, licensing of opium sellers and operation

---

[28] See, for example, interrogation of General Tanaka, Ryukichi by Col. W.M.T. Hornaday, see Interrogation of Tanaka (8 March 1946), 2–8, reproduced in R. J. Pritchard, ed., *The Tokyo Major War Crimes Trial: The Records of the International Military Tribunal for the Far East with an Authorised Commentary and Comprehensive Guide* vol. 124A, (Lewiston: Edwin Mellen, 1998–2005), 4.
[29] IMTFE Transcript, vol. 14, 4669.
[30] IMTFE Transcript, vol. 14, 4667.
[31] IMTFE Transcript, vol. 14, 4670.
[32] IMTFE Transcript, vol. 14, 4671.

of opium dens. Official sanction was established by evidence of the issuing of Japanese bonds against opium profits and through contributions to budgets.³³ A secret telegram from the chief of staff of the Kwantung Army to the vice-minister of war of 4 June 1932 revealed that initially ¥10 million of the estimated ¥64 million required per annum to administer Manchukuo was to come from opium revenues, an estimated total cost increase to ¥93 million which required rapidly increased opium revenue.³⁴ A ¥30 million Manchukuo Government bond issued on 19 November 1932 was 'secured by the profits of the opium monopoly office.'³⁵ It was signed by the accused Hoshino Naoki (then a member of Japan's Finance Ministry).

Further US reports were then read into the record, detailing cultivation and sale. A report from the consul general in Mukden in 1936 provided a translation of the Manchukuo Opium Monopoly Bureau's announcement concerning the authorization of poppy cultivation in 1937 which showed an increase in production. It also recorded the visit to Mukden in 27–28 October 1937 of B. M. Thompson, special assistant to the US Treasury secretary, who was surprised to find that upon entering an opium den the 'attendants without question started to lead [him] to a smoking compartment, in much the same way as one could be led to a table in a restaurant.'³⁶ He concluded: 'Demonstrating with peculiar force the relation of cause to effect, there lay on an ash heap behind the narcotic brothels seven naked corpses which had evidently been stripped of their rags by fellow addicts.'³⁷ Drawing in the other Japanese monopolies, a 1937 report from the consul general in Seoul about a surge in opium imports from Korea to Manchuria was tendered, followed by evidence of a 1933 Japanese Cabinet decision to supply opium from Korea to Manchukuo.³⁸

The prosecution then introduced statements in the OAC's 22nd session in 1937 by the US Representative Stuart Fuller noting the rise in production, recounting Japanese criticism of Manchukuoan drugs policy and dismissing efforts to stamp out illicit cultivation as 'an effort to destroy business competition.'³⁹ Fuller's conclusions were quoted at length:

---

³³ IMTFE Transcript, vol. 14, 4671–4693.
³⁴ IMTFE Transcript, vol. 14, 4682. vol. 57, 20340.
³⁵ IMTFE Transcript, vol. 14, 4683–4685.
³⁶ IMTFE Transcript, vol. 14, 4702.
³⁷ IMTFE Transcript, vol. 14, 4705.
³⁸ IMTFE Transcript, vol. 14, 4706. 4708.
³⁹ IMTFE Transcript, vol. 14, 4713–14.

> Mr Chairman I put it to you that this is a sad but most illuminating example of the results of greed, of large scale poisoning of one's fellow man for gain and an example of the total disregard of the obligations which any government, de facto or de jure, which hopes to enjoy respect, confidence or recognition, has towards other governments of the world.[40]

A reprise to Fuller from the Egyptian representative Russel Pasha, described Manchukuo's drug policy as a menace 'to the rest of the civilised world,' with Darien as the source of 'thousands of letters containing drugs ... posted to the United States, Egypt and elsewhere,' and Tientsin 'as the nerve centre of heroin manufacture and addiction in the world,' and culminated with the unsupported claim that 90 % of all white drugs were Japanese in origin and 90 % were going to the USA.[41] Japanese sanction of this illicit traffic was according to the prosecution established by the failure of Japanese consular authorities to punish trafficking into China adequately, in contrast to the severity meted out for trafficking into Japan.[42] Evidence described the Manchukuo Opium Monopoly's fruitless complaints to the Manchukuoan Government to close the illegal factories down[43] and reports from the US consul general in Mukden in 1939 condemning as a fraud new drug laws in Manchukuo claimed to be aimed at eradication.[44]

North China

The prosecution then turned to North China, where it led evidence that Japan's occupation was followed by increases in use, production (first voluntary and then compulsory) and revenue.[45] Late in the trial a witness, Chinese Judge Advocate Kiang Cheng-Ting, noted that while prior to the invasion attempts to expel Japanese and Korean drug traffickers were hindered by the Japanese authorities, after the invasion 'large-scale narcotization in China' had been carried out under the auspices of the Japanese established Board of Opium Suppression.[46]

---

[40] IMTFE Transcript, vol. 14, 4722.
[41] IMTFE Transcript, vol. 14, 4724–4729.
[42] IMTFE Transcript, vol. 8, 2680, vol. 11, 3890.
[43] IMTFE Transcript, vol. 14, 4734.
[44] IMTFE Transcript, vol. 14, 4745–4750.
[45] IMTFE Transcript, vol. 108, 39310–39325.
[46] IMTFE Transcript, vol. 14, 4631–32.

Returning to the international stage, the prosecution read statements made by the Chinese representative Dr Hoo Chi-Tsai from the 24th session of the OAC in 1939 about the improved prohibition of drugs in China itself,[47] and contrasted these with more from US Representative Fuller, who cited the export of 650 kg of heroin from Tienstin to the USA in a 15-month period (sufficient 'to supply some 10,000 addicts for a year') and who recorded the flood of Iranian opium into Japanese-occupied China.[48]

To firm up the official connection, the prosecution witness Oikawa Genshichi, former vice president and director of political affairs in the Kōain (Asia Development Board) branch in Shanghai detailed the board's and the Japanese Special Services Organization's (SSO) role in analyzing demand and arranging supply.[49] Japanese Cabinet reports were relied upon to indicate high-level awareness about the drug control situation in China.[50]

A sheaf of reports from the UAA's Shanghai Treasury Attaché Nicholson detailed events on the ground. A 1940 report indicated a surge in opium cultivation in occupied North China. A May 1936 report indicated the growth of heroin manufacture in Chahar and Jehol. A June 1936 report charted the rise in opium sales. An April 1937 report detailed tax and military service exemptions for cultivation and the death penalty for adulteration of product. A July 1940 report revealed enforced planting. Then a July 1936 report spoke of 'Japan's narcotization policy in North China.'[51] A May 1940 State Department report commented that the efforts by Chinese puppets to control opium were being resisted by the SSO.[52] In 1941 the US consul general in Tsingtao reported the establishment of a new opium prohibition bureau.[53] A former manager of an opium den, Kuo Yu-San, deposed that everything was under Japanese control, while an Austrian dentist, Leo Kandel, opined in oral testimony that Japan supported the traffic into China to undermine the 'strength of the Chinese people.'[54]

---

[47] IMTFE Transcript, vol. 14, 4751–55.
[48] IMTFE Transcript, vol. 14, 4756–58.
[49] IMTFE Transcript, vol. 14, 4761.
[50] IMTFE Transcript, vol. 14, 4776–68.
[51] IMTFE Transcript, vol. 14, 4779–4791.
[52] IMTFE Transcript, vol. 14, 4794.
[53] IMTFE Transcript, vol. 14, 4797.
[54] IMTFE Transcript, vol. 14, 4810, 4813.

Central China

In regard to occupied Central China, the prosecution relied even more heavily on Nicholson's reports. A November 1934 report related a deal to move a large quantity of Persian opium held in Formosa to South China to be used to finance Chinese pro-Japanese bandits transported by the Japanese navy.[55] An April 1936 report confirmed that the cheap sale of Persian opium was being used to finance the Japanese sponsored autonomy movement. His July 1936 report recorded the formation of trade unions to protect Formosan–Japanese drug interests in Amoy. A November 1936 report recorded maintenance of secret plants in the hills for manufacture of heroin. A July 1937 report revealed Japanese attempts to intervene in the trial of the opium king Paul Yap.[56] A July 1938 report recorded the fall in opium prices after the occupation in Shanghai.[57] A 1939 report from the US consul at Amoy, contrasted the considerable success of Chinese efforts to eradicate the traffic with 'legalisation of the use of opium' under Japanese occupation.[58] A March 1940 report from the US consul at Canton drew attention to the Formosan connection and detailed monthly incomes to Japanese authorities, some dispersed to the Japanese puppet government and some to the army.[59]

Prior to occupation, a February 1937 report by the US consul general noted an increased number of Japanese and Koreans engaging in the traffic in Shanghai. The Shanghai Municipal police, it recorded, were receiving poor cooperation from Japanese consulate police who were unwilling to go on night raids, and it commented on the imposition of light penalties on Japanese subjects, including a caution for the first offence, fines for the third offence and deportation for a flagrant offence.[60] The former Chief of the Shanghai International Settlement's Narcotics Bureau Harold Gill testified to similar practices[61] and the prosecution backed this up with statement by Fuller to the 24th session of the OAC, who drew attention to the continued disparity between offenders sentenced by Japanese authorities and by Chinese courts in Shanghai (fines versus death).[62]

---

[55] IMTFE Transcript, vol. 14, 4820.
[56] IMTFE Transcript, vol. 14, 4824–4830.
[57] IMTFE Transcript, vol. 14, 4832.
[58] IMTFE Transcript, vol. 14, 4834.
[59] IMTFE Transcript, vol. 14, 4837–4842.
[60] IMTFE Transcript, vol. 14, 4845–48.
[61] IMTFE Transcript, vol. 14, 4407.
[62] IMTFE Transcript, vol. 14, 4852.

A report from Nicholson in January 1938 indicated the formalization of the trade in Shanghai under Japanese occupation.[63] A 1939 report of the Japanese Foreign Ministry's treaty bureau recorded the import of Persian opium for distribution by the Japanese conglomerate Mitsui Bussan.[64] Very detailed reports from Nicholson in 1938 indicated that the Japanese SSO had been sending Persian opium into the international settlement for sale in opium businesses, while a 10 December 1939 report detailed Japanese ships delivering opium in Shanghai.[65]

In December 1939 Nicholson reported the establishment of a central opium monopoly bureau in occupied China by the 'puppet regime in Nanking' and recorded a Ministry of the Interior official's explanation that Japan had transferred the administration of the opium trade to it 'to avoid international criticism for their part in the narcotisation of China.'[66] In earlier testimony, the former professor of history at Nanking University, M. E. Bates, gave evidence of the rapid expansion of narcotics as a public enterprise after the occupation.[67]

The prosecution recorded Nicholson's view that the 'puppet government' had set aside US$4000 per month to fund opium suppression propaganda as a whitewash 'to cover their narcotization crimes.'[68] An affidavit from Harada Kumakichi, a Japanese attaché in Shanghai in 1937, set out how the Japanese advised the puppet Chinese government to establish the opium suppression board.[69] Nicholson's report of February 1939 details opium profits to the SSO (US$300 million per annum).[70] A January 1939 report notes the Japanese use of a Chinese charity, the Hung Chi Shan Tang, to front the traffic.[71] The prosecution's witness, Satomi Hajima, vice president of the Hung-Chi-Shan-Tung clarified that profits went to the SSO.[72] A report from Nicholson of July 1939 described the opium monopoly in central China and asserted that it was the same system employed in Formosa.[73] A September 1939 report recorded the Japanese

---

[63] IMTFE Transcript, vol. 14, 4854.
[64] IMTFE Transcript, vol. 14, 4860.
[65] IMTFE Transcript, vol. 14, 4866.
[66] IMTFE Transcript, vol. 14, 4868, 4870.
[67] IMTFE Transcript, vol. 8, 2649.
[68] IMTFE Transcript, vol. 14, 4871.
[69] IMTFE Transcript, vol. 4, 4875.
[70] IMTFE Transcript, vol. 14, 4871.
[71] IMTFE Transcript, vol. 14, 4874.
[72] IMTFE Transcript, vol. 14, 4881.
[73] IMTFE Transcript, vol. 14, 4894.

military's reluctance to give complete control of sale to the puppet Chinese government and its intention to retain supply control in order to guarantee profits.[74] Statements from the record of the Chinese prosecution of Mei Szi Ping, an official in charge of the puppet regime's opium monopoly, were adduced to indicate that Japan escaped from formal difficulties in China by having no official involvement in profit-taking and that such taking was done in secret.[75] Student riots had prompted the Japanese to offer restoration of pre-war suppression measures, and the Chinese had reduced supply, wound up the Hun-Chi-Shan-Tang and cracked down on former Chinese 'associates' of the Japanese, all without Japanese interference.

Returning to the international stage, the prosecution then contrasted US evidence from occupation forces of large-scale heroin manufacture in Korea with the declaration by Japan recorded in the report of the Permanent Central Opium Board of 29 January 1946 that Japan had not engaged in heroin manufacture in Korea from 1939 to 1945.[76] A letter from the chief of the league's drug control service, Bertil A. Renborg, revealed a complete breakdown in Japan's reporting obligations under the drug conventions during the war.[77] A letter from the US Ambassador to Japan, Joseph C. Grew, written in April 1939, revealed a complete absence of response by Japan to accusations about its drug policies made directly to it in an official diplomatic protest by the USA.[78]

THE DEFENCE RESPONSE

The defence tried to show that the opium policy of Manchukuo was established for control and suppression[79] and that 'sincere efforts' had been made to enforce it.[80] It did not deny the existence of a monopoly system, but led evidence that the policy adhered to article 6 of the 1912 Convention's provision for 'gradual and efficacious suppression' and League of Nations recommendations to the same effect, and stated how Japan had tried to emulate the positive results of the Formosan system.[81] It placed

---

[74] IMTFE Transcript, vol. 14, 4896.
[75] IMTFE Transcript, vol. 15, 4912–4918.
[76] IMTFE Transcript, vol. 15, 4920.
[77] IMTFE Transcript, vol. 15, 4924–5.
[78] IMTFE Transcript, vol. 15, 4927–41.
[79] IMTFE Transcript, vol. 57, 20245.
[80] IMTFE Transcript, vol. 116, 42612.
[81] IMTFE Transcript, vol. 57, 20246.

in evidence the 1925 Closed Geneva Agreement which had been ignored by the prosecution. Article 1 provides for a government monopoly on supply, and according to the defence this was of the kind used in Formosa and in Manchukuo.[82] The defence also introduced a 1930 report from the League of Nations Commission of Enquiry for the Control of Opium Smoking in the Far East which suggested that total prohibition, as practised in the Philippines, was ineffective.[83] They quoted:

> Experience has proved that total rigorously applied prohibition of opium-smoking does not lead to total suppression of the opium-smoking habit, in view of the persistence of the deeply rooted vice and the great difficulties in preventing imports of illicit opium and its distribution to illegal consumers. It seems better that the opium-smoking habit should be gradually suppressed by legalising smoking by confirmed addicts and by supplying such smokers with government opium. This method only offers the possibilities of limiting individual consumption and preventing the spread of the habit to more and more individuals. Whether the system be prohibition or Government control, limitation and, as far as possible, eradication of the illicit traffic is indispensable to success.[84]

Turning to the situation in Japanese-occupied China, the defence introduced excerpts from the Manchukuo Yearbook of 1942, which sets out that the purpose of the opium monopoly in Manchukuo was licensed control of cultivation and use while suppressing illicit supply.[85] It argued that the policy in Formosa was a success, pointing out that the register of users had to be reopened twice, suggesting that an upsurge of use as happened in Manchukuo was a feature of a monopoly system.[86] However, when it wanted to introduce into evidence former governor of Formosa Sagatoro Kaku's book, *Opium Policy in Japan*, which it maintained provided relevant details on the transfer of the monopoly policy, a majority denied admissibility, with President Webb commenting, 'The Formosan example may have been a bad one, not necessarily a good one.'[87] In order to illustrate that Manchukuo was serious about controlling opium,

---

[82] IMTFE Transcript, vol. 57, 20246, vol. 116, 42606.
[83] IMTFE Transcript, vol. 57, 20251, vol. 116, 42606.
[84] IMTFE Transcript, vol. 57, 20252–3.
[85] IMTFE Transcript, vol. 57, 20254.
[86] IMTFE Transcript, vol. 57, 20258.
[87] IMTFE Transcript, vol. 57, 20261–20256.

the defence then introduced the Opium Law of 1932 and associated regulations as suppression measures for gradual decrease of usage.[88] It tried to buttress the argument that monopoly control leads to a rise then gradually a fall in use over time by introducing excerpts from the League Opium Commission's report that the number of addicts had increased and then decreased in Formosa from 50,597 (1897) to 165,752 (1900) to 24,626 (1929).[89] The defence recorded the commission's view 'that all governments concerned are endeavouring to fulfil their international obligations as regards control of opium smoking, and attempting to control and reduce as soon as possible the consumption of opium smoking purposes.'[90] In an attempt to show that Japan's approach was not exceptional, excerpts from the report were introduced to show how all Far East territories ran some version of a monopoly system and relied on opium revenue.[91]

After the defence referred to article 12 of the Narcotics Laws of 1937 which provided that narcotics shall not be used except for medical and scientific purposes,[92] a defence witness Namba Tsunekazu, the vice director of the monopoly bureau from 1933, gave evidence that in spite of the continuity of the illicit traffic the decision was made not to lend it impetus by imposing strict prohibition which they thought would result in corruption of officials and uncontrolled use.[93] An excerpt from the Manchukuon Yearbook of 1942 was introduced to suggest that Japanese officials recognized that revenue from opium came at an overall cost to society.[94] An excerpt from the *Tokyo Gazette* stated that the number of addicts had fallen in the period 1932 to 1941 from 3 million to 500,000.[95] The evidence gave details of registration of addicts, improved treatment facilities and the ostensible profit of 150 million yuan actually being a loss of 100,000 yuan because of negative impact.[96] Further similar evidence was rejected as irrelevant by the tribunal.[97] When the defence tried to lead

---

[88] IMTFE Transcript, vol. 57, 20288
[89] IMTFE Transcript, vol. 57, 20271.
[90] IMTFE Transcript, vol. 57, 20273.
[91] IMTFE Transcript, vol. 57, 20275–76.
[92] IMTFE Transcript, vol. 57, 20301.
[93] IMTFE Transcript, vol. 57, 20325, 20307.
[94] IMTFE Transcript, vol. 57, 20358.
[95] IMTFE Transcript, vol. 57, 20359.
[96] IMTFE Transcript, vol. 57, 20371.
[97] IMTFE Transcript, vol. 57, 20360.

evidence of opium monopolies in European colonies in Asia, a majority of the tribunal upheld a prosecution objection.[98] Attempts at cross examination of prosecution witnesses to historically implicate Western states in opium supply had been rejected early on in the trial.[99]

Closing Arguments

In closing, the prosecution pursued the narcotization and exploitation theses, condemning Japanese policy as uncivilized and intending to debauch the Chinese, the monopoly system as a fraud designed to encourage use rather than suppress it, and pointed out that use, production and government revenue had gone up significantly after occupation.[100] Japan had enforced a 'policy of narcotization in the occupied areas for purposes of raising revenue for Japan's plans of aggression and of debauchery of the people to keep them subservient to the will and desire of Japan.'[101]

The defence responded by arguing that Japan's anti-opium policy was not 'a gesture to the League ... but a preparation for total abolition.'[102] It denied that Japan's goal was to impair the health of the Chinese population.[103] It denied a connection between the traffic[104] and the Japanese Government or the accused.[105] It suggested that those individuals whose evidence was relied on by the prosecution were opponents of the monopoly system:[106]

> In our submission, all the prosecution evidence ... consists of information gathered by persons taking an opposite view to the governmental monopoly as sanctioned by the Geneva Treaty of 1925, in particular of information given by the consular authorities of the United States, who did not join the said treaty.[107]

---

[98] IMTFE Transcript, vol. 61, 22082–22090.
[99] IMTFE Transcript, vol. 8, 2671–72.
[100] IMTFE Transcript, vol. 107, 39178–39190.
[101] IMTFE Transcript, vol. 108, 39309.
[102] IMTFE Transcript, vol. 116, 42512.
[103] IMTFE Transcript, vol. 117, 42536.
[104] IMTFE Transcript, vol. 117, 42536.
[105] IMTFE Transcript, vol. 128, 47245–46.
[106] IMTFE Transcript, vol. 116, 42608.
[107] IMTFE Transcript, vol. 116, 42608.

Judicial Responses

After reiterating Japan's international drug control treaty obligations,[108] a majority of the tribunal (without the members for France, India and the Netherlands) noted that by taking up these obligations Japan had claimed a place as a 'Member of the Family of Nations ... a place among the civilized communities of the world.'[109] It then confirmed the prosecution's narcotization and exploitation theses, finding that Japan had sanctioned and developed the traffic in opium and narcotics in Manchuria in order to finance her operations in Manchuria and weaken Chinese resistance.[110] It construed the Japanese policy of gradual suppression as a 'cover' for establishing a distribution monopoly and then collecting revenue from it.[111] Japan had 'found in the alleged but false independence of Manchukuo a convenient opportunity to carry out a world-wide drug traffic and cast the guilt upon that puppet state.'[112] The policy imposed in occupied China was similar in nature and deleterious effect. Addiction increased,[113] the Kōain took control,[114] revenue was used to fund local governments,[115] and Iranian opium imported to meet demand.[116] The majority labeled the renovation government's establishment of a General Opium Suppression Bureau and its funding of opium suppression propaganda 'ostensible' measures.[117] In Central China the majority found that the Japanese had reversed a situation where the trade had been practically extinguished under the Chinese[118] to one that generated monthly revenues by 1939 of $3 million once it became 'public.'[119] These findings condemned Japan as a state; there was no mention of Japan's drugs policy in the individual verdicts.[120]

---

[108] IMTFE Transcript, vol. 132, 48454–59, 48572.
[109] IMTFE Transcript, vol. 132, 48512(a).
[110] IMTFE Transcript, vol. 135, 49159.
[111] IMTFE Transcript, vol. 135, 49162–63.
[112] IMTFE Transcript, vol. 135, 49164.
[113] IMTFE Transcript, vol. 136, 49322.
[114] IMTFE Transcript, vol. 136, 49280.
[115] IMTFE Transcript, vol. 136, 49322.
[116] IMTFE Transcript, vol. 136, 49323.
[117] IMTFE Transcript, vol. 136, 49324.
[118] IMTFE Transcript, vol. 136, 49326.
[119] IMTFE Transcript, vol. 136, 49326.
[120] Hoshino was condemned for 'making the resources of Manchukuo serve the warlike purposes of Japan,' see IMTFE Transcript, vol. 138, 49793.

Dissenting, Judge Pal dismissed their relevance to crimes against peace, pointing out that their violation in occupied territory during a war might amount at most to a war crime.[121]

The prosecution evidence revealed a policy of exploitation by the Japanese Government in Manchuria, but it was tenuously linked to the alleged conspiracy to wage aggressive war in any way. Why then was this evidence about drugs adduced at Tokyo? The answer, it is suggested, was not to establish Japanese aggression, but to engage in public condemnation of Japan's drug policy.

The 'Fuller' Story

The history of Japan's encounter with opium is more complex than the story accepted by the majority of judges at Tokyo.[122] When Japan occupied Taiwan, the withdrawing Chinese authorities warned the Japanese of the trouble they would encounter once they had to manage Taiwanese use of opium themselves.[123] Japan opted for a government-controlled monopoly to slowly wean existing users from the drug while prohibiting new use.[124] The brainchild of the Director of the Health Administration Board of Japan Goto Shimpei, the policy was chosen in preference to the necessity for large-scale law enforcement to impose prohibition. It had the added benefit initially of covering the costs of occupation, though this revenue declined steadily.[125] Japan introduced a similar monopoly in Korea.[126] Although adopted for partly instrumental purposes and notoriously poorly regulated,[127] the arguably enlightened (in conception) policy[128] was then exported to Japanese concessions in Manchuria where it

---

[121] See Justice Pal's dissenting Judgment reported as *United States v Araki, Sadao, Judgment for the Member for India*, 272, reproduced in Boister and Cryer, *Materials*, 926.

[122] See Jennings, *The Opium Empire*, 7; Meyer, 'Japan and the World Narcotics Trade', 186.

[123] Jennings, *The Opium Empire*, 17; Meyer, 'Japan and the World Narcotics Trade', 201.

[124] Jennings, *The Opium Empire*, 19–22; Meyer, 'Japan and the World Narcotics Trade', 189.

[125] Jennings, *The Opium Empire*, 27–28.

[126] Jennings, *The Opium Empire*, 32.

[127] Jennings, *The Opium Empire*, 22–23.

[128] Alfred R. Lindesmith, *The Addict and the Law* (Bloomington: Indiana University Press, 1965), chapter 7.

slowly disintegrated into what the former Chinese Emperor Henry Pu Yi labeled a 'contradiction.'[129]

Failure seemed inevitable when official control of production and supply was incomplete and left to compete with an illicit trade that soaked up production and undercut official prices.[130] Japanese traffickers began operating out of Japan's concessions where official control was weak, transport networks good and drug production licensed to private individuals.[131] License holders began to exploit the system to feed illicit markets.[132] Officially sanctioned monopolies merged symbiotically with a burgeoning illicit traffic.

A policy functional in times of comparative peace where there were other sources of finance (Taiwan and Korea) became dysfunctional during the colonial war in China because of the heavy demands on it made to finance the securing of colonization. Control of the trade, originally in the hands of semi-autonomous right-wing idealists, was lost to military technocrats.[133] Faced with the challenges of peace-making and of funding government, Jennings notes that 'the Kwantung Army, like its Chi'ing and warlord predecessors in Manchuria, found opium to be an irresistible source of revenue.'[134]

Japan's opium policy in China was also dogged by its Western antagonists. During the Shanghai Opium Commission Japanese delegates had side-stepped questions about the role of opium in Taiwan's finances.[135] But from 1918 Japan was attacked in international fora because of its unwillingness to take steps to stop the increasing incidence of trafficking by Japanese nationals.[136] Japan and Britain supported gradual suppression under monopoly control, and Japan tacitly supported British resistance to the US drive towards global prohibition in the 1920s.[137] It came under fire from the International Opium Association, an NGO composed of missionaries and Western residents in China[138] and at the second session of

---

[129] IMTFE Transcript, vol. 12, 4043.
[130] Jennings, *The Opium Empire*, 102.
[131] Jennings, *The Opium Empire*, 40, 47.
[132] Jennings, *The Opium Empire*, 50.
[133] Meyer, 'Japan and the World Narcotics Trade', 197–99.
[134] Jennings, *The Opium Empire*, 81.
[135] Jennings, *The Opium Empire*, 63.
[136] Jennings, *The Opium Empire*, 61.
[137] Jennings, *The Opium Empire*, 64.
[138] Jennings, *The Opium Empire*, 67.

the OAC, was criticized for lack of control over import and export of drugs; the OAC's report to the League's Council suggested that increases in production were feeding the illicit traffic in China.[139]

After the termination of the Anglo-Japanese Alliance, British and dominion delegates became Japan's most tenacious critics in the OAC (China was also heavily criticized for similar reasons).[140] At the fifth session in 1923 Japan was criticized for not being able to explain where large quantities of imported morphine were located in Taiwan. It was accused of allowing the exportation of morphine to China, Japan's critics pointing out that Japan could not logically claim that the number of Taiwanese addicts was decreasing while their morphine use was increasing.[141] While the USA and Britain were in conflict over the direction drug control should take in 1925 in Geneva (a victory for Japan because of the closed conference's acceptance of the monopoly system), Britain and Japan were in increasing conflict over the Indian exports to Taiwan and Kwangtung apparently being diverted into Japan's traffic into China.[142] The League of Nations held a Commission of Enquiry into Opium between 1929 and 1930, which, as noted, favored gradual suppression but pointed out the potential ill effects of a global trade in narcotics.[143] Ironically, it was a Japanese suggestion which formed the basis of the 1931 Convention's estimates system, driven by Japan's concern that it would be shut out of the licit trade in narcotics if—as was originally proposed—only certain designated states would be permitted to export.[144]

In 1930, the US Secretary of State Henry Stimson clarified that US policy was complete prohibition except for medical and scientific use.[145] The establishment of the opium monopoly in Manchukuo resulted in the OAC becoming a forum for vociferous criticism by the USA of Japan's

---

[139] Jennings, *The Opium Empire*, 71 citing the League of Nations Opium Advisory Committee (hereinafter OAC), Minutes of the Second Session: Held at Geneva from 19 to 29 April, League of Nations Official Document (hereinafter L.N. Doc.), C.416.M.254.1922.XI (Geneva 1922), 2930; OAC, Report on the Work of the Committee during its Second Session held at Geneva from 19–29 April 1922, L.N. Doc. A.15.1922 (Geneva, 1922), 7.

[140] Jennings, *The Opium Empire*, 71, 73.

[141] Jennings, *The Opium Empire*, 71, citing OAC, Minutes of the Fifth Session: Held at Geneva from 24 May to 7 June 1923, C.418.M.184.1923.XI (Geneva, 1923), 73, 76.

[142] Jennings, *The Opium Empire*, 72.

[143] Walker, *Opium and Foreign Policy*, 55, citing League of Nations, Commission of Enquiry, Report to the Council of the League of Nations, Geneva 1929–1930, 138.

[144] Jennings, *The Opium Empire*, 75.

[145] Walker, *Opium and Foreign Policy*, 56.

policy (with the benefit of discouraging recognition of Manchukuo).[146] The US Government established the FBN in 1930. Its first commissioner, Harry Anslinger, linked domestic drug policy to foreign drug policy and saw the threat to the USA as primarily external in origin.[147] From the 1932 meeting of the OAC onwards he worked closely with the US delegate Stuart J. Fuller, who had been US consul-general in Tientsin from 1919–1923 and had rejoined the State Department as a narcotics expert. Anslinger provided Fuller with domestic authority; Fuller helped to use the international arena to bolster the FBN's position and to relieve pressure on it from the Democrats' plans to consolidate it into other federal structures.[148] They relied on consular reports to target foreign states and territories soft on drug control.[149]

They also found an ally in China. At the 1930 and 1931 OAC meetings China's representative Dr Ji Kyuin (Ku Wei-chiun) Wellington Koo,[150] a former ambassador to the USA, had been forced to defend China's incapacity to take control of the problem. The Guomindang used the Japanese invasion to deflect the world's attention.[151] At the Permanent Central Opium Board in 1931, Japan was criticized about high rates of heroin consumption in its Chinese territories.[152] In 1932, acting as China's representative on the Lytton Commission, Koo opined that the evidence of increased traffic by Japanese nationals implicated the Japanese in a deliberate policy of undermining the health of the Chinese population.[153]

Japan's policy was put under the microscope at the 17th session of the OAC held in 1933.[154] Driven by US concerns about narcotics flooding

---

[146] Jennings, *The Opium Empire*, 77.
[147] Walker, *Opium and Foreign Policy*, 57.
[148] McAllister, *Drug Diplomacy*, 107.
[149] McAllister, *Drug Diplomacy*, 109.
[150] Walker, *Opium and Foreign Policy*, 28.
[151] Walker, *Opium and Foreign Policy*, 59–62.
[152] Permanent Central Opium Board (PCOB), Report to the Council on the proceedings of the eighth, ninth, and tenth sessions of the Permanent Central Board containing an analysis of the narcotics statistics forwarded by governments for 1930, together with errata, L.N. Doc., C.439.M.186.1931.XI, 6–12.
[153] Wellington VK Koo, *Memoranda Presented to the Lytton Commission*, Vol. II, (New York: The Chinese Cultural Society, 1952), 903.
[154] Jennings, *The Opium Empire*, 85 citing OAC, Minutes of the Seventeenth Session: Held at Geneva from 30 October to 9 November, 1933, L.N. Doc. C.661.M.316.1933.XI (Geneva, 1933), 14.

into its domestic market, Fuller challenged Japanese control of the situation in Manchuria and alleged that imports into Manchuria resulted in illicit exports to the rest of the world including the USA.[155] The Chinese delegates Victor Hoo Chi-Tsai and Koo also tried to draw the focus onto Manchuria.[156] The OAC declined to condemn Japanese policy, considering it a political question beyond the OAC's competence.[157] Anslinger and Fuller knew the Chinese were also heavily implicated in the trade and drugs from China were flowing into the USA. They knew China's efforts at control were as inauthentic as those in Japanese-occupied Manchuria. Yet Walker notes they 'virtually denied it' and blamed Japan.[158] By 1933 Japan had already lost the struggle within the OAC to win over Western powers to its way of thinking about drugs.[159]

Given that US officials were aware of heavy Chinese involvement in the trade, why was the USA so eager to blame Japan and so quick to embrace the Chinese thesis that Japan was deliberately poisoning the Chinese? Walker notes that '[e]xcessive opium growing in Jehol and the existence of opium factories in Mukden does not prove conclusively that Japan deliberately sought to use drugs as a weapon of war against China.'[160] He believes that the accumulation of consular reports laying the blame on the Japanese led to a simplified perception of a complex problem by US policymakers thus limiting their responses.[161]

Japan withdrew from the League in 1935 but remained an invited participant in the OAC.[162] Consular reports of significant outflows of drugs from China to the USA continued to arrive from Nicholson.[163] At the 1936 OAC meeting Fuller criticized China as a narcotics menace to the rest of the world.[164] The USA and Britain considered the OAC's resolution expressing satisfaction with China's control efforts as without foundation. None of this information made it into the evidence at Tokyo. Fuller continued to attack Japanese policy, concluding that wherever Japan advanced

---

[155] Walker, Opium and Foreign Policy, 57.
[156] OAC, Minutes of the Seventeenth Session, 13, 17.
[157] Walker, *Opium and Foreign Policy*, 57.
[158] Walker, *Opium and Foreign Policy*, 31.
[159] Jennings, *The Opium Empire*, 86.
[160] Walker, *Opium and Foreign Policy*, 91.
[161] Ibid.
[162] Jennings, *The Opium Empire*, 89.
[163] Walker, *Opium and Foreign Policy*, 98.
[164] Walker, *Opium and Foreign Policy*, 99.

in the Far East, so too did the drug traffic.[165] At the 1937 OAC meeting this criticism was again put by Fuller in very forthright terms.[166] Jennings notes that Fuller's rhetorical flair rubbed off on others including Thomas W. Russell (Russell Pasha), who outdid Fuller by drawing a lurid picture of the ash heaps of Harbin festooned with dead addicts and claiming that Japan was responsible for manufacturing 90 % of the world's illicit drugs.[167] As we have seen, this material was used by the prosecution at the Tokyo Trial. Anslinger supported this oversimplified and under-verified position, but it caused alarm in the US State Department and was condemned by Nicholson as loose and dangerous to the cause of drug suppression.[168] The Japanese delegate, Yokoyama, could only complain at the lack of diplomacy in these condemnations. Nicholson continued to file reports, some of which showed Japanese anti-drug activity in Manchuria[169] and Britain's undersecretary of state for foreign affairs told the House of Commons that Britain 'had no evidence that the increased drug traffic … is the outcome of any deliberate plan on the part of the Japanese Government, or that it is aimed at the systematic demoralization of the Chinese people.'[170] But these statements were not put into evidence at Tokyo.

At the 23rd session of the OAC in 1938, Japan's new OAC representative, Amo Eiji, criticized Japan's antagonists for introducing unverifiable materials into the OAC's discussions, citing Machukuoan activity against illicit smugglers and attacking the Nationalist Chinese record on drug control.[171] Fuller responded that there had been no improvement in Manchukuo and accused Japan of smuggling opium from Iran into occupied areas where the situation was deteriorating.[172] The OAC's response was muted, and Fuller was deeply critical of it. Pushing the narcotization thesis, China's representative Wellington Koo reiterated that

---

[165] Walker, *Opium and Foreign Policy*, 100.
[166] Walker, Opium and Foreign Policy, 102.
[167] Jennings, *The Opium Empire*, 89, OAC, Situation in the Far East: Extracts from the Minutes of the Twenty-Second Session: Held at Geneva from 24 May to 12 June, 1937, C.L.203, 1937 XI (Geneva, 1937), 9.
[168] Walker, *Opium and Foreign Policy*, 103, citing NARA, RG 59, 500 C1197/1094, Nicholson to Customs, 12.
[169] Walker, *Opium and Foreign Policy*, 115–16, 122.
[170] Walker, *Opium and Foreign Policy*, 120, citing 342 House of Commons Debates (Great Britain), 22 December 1938, 3204.
[171] Walker, *Opium and Foreign Policy*, 125, citing OAC, Minutes of the Twenty Third Session: Held at Geneva from 7 to 24 June, 1938, L.N. Doc. C.249.M.147.1938, XI (Geneva 1938), 46–47.
[172] Jennings, *The Opium Empire*, 90.

invasion by dangerous drugs went hand in hand with military invasion.[173] The League Council imposed economic sanctions and in November Japan withdrew from all cooperation with the League. By this time Japan's critics in the USA believed Japan's inability to control narcotics in China proved its malicious intent and that the USA was entitled to take action in self-defence.[174] By 1943 the USA was viewed as the guardian of order in postwar Asia and its explicit policy was to dismantle the colonial opium monopolies.[175] Cajoled in a meeting held by Anslinger in Washington (the League's drug control administration had withdrawn to the USA at that time), the British and the Dutch capitulated and accepted total prohibition after the war.[176]

Much of the information on which the Tokyo Tribunal developed its opium case was furnished by the USA, which had begun to assemble evidence of the narcotization thesis in the 1930s.[177] In Walker's view the case 'provided an additional means of restructuring Japanese politics and society so that Japan might ultimately take its place in the Western security regime in Asia.'[178] On 16 October 1945 in a meeting with members of the War Crimes Office, Anslinger (who tried unsuccessfully to get provisions on drug prohibition into the US peace treaty with Japan)[179] laid out the steps necessary to hold Japan accountable in this regard, itemizing all of the evidence that he knew was available and from where it could be retrieved.[180] Most of the steps he refers to, including, for example, obtaining all of the reports from the Opium Advisory Committee to the League Council on violations by the Japanese Government and all US Consulate reports from Manchuria during the Japanese occupation relating to narcotics, were taken. This is unsurprising given that Major John

---

[173] See OAC, Report to the Council on the Work of the Twenty-Third Session, L.N. Doc. C.237.M.136.1938.XI. Geneva, 1938, 14.
[174] Walker, *Opium and Foreign Policy*, 150.
[175] Walker, *Opium and Foreign Policy*, 153–6, citing a US Department of State Memorandum of September 1943.
[176] They apparently did so in exchange for access to medical opium—see report with no title or date, Pennsylvania State University, Special Collections, Historical Collections and Labor Archive, Harry Anslinger Papers, Box 5, File 9, Scrapbook.
[177] Walker, *Opium and Foreign Policy*, 125.
[178] Walker, *Opium and Foreign Policy*, 165.
[179] McAllister, *Drug Diplomacy*, 163.
[180] NARA, RG 59, 894.114 Narcotics/10-1645, Herbert E. Gaston (Treasury) to George. E. Morlock (State) with a Memorandum of a Conversation between the Commissioner of Narcotics and Members of the War Crimes Office, 16 October 1945; see McAllister, *Drug Diplomacy*, 163.

F. Hummel, who attended that meeting, led the prosecution's case on Japan's violation of the drug conventions at Tokyo. It is not clear if the idea to pursue the charges came from the War Crimes Office or whether they were prompted to do so (General MacArthur was directed to set up the trial on 10 November 1945).[181] From the Chinese side, Wellington Koo was chair of the ad hoc Special Far Eastern Committee that made recommendations on Japanese war criminality to the UN War Crimes Commission and may have had an input.[182] So too may Victor Hoo, an Assistant Secretary General of the UN based in New York by June 1946 and on friendly terms with Anslinger.[183] However, the theory that Japan had used opium 'to stupefy and imperialise' in Asia was widely subscribed to within the USA both in government and in the press.[184] Anslinger had already in 1942 made a statement (release of which was approved by then Secretary of the Treasury Henry Morgenthau) in which he explained the Japanese intentions as being three-fold:

1. To gain additional revenue for war purposes.
2. To corrupt occidental nations, which are regarded by the Japanese as peculiarly susceptible to the higher concentrations of narcotics, such as morphine, heroin and cocaine.
3. To demoralize and enslave the peoples of lands already invaded or marked for eventual invasion.[185]

---

[181] US Directive, *Apprehension and Punishment of War Criminals*, Serial No. 19, 10 November 1945, attached to Archives New Zealand, FEC 007/8, 23 May 1946, File no. EA 106/3/22, Part 2.
[182] UNWCC, *The History of the United Nations War Crimes Commission and the Development of the Laws of War* (London: HMSO, 1948), 129–131.
[183] Letters between them suggest they were close—Pennsylvania State University, Special Collections, Historical Collections and Labor Archive, Harry Anslinger Papers, Box 9, File 59, Opium (1924–1945), Box 2, File 21 (Correspondence 1944–5).
[184] Pennsylvania State University, Special Collections, Historical Collections and Labor Archive, Harry Anslinger Papers, Box 4, File 2, Notes for the Opium Question, under title 'International,' p. 2; article in *Wall Street Journal*, 18 November 1944, Harry Anslinger Papers, Box 5, file 4, Scrapbook. A similar charge of use of this 'old but effective weapon' was made against the 'Red' Chinese in the early 1950s—see, id, Box 5, File 5, untitled newspaper article dated 11 May 1954 reporting this charge being made by Anslinger in the CND.
[185] Reported in article by Cabell Phillips, 'Jap Secret Weapon: Dope,' 11 February 1942, no title but at that stage Phillips wrote for *The New York Times*, Pennsylvania State University, Special Collections, Historical Collections and Labor Archive, Harry Anslinger Papers, Box 5, File 7, Scrapbooks; the same report is referred to in an untitled article dated 27 January

Japan was not the only target however. In late 1945 US authorities were concerned that the British and Dutch were dragging their feet in regard to the breaking up of their drug monopolies and they were keen to drive home their policy of absolute prohibition for all but medical and scientific purposes in territories where they had no direct control.[186]

Conclusion

Drug control policy suborned international criminal justice at the Tokyo Tribunal. Through a symbolic prosecution of Japan (rather than a legal prosecution of the accused on trial), the tribunal was used to inscribe the social policy of drug prohibition and isolate the world against other possible ways of dealing with this particular social problem. The US Government, increasingly wedded to absolute prohibition, had been frustrated at the international community's decision to maintain a gradualist approach to phasing out non-medical supply and use in the 1925 Geneva Convention, and by its inability in the OAC to get the Japanese to abandon its monopoly control position. The Tokyo Tribunal provided an unusual public forum to scrutinize and condemn this policy. The prosecution's complaint that Japan had extended its 'activities into fields abhorred by all civilized mankind ... the traffic in opium and narcotics' implies that Japan had morally and legally breached its international obligations.[187]

At a factual level the Tokyo Trial's acceptance of the narcotization and exploitation theses over-simplified a complex issue.[188] Contradictory evidence of Japanese struggles to suppress the illicit trade[189] while struggling to control opium[190] was omitted or rejected.

The legal position was also distorted. Prohibition was not clearly articulated in the drug conventions. Japan's was a permissible interpretation of its obligations, something which the defence at Tokyo tried without success to point out. It was the normative interpretation of these conventions

---

1942 in the *Bangor Daily News*, Historical Collections and Labor Archive, Harry Anslinger Papers, Box 5, File 12, Scrapbooks.
[186] See the Resolution of Rep Walter H Judd in the US Congress, 15 October 1945—Pennsylvania State University, Special Collections, Historical Collections and Labor Archive, Harry Anslinger Papers, Box 5, File 4, Scrapbook.
[187] IMTFE Transcript, vol. 107, 39177–78.
[188] Jennings, *The Opium Empire*, 110.
[189] Walker, *Opium and Foreign Policy*, 156.
[190] Walker, *Opium and Foreign Policy*, 136–37.

developed by the USA and pressed in the OAC which provided the standard against which Japan was measured in the Tokyo Trial.

Finally, the prosecution's cover-up thesis allowed the USA to implicitly criticize the League's handling of the problem, and left the USA to direct the institutionalization of prohibition in the UN. The much stricter drug control regime that emerged in the postwar period through the 1953 Opium Protocol[191] and the Single Convention in Narcotic Drugs[192] is testament to the success of this transformative enterprise.

---

[191] 20 February 1957; 309 United Nations Treaty Series (U.N.T.S.) 65.
[192] 30 March 1961; 520 U.N.T.S. 204.

CHAPTER 3

The French Prosecution at the IMTFE: Robert Oneto, Indochina and the Rehabilitation of French Prestige

Beatrice Trefalt

Early in April 1946, after a number of delays, French prosecutor Robert Oneto arrived in Tokyo to join the prosecution team of the International Military Tribunal for the Far East (IMTFE). When he sat down to read the draft of the indictment, Oneto was shocked to find French Indochina listed as one of the wartime allies of Japan, rather than as an early victim of Japanese aggression. Though this 'misunderstanding' was soon cleared up, the incident underscored for Oneto, and for the chief of the French mission in Tokyo, Ambassador Zinovi Pechkoff, France's precarious image as an ally of the victorious powers. It also highlighted for both men Oneto's importance, as a member of the prosecution team, in establishing in a court of law that French Indochina had been invaded by Japan in 1940, and that France, as an early victim of Japanese aggression, had a proper claim to any subsequent reparations.

B. Trefalt (✉)
Monash University, Melbourne, Australia

© The Author(s) 2016
K. von Lingen (ed.), *War Crimes Trials in the Wake of Decolonization and Cold War in Asia, 1945–1956*,
DOI 10.1007/978-3-319-42987-8_3

Oneto's preparation of his case, as well as his commentary on his own accusation, the defence's arguments, and the IMTFE in general, reveal a dimension of the tribunal that has only recently begun to receive attention: namely, its role as an international arena for 'cultural diplomacy.' I argue here that for the French prosecution, and the French Government representation in Tokyo, the Tokyo Tribunal had a central dimension as a stage upon which the French Government demanded to record its assertions of victimhood, and justified its presence amongst the nations now joined in punishing Japan's wartime leadership. Thus it could purge the shadow of Vichy collaboration, shore up postwar France's international power and stake a claim for any future reparations. In that sense, for France, the Tokyo Tribunal afforded an opportunity to record and rewrite wartime history: what was on trial in Tokyo was not only the government of Japan, but the government of wartime French Indochina. The French prosecution was aimed not just at Japanese defendants, but at the world at large. Importantly, the French prosecution also asserted France's position as an equal amongst the Allies, which in turn implied an assertion of the French Government's right to continue claiming Indochina as an unalienable part of the French colonial empire. Perhaps because France's grasp on its Asian colonies was already so clearly slipping, such assertions were especially urgent, and their elaboration especially visible in official correspondence between Oneto, the Chief of the French Mission Pechkoff and the Ministry of Foreign Affairs in Paris, as we will see.

Although early debates about the nature of the Tokyo trials focused particularly on the charge that it constituted victor's justice, more recently scholarly attention has expanded to include analysis of its role in determining postwar hierarchies amongst the victorious nations.[1] Here, the focus is on the Tokyo Trial as a stage upon which the governments of nations emerging from the war could voice grievances, justify previous and current actions and, thus, attempt to claim visibility in a world order fundamentally transformed by the war and now dominated by the USA. Yuma Totani has made this point in relation to the representation of 'victim' countries in

---

[1] Richard Minear, *Victors' Justice: The Trials at Tokyo* (Princeton, NJ: Princeton University Press, 1971); Tim Maga, *Judgment at Tokyo* (Lexington, KY: The University Press of Kentucky, 2001); Yuma Totani, *The Tokyo War Crimes Trials: the pursuit of Justice in the Wake of World War II* (Cambridge, MA: Harvard University Press, 2008), 1; Neil Boister, 'The Tokyo Military Tribunal: A show trial?,' in *Historical Origins of International Criminal Law: Volume 2*, eds. Morten Bergsmo et al. (Brussels: Torkel Opsahl Academic EPublishers, 2014), 3–29.

the trials, especially the Philippines, which were able thanks to the trials 'to voice publicly their grievances against the former victimizer in the international area.'[2] As Hitoshi Nagai has shown in the case of the Philippines, both Justice Delfin Jaranilla and prosecutor Pedro Lopez aimed to emphasize the extent of Japanese atrocities in the Philippines as unique.[3] The ability to remind the Allies of the nature of Filipino suffering in during the Japanese occupation, as it had been established during the Tokyo Trial, was crucial in negotiating the Philippines' position within the international hierarchies emerging during and after the end of the trial.[4]

The French participation in the Tokyo Tribunal has largely been ignored, apart from some scholarship on the dissenting opinion of French Justice Henri Bernard on the tribunal's final judgment. In comparison to the voluminous materials available on the other dissenting justices, however, even Bernard's opinion remains under-researched, though Mickaël Ho Foui Sang has recently provided a fresh analysis of the basis for his dissention.[5] There is little written in detail about the French prosecution: Yves Beigbeder, who has written on the French Government's participation in international tribunals since 1940, argues without extensive detail that Oneto made a flimsy case at the Tokyo Tribunal.[6] A rare article on the French participation in the Tokyo trials, focusing especially on the character of Justice Bernard and the nature of his dissenting opinion, also touches on the problematic nature of the French case for the prosecution.[7] Admittedly, France had only played a minor role in the war in the Pacific, and was invited to participate at the Tokyo tribunal because it had been one of the Allies participating the United Nations War Crimes Commission, and because it was sitting in judgment of Germany's leadership at Nuremberg at the time the preparations for the Tokyo Trial were underway. France's participation in the Tokyo Trial was, in that

---

[2] Totani, *The Tokyo War Crimes Trials*, 12.
[3] Hitoshi Nagai, 'The Tokyo War Crimes Trial,' in *Philippines-Japan Relations*, ed. Ikehata Setsuho and Lydia N. Yu Jose (Manila: Ateneo de Manila University Press, 2003), 261–298.
[4] Beatrice Trefalt, 'Hostages to international relations? The repatriation of Japanese war criminals from the Philippines,' *Japanese Studies*, vol. 31 no. 2 (2011): 193.
[5] Mickaël Ho Foui Sang, 'Justice Bernard (France),' in *Beyond Victor's Justice? The Tokyo War Crimes Trials revisited*, eds. Toshiyuki Tanaka et al. (Leiden: Martinus Nijjhof Publishers, 2011), 93–102.
[6] Yves Beigbeder, *Judging War Crimes and Torture: French Justice and International Criminal Tribunals and Commissions (1940–2005)*, (Leiden: Martinus Nijjhof, 2006), 265.
[7] Jean Esmein, 'Le Juge Bernard au procès de Tokyo,' *Vingtième Siècle: revue d'histoire* (Summer 1998) no. 59: 3–14.

sense, tokenistic, and has largely been forgotten. In France, as Sébastien Verney has shown, only a small proportion of scholarship has addressed France's Asian colonies, and the history of wartime Indochina, linked as it is with the Vichy government, has been the subject of bitter memoirs rather than sustained analysis, because of the 'double taboo' of colonial history and collaboration history.[8] Since Oneto was prosecuting the leadership of Japan in Tokyo on behalf of a colony that France was shortly about to lose in bitter defeat, there is perhaps little reason to remember France's role in Tokyo.

When Oneto arrived in Japan, he became an associate prosecutor in an international team headed by (American) Chief Prosecutor Joseph Keenan, which also included representatives from Australia, Canada, China, India, the Netherlands, New Zealand, the Philippines and the USSR. The prosecutions' selection of accused and its preparation of an indictment had been a hurried affair, the International Prosecution Section having been in existence in Tokyo only since 8 December 1945.[9] Oneto arrived in Tokyo late in the game, on 4 April 1946, just over three weeks before the indictment was formally delivered to the tribunal on 29 April.[10] Although the French Government had been asked to nominate its representatives to the International Military Tribunal on 21 October 1945, this request had initially prompted uncertainty about whether French participation in the trials in Tokyo would invalidate France's right to conduct, independently, war crimes trials in Indochina. This uncertainty was not cleared up until late December 1945.[11] Once the possibility of doing both had been established, the French Government had difficulty filling the positions, compounding delays in nomination. The USA had made it a requirement that the nominees be fluent in English. In addition, the French Government sought to be represented by individuals familiar with French colonial administration, untainted by wartime collaboration and able to

---

[8] Sébastien Verney, *L'Indochine sous Vichy : Entre Révolution nationale, collaboration et identités nationales, 1940–1945* (Paris: Riveneuve, 2013), 20–21.
[9] Neil Boister and Robert Cryer, *The Tokyo International Military Tribunal: a reappraisal* (Oxford: Oxford University Press, 2008), 49–50, 77.
[10] Boister and Cryer, *The Tokyo International Military Tribunal*, 69.
[11] Archives Diplomatiques (La Courneuve) (henceforth AD), Asie-Océanie. Japon.130: Criminels de Guerre , Author unclear, 'Pour Monsieur Gaucheron', Secrétariat des Conférences, 15 November 1945.; Archives Nationales d'Outre-Mer (Aix-en-Provence) (henceforth ANOM), INF1364.G407.4 , 'Télégramme de Washington,' 21 December 1945.

put France's national interests above retribution against collaborators.[12] A number of other candidates for both judge and prosecutor positions refused the appointment at the last minute for personal reasons.[13] Neither Bernard nor Oneto were thus the French Government's first choice of representation. Bernard, whose English language skills were wanting, had at least good credentials as a colonial magistrate, and was willing to go to Tokyo. Oneto had participated in the Resistance, was an experienced prosecutor and was able to leave for Tokyo at short notice, but like Bernard had limited fluency in English.[14] Oneto's contribution to the Tokyo Tribunal has been known best up to now for the contretemps that occurred when he insisted on his right to read his accusation in French, the most famous incident of linguistic and cultural competition at the trials.[15] In any case, Oneto's late appointment delayed his arrival in Tokyo, and when he finally joined the prosecution team the first draft of the indictment had already been created, as we have seen, in a way that clashed with Oneto's own sense of Indochina's recent history.

From the moment of Japan's defeat, France's participation in the pursuit of Japanese war criminals had been understood by its government as crucial to the recovery of French prestige in the Asian region and the world generally. More immediately, in Indochina itself, it was seen as a symbol of the recovery and assertion of legitimate authority.[16] This authority had been weakened by the French Government's immediate postwar military and economic deficiencies. Such deficiencies limited, for a short period at least, metropolitan interests in the conditions of the colony, and also

---

[12] Esmein, 'Le Juge Bernard,' 4–5.

[13] AD, Asie-Océanie. Japon.130: Criminels de Guerre, 'Note pour la direction du personnel et de la comptabilité,' 1 March 1945. See also Esmein, 'Le Juge Bernard,' 4–5; Sang, 'Justice Bernard (France),' 95–96.

[14] Boister and Cryer, *The Tokyo International Military Tribunal* (Oxford: Oxford University Press, 2008), 77; Ann-Sophie Schoepfel, 'The War Court as a form of State building: The French Prosecution of Japanese War crimes at the Saigon and Tokyo trials,' in *Historical Origins of International Criminal Law: Volume 2*, eds. Morten Bergsmo et al. (Brussels: Torkel Opsahl Academic EPublishers, 2014), 137.

[15] See records of the International Military Tribunal for the Far East, 30 September 1946, *The Records of the International Military Tribunal for the Far East*, ed. John Pritchard (Lewiston, Edwin Mellen, 1998), vol. 15, 6695–6708; Kayoko Takeda, *Interpreting the War Crimes Trials: a socio-political analysis* (Ottawa: University of Ottawa Press, 2010), 22–26.

[16] See for example ANOM, INF 159/1364 G.407.4, Direction de l'Indochine, Direction des Affaires Politiques to the Secrétaire Général du Comité de l'Indochine, 30 October 1945.

required Japanese disarmament to be managed by British and Chinese troops.[17] The Vietnamese declaration of independence in the wake of the Japanese defeat rendered even more urgent the practical and symbolic return of the French Government as the legitimate authority in Indochina. Oneto linked France's punishment of Japanese war crimes with the recovery of French national prestige, and his preparations for the French contributions to the indictment were colored, as he constantly reminded his government, by the need to recover France's reputation in Asia and to avoid as much as possible any harmful debate about the fate of Indochina as part of the French Empire.

The focus on prestige underlines the deep apprehension, held by Oneto and shared by many others in the postwar French Government, that wartime France would forever be linked with the wartime government of Maréchal Pétain in Vichy, rather than with General De Gaulle's Free France. The defeat of Germany and Japan brought with it a reassertion of France's status as a key ally of the USA and a major combatant during the war.[18] Unlike other French colonies, Indochina had not recognized De Gaulle's Free France but had remained allied with the collaborationist Vichy government. Eric Jennings has shown that the colonial government in Indochina was even more stridently aligned with Pétainist ideas than Vichy France itself; and it was this government that had allowed the Japanese to station troops on Indochinese soil from September 1940, ostensibly to allow Japan to encircle and weaken the Chinese nationalist resistance in Chongqing and to hinder the passage of American aid to Free China.[19] It wasn't until the night of 9–10 March 1945 that the Japanese military forces violently dislodged the French civilian government in Indochina and put its governor under house arrest, thus ending a long period of apparent French collaboration.

Those associated with the French Government in Indochina between 1940 and 1945 argued vehemently that they had not collaborated willingly with the Japanese government, that they did not have the means

---

[17] David Marr, *Vietnam 1945: the Quest for Power* (Berkeley, 1995), 476.

[18] Marr, *Vietnam 1945*, 310. See also Fréderic Turpin, *De Gaulle, Les Gaullistes et l'Indochine* (Paris: Les Indes Savantes, 2005), quoted in Yuichirō Miyashita, 'La France face au retour du Japon sur la scène internationale' (PhD diss., Institut d'Etudes Politiques de Paris, 2012).

[19] Eric Jennings, *Vichy in the Tropics: Pétain's National Revolution in Madagascar, Guadeloupe, and Indochina, 1940–1944* (Stanford: Stanford University Press, 2001), 130–41. See also Verney, *L'Indochine sous Vichy*.

to resist Japanese demands and could not rely on external help to fight Japanese threats. Throughout the period, tensions simmered between those who collaborated, however reluctantly, with the Japanese military and those who prepared for an eventual assault against Japan, itself preempted and prevented by the Japanese coup d'état.[20] After the Japanese defeat, quite apart from emerging warfare between Vietnamese nationalists and the French Government, tensions persisted within the French community between those who had worked for the colonial government up until 1945 and the representatives of Free France arriving in Indochina. The latter found that, far from being able to dismiss those they might suspect of collaboration, they had to rely on their local knowledge and experience.[21] As Esmein suggests, it was those kinds of tensions that complicated, both in Paris and in Indochina, the French choice of representation at international and local war crimes trials: the question was who could best represent the colony in Tokyo and the French Government in Indochina, and focus on Japanese war crimes without being distracted by issues of collaboration.[22]

Oneto's correspondence reveals how delicate such issues remained in 1946. He had spent the war years as a *juge d'instruction* in occupied France (first in Corbeil, then in Pontoise), then as a prosecutor at the Special Versailles Court,[23] so he was particularly sensitive about collaboration. In candid correspondence with his own government, he expressed surprise about the courteous reception he had received in Washington on the way to Tokyo, and wrote of his relief at hearing General MacArthur praise the French Resistance when he attended his first reception in Tokyo.[24] At the same time, however, his disquiet was vindicated when he saw that the draft of the indictment placed Indochina, and by extension, France, not on the side of the victims, but on the side of Japan's wartime allies. He thought Americans especially were ill-informed about Indochina's

---

[20] Marr, *Vietnam 1945*, 312–314.
[21] Marr, *Vietnam 1945*, 472–543; Jean Sainteny, *Histoire d'une Paix Manquée* (Paris: Amiot-Dumond, 1954); Paul Mus, 'L'Indochine en 1945 : Quelques Souvenirs et une opinion', *Politique Etrangère*, no. 4 (1946): 349–374.
[22] Esmein, 'Le Juge Bernard', 3.
[23] 'Fiche Magistrat : Robert Lucien Oneto,' Annuaire Rétrospectif de la Magistrature, http://tristan.u-bourgogne.fr:8080/4DCGI/Fiche/56382 (accessed 10 February 2015).
[24] AD, Secrétariat des Conférences, Nations Unies et Organisations Internationales (henceforth NUOI) 372Q099, Le Procureur Français près le Tribunal Militaire des Crimes de Guerre en Extrême Orient à Monsieur le Ministre des Affaires Etrangères, 7 May 1946.

position during the war: in Oneto's view, they seemed to assume that the wartime government of Indochina's connection with Vichy meant that it had willingly entered into arrangements with Japan to allow the presence of Japanese troops. Oneto paraphrased the most brutal reaction to his arrival as 'Actually, what IS France doing here? You've never been at war with Japan, and you gave Japan everything it wanted.'[25]

It became crucial for Oneto to redress that misunderstanding, to prove that Japan invaded Indochina in 1940, that the Japanese government intended to do so already in 1939 and that France was not only a victim of Japanese wartime aggression but actually the first among its Western victims, not the USA, nor Great Britain or the Netherlands. Oneto wanted his part in the prosecution of Japanese war crimes in the Tokyo Tribunal to correct the assumption that Indochina, and by extension, France, had been a willing ally of Japan, an assumption which was 'dangerous for our position in the Far East, and for the favourable outcome of the problem of reparations.'[26] In his mission to rehabilitate France, Oneto was supported by the Chief of the French Mission to the Occupation Brigadier Zinovi Pechkoff, who met with Supreme Commander of the Allied Powers General Douglas Macarthur in mid-May 1946: Pechkoff expressed his dismay at the extent of American suspicions regarding France and its role in Indochina, and reported that he was able to secure MacArthur's sympathy for the French position.[27]

The problem, for Oneto, was building a convincing case. Not only had Oneto arrived in Tokyo late, but he struggled to find appropriate evidence to support his claims. First, he had requested information from Saigon before his departure for Tokyo, but found once he arrived in Tokyo that the material had not turned up; he then had to leave again, flying to Saigon to try and find evidence. Once there he found little of use: French bureaucrats in Saigon had burned large numbers of documents on the night of 9–10 March 1945, during the Japanese coup.[28] From Saigon,

---

[25] My translation. AD (NUOI) 372QO99, Le Procureur Français près le Tribunal Militaire des Crimes de Guerre en Extrême Orient à Monsieur le Ministre des Affaires Etrangères, 22 October 1946.

[26] My translation. AD (NUOI) 372QO99, Le Procureur Français près le Tribunal Militaire des Crimes de Guerre en Extrême Orient à Monsieur le Ministre des Affaires Etrangères, 22 October 1946.

[27] ANOM HCI124.382 Tokio, 1946–1951, Pechkoff to Président Gouin, 21 Mai 1946, reported in Président Gouin to Haut Commissaire D'Indochine, 29 Mai 1946.

[28] Mus, 'L'Indochine en 1945,' 358.

faced with a dearth of material to work with, Oneto sent a telegram to Paris to request relevant copies of correspondence in the Ministry of Foreign Affairs or the Ministry of Colonies.[29] In the end, he had to support his case at least in part with unsatisfactory newspaper clippings and French military communications.[30] Esmein claims that the American prosecution suggested that Admiral Decoux be called as a witness, but that Oneto refused to allow the presence in the tribunal of a person whom he considered as a 'national disgrace'; in any case, Decoux was by then under guard in France, facing trial as a collaborator.[31] Oneto also found it difficult to find witnesses, and he suspected that many relevant papers had been burned by the Japanese military forces after 15 August 1945, or had been seized by the Việt Minh.[32] It is also possible, though Oneto does not mention it, that he failed to gain the cooperation of many in Saigon who worried that his investigations might make them vulnerable to accusations of collaboration in the future, and who were therefore evasive.

In his prosecution, Oneto meant to demonstrate that Japan had conducted an aggressive war against Indochina and France. He accused the Japanese leadership of having planned the invasion of Indochina as early as 1939, supported by the tripartite alliance with Germany and Italy, because of Indochina's importance as a pivot of communications in Southeast Asia, as a strategic vantage point for its war on China and because of its riches in rice and rubber.[33] Central to Oneto's argument was the point that whatever treaties had been signed between the French Government and Japan after 1939 were signed under duress: the Matsuoka–Henry agreement of 30 August 1940, which was an in-principle agreement between Japan and France for the control of the Indochina–Chinese border, had been the result of an ultimatum, implying strongly the use of military force unless France agreed to Japanese demands. The details of the agreement were to be worked out on the ground between the French High Commission and Japanese advisers; it was this agreement, eventually signed by Admiral Decoux on 22 September 1940 that enabled the

---

[29] AD Asie-Océanie. Japon.130: Criminels de Guerre, Oneto, 'Télégramme à l'arrivée,' 16 May 1946.
[30] Esmein, 'Le juge Bernard,' 6.
[31] Verney, *L'Indochine sous Vichy*, 453–454; Esmein, 'Le juge Bernard,' 8. See also Schoepfel, 'The War Court,' 129.
[32] AD (NUOI) 372QO99, Oneto to Minister of Foreign Affairs, 22 October 1946, 2.
[33] Robert Oneto, International Military Tribunal for the Far East, 30 September 1946, in *The Records of the International Military Tribunal for the Far East*, vol. 15, 6708–6710.

Japanese deployment of troops in northern Indochina. Oneto maintained in his accusation that it was also signed under duress, because the war in Europe had isolated the colonial government in Saigon and prevented assistance from other powers. The best proof, argued Oneto, that Japan meant to use force against Indochina was found in the events surrounding the agreement of 22 September: the Japanese had issued an ultimatum on 19 September demanding the signature of the agreement by midday on 22 September, but documents were signed two hours later, at two in the afternoon. The delay meant that, on the night of 22 September, unaware that the documents had been signed after all, Japanese troops attacked the border in Tonkin at Lạng Sơn and Japanese planes bombarded the port of Haïphong. It was this attack, claimed Oneto in his accusation, that was the ultimate proof of the intention to use force had the treaty not been signed.[34] At the time, Oneto recounted bitterly, Japanese propaganda called this invasion 'a friendly and peaceful penetration into Indochina' and the battle of Tonkin 'a local skirmish due to a misunderstanding,' but in reality at that moment France became the first Western victim of Japanese aggression.[35]

The penetration of Japan into the south of Indochina in the months that followed, Japan's mediation in the Franco–Thai border dispute of 1941 and the violent coup-d'état of March 1945 were, in Oneto's accusation, the logical subsequent steps in the complete subjugation of France in Indochina, accompanied by numerous atrocities committed against French and local populations. In short, the Japanese threat that became manifest on the night of 22–23 September, building on Indochina's isolation in the wake of the French defeat to Germany, forced a helpless government to allow the entry of Japanese troops on its territory. This was an invasion, not an agreement, as Oneto argued in court on 30 September 1946:

> France was thus the first of the Western nations to fall victim to Japanese aggression. The acts of violence which, at a later period, were to be repeatedly carried out by Japan, were the consequence of this oppression.[36]

---

[34] Robert Oneto, IMTFE, 30 September 1946, in *The Tokyo Major War Crimes* Trial, vol. 15, 6716–6717. See also AD (NUOI) 372QO100, Oneto, 'Relation du Japon avec la France et le Siam, aggression contre l'Indochine: exposé préliminaire,' 9–10.
[35] Robert Oneto, IMTFE, 30 September 1946, in *The Tokyo Major War Crimes* Trial, vol. 15, 6717; see also AD (NUOI) 372QO100, Oneto, 'Relation du Japon,' 10.
[36] Robert Oneto, IMTFE, 30 September 1946, in *The Tokyo Major War Crimes* Trial, vol. 15, 6717.

Keeping in mind Oneto's conviction that many at the IMTFE saw France's agreements with Japan in 1940 as willing collaboration, he appears to have been unsure that his arguments would be convincing. His concerns were shared by Pechkoff, who reported to his government with barely disguised relief that Oneto's arguments had not been questioned by others in the prosecution or on the bench; he even noted that American Chief Prosecutor Keenan had been impressed by the ability of Oneto to prove aggression against the French colony.[37] Oneto was buoyed on 8 October 1946 by a highly complimentary personal letter from Keenan, in which Oneto was praised for the quality of his preparation and the convincing nature of his arguments, as well as his courteous cooperation with the prosecution team.[38] Oneto reported to Paris that his part in the prosecution had worked to inform not only Keenan but American public opinion as a whole on the question of Indochina, and that, therefore 'a good result had been obtained on the point of the international position of France in the Far East […] which will allow us more authority to discuss the problem of reparations.'[39] Justice Bernard concurred: he wrote to his government in praise of Oneto suggesting that 'his work will contribute in no small part to the restoration of French prestige.'[40]

The next hurdle was dealing with the arguments for the defence. Oneto, who had struggled to find the materials to support his case, was concerned about the nature of the proof the defence might bring to its arguments. Not surprisingly, perhaps, the defence argued that countries that had signed treaties allowing the presence of Japanese troops on their territory (such as Indochina and Thailand) could not now suggest they had been victims of crimes against peace.[41] Oneto, who sent regular commentaries on the trials to the Ministry of Foreign Affairs, noted with relief, however, that the defence relied on familiar documents, such as the Matsuoka–Henry agreement of 30 August 1940, the Decoux–Nishimura agreement of 22 September 1940, and various pieces relating to the settling of the Franco–Siam dispute of 1941, which did not challenge

---

[37] AD Asie-Océanie. Japon.130: Criminels de Guerre, Pechkoff, to Minister of Foreign Affairs, 17 October 1946 ; Pechkoff to Minister of Foreign Affairs, 9 October 1946.
[38] AD (NUOI) 372QO99, Joseph Keenan to Robert Oneto, 8 October 1946.
[39] AD (NUOI) 372QO99, Oneto to Minister of Foreign Affairs, 22 October 1946, 8.
[40] AD (NUOI) 372QO99, Justice Henri Bernard to Minister of Foreign Affairs. 11 October 1946, 3.
[41] Esmein, 'Le Juge Bernard,' 6. See also the testimony of accused Tōjō Hideki, IMTFE, 29 December 1947, in *The Tokyo Major War Crimes Trial*, vol. 76, 36198–36199.

Oneto's argument that these had been signed under duress.[42] In particular, the testimony of former staff officer General Sawada Shigeru revealed unintentionally that the Japanese had been considering the use of force in September 1940, making clear that on the Japanese side, French prevarication about signing the 22 September accord signified the possibility that Indochina might yet join Free France, making the stationing of Japanese troops there even more urgent.[43] Even so, Sawada maintained that the military engagements at Lạng Sơn and Haïphong were not part of Japan's broader strategy, but were the result of miscommunications within the Japanese army itself, for which Japanese troops were court-martialled or otherwise punished. Sawada's testimony on that point was supported by former Prime Minister and General Tōjō Hideki in his own, famously articulate defence of December 1947 and January 1948: he maintained that French Indochina had voluntarily permitted the presence of Japanese troops on its territory, and that Japan's involvement in the Franco–Thai border dispute of 1941 was that of a legitimate mediator between these two countries for a peaceful settlement of the border region. Tōjō reiterated the point made by Sawada earlier that Japanese troops and commanders involved in the battles of Lạng Sơn and Haïphong had been severely punished, and so rejected Oneto's argument that these battles signalled the beginning of a coherent plan of aggression.[44] In short, Tōjō argued, Japan had no intention to invade French Indochina in 1940, and installed a relatively small number of troops in northern Indochina, with French permission, in order to prosecute its war with China, not as a first attack on Western powers. Though Oneto noted that Tōjō was a gifted orator, he considered that Sawada's testimony had conclusively played into the hands of the prosecution, because it supported the contention that French authorities had been forced into signing any agreements with Japan.[45]

---

[42] AD(NUOI) 372QO 100, Oneto to Minister of Foreign Affairs, 19 September 1947, 1.
[43] Testimony of Sawada Shigeru, IMTFE, 26 August 1947, *The Records of the International Military Tribunal for the Far East*, vol. 56, 26851–26852; see also AD(NUOI) 372QO 100, Oneto to Minister of Foreign Affairs, 19 September 1947, 3.
[44] Testimony of accused Tōjō Hideki, IMTFE, 29 December 1947, in *The Tokyo Major War Crimes Trial*, vol. 76, 36198–36199; see also AD (NUOI) 372QO 100, 'Affidavit of Tōjō Hideki,' paragraphs 13–16, attached to Oneto to Minister of Foreign Affairs, 29 December 1947.
[45] AD (NUOI) 372QO 100, Oneto to Minister of Foreign Affairs, 19 September 1947, 7–8, 7–8.

The argument that underpinned Oneto's accusation, namely that the Japanese government had had a long-term plan to invade southeast Asia in which the occupation of Indochina was the first step, accorded with the narrative of war woven by the prosecution as a whole. This aspect of the trial, relying on the concept of conspiracy, was criticized at the time, and has continued to be criticized since.⁴⁶ Notably, Indian Justice Pal wrote in his dissenting opinion that the series of events recounted by the prosecution in its description of Japanese actions in Indochina, while it did happen, 'did not happen pursuant to any policy of the conspirators.'⁴⁷ More specifically in relation to Indochina, Franck Michelin has discussed in detail the complexity of the decision-making process that led the Japanese army commands in Southern China to cross the border at Lạng Sơn in September 1940, and the extent to which this attack was supported in Tokyo: he shows that while the Japanese military command was united in its understanding of the importance of controlling the border in Indochina, there was no agreement in the Japanese leadership or even within the army on the desirability of military intervention against France.⁴⁸

Debatable as was Oneto's contention that the military engagements of 23 September onwards signalled clearly Japan's readiness to invade Indochina at that point, it was nevertheless crucial for this part of the indictment to remove any lingering doubt about French collaboration in Indochina. If France 'gave Japan everything it wanted' as some might have thought before the trial, it was because it was forced to do so at gunpoint. The majority judgment of the tribunal accepted that point, and noted that the French governor general, 'faced with an actual invasion, was forced to accept Japanese demands.'⁴⁹ As Yuma Totani has shown, the tribunal's acceptance of Oneto's argument that a threat of force was as much a crime against peace as an actual invasion, mirrored the findings of the Nuremberg Tribunal in the definition of a crime against peace.⁵⁰

---

⁴⁶ John Dower, *Embracing Defeat. Japan in the Aftermath of World War II* (London: Penguin, 1999), 463; Totani, *The Tokyo War Crimes Trial*, 90.

⁴⁷ Radhabinod Pal, 'Dissenting Opinion of the Member from India (Justice Pal)' in *Documents on the Tokyo International Military Tribunal: Charter, Indictment and Judgments*, ed. Neil Boister and Robert Cryer (Oxford: Oxford University Press, 2008), 1239.

⁴⁸ Franck Michelin, 'Décider et Agir: l'intrusion Japonaise en Indochine française, Juin 1940,' *Vingtième Siècle: Revue D'Histoire*, no. 83 (2004): 75–93.

⁴⁹ Boister and Cryer (eds), *Documents*, 478.

⁵⁰ Totani, *Tokyo War Crimes Trials*, 94–95.

In that sense, Oneto's accusation and the findings of the tribunal buried the fact that in Indochina at least, France was not at war with Japan after 1940 (though Free France declared war on Japan in the wake of the Pearl Harbor attack), that after the battles of Lạng Sơn and Haïphong, the French colonial government continued its administration of the colony, that Japanese and French soldiers coexisted peacefully and French soldiers continued to guard borders, including at Lạng Sơn, until the Japanese coup of the night of 9–10 March 1945.

During the period when Oneto was preparing and delivering his indictment in Tokyo, accusing Japanese leaders of aggression against France in September 1940, in Saigon a French permanent military tribunal tried Japanese individuals for war crimes. There, however, a different interpretation was underlying the definition of war crimes. As the jurisdiction of the pursuit of war crimes was being determined, a note from the judicial office of the high commissioner suggested that war crimes to be pursued in Indochina should be limited to those that occurred between 9 March 1945 and the Japanese defeat. Attempting to pursue Japanese war crimes committed before the Japanese coup d'état, mused the commentator, was to invite the question of whether there existed, in fact, a state of war between Japan and France in Indochina before that moment, since General De Gaulle's 1941 declaration of war against Japan had not even been published in Indochina.[51] While such considerations were important in limiting the number of possible cases brought to the permanent military tribunal of Saigon as a whole, they also functioned to short-circuit any possible conflation of war crimes with collaboration. In that sense, the prosecution of war crimes at the local level in Saigon and at the international level in Tokyo had to adopt different time frames in order to achieve the same result: punishing Japanese war crimes and re-establishing French prestige, the one in Saigon for the benefit of France's position in the colony itself, and Oneto's prosecution in Tokyo for the benefit of France's position in the world at large.[52]

Oneto made a number of consciously political choices in his case for the prosecution, again with the prestige of France in mind, and the safeguarding of its future as an imperial power in the region. He reported to

---

[51] ANOM. INDO HCI ConsPol 153, Conseiller Juridique Torel, pour le Conseiller Politique, 24 December 1945.

[52] Beatrice Trefalt, 'Japanese war criminals in Indochina and the French pursuit of justice: Local and International Constraints,' *Journal of Contemporary History*, vol. 49 no. 4 (October 2014): 727–742.

his government that while some of the material he had available could have been useful for the prosecution, he had chosen to ignore it when it contained information that reflected badly on French military operations or discipline.[53] In at least one case, he had been told by his government not to include in the documents presented to the court the affidavit of General Mennerat, who had been in command of French troops at Lạng Sơn because, while the information was important for Oneto himself, it cast the French military forces in a bad light.[54] In addition, Oneto was not only considering the past when making his choice of documents, but also the future of France as a colonial power. He explained to his government that he chose not to include material that revealed 'the lack of loyalty of local populations' to France and 'the participation of indigenous people in independence movements.' His choice, he said, was dictated by his understanding that it would be dangerous to accuse the Japanese government of having deliberately inflamed local populations against French authority, when the Japanese side was using the liberation of local populations from the colonial yoke of Western powers as a justification for its own actions. An argument about whether or not the Japanese authorities encouraged Vietnamese independence, Oneto mused, was unlikely to be won by France when 'anti-colonialism, already traditionally strong amongst the Americans, has recently become even stronger.' Oneto was also concerned to avoid provoking debate on the issue of Vietnamese independence when 'negotiations in Indochina on this point are delicate.'[55]

As Oneto was highly sensitive to the political context of the trial, he was also likely to see the manifestation of similar sensitivities in the actions of others around him. For example, he explained that while some might consider 'despotic' Tribunal President Justice Webb's limits on the number of documents produced by the defence, he appreciated such limits as motivated by the need to speed up the trial. Oneto considered that the trial risked becoming anachronistic, and that the political situation between Japan and the USA was evolving so rapidly that '"sentences" that might have appeared normal even 6 months ago might well become entirely shocking in another 6 months.'[56] He also noted with interest how contextual politics

---

[53] AD (NUOI) 372QO99, Oneto to Foreign Minister, 22 October 1946, 2.
[54] AD (NUOI) 372QO100, Foreign Minister to Mr. Naggiar, 29 Mai 1946.
[55] AD (NUOI) 372QO99, Oneto to Foreign Minister, 22 October 1946, 2.
[56] AD (NUOI) 372QO100, Oneto, 'Le Tribunal Militaire international de Tokyo: Développement du procès du 24 Février au 20 Mars 1947,' no other date, 5.

affected other participants in the trial—especially how ideologically tainted some of the debates were between American defence counsels and Soviet prosecutors.[57] He also considered it a small victory when he was allowed to use his own language during the trial, leaving a precedent for his Russian counterpart to do the same. This victory was couched again as a matter of French prestige.[58] Though it might easily be dismissed as an absurd anecdote by some, for Oneto it symbolized resistance against Anglophone imperialism, and more broadly against the American domination of the postwar world which he saw as manifest in the trials.

Neil Boister has recently appraised the nature of the IMTFE as a 'show trial,' defining a show trial as having the broad characteristics of outcome predictability and audience management. Boister concludes that while the Tokyo Trial had some of the characteristics of a show trial, competition amongst the participants, and the autonomy of many of its parts made it an unreliable show, and thus, perhaps, not a very successful one.[59] In his analysis, Boister also raises the notion of impartiality in his discussion of the distinction between victors' justice and show trials, noting that for scholars like Alejandro Chehtman, a trial's overall impartiality depends on 'whether the participants in the trial expressed the partiality of the state and their political masters.'[60] French prosecutor Oneto expressed such a partiality with his explicit choice in the presentation of evidence, which avoided debate about Vietnamese claims to independence and drew attention away from French military failure, selectively excluding documentation, as we have seen, when required by his government. Oneto might well have had a much stronger case had he accused the Japanese leadership of breaking, in March 1945, the agreements made in 1940 with respect to French territorial integrity. But to do so would have disrupted 'the show' because it would have made a much more complicated and murky story out of what happened in Indochina between 1940 and 1945. The point for Oneto was to avoid any ambiguity in the story of France's participation on the side of the Allies in the war against Japan: Indochina was invaded in 1940, not in 1945.

---

[57] AD (NUOI) 372QO100, Oneto to Minister of Foreign Affairs, 14 June 1947, 6.
[58] See AD, Asie-Océanie. Japon. 130:Criminels de Guerre, Pechkoff, 'Télégramme,' 9 October 1946.
[59] Boister, 'The Tokyo Military Tribunal,' 3–29.
[60] Alejandro Chehtman, *The Philosophical Foundations of Extraterritorial Punishment* (Oxford: Oxford University Press, 2010), 160, quoted in Boister, 'The Tokyo Military Tribunal,' 11.

In conclusion, Oneto understood his participation in the prosecution of Japanese war criminals as having an important political dimension, one aiming to remove any lingering doubt about the collaboration of France with the Axis in Asia. Only by establishing this point could France hope eventually to claim reparations. As the trial ground on, however, both Oneto and Pechkoff noted the rapid transformation of postwar international relationships: by the time the trial was finished, the question of reparations was no longer relevant and France's position in Indochina was as difficult as ever. Pechkoff was particularly cynical about the ability of the trial to fulfill its pedagogical function of assigning guilt. He noted in January 1948 the effect that the testimony of former General Tōjō had on the Japanese public:

> The difficulties currently faced by the Western Powers in their Far Eastern possessions show that even if Japan lost the war in the Pacific, it has won the war in greater Asia. It is this of which Japanese are conscious, and this which Tōjō has, ironically, drawn attention to.[61]

While Pechkoff foretold France's defeat in Indochina at that point, his commentary shows that he also recognized the trial as a show that had not managed in the end to convey the right message.

The French prosecution at the IMTFE was a small part of a much larger process, and if we consider Oneto within the metaphor of the 'trial as show,' he was a mere bit-part actor, certainly not a large, central presence. However, attention to all the actors in this tribunal allows a better sense of the trial as a long process in a mutable political environment. Just as research on the French participation in the Tokyo Tribunal has been dwarfed by the amount of material written on more powerful actors, a focus on the final judgment and its dissenters has drawn attention away from the varied aims of participants in the prosecution. As we have seen here, individual prosecutors had specific intentions, not always in the end congruent with each other, but nestled within competing national agendas. For Oneto, the aim of punishing Japanese leaders for crimes against peace was contained within the broader one of rehabilitating France's image. As a single actor in a bigger show, Oneto jostled with others to have France's own 'victim statement' heard, not for the benefit of the accused in the dock as much as for the instruction of a much broader audience.

---

[61] My translation. AD (NUOI) 372QO100, Pechkoff to Foreign Minister, 7 January 1948, 2.

CHAPTER 4

Decolonization and Subaltern Sovereignty: India and the Tokyo Trial

Milinda Banerjee

INTRODUCTION

The present chapter explores the ambiguous relationship between ideals of justice, rule of law and the question of non-European sovereignty through a case study of Indian engagements with the Tokyo Trial. If colonial authority rested, among other things, on a 'rule of colonial difference,'[1] denying to the colonized juridical, political and cultural equality with the imperial masters, then decolonization would represent a deep unsettling of such asymmetries. I argue in this chapter that the International Military Tribunal for the Far East (IMTFE), popularly known as the Tokyo Trial (1946–48), represented, at least from the perspective of India, a key component of such decolonization. A study of certain strands in India's role

---

[1] The quoted phrase is taken from Partha Chatterjee, *The Nation and its Fragments* (Delhi: Oxford University Press, 2001), 16–8. On the construction of colonial difference, see also Thomas R. Metcalf, *Ideologies of the Raj* (Cambridge: Cambridge University Press, 1995).

M. Banerjee (✉)
Presidency University, Kolkata, India
Heidelberg University, Heidelberg, Germany

© The Author(s) 2016
K. von Lingen (ed.), *War Crimes Trials in the Wake of Decolonization and Cold War in Asia, 1945–1956*,
DOI 10.1007/978-3-319-42987-8_4

in the trial promises to raise broader questions about what decolonization implied in terms of an insurgent expropriation of European-colonial formats of state sovereignty and law.

To achieve this, the theoretical angle on decolonization adopted in this chapter is first discussed. I then offer a historiographic survey centering on the dissenting opinion of the Indian judge in Tokyo, Radhabinod Pal (1886–1967), in order to identify a basic lacuna in the historiography, which has impeded our ability to relate the dissent to the intellectual complexities of India's decolonization. Next, I offer my own take on the Pal dissent, while also relating it to political debates surrounding Tokyo. I focus especially on the ambiguous relationship between the British Government and the newly independent Government of India, and on the role of the Indian Prime Minister Jawaharlal Nehru (1889–1964). Following that, Pal's attitude towards decolonization in the years following the trial is examined. And finally, in the conclusion, I return to the question of how this study can complicate our appreciation of the conceptual ambiguities inherent in decolonization, especially on the issue of transfer of sovereignty.

Placing the Theoretical Stakes: Decolonization and the Problem of Sovereignty

There exists a long and sophisticated tradition of dealing with legal and political histories of the Tokyo Trial; in contrast, there has been a relative lack of intellectual historical investigations. An earlier essay by this author sought to unpack some of the intellectual assumptions that animated the trial: it focused especially on the debate on natural law and the role of Pal.[2] This chapter focuses more closely on a conceptual problem regarding decolonization, namely, as to why anti-colonial actors of the twentieth century chose not to reject the framework of modern state sovereignty which was first imposed in many extra-European societies by European empires, even though the violence and exclusion inherent in such formats should have been obvious to them. What was so compelling about what

---

[2] Milinda Banerjee, 'Does International Criminal Justice Require a Sovereign? Historicising Radhabinod Pal's Tokyo Judgment in Light of his 'Indian' Legal Philosophy,' in *Historical Origins of International Criminal Law*, vol. 2, Morten Bergsmo, Cheah Wui Ling, and Yi Ping, eds. (Brussels: Torkel Opsahl, 2014), 67–117. The present chapter draws in part on that earlier article, while adding new empirical and theoretical strands.

David Armitage has called the 'contagion of sovereignty'?[3] The idea of contagion implies almost a state of involuntary malady: if sovereignty was indeed a malady, then why did many non-European actors choose not to be inoculated against it? The most popular account of this diffusion of the format of nation-state sovereignty, by Benedict Anderson, does not address this issue: no amount of faith in pre-existing modules and their mimesis can adequately explain the agency of non-Europeans in the age of decolonization.[4] Unless we present the latter as deploying the format of state sovereignty as a strictly cynical instrument for gaining power, we would have to probe deeper into their moral motivations.

Samuel Moyn has recently highlighted the urgency of this problem for those interested in global intellectual history, by focusing on the competing claims of collective self-determination (nation-state sovereignty) and human rights among political actors in the twentieth century. He argues that intellectual historians need to remain acutely sensitive to the contingency of such choices, in studying how actors, including anti-colonial ones in the decolonizing world, have navigated across time between competing claims for rights (collective/state rights versus human rights, for example). Thereby, he distances himself from those narratives which assume an a priori inevitability to the spread of certain forms of rights consciousness (here he particularly targets those who identify a teleological and irresistible march of progress in the universalization of human rights claims).[5]

By focusing on the Tokyo Trial and its long intellectual aftermath, and relating this to India's decolonization, I shall try to address why, in specific strands of anti-colonial intellection, nation-state sovereignty appeared as the least worst political option, even if the tragic potential of sovereign violence was never lost sight of. The role of legal discourse in mediating this critical moment will be underscored, even as I shall highlight not just the contingency, but also the plurivocality of the choices made. A cue shall be taken from Moyn's own characterization of Pal's dissenting opinion in Tokyo as forming 'a subaltern critique of Western international law".'[6]

---

[3] David Armitage, *The Declaration of Independence: A Global History* (Cambridge, MA: Harvard University Press, 2007).
[4] Benedict Anderson, *Imagined Communities: Reflections on the Origin and Spread of Nationalism* (London: Verso, 2006)
[5] Samuel Moyn, 'On the Nonglobalization of Ideas,' in *Global Intellectual History*, Samuel Moyn and Andrew Sartori, eds. (New York, NY: Columbia University Press, 2013), 187–204.
[6] Samuel Moyn, 'Judith Shklar versus the International Criminal Court,' *Humanity* 4 (2013), 485.

The act of decolonization, in India as elsewhere in mid-late twentieth century Asia and Africa, constituted a peculiar moment in subalternity: the subaltern—or to phrase this more historically, the non-European actors/ societies—threw off their colonial masters, but only by appropriating their masters' apparatuses of state sovereignty. Here, the term 'subaltern sovereignty' is used as a heuristic tool for tracking this gesture. I argue that, at least in the case discussed here, there was a strange episode of unhappiness involved, rather than the jubilation that one might associate with the decolonizing moment.[7]

Sudipta Kaviraj has used an iconic term from G. W. F. Hegel's *Phenomenology of Spirit* (*Phänomenologie des Geistes*) to describe the anticolonial Bengali discourses of Bankimchandra Chattopadhyay, arguing that the latter exhibited an 'unhappy consciousness' (in Hegel's original, *das unglückliche Bewußtsein*). Bankimchandra's unhappiness lay in the fact that he could neither disavow the promise of Enlightenment modernity, nor be completely at ease with it, given that a discursive acceptance of the European civilizing mission would also entail a political recognition of British colonial tutelage.[8] Kaviraj's is a classic subaltern studies and postcolonial analysis of late nineteenth-century India's most famous nationalist litterateur. I shall take a cue from it to discuss a later moment of indecision and melancholy. We shall see that, like his compatriot Bankimchandra, Pal was also caught in incertitude and hesitation: he could neither accept the Western-origin promise of modern state sovereignty, nor deny it altogether. This created in him a schizophrenia towards international criminal law. Pal shall be compared with actors associated with the Government of

---

[7] The expression 'subaltern sovereignty' has also been used in M. Madhava Prasad, "Fan Bhakti and Subaltern Sovereignty: Enthusiasm as a Political Factor", *Economic and Political Weekly* 44 (2009): 68–76; however my focus and argument about subaltern sovereignty is quite different from Prasad's. In case of India, and especially for Bengal (from where Pal came), the experience of decolonization was also marked by the violence and displacements unleashed by Partition. Many (on both 'right' and 'left' strands of the political spectrum) also lamented the inadequacy of a transfer of power that left intact much of the framework of British governance. On the ensuing complexities, including in terms of emotional expression, see Sekhar Bandyopadhyay, *Decolonization in South Asia: Meanings of Freedom in Post-Independence West Bengal, 1947–52* (Abingdon: Routledge, 2009).

[8] Sudipta Kaviraj, *The Unhappy Consciousness: Bankimchandra Chattopadhyay and the Formation of Nationalist Discourse in India* (Delhi: Oxford University Press, 1995); Georg W. F. Hegel, *Phenomenology of Spirit*, A. V. Miller, trans. (Oxford: Oxford University Press, 1977), 119–138.

India who displayed analogous complexities that stemmed from the inherent and ineradicable intellectual contradictions involved in decolonization.

INDIA'S ENTRY INTO TOKYO

Pal's entry into Tokyo was itself the product of a decolonizing moment. Yuki Takatori and James Burnham Sedgwick have briefly noticed the contribution of Sir Girja Shankar Bajpai (1891–1954), the agent general for India in Washington, in ensuring the entry of an Indian judge into the trial, in the face of strong American opposition.[9] It is not possible here, for reasons of space, to elaborate on Bajpai's intellectual stance, or the debates on race politics he provoked in the US State Department.[10] What will be stressed here was that the entry of a judge to represent India at the trial, and a non-white one at that, was by no means a foregone conclusion.

This was especially because, in 1945–46, India was not yet an independent state. However, in October 1945, with the support of the British government (communicated through the British Secretary of State for Foreign Affairs, Ernest Bevin) and the agreement of the USA, India entered the Far Eastern Commission. Bajpai was the Indian representative in the commission.[11] This did not imply, however, that India would also gain entry into the Tokyo Trial. The initial position of the USA was that, in the context of war crimes and atrocities suffered by its citizens, India (like Philippines) could send an associate prosecutor to the trial, but not a judge. Only the states which had been signatory to the Japanese surrender—USA, China, UK, USSR, Australia, Canada, France, Netherlands

---

[9] Yuki Takatori, '"America's" War Crimes Trial? Commonwealth Leadership at the International Military Tribunal for the Far East, 1946–48,' *The Journal of Imperial and Commonwealth History* 35 (2007): 557; James Burnham Sedgwick, 'The Trial Within: Negotiating Justice at the International Military Tribunal for the Far East, 1946–1948,' University of British Columbia PhD Dissertation, 2012, 269.

[10] I intend to expand on this in a forthcoming essay. Milinda Banerjee, 'India's "Subaltern Elites" and the Tokyo Trial' (forthcoming), draft paper presented at the conference 'Law, Biography, and a Trial: The Tokyo Tribunal's Transnational Histories,' Heidelberg University, 6–8 December 2015.

[11] 'Statement on the Establishment of a Far Eastern Commission to Formulate Policies for the Carrying Out of the Japanese Surrender Terms,' issued in London by James F. Byrnes, US secretary of state on 29 September 1945, and released to the press on 1 October 1945, in *United States The Department of State Bulletin*, 1945, vol. 13, 545; 'Appointment of Indian Representative,' 29 October 1945, in *United States The Department of State Bulletin*, 1945, vol. 13, 728.

and New Zealand—could send judges.¹² Bajpai had to fight to gain for India 'a footing of equality' (to quote from a letter sent by him to the US secretary of state on 4 January 1946),¹³ a process which involved not only timely British support,¹⁴ but also protracted and crucial negotiations within the US State Department.¹⁵ Only after these was the IMTFE Charter amended on 25 April 1946,¹⁶ and the path was laid clear for the entry of Radhabinod Pal, 'formerly Judge of the Calcutta High Court,'¹⁷ to represent India at Tokyo.

The entry of an Indian judge was itself, in the broadest sense, a part of the decolonization of legal regimes, allowing non-white actors to gain recognition within white-dominated legal domains. It marked one step, perhaps minor but certainly significant, in the transformation of India into a sovereign legal and political space. It was the dissenting opinion of the Indian judge which would, however, leave the most lasting memorial to the complex links between Indian decolonization and the Tokyo Trial. Even more than the dissents of the Dutch and the French judges, Pal's judgment would achieve durable fame and notoriety, because of its seeming exculpation of the top Japanese political-military leadership with respect to their role in war crimes. In the conclusion of his dissent, Pal sonorously proclaimed that he held that 'each and everyone of the accused must be found not guilty of each and every one of the charges in the indictment and should be acquitted of

---

[12] National Archives at College Park, College Park, MD (hereafter NARA), General Records of the Department of State, RG 59, Letter from the Acting Secretary of State to the Agent General for India, 23 January 1946, File No. 740.00116 PW/1-446 CS/LE, Box 3631, Decimal File, 1945–49.

[13] NARA, General Records of the Department of State, RG 59, Letter from the Agent General for India to the Secretary of State, 4 January 1946, File No. 740.00116 PW/1–446 CS/LE, Box 3631, Decimal File, 1945–49.

[14] Sedgwick, 'The Trial Within,' 265–9, 305.

[15] Banerjee, 'India's "Subaltern Elites".'

[16] International Military Tribunal for the Far East Charter, available at http://www.jus.uio.no/english/services/library/treaties/04/4-06/military-tribunal-far-east.xml (accessed on 13 October 2014); NARA, General Records of the Department of State, RG 59, Telegram Sent, Department of State, 22 April 1946, File No. 740.00116 PW/4-2246 CS/A, Box 3631, Decimal File, 1945–49.

[17] NARA, General Records of the Department of State, RG 59, Letter from the Agent General for India to the Secretary of State, 29 April 1946, File No. 740.00116PW/4-2946 CS/A, Box 3631, Decimal File, 1945–49.

all those charges.'[18] The aim of the rest of this chapter is to conceptually relate this strange judgment to the wider complexities, intellectual and political, of decolonization. But for that, we first need a historiographic review of the dissent.

Radhabinod Pal's Tokyo Dissent: Problematizing the Historiography

I cannot offer an exhaustive bibliographic survey, but shall outline some of the main paradigms; the lack of an analytically detailed historiographic survey on Pal's dissent in existing scholarship renders this all the more urgent. In the secondary literature on Pal, one dominant suggestion has been that his judgment was designed to protect the top Japanese political-military leadership, and that this was done from a broadly positivist stance, thereby to challenge the claims of international criminal justice, in part embedded in naturalist philosophy, that was upheld by the prosecution. From this position, some have seen Pal (with a mixture of praise and criticism) as an *avant la lettre* champion of third world approaches to international law. Pal is represented as having denounced the dominant Allied position in Tokyo which aimed at using the trial to justify the preservation of a white-dominated imperial status quo in the international system. Exegetes range from those who view Pal as an untainted positivist to those who see in him some shades of a quasi-naturalistic anti-colonial moral fervour that was, somewhat sanctimoniously, directed against Western state power.[19] Others criticize Pal's positivism more strongly for failing to recognize

---

[18] International Military Tribunal for the Far East (IMTFE) Transcripts, *United States of America et al. v. Araki Sadao et al.*, Judgment of The Hon'ble Mr. Justice Pal, Member from India ('Pal Judgment') (https://www.legal-tools.org/en/go-to-database/ltfolder/0_29521/#results), 1226. All citations from the Tokyo Trial have been given from the International Criminal Court Legal Tools Database.

[19] Judith N. Shklar, *Legalism: An Essay on Law, Morals and Politics* (Cambridge, MA: Harvard University Press, 1964), 181–90; Richard H. Minear, *Victors' Justice: The Tokyo War Crimes Trial* (Princeton: Princeton University Press, 1971); Elizabeth S. Kopelman, 'Ideology and International Law: The Dissent of the Indian Justice at the Tokyo War Crimes Trial,' *New York University Journal of International Law and Politics* 23 (1990/91): 373–444; Neil Boister and Robert Cryer, *The Tokyo International Military Tribunal: A Reappraisal* (Oxford: Oxford University Press, 2008); Robert Cryer, 'The Doctrinal Foundations of International Criminalization,' in *International Criminal Law*, vol. 1, Mahmoud C. Bassiouni, ed. (Leiden: Martinus Nijhoff, 2008), 112; Robert Cryer, 'The Philosophy of

the sovereign violence committed by a non-white power (Japan), and thereby in morally failing to admit the claims of international criminal and humanitarian justice.[20]

These divergent strands (by and large) focus on Pal's Tokyo dissent to the exclusion of his broader oeuvre of writings and speeches; they also do not relate the legal philosophy outlined in Pal's dissent to that laid out in his other juridical works. Thus, Pal largely appears as a 'mimic man' (to borrow a celebrated phrase from Homi Bhabha),[21] someone who appropriated age-old European assumptions (in this case, about state sovereignty) to challenge the colonial powers. Pal, as the representative of the colonized subject, seemingly replicated the imperial master without challenging the basic grammar of sovereignty through which the master–subaltern relation was implemented in colonial power structures. To tease out the broader implications of this for processes of decolonization, it would appear from this vantage point that Pal's mimicry, in seeking to defend Japanese state sovereignty despite the latter's brutal complicity with imperial violence, was symptomatic of a broader anti-colonial mimesis. In other hands, this would ensure that extra-European nationalist actors would seek to raise scaffolds of sovereignty: their acts of decolonization would create, defend and strengthen extra-European state sovereignty even if postcolonial statehood was complicit with large-scale violence and exclusion. Decolonization would dismantle old-style imperialism, no doubt, but substitute it with another order of

---

International Criminal Law,' in *Research Handbook on the Theory and History of International Law*, Alexander Orakhelashvili, ed. (Cheltenham: Edward Elgar, 2011), 243; Kirsten Sellars, 'Imperfect Justice at Nuremberg and Tokyo,' *The European Journal of International Law* 21 (2011): 1096; Kirsten Sellars, *'Crimes against Peace' and International Law* (Cambridge: Cambridge University Press, 2013); Latha Varadarajan, 'The Trials of Imperialism: Radhabinod Pal's Dissent at the Tokyo Tribunal,' *European Journal of International Relations* 2014: 1–23.

[20] Yuma Totani, *The Tokyo War Crimes Trial: The Pursuit of Justice in the Wake of World War II* (Cambridge, MA: Harvard University Press, 2009), especially 218–45. This is presumably also the opinion of Nariaki Nakazato, *Paru Hanji: Indo nashonarizumu to Tokyo Saiban* (Tokyo: Iwanami Shoten, 2011), which, like other Japanese literature on Pal, I have not studied. On Nakazato's views: Yuma Totani, 'Japanese Receptions of Separate Opinions at the Tokyo Trial,' 2015, http://ceas.yale.edu/sites/default/files/files/events/2014-2015/Totani%20Paper%20for%20CEAS%20copy.pdf, 16–17, accessed 24 October 2015.

[21] Homi K. Bhabha, 'Of Mimicry and Man: The Ambivalence of Colonial Discourse,' in his *The Location of Culture* (London: Routledge, 1994), 85–92.

state sovereignty. Sovereignty would embody the secret conspiracy linking empire and postcolony.

An entirely different explanation of Pal's dissent is given by Ashis Nandy, Barry Hill and, to some extent, by Nakajima Takeshi, who highlight Pal's adherence to an old, presumably unchanging, Hindu/Indic mythic-religious vision of the world. For Nandy, Pal represented an ancient Hindu ideology that refused to distinguish between good and evil in the manner of the West, and, in the context of the Second World War, of the Allied Powers. This assessment is not based on any detailed examination of Pal's writings on Hindu law, in which Nandy observes an 'overdone attempt to provide a comparative picture and to explain India in Western terms.'[22] In a less extreme way, Takeshi suggests, without going into legal-philosophical details, that 'Pal was a believer of humanism based on the philosophy of "dharma" from ancient India.'[23]

Hill has offered a more sophisticated interrogation of Pal's Hindu law writings. However he is equally extreme in suggesting that Pal, like his fellow Bengali, the poet Rabindranath Tagore, 'sought to ground their ethics in traditional Indian culture, rather than the universalism of the West: they would in the end place their trust in the ancient Dharma, which rested in kinship rather than a notion of sovereignty.'[24] Hill anachronistically lumps together the *Vedas*, the *Upanishads* and the *Dharmasutras* (which were written across different time periods, and all of which Pal commented on, but with rather varying attitudes). Hill's self-proclaimed 'leftist Buddhistic'[25] stance offers important insights. I certainly agree with his observation on the way in which Pal was critical towards legal dogmatism[26]; we seem to have arrived at this discovery through parallel, if simultaneous, routes. However, Hill's overall schema is too monochromatic; he focuses on one (important) facet of Pal and completely suppresses others. This has partly to do with the ambiguities in the Tokyo judgment itself, and partly with the complexities in the Vedic/Sanskrit texts and their

---

[22] Ashis Nandy, 'The Other Within: The Strange Case of Radhabinod Pal's Judgment on Culpability,' in *New Literary History* 23 (1992): 60.
[23] Nakajima Takeshi, 'Justice Pal (India)' in *Beyond Victor's Justice?: The Tokyo War Crimes Trial Revisited*, Yuki Tanaka, Tim McCormack and Gerry Simpson, eds. (Leiden: Martinus Nijhoff, 2011), 140.
[24] Barry Hill, 'Reason and Lovelessness: Tagore, War Crimes, and Justice Pal,' in *Postcolonial Studies* 18 (2015): 156.
[25] Ibid., 157.
[26] Ibid., 159.

location within shifting South Asian discourses and legal cultures which have escaped Hill's literary and Anglophone perspective.

I do not, of course, wish to dismiss or minimize the impressive scholarship of previous generations of study on Pal. But I shall underscore the sense of aporia we feel when confronted by the contradictions in historiography: Pal is differentially cast as a positivist defender of state sovereignty against naturalism, and as a believer in moral law (*dharma*) rather than in state sovereignty; as an imitator of Western statehood and as a disciple of ancient Hindu beliefs. There is a puzzling multiplicity to Pal, and indeed to his dissenting judgment, which calls for a deeper explanation.

The Paradoxes of Sovereignty: Revisiting the Pal Dissent

I attempted in an earlier essay to explain the seemingly contradictory, and often paradoxical, multiple facets of Pal's legal worldview. I shall not repeat those findings here, except in a summary form, to relate them to the politics of decolonization. I have suggested that Pal's writings on 'Hindu' (in his words) legal history and philosophy were motivated by a quest to find an alternative source of law than in divine or human sovereignty. Such a motivation is visible as early as the late 1920s, and is articulated in an elaborate manner in his 1958 book. Pal identified in certain ancient Indian legal texts, especially in Manu, as well as in European discussions, including about Christian concepts of divine authority and early modern and modern references to state sovereignty, a problematic sanction for authoritarian violence. In contradistinction to this, he championed ideas of natural law, which he identified especially in *rta* of the *Rgveda*, as well as in various European Christian concepts of natural law. He felt that such a horizon of natural law reflected rationality and was open-ended enough to take into account social transformation. Laws had to remain dynamic to respond to social needs: *vrata* of the *Rgveda* was one such order of legality where he found this flexibility. In a nuclear form in the 1920s writings, and elaborately in the 1958 book, we see that Pal was anxious to critique notions of authoritarian sovereignty by invoking concepts of cosmic and ethical law. This also helped him negate the suggestion that India lacked in law simply because state-backed legal regimes had largely been absent in its precolonial past. Making a virtue out of necessity, he combated colonial suppositions about state-supported rule of law by upholding the superiority of a rule of law that could exist independent of sovereign force, by being embedded in ethical principles.[27]

This leaves us with the question as to why Pal became a positivist in Tokyo, defending Japanese state sovereignty. In my earlier essay, I have identified a key, and till then largely un-noticed, part of the Tokyo dissent, where Pal confessed: 'I, myself, am not in love with this national sovereignty and I know a strong voice has already been raised against it.'[28] Equally interesting is the fact that Pal affirmed the desirability of an impartial international criminal court. furthermore, he aligned himself with Hersch Lauterpacht to assert that the goal of international law was to protect the individual human being's rights.[29] Despite this anti-sovereignty tone, Pal also noted: 'But even in the postwar organizations after this Second World War national sovereignty still figures very largely.'[30]

Pal's position on state sovereignty and natural law in Tokyo was in fact largely constituted through an adversarial mode. He was opposing the views of the chief (American) prosecutor, Joseph B. Keenan (1888–1954), and more generally of the prosecution, when they sought to circumvent the absence of definitive positive laws that might enable them to prosecute the Japanese leaders (and therefore the whole matter of *nullum crimen nulla poena sine lege*: no crime, no punishment, without a law) by invoking a universalist stance embedded in natural law. This ideological position can be found in particular detail in the opening and summation speeches of the prosecution as well as in a 1950 volume on international criminal law, written by Keenan and his juridical associate at Tokyo, Brendan Brown. There was, arguably, an emerging Cold War context behind this invocation of Christian natural law principles; in any case, by 1950, this was being consciously deployed by Keenan and Brown to condemn not just the Axis Powers, but also the Soviet Union, and thereby to legitimate America's role in the war in Korea. Proximate to Keenan's position in

---

[27] Banerjee, 'International Criminal Justice ' 72–86. The main sources for my interpretation are: Radhabinod Pal, *The Hindu Philosophy of Law in the Vedic and Post-Vedic Times Prior to the Institutes of Manu* (Calcutta: Biswabhandar Press, 1927?); Radhabinod Pal, *The History of Hindu Law in the Vedic Age and in Post-Vedic Times down to the Institutes of Manu* (Calcutta: Biswabhandar Press, 1929?), enlarged edition: (Calcutta: University of Calcutta, 1958).

[28] Pal Judgment, 186.

[29] Ibid., 10–5, 145.

[30] Ibid., 186 (underlining in the original here and elsewhere in citations in this chapter).

Tokyo was also that of the (Australian) President Judge William Webb, whose separate judgment also references Christian and natural law principles. On the question of sovereignty, Keenan as much as Webb suggested that the Allied Powers, and specifically the supreme commander for the Allied Powers and his administration, could act in a sovereign capacity to enforce natural law principles and prosecute the Japanese.[31] The majority judgment (representing the views of judges from the UK, USA, USSR, Canada, New Zealand and China) did not invoke such explicit naturalist argumentation, but nevertheless drew legitimacy from the surrender of Japan and from the IMTFE charter, reinforcing Allied hegemonic claims over Japan.[32]

Pal's attitude makes sense only within this landscape. He deliberately opposed Keenan's opening statement at the trial, where Keenan claimed legitimation for the prosecution's legal stand from what was variously known as 'common law,' 'general law' or 'natural law.'[33] Even as he accepted the legitimacy of a naturalist viewpoint, Pal negated the possibility that the Allied Powers could claim to truly give voice to natural-moral law.[34] In Pal's words:

> I should only add that the international community has not as yet developed into 'the world commonwealth' and perhaps as yet no particular group of nations can claim to be the custodian of 'the common good'. International life is not yet organized into a community under a rule of law. A community life has not even been agreed upon as yet. Such an agreement is essential before the so-called natural law may be allowed to function in the manner suggested. It is only when such group living is agreed upon, the conditions required for successful group life may supply some external criteria that would furnish some standard against which the rightness or otherwise of any particular decision can be measured.[35]

From this oppositional stance, Pal also unmasked the colonial uses of natural law arguments. He observed how European powers had traditionally justified imperial conquest 'as a right derived from natural law and

---

[31] Banerjee, 'International Criminal Justice,' 104–8; Sellars, *Crimes*.
[32] IMTFE Transcript, *United States of America et al. v. Araki Sadao et al.*, Judgment (https://www.legal-tools.org/en/go-to-database/ltfolder/0_29521/#results), 1 November 1948, especially 23–37.
[33] Pal Judgment, 24–25.
[34] Ibid., 147–51.
[35] Ibid., 151.

justified by the fiction of the territorium nullius, territory inhabited by natives whose community is not to be considered as a state.'[36]

In a related manner, Pal denied that the Allied Powers could claim sovereignty over Japan on the basis of military conquest.[37] Neither could they pretend to embody a universalistic sovereign force. Pal condemned the notion that a victor nation could claim to be 'a sovereign of the international community. It is not the sovereign of that much desired superstate.'[38] The critique of sovereignty that is visible in Pal's Hindu law writings was thus equally present in his Tokyo dissent; only it had turned into a critique of the sort of global super-sovereignty that he feared the Allied Powers were trying to establish in Japan and beyond. He thought that such a regime would claim an ersatz divinity, declaring itself as 'a valiant god struggling to establish a real democratic order in the Universe,' when it was merely maintaining 'the actual plague of imperialism' by conserving a 'political status quo' that reinforced 'political dominations' over much of the world, denying to other societies the 'political freedom' that the dominant Allied Powers themselves enjoyed.[39] Pal also challenged Allied rhetoric of waging a just war by noting how Western powers had acquired 'territories in the Eastern Hemisphere' through 'armed violence.'[40] The Second World War, at least in Asia, could not be cast, in his opinion, in Manichean binaries; it was the fatal product of 'the combined impact of democracy and industrialism.'[41]

While condemning Allied hypocrisy, however, Pal also provided something of an apologia for Japan. He denounced the 'devilish and fiendish' nature of Japanese war crimes,[42] but he also suggested that Japanese imperialism was ultimately overdetermined by Western imperialism and racism. Further, in his historic map of crimes, Kaiser William II (during the First World War), the major war criminals of the European Axis Powers and especially the Nazi leaders, as well as the American leadership (in the context of the atomic bombing of Japan) had been directly responsible for war crimes, whereas he felt that the Japanese leadership had not been

---

[36] Ibid., 342.
[37] Ibid., 29, 55, 57, 60–1.
[38] Ibid., 55.
[39] Ibid., 238–9.
[40] Ibid., 70.
[41] Ibid., 736.
[42] Ibid., 1070, 1089.

so directly responsible. In absolving them, with rhetorical hyperbole, Pal exposed himself to the charge of covering up Japanese war guilt.[43]

What was at stake in adopting such a posture? I would argue that Pal's Tokyo dissent serves as a microcosm for some of the major intellectual contradictions in decolonization. Pal was typical of an anti-colonial actor who was acutely aware of the problem of sovereign violence, of the violence necessarily characteristic of any form of organized power, including that of the modern sovereign state. However, a supranational power structure was no solution for him. Rather than transcending sovereignty, he felt that such a framework—instantiated through a juridical context, like the Tokyo Trial, or, more broadly, through mechanisms of international criminal justice and policing—would merely replicate on an even more dangerous scale the problem of sovereignty, creating a monstrous super-sovereignty of colonial powers masquerading as a universal peacekeeping force. In defence against such a possibility, Pal was ready to accept what he thought was a lesser evil: the possibility of a non-European sovereign state, even if that state committed violence. Hence his anguish at the prospect of Allied sovereignty over Japan, as well as his morally dubious defence of the Japanese leadership. In defending Japan out of fear about Western imperial sovereignty, Pal's judgment reveals a trick to preserve and sublate the grammar of sovereignty, rather than overthrow it. This was a schizophrenic and unhappy acceptance of sovereignty, but one with profound historical consequences.

Anxieties of (Post-)Coloniality: Britain, India and Pal's Tokyo Dissent

Our discussion on 'subaltern sovereignty' gets added depth when we track perceptions towards Pal's Tokyo dissent within British and Indian governmental circles. Through the microcosm of the Pal dissent, one can chart in fascinating ways the anxieties of humiliation which accompanied decolonization for British ruling classes, as well the desperation and desire, among sections of the new rulers of India, to get rid of their subalternity by making their state respectable to its former masters.

The prospect of humiliation loomed large from early on. Pal's hostile stance could, after all, be detected from near the outset in Tokyo.[44] In

---

[43] Ibid., 9, 137–8, 1089–91; Banerjee, 'International Criminal Justice,' 99–100.
[44] Sellars, *Crimes*, 234–35; Sedgwick, 'The Trial Within,' 83. Many of the archival documents cited from now on in this essay have been interrogated by previous scholars; however, I add new theoretical dimensions.

April–May 1947, British governmental circles feared some special 'back-slaps' towards Britain. There was a great deal of discussion mediated through the networks that linked Tokyo (the British judge Lord Patrick and the United Kingdom Liaison Mission in Japan) with London (the Lord Chancellor, the Attorney General, the Dominions Office and the Foreign Office). The British Prime Minister Clement Atlee was kept in the loop. Others, including Keenan and Webb, also created controversy and panic; however, Pal's role was quite significant in provoking counter-moves to construct a cohesive majority judgment.[45] The language of imperial-racial humiliation is visible from the way in which the British Foreign Secretary Ernest Bevin seemingly feared 'a shattering blow to European prestige' and justification of 'Japanese militarism' if the trial failed.[46]

To add to this specter, Pal's friendship with the Dutch judge B. V. A. Röling, along with Röling's nascent (partly Orientalist) affection for Japan, turned the latter increasingly sceptical towards the hegemonic and imperial nuances of Allied war crimes trial policy, differentiating him from the majority of the judges.[47] However Röling soon faced pressure; a British Foreign Office note laconically observed: 'If the Indian is unsupported he may in the end toe the line.'[48] Eventually Röling moderated his position, but the result was still a dissent. As for Pal, the British hoped, even in September 1947, to influence him through Lord Patrick, and to bring him 'into Nuremberg fold.'[49] This was a pipe dream. Even as India underwent political decolonization in 1947, Pal made his own decolonizing move in Tokyo.

But just as Pal's decolonizing gesture concealed a certain complicity with the imperial grammar of state sovereignty, similar was the case with the newly independent Government of India. V. K. Krishna Menon, a close Nehru aide and then the high commissioner for India to the United Kingdom (he would be an influential defence minister of India from 1957

---

[45] Quote from The National Archives, United Kingdom (hereafter TNA), FO 371/66552, From United Kingdom Liaison Mission in Japan to Foreign Office, 25 April 1947. The trial provoked juridical conflicts which were rooted in ideological and private quarrels, in turn resulting in attempts to negate differences. See, for example, TNA, LCO 2/2992, FO 371/63820, FO 371/66552, FO 371/66553.
[46] TNA, FO 371/66553, U 666/1/73, Foreign Office, 22 May 1947.
[47] Lisette Schouten, 'From Tokyo to the United Nations: B. V. A. Röling, International Criminal Jurisdiction and the Debate on Establishing an International Criminal Court, 1949–1957,' in Bergsmo et al. (eds.), *Historical Origins*, 184–92.
[48] TNA, FO 371/66553, Foreign Office Note, 23 May 1947.
[49] TNA, FO 371/63820, From United Kingdom Liaison Mission in Japan to Foreign Office, 21 September 1947.

to 1962), contacted the British Secretary of State for Commonwealth Relations Philip Noel-Baker in August 1948, asking 'whether the Indian Government should issue a statement dissociating themselves from the opinions published by Justice Pal.' Noel-Baker 'mildly encouraged' Menon, while he also sought the advice of other British authorities.[50] The fear of 'thinly concealed backslaps at Great Britain' by Pal continued to haunt some British governmental circles.[51] However, the Foreign Office felt overall that 'silence seems to be the best rejoinder'; it was best not to publicize Pal's opinion, especially given the lack of any stir in Japan. If things changed, and Pal's opinion about 'Japanese war-innocence' was regarded in Japan as the official Indian view, then the Indian government could reconsider the matter.[52] The United Kingdom Liaison Mission in Japan agreed. Lord Patrick felt the same since the matter was *sub judice*.[53] Alvary Gascoigne, the British political representative in Tokyo, also thought that the Indian government should not make a statement.[54] Noel-Baker ultimately communicated this view to Menon.[55]

While the Government of India thus projected itself as a respectable partner (in league with its former master) in the project of international justice, it could not wholly get rid of its subalternity as an Asiatic power. Gascoigne speculated that the Indian government had, in line with its 'Asiatic policy,' prompted Pal to take his stand.[56] Pal was suspected of being aligned with the anti-British Indian National Army, or (on the basis of impressions collected from the British prosecutor in Tokyo Arthur Comyns Carr) of being 'an agreeable and sincere individual who unfortunately has a bee in his bonnet about "Asia for the Asiatics."' There

---

[50] TNA, DO 35/2938, Record of Conversation between the Secretary of State and the High Commissioner for India, 3 August 1948.

[51] TNA, DO 35/2938, F. 3151/17, 5 August 1948 (quote from here); also TNA, DO 35/2938, F. 3151/17, Letter from Commonwealth Relations Office to F. S. Tomlinson, Foreign Office, and F 12157/48/G, Telegram from Foreign Office to UK Liaison Mission in Japan.

[52] TNA, DO 35/2938, F 10950/48/G, Letter from F. S. Tomlinson, Foreign Office, to J. M. C. James, Commonwealth Relations Office, 20 August 1948.

[53] TNA, DO 35/2938, Telegram from United Kingdom Liaison Mission in Japan to Foreign Office, 7 September 1948.

[54] TNA, FO 371/69833, F 15996/48/23, Minutes, 15 November 1948.

[55] TNA, DO 35/2938, Letter from Philip Noel-Baker to V. K. Krishna Menon, 2 October 1948.

[56] TNA, DO 35/2938, P. A. 39/13/48, Letter from United Kingdom Liaison Mission in Japan to M. E. Dening, Foreign Office, 25 November 1948.

was some fear about whether India and Japan were uniting in some anti-Western front.⁵⁷

To negate such doubts, Nehru monitored Indian political statements, as evident in a cable he sent in November 1948 to the Governor of West Bengal Kailash Nath Katju, where he asked the latter not to 'send any telegram to General Macarthur,' since he was a 'mere mouthpiece of other Governments.' Nehru feared being associated 'with Justice Pal's dissenting judgment,' where 'wild and sweeping statements have been made with many of which we do not agree at all. In view of suspicion that Government of India had inspired Pal's judgment, we have had to inform Governments concerned informally that we are in no way responsible for it.'⁵⁸ The same anxiety is manifest in a letter sent by Nehru on 6 December 1948 to the premiers of the provincial governments of India. He noted that the death sentences passed on Japanese war leaders had 'met with a great deal of adverse criticism in India.' Pal's opinion however expressed *'many opinions and theories with which the Government of India could not associate itself.'* To distance the Indian government from the judgment, Nehru underlined that Pal was 'not functioning in the Commission as a representative of the Government of India but as an eminent judge in his individual capacity.' But Nehru also confessed that 'most of us' regarded the death sentences as 'unfortunate'; however, 'an official protest would not do any good either to the persons concerned or to the cause we have at heart, and therefore we have not intervened officially.'⁵⁹

There were contradictions in Nehru. On the one hand, he condescendingly dismissed Pal's judgment, mirroring colonial aspersions about Pal's lunacy. The non-European, Pal, in seeking to emulate the white man's language of command, had copied it to the point of a dangerous and 'wild' surplus, which another of his more gentrified compatriots felt compelled to denounce. On the other hand, there was also a tone of sympathy, embedded in Indian political criticism of the death sentences. Nehru's December letter notwithstanding, in November 1948, the Government of India representative had asked in a meeting of the Far Eastern Commission powers that the death sentences at Tokyo be commuted to life imprisonment.

---

⁵⁷ TNA, DO 35/2938, Notes of Commonwealth Relations Office.
⁵⁸ Jawaharlal Nehru, *Selected Works of Jawaharlal Nehru*, vol. 8 (Delhi: Jawaharlal Nehru Memorial Fund, 1989), 415.
⁵⁹ Jawaharlal Nehru, *Letters to Chief Ministers (1947–1964)*, vol. 1 (Delhi: Jawaharlal Nehru Memorial Fund, 1985), 234–5.

He had been rebutted by MacArthur.⁶⁰ This move shows all the schizophrenias of a postcolonial state that oscillated between sympathy for a defeated Asian power and a desire to conform to notions of legal propriety propagated by the dominant Allied nations. At any rate, this intensified suspicion in the British Foreign Office about Indian public support behind Pal's dissent, and about the extent to which the Indian government could sincerely criticize the judgment in view of this public opinion.⁶¹

Interestingly, we see in Nehru's foreign policy towards Japan, in the immediate years after the trial, a sympathetic concern for Japanese sovereignty and desire to enable its postwar reconstruction. This culminated in India's refusal to be party to the San Francisco Peace Treaty with Japan (1951), since Nehru saw there an attempt to maintain Western control in East Asia (ignoring also the concerns of the Soviet Union and of the People's Republic of China), including through maintenance of foreign troops and bases in Japan. Though this caused friction between America and India (prefiguring later Cold War polarities), Nehru claimed that the Indian policy was appreciated by the Japanese government and people. India negotiated a bilateral peace treaty with Japan in 1952: this showed a pro-Japanese stance in issues like waiving reparations claims.⁶² Thus, the Indian state's foreign policy revealed a concern for protecting the sovereignty of an Asian state in a manner that may be compared with Pal's dissent. In both the dissent and in the foreign policy, we see the international ramifications of decolonization, or to be more specific, of the emergence of India as a major postcolonial sovereign state, with all the contradictions and complexities that this entailed.

FROM TOKYO TO THE POSTCOLONIAL WORLD: PAL'S LEGAL THINKING IN THE 1950S AND 1960S

To appreciate the full ramifications of this process of decolonization in relation to Pal's Tokyo dissent, we need to return to Pal's post-Tokyo interventions. Critical here is the way that he abstained from voting on a draft code of international criminal law, Draft Code of Offences against

---

⁶⁰ TNA, FO 371/69833, Telegram from Tokyo to Foreign Office, 22 November 1948.
⁶¹ TNA, FO 371/69834, F 17460/48/23, Minutes.
⁶² Banerjee, 'International Criminal Justice,' 91–2; Robert J. McMahon, *The Cold War on the Periphery: The United States, India, and Pakistan* (New York, NY: Columbia University Press, 1994), 103–8.

the Peace and Security of Mankind, which was debated at the sixth session of the International Law Commission, held in Paris in 1954. An elaborate explanation for his abstention was provided in a 1955 book. In this volume, he had two cases of decolonization especially in mind: Indonesia and Indochina. Pal observed that the Dutch and the French had sought to legitimate re-imposition of their authority in these colonies, and with tacit support from other Western powers; in the case of Indochina, he noted, the situation was aggravated by the charge of collaboration with the Japanese brought against the anti-colonial nationalists. Pal related these scenarios to American and Soviet competition over Korea, in order to suggest that Allied rhetoric of righteousness only aimed at creating an international status quo that benefited the dominant (white) powers. Hence he remained sceptical towards top-down processes of codifying international criminal law and of thereby criminalizing all forms of militancy, including anti-imperial rebellions like the ones in Southeast Asia.[63]

If the imperative of decolonization made Pal denounce one sort of legal universalism, then it made him more open to another, as can be seen from his report on the fifth session of the Asian–African Legal Consultative Committee held in Rangoon in Burma in 1962. It was decolonization itself, he believed, which would mould a novel legal world, replacing the earlier false rhetoric of universalism with a new and more genuine one. Hence his request before the committee that 'all the Asian–African nations would join the organization and help building up this new wholeness, always remembering that our environment now is no longer the world about us but rather the world.' A new sense of the global, of 'the world' itself as the space for unified legal thinking, was the bedrock of Pal's hope; yet this was a world not codified from above by colonial and neo-colonial powers but fashioned from below, especially by people from the decolonizing world. This was 'the popular will of the world,' provoked by a 'sense of injustice [...] universally felt,' and propelling people to 'weld their souls and spirits in one flaming effort,' constituting new 'legal provisions' which

---

[63] Official Records of the UN General Assembly, Ninth Session, Supplement No. 9, Report of the International Law Commission Covering the Work of its Sixth Session, 3, 28 July 1954, and Summary Record of the 276th Meeting of the International Law Commission, Document No. A/CN.4/SR.276, in International Law Commission database, http://legal.un.org/ilc/index.html (accessed 8 March 2015); Radhabinod Pal, *Crimes in International Relations* (Calcutta: University of Calcutta, 1955), especially 44–52.

would be 'the instruments of the conscience of the community.'[64] Variants of such a globally inflected vision can be found in his writings and public lectures dating from this period on Hindu law, on international law and on human rights. These emphasized laws as dynamic mechanisms which would be transformed by political struggles and contribute to the diminution of asymmetries of racial and imperial power and economic disparity.[65]

Epistemologies of Decolonization

I have argued in my earlier essay that Pal was driven by a juridical epistemology and soteriology that drew in part on ancient Indian Vedic and Upanishadic texts. In this perspective, justice was not about sovereignty-driven legitimation of power, but rather about relativizing existing knowledges to expand one's moral horizon.[66] As he summarized in his 1958 book on Hindu law: 'Justice is indeed a mutual limitation of wills and consciousness by a single idea equally limitative of all, by the idea of limitation itself which is inherent in knowledge, which is inherent in our consciousness as limited by other consciousnesses. In spite of ourselves we stop short before our fellow man as before an indefinable something which our science cannot fathom, which our analysis cannot measure, and which by the very fact of its being a consciousness is sacred to our own.'[67] This concern about the sacredness of the other should be related to Pal's perspective about deliberations among decolonizing Asian and African countries; it was through an encounter with alterity, and especially with formerly subjugated alterities, that a new global justice could be forged.

Let us return to Hegel's *Phenomenology of Spirit* (from which Kaviraj derived his concept of unhappy consciousness), but in a moment prior to the formation of the unhappy consciousness, to the dialectic between the lord (*Herr*) and the bondsman (*Knecht*).[68] For Hegel the process of mutual recognition between two consciousnesses entailed a deadly fight

---

[64] Report on the Fifth Session of the Asian–African Legal Consultative Committee (Rangoon, January 1962) by Mr. Radhabinod Pal, Observer for the Commission, 153–4, in International Legal Commission database (accessed 8 March 2015).
[65] Pal, *History*, 1958; Radhabinod Pal, *Lectures on Universal Declaration of Human Rights* (Calcutta: Federation Hall Society, 1965); Radhabinod Pal, *World Peace Through World Law* (Tokyo: United World Federalists of Japan, 1967).
[66] Banerjee, 'International Criminal Justice,' 116–7.
[67] Pal, *History*, 1958, 172.
[68] Hegel, *Phenomenology*, 111–9.

culminating in the mastery of the lord over the bondsman. In contrast, Pal emphasized a recognition of the sacredness of the Other on encountering another consciousness. I would suggest that this ethical gaze also inspired in him a 'global' vision, a sense of the world as united in a common quest for justice, beyond imperial and national borders. It was also from this perspective that Pal, in his Tokyo judgment, visualized the nation-state as a destructive agent that provoked 'the evil of warfare,' as democracy 'turned "the sport of kings" into the wars of Nationality passionately.' For Pal, this nationalist 'spirit' mobilized ordinary people as much as soldiers, enabling the 'totalitarian character of war.'[69]

Such a critical stance towards bordered conceptions of state sovereignty and nationhood existed alongside Pal's alternate position, his second subjectivity, which wished to appropriate the colonial lord's grammar of sovereignty for pragmatic political ends, to transform the colonized people into a sovereign state. This latter aspect was a derivative, dependent and terrified consciousness, moulding its subject position on sovereignty out of fear of colonialism, and thereby becoming complicit with the most brutal expression of Japanese state violence. It is important to recognize the simultaneity, the contradictions, as well as the intertwining of the two subjectivities.

The colonizers, such as the British in India, had constructed centralized structures of sovereign statehood, and it was tempting for the colonized to simply adopt these structures of sovereignty whole-scale by (to cite Marx's famous phrase) expropriating the expropriators.[70] But this transfer of power from the colonial sovereign state to the postcolonial sovereign state was never a satisfactory solution. Pal was tormented by the contradictions that it entailed, and denied the possibility, as he noted in a meeting of the International Law Commission in 1954, of 'seeking any premature escape from the guilt of history.'[71]

Conclusion

Can one make any generalization from this case study which has related India's relation with the Tokyo Trial to the wider politics of decolonization? I have tried to address one paradox. Many of late colonial India's most

---

[69] Pal Judgment, 736.
[70] Karl Marx, *Capital*, vol. 1, Chapter 32, available at Marxists Internet Archive, https://www.marxists.org/archive/marx/works/1867-c1/ch32.htm (accessed 23 March 2015).
[71] Pal, *Crimes*, viii.

prominent politicians and intellectuals, including Rabindranath Tagore, Mahatma Gandhi and Jawaharlal Nehru, were deeply skeptical about the violent potential of the modern sovereign state, including the nation-state. Many of the subcontinent's popular movements, including left-democratic ones as well as lower-caste politics, produced creative critiques of the elite dominance that underpinned structures of state sovereignty. Various strands of internationalism and transnational solidarity-building, from communist to pan-Islamic ones, animated South Asians. Yet what resulted out of decolonization was the creation of sovereign nation-states which soon demonstrated their capability to commit unprecedented violence and reinforce social hierarchies.

I would suggest that the imperial institutional legacies of the transfer of power—the carry-over of military, police and bureaucratic apparatuses—cannot suffice to explain this irony. Nor is it enough to talk about the mimesis of nationalist modules (*pace* Anderson). If the contagion of sovereignty needs to be explained, it has to be done also at the level of intellection and political ethics. I have suggested, through the case study of Pal, that anti-colonial thinking was often acutely conscious of the inadequacy of translating imperial sovereignty into postcolonial national sovereignty. However, what motivated many anti-colonial actors to see the nation-state as a necessary evil was the fear that a global authority would create a more monstrous super-sovereignty. It was a Hegelian bondsman's fear, and not always a mimetic desire, that drove the contagion of sovereignty. In the mirror of this fear, of which Pal is so representative, even a brutal imperial state like Japan could be exculpated to a degree if that meant protecting its sovereignty. The prospect of colonial warfare relentlessly haunted such minds, as visible from the manner in which Pal regarded Indonesia and Indochina. The translation of sovereignty was equally, if in a very divergent way, accompanied by anxiety for someone like Nehru, who was afraid that Pal's Tokyo dissent would compromise the Indian state's international respectability; it was fear again that later animated his foreign policy and its protective concern for Japanese sovereignty.

Thus, fear, as much as desire, needs to be factored in to explain the conservative trajectory of decolonization in preserving the state form. The adoption of sovereignty was, sometimes at least, the expression of a semi-voluntary, rather than enthusiastic, choice for anti-colonial actors who were enchanted by alternate, more utopian, possibilities. But this fear was also riven by guilt, as well as hope. Hence the revolutionary ferment of decolonization, which was seemingly tamed by the proliferation of sovereign states (each with its own future of sovereign violence), also left open ineradicable apertures of thinking about transnational solidarity, about forging justice from below. The translation of sovereignty thus remained inherently self-contradictory, and open to re-negotiation.

CHAPTER 5

The Legacy of Extraterritoriality and the Trial of Japanese War Criminals in the Republic of China

Anja Bihler

INTRODUCTION

As one of the victorious nations in the Second World War, the Republic of China was called upon to participate in the Allied effort to seek justice for the unspeakable atrocities committed during the war years. The Chinese Nationalist government, the officially recognized government at the time, was represented at the International Military Tribunal for the Far East (IMTFE) in Tokyo and held a series of domestic trials between 1946 and 1948. Beginning in February 1946, military courts for war criminals were established in the cities of Beijing, Taiyuan, Shenyang, Jinan, Xuzhou, Hankou, Shanghai, Nanjing, Guangzhou and Taipei. Japanese and a small number of Taiwanese defendants were tried for class B and

C war crimes including[1]: unlawful detention, torture, rape and killing of civilians, torture of prisoners of war as well as a number of non-violent offenses such as looting and extortion of money. Out of a total of 871 defendants 147 received the death penalty, 83 were given life sentences and 276 received prison terms of varying lengths. The remaining 365 were found not guilty.[2] In Asia, the overall number of defendants tried in Chinese courts was lower than those tried by the Western Allies, including the Americans (1400), the Dutch (1038), the British (978) and the Australians (949).[3]

The trials took place in a tumultuous period in Chinese history following the Second Sino–Japanese War that was characterized not only by the looming civil war between the Nationalists and the communists, but was also influenced by the early Cold War and a wave of decolonization in Asia. In the nineteenth and early twentieth century, colonialism in China took many different forms ranging from classical colonies such as Hong Kong, Macau and Taiwan to land lease and treaty ports and various other spheres of influence. In the words of Bryna and David S. Goodman, 'colonialism in China was a piecemeal agglomeration' with a 'diversity of […] colonial arrangements across China's landscape (that) defies systematic characterization.'[4] With scholars divided over the nature and degree of China's colonization, decolonization remains an equally difficult concept to grasp.[5] The following chapter will focus on one aspect, the relinquishment of extraterritoriality in China, and explore its impact on the trials of Japanese war criminals.[6] Extraterritoriality, in this context,

---

[1] Wada Hideo 和田英穂, 'Hi-shinryakukoku ni yoru tainichi senso hanzai saiban – kokumin seifu ga okonatta senpan saiban no tokucho 被侵略国による対日戦争犯罪裁判-国民政府が行った戦犯裁判の特徴,' 中国研究月報 645 (2001): 25. According to a statistic used in the article 58 Taiwanese war crimes suspects were sentenced in Chinese military courts.

[2] The number of defendants and trial outcomes vary between different authors. For the numbers used here, see: Chaen Yoshio 茶園義男 and Shigematsu Kazuyoshi 重松一義, *Hokan senpan saiban no jisso* 補完戦犯裁判の実相, (Tokyo: Fuji Shuppan, 1987), 24.

[3] For an overview of trial locations and number of defendants see: ibid., 9.

[4] Bryna Goodman and David S. Goodman, 'Introduction: Colonialism and China,' in *Twentieth Century Colonialism and China-Localities, the Everyday, and the World*, Bryna Goodman, David S. Goodman, eds. (Oxon: Routledge, 2012), 1.

[5] For an overview of interpretations of the forms of colonialism in China over time see: ibid., p. 3–9.

[6] For an introduction to the war crimes trials programme see: Barak Kushner, *Men to Devils, Devils to Men: Japanese War Crimes and Chinese Justice* (Cambridge, MA: Harvard University Press, 2015), 162 or Liu Tong 刘统, 'Guomin zhengfu shenpan riben zhanfan gaishu (1945–1949) 国民政府审判日本战犯概述(1945–1949) (A brief account of the National Government's trial of Japanese war criminals (1945–1949)),' *Minguo dang'an* (2014):

denotes the practice of foreign powers to apply criminal and civil legislation to their nationals abroad who were, at the same time, exempt from the local laws of their temporary country of residence. Following Turan Kayaoglu's approach, this chapter treats extraterritoriality as a form of legal imperialism and argues that while extraterritoriality ended in 1943,[7] the legacy of extraterritoriality continued to influence the legal and political sphere in China for several years after this date. In theory, the year 1943 reinstated China with full legal sovereignty and gave her jurisdiction over all foreign nationals on her territory.[8] In particular the USA, however, retained partial extraterritoriality and continued to exert influence on the reform and modernization process of the Chinese legal system. During the war, the Nationalist government's jurisdiction was severely limited due to the existence of the puppet state of Manchukuo, Japanese military occupation, collaborationist governments and communist-controlled areas. Therefore, the right to try foreigners in Chinese courts of law could only be fully exercised after the Japanese surrender in 1945. This makes the trials against Japanese war criminals the first occasion in the history of the Republic of China that a sizeable number of foreign nationals were tried in Chinese courts, thereby bringing extraterritoriality to its practical conclusion.

72–84. This chapter exclusively discusses the treatment of war crimes suspects. For information on the trials of alleged traitors see: Xia Yun, 'Traitors to the Chinese Race (Hanjian): Political and Cultural Campaigns Against Collaborators during the Sino-Japanese War of 1937–1945' (PhD diss., University of Oregon, 2010), Lo Jiu-jung, 'Trials of the Taiwanese as Hanjian or War Criminals and the Postwar Search for Taiwanese Identity,' in *Constructing Nationhood in Modern East Asia*, ed. Chow Kai-wing et al. (Ann Arbor: University of Michigan Press, 2001), 279–316, Margherita Zanasi, 'Globalizing Hanjian: The Suzhou Trials and the Post-World War II Discourse on Collaboration,' *American Historical Review* 113 (2008): 731–751.

[7] Turan Kayaoglu, *Legal Imperialism: Sovereignty and Extraterritoriality in Japan, the Ottoman Empire, and China* (Cambridge: Cambridge University Press, 2010), 6. I follow Kayaoglu, who defines legal imperialism as 'the extension of a state's legal authority into another state and limitation of legal authority of the target state over issues that may affect people, commercial interests, and security of the imperial state' and concludes that 'extraterritoriality was quintessential legal imperialism.' Compare to: Teemu Ruskola, 'Colonialism without Colonies: On the Extraterritorial Jurisprudence of the U.S. Court for China,' *Law and Contemporary Problems* 71, 3 (2008): 236. Here, the author interprets the practice of extraterritoriality as a form of 'colonialism without colonies.'

[8] Note that several countries, including France, Italy, the Netherlands, Belgium and Denmark only relinquished extraterritorial rights after the end of the war. For an overview see: Kayaoglu, *Legal Imperialism*, 151.

The Nationalist government's war crimes program may serve as a case study for the transition process from extraterritoriality to legal sovereignty and allow for a better understanding of the continuing effects of extraterritoriality in the Republic of China after 1943. To highlight the special legal historical background of the trials helps explain some of the unique features of the Chinese war crimes program that differed markedly from those held by the other Allies in the Asia Pacific.

Part 1 contains a short overview over the history of extraterritoriality in China and some of the efforts made to bring about its abolition. Part 2 will show to what extent the treatment of Japanese war crimes suspects was influenced by the legacy of extraterritoriality by focusing on two aspects of the Chinese war crimes program: first, China's participation in the United Nations War Crimes Commission (UNWCC); second, the war crimes legislation and procedural standards applied during the trials.

Extraterritoriality in China and Its Legacy

In the mid-nineteenth century, following the defeat of the Chinese Empire in the First and Second Opium Wars, China signed treaties with several Western powers institutionalizing a range of privileges for foreign nationals, including the right to be exempt from the application of Chinese laws.[9] The idea of a standard of 'civilization' required that all foreign nationals had to be treated according to legal ideals held by the West.[10] As long as countries such as China were either unable or unwilling to guarantee such treatment, the Western powers thought themselves justified in applying their own national laws to their citizens residing in

---

[9] Treaty of the Bogue, 8 October 1843, Article 13, Disputes between British subjects and Chinese, full text to be found at: Treaties, Conventions, ETC., between China and Foreign States, vol. 1 (Shanghai: Statistical Department of the Inspector General of Customs, 1917), 383–9. Article 13 reads: 'Regarding the punishment of English criminals, the English Government will enact the laws necessary to attain that end, and the Consul will be empowered to put them in force; and regarding the punishment of Chinese criminals, these will be tried and punished by their own laws, in the way provided for by the correspondence which took place at Nanking after the concluding of the peace.'

[10] Gerrit W. Gong, *The Standard of 'Civilization' in International Society* (Oxford: Clarendon Press, 1984), 14.

such places.[11] A very clear expression of this thinking can be found in a series of treaties signed between the Chinese Empire and the USA,[12] the British Empire[13] and Japan in 1902 and 1903.[14] The treaties stipulated that extraterritoriality would be upheld to the day these powers were satisfied that China had reformed and modernized her legal system to conform to Western ideals and standards. In order to successfully renegotiate, the countries affected by extraterritoriality had to demonstrate that they possessed a 'civilized' form of government, 'civilized' codes of civil and criminal law and the willingness to adhere to international agreements on civilized warfare.[15] The Japanese Empire renegotiated its position with respect to the major powers and rid itself of the unequal treaties and Western extraterritorial rights by 1899. The Republic of China, on the other hand, had to wait until 11 January 1943 before the USA, followed by the British, finally decided to grant the Chinese their long-awaited freedom from extraterritoriality.[15]

---

[11] Ibid., 64.

[12] Treaty for the Extension of the Commercial Relations between them [United States and China], 8 October 1903, Article 15 reprinted in: John V.A. MacMurray, *Treaties and Agreements With and Concerning China 1894–1919*, vol. 1 (New York, NY: Oxford University Press, 1921), 423–52.

[13] Treaty Respecting Commercial Relations etc. [Great Britain and China], 5 September 1902, Article 12, reprinted in: ibid.. 342–56.

[14] Supplementary Treaty of Commerce and Navigation (with annexes) [Japan and China], 8 October 1903, Article 11, reprinted in: ibid., 411–22. The treaty with Japan differed slightly from that with the USA and reads: 'China having expressed a strong desire to reform its judicial system and to bring it into accord with that of Japan and Western nations.'

[15] Douglas Howland, 'Japan's Civilized War: International Law as Diplomacy in the Sino-Japanese War (1894–1895),' *Journal of the History of International Law 179* (2007): 183. This chapter will not discuss constitutional reform in the Republic of China, for an introduction on the topic see: Xiaohong Xiao-Planes, 'Building Constitutionalism in China,' in *Of Constitutions and Constitutionalism: Trying to Build a New Political Order in China, 1908–1949*, ed. Stephanie Balme et al. (New York: Palgrave MacMillan, 2009), 37–57 or Zhang Qianfan, *The Constitution of China – A Contextual Analysis* (Oxford: Hart Publishing, 2012).

[16] Scholars have found a range of possible explanations for this sudden change in policy ranging from gestures of support for China to an attempt to counter Japanese propaganda, to a de facto end of extraterritoriality during the Japanese occupation, see: Kayaoglu, *Legal Imperialism*, 149. Kayaoglu argues that the decision was mainly a result of legal institutionalization in China in the 1930s.

Legal Reforms

The late Qing had already started tentative reforms to modernize Chinese laws and legal institutions, often looking towards Japan for guidance.[17] The fall of the last dynasty and the birth of the Republic of China in 1912 only temporarily interrupted this process. During the Washington Arms Conference in 1921 the Chinese delegation again raised the question of extraterritoriality and in 1926 an international commission[18] assembled in Beijing to inquire into the practice of extraterritorial jurisdiction in China.[19] In its final report, the commission concluded that extraterritoriality should be further upheld 'until the evolution of the laws and legal conceptions of China should render it unnecessary.'[20] In the 1920s and 1930s, especially after the consolidation of the Nationalist government, legal sovereignty became an important goal in the state building[21] and foreign policy[22] agenda and at the same time an important motivation for Chinese legal reform and modernization efforts.[23] Western criticism and demand for a modern legal system in the Western sense had a direct and long-lasting effect on the Republican legal system. Major reforms, such as codification of civil and criminal law as well as reforms of the court system were carried out[24] with the explicit aim of achieving the relinquishment of extraterritoriality.[25] The Western powers not only determined the ultimate goal for the reform project but were also in a position to 'supervise

---

[17] Jianfu Chen, *Chinese Law: Context and Transformation* (Leiden: Martinus Nijhoff Publishers, 2008), 27.
[18] Countries with representatives were: United States of America, Belgium, the British Empire, China, France, Denmark, Italy, Japan, the Netherlands, Norway, Portugal, Spain and Sweden.
[19] Commission on Extraterritoriality in China, *Report of the Commission on Extraterritoriality in China* (Washington, DC: Government Printing Office, 1926), v.
[20] Ibid., 20.
[21] Edmund S.K. Fung, 'The Chinese Nationalists and the Unequal Treaties 1924–1931,' *Modern Asian Studies* 21, 4 (1987): 817.
[22] Julia C. Strauss, *Strong Institutions in Weak Polities – State Building in Republican China, 1927–1940* (Oxford: Clarendon Press, 1998), 156–57.
[23] Li Qicheng 李启成, 'Zhiwai faquan yu zhongguo sifa jindaihua zhi guanxi 治外法权与中国司法近代化之关系' (The Relation between Extraterritoriality and the Legal Modernisation in China), *Xiandai faxue* 28, 4 (2006): 35.
[24] Turan Kayaoglu, 'The Extension of Westphalian Sovereignty: State Building and the Abolition of Extraterritoriality,' *International Studies Quarterly* 51, 3 (2007): 666–7.
[25] Compare: Klaus Mühlhahn, *Criminal Justice in China – A History* (Cambridge, MA: Harvard University Press, 2009), 71. The author argues that 'in the mid-1930s the wish to

and judge' every reform step the Chinese were taking.[26] Frustrated with Western refusal to make good on their promise, the Nationalist government publicly announced their resolve to abolish extraterritorial rights unilaterally in May 1931,[27] before the Mukden incident and the Japanese invasion of Manchuria put a stop to further negotiations until the 1940s.[28]

Adherence to International Law and the Laws of War

By the nineteenth and twentieth centuries a body of rules regulating warfare emerged under international customary as well as treaty law.[29] Knowledge of and adherence to these rules were another important criterion to gauge the level of 'civilization' a country had attained. Leading up to, and for several years after the relinquishment of extraterritoriality, Japan made a conscious effort to adhere to the laws of war. During the First Sino–Japanese War, Japan used it as a diplomatic tool, showcasing her own civility while at the same time portraying China as a barbaric and backward country.[30] Japan acquired a 'reputation for impeccable behavior on the battlefield' and went to great length to showcase 'their country's high degree of civilization through the humane treatment of civilians and prisoners of war.'[31] Finally, during the First World War, Japan accorded German and Austrian prisoners of war a treatment generous enough to lead many scholars to conclude that 'prisoners in Japan were, if anything, being too well

---

bring to an end extraterritoriality still formed a major incentive for the reform of criminal justice in China.'

[26] Kayaoglu, *Legal Imperialism*, 161.

[27] Tao-tai Hsia and Wendy Zeldin, 'Wartime Judicial Reform in China,' in *China's Bitter Victory: The War with Japan, 1937–1945*, James C. Hsiung and Steven I. Levine, eds. (Armonk, NY: M. E. Sharpe, 1992), 276.

[28] K.C. Chan, 'The Abrogation of British Extraterritoriality in China 1942–1943: A Study of Anglo-American–Chinese Relations,' *Modern Asian Studies*, 11, 2 (1977): 266. The British and the Americans promised in 1940 and 1941 to further discuss the question after the war.

[29] For a discussion of individual legal issues and relevant treaty law see: Dietrich Schindler and Jiri Toman, eds., *The Laws of Armed Conflicts – A collection of Conventions, Resolutions and Other Documents* (Dordrecht: Martinus Nijhoff Publishers, 1988) or Alexander Gillespie, *A History of the Laws of War* (Volume I–III), (Oxford: Hart Publishing, 2011).

[30] Howland, 'Japan's Civilized War,' 189.

[31] S. C. M. Paine, *The Sino–Japanese War of 1894–5: Perceptions, Power, and Primacy* (Cambridge: Cambridge University Press, 2003), 209.

treated.'[32] During the Second Sino–Japanese War, however, the tables had turned. Now it was for China to showcase their faithful adherence to the laws of war, while pointing out Japan's relapse into a state of barbarism. Both after Japan's invasion of Manchuria and the outbreak of full-scale war in 1937, China brought its grievances with Japan before the League of Nations, attempting to achieve recognition of Japan's invasion as an act of aggression and her conduct in warfare as contrary to international law.[33] With a distinction between combatants and non-combatants already firmly established under international law, China concentrated her case on Japan's use of aerial bombing of civilian targets. The Chinese representative Wellington Koo addressed the Far East Advisory Committee on 27 September 1937 stating that 'the Japanese air force has intensified its inhuman method of terrorisation and mass murder of the civilian population [...]. This method of aerial bombardment is so revolting to the conscience of mankind.'[34] He thus pointed out that, 'Since the announcement of the sinister intention to resort to wholesale butchery of the Chinese civilian population, Japanese warplanes have already made nine bombing raids on Nanking, five on Canton and extended their ruthless attacks to Soochow, Hankow, Nanchang, Tsinan, Hsuchow and a dozen other cities, levying in only a few days a toll of death of perhaps Io,000 innocent men, women and children.[...] Japan's persistent resort to this form of indiscriminate slaughter of non-combatants is a challenge to civilization.'[35]

After the outbreak of the war and in support of the International Peace Campaign, China organized an 'Anti-Aggression Publicity Week.' On the occasion Chiang Kai-shek is quoted as saying: 'What Japan is doing is nothing less than the destruction of law, order and civilization and leading the world back into medieval barbarism.'[36] He went on to stress China's

---

[32] Mahon Murphy, 'Brücken, Beethoven und Baumkuchen: German and Austro-Hungarian Prisoners of War and the Japanese Home Front,' in Other Fronts, Other Wars? – First World War Studies on the Eve of the Centennial, ed. Joachim Bürgschwentner et al. (Leiden: Brill, 2014), 130.

[33] Thomas W. Burkman, *Japan and the League of Nations: Empire and World Order, 1914–1938* (Honolulu: University of Hawaii Press, 2008), 207.

[34] League of Nations Official Journal, Special Supplement No. 177, Sino–Japanese Conflict, Appeal by the Chinese Government (Geneva, 1937), Minutes of the third session of the Far-East Advisory Committee, Second Meeting 27 September 1937, p. 9–16, at p. 10.

[35] Ibid., 12.

[36] Anti-Aggression Publicity Week (The China Information Committee, Hankow, undated), Generalissimo Chiang Kai-shek's Message to the International Peace Campaign Conference, 'Japan is Destroying Law and Order, Civilization, Violating Treaty Sanctity and Leading Mankind Back Into Barbarism,' p. 4.

devotion and willing adherence to international law and the importance of the war for the international community and the international legal order. 'We are fighting not only for our own liberty and existence and for the preservation of our own sovereignty and national integrity, but also for the sanctity of international treaties as well as for the common security of all nations. If Japan is permitted to tear up the treaties as scraps of paper and violate with impunity the territorial integrity of her neighbor which she pledged to respect, soon the whole world will be plunged into the greatest catastrophe yet known in human history.'[37] In contrast to Japan, the Chinese central government was also 'keen to abide by internationally agreed standards of treatment of prisoners of war.'[38] China allowed inspection of camps by the International Committee of the Red Cross and the representative in China, Ernest Senn, 'observed that the central government was keen to live up to the Geneva Convention on the conduct of warfare, a determination based on the desire to "put themselves in line with civilized nations in the observance of humanitarian conventions".'[39] While the government frequently failed to live up to the requisite standard, its 'desire to show its compliance with international standards and the active involvement of international agencies ensure(d) that POWs were better off than their counterparts serving in the army.'[40]

Part 1 has briefly discussed China's desire to bring about the relinquishment of extraterritoriality through legal reforms and her adherence to the laws of war. Part 2 explores to what extent the legacy of extraterritoriality continued to influence the way in which the Chinese Nationalist government engaged with the international community on the topic of war crimes and the national war crimes trials program in the Republic of China after 1943.

Joining the International Discussion—China at the United Nations War Crimes Commission

From the 1940s onwards various legal circles in Europe began deliberating how war criminals were to be punished after the war.[41] The semi-official London International Assembly, for instance, was regularly

---

[37] Ibid., p. 5.
[38] Frank Dikötter, *Crime, Punishment and the Prison in Modern China* (New York, NY: Columbia University Press, 2002), 345.
[39] Ibid., 346–347.
[40] Ibid., 348.
[41] The United Nations War Crimes Commission, *History of the United Nations War Crimes Commission and the Development of the Laws of War* (London: His Majesty's Stationery

attended by the Chinese delegate Dr. Liang Yunli.[42] In January 1942 nine member states of the Allies[43] signed the St James's Declaration, criticizing acts of the German forces to be contrary to international law and stating that the signatories 'place(d) amongst their principal war aims the punishment, through the channel of organized justice, of those guilty and responsible for these crimes.'[44] The Republic of China was not a signatory to the declaration, but the Chinese government confirmed that they 'intended, when the time comes, to apply the same principles to the Japanese occupying authorities in China.'[45] The following year, on 20 October 1943, Dr. Wellington Koo and Dr. Liang attended the first meeting of the United Nations War Crimes Commission (UNWCC) for China.[46] The UNWCC's main responsibility was to collect and review evidence on war crimes and to draw up lists of suspects for apprehension after the war. With the exception of India and Australia, that were only infrequently represented in London, the Republic of China was the only country representing the Asia Pacific region in the commission. In parallel to these developments in Europe, the Chinese government set up a first body for the investigation of war crimes in China.[47]

Office, 1948), 95. An example: The International Commission for Penal Reconstruction and Development, a semi-official group made up of members of the Law Faculty at the University of Cambridge and important scholars of international and criminal law, including: M. Aulie (Norway), Dr. Benes (Czechoslovakia), M. Bodson (Luxembourg), Prof. Cassin (France), M. de Baer (Belgium), Dr. de Moor (Netherlands), Dr. Glaser (Poland), M. Kaeckenbeck (Belgium), M. Stavropoulos (Greece), Dr. Vlajic (Yugoslavia).

[42] The following members of the London International Assembly were also members of the United Nations War Crimes Commission founded in 1943: De Baer (Belgium), Liang (China), Ečer (Czechoslovakia), Stavropoulos (Greece), de Moor (Netherlands), Bodson (Luxembourg) and Colban (Norway).

[43] Signatory nations: Belgium, Czechoslovakia, the Free French National Committee, Greece, Luxemburg, the Netherlands, Norway, Poland, Yugoslavia; Present as observers: Britain, the USA, the USSR, China and India.

[44] Full text of the Declaration reprinted in 'The Inter-Allied Conference, January 13 1942,' in *Bulletin of International News* 19, 2 (1942): 50–3.

[45] Telegram, The Ambassador to the Polish Government in Exile to the Secretary of State, 14 January 1942, reprinted in: United States Department of State, *Foreign Relations of the United States Diplomatic Papers, 1942 General; the British Commonwealth; the Far East* (Washington, DC: US Government Printing Office, 1960), 45.

[46] The United Nations War Crimes Commission, *History of the United Nations War Crimes Commission and the Development of the Laws of War* (London: His Majesty's Stationery Office, 1948), 112.

[47] Zuo Shuangwen 左双文, 'Guomin zhengfu yu chengchu riben zhanfan jige wenti de zai kaocha 国民政府与惩处日本战犯几个问题的再考察'(A re-examination of Several Questions

Soon, Wellington Koo started to lobby for a new UNWCC panel for the investigation of Japanese war crimes in Asia Pacific and eventually the UNWCC expanded into Asia with a Far Eastern and Pacific Sub-Commission in Chongqing. The inaugural meeting on 20 November 1944 was chaired by the eminent jurist Dr. Wang Chonghui. The option of setting up additional panels besides the main commission London was discussed from the beginning, but the Republic of China was the only member state of the UNWCC insisting on exercising this right.

The efforts to end extraterritoriality led to a marked 'professionalization of international law in modern China'[48] and brought about a generation of international law scholars educated at top law schools in the USA and Europe. Wellington Koo, the main delegate for China at the UNWCC in London had graduated from Columbia University with a thesis on the legal status of foreigners in China[49] and always considered international law as the one tool that might free China from humiliation and make her a true member of the family of nations.[50] Dr. Wang Chonghui who acted as the chairman of the Far Eastern and Pacific Sub-Commission had graduated at the top of his class from Yale Law School[51] and served as minister of foreign affairs when the conflict with Japan escalated to a war in 1937.[52] He was also involved in all efforts of trying to renegotiate foreign extraterritorial rights and was one of the most important contributors to the attempts to modernize the national legal system. Wang Chonghui, Wellington Koo, Liang Yunli and Wunsz King, who represented the Republic of China at the UNWCC, were all members of the generation of legal experts who had pursued the study of international law with the intention of freeing their home country from the 'shame of extraterritoriality.' With this important milestone accomplished and given their professional background and belief in the power of international law,

---

concerning the Nationalist Government's Punishment of Japanese War Criminals), *Shehui kexue yanjiu* 6 (2012): 146.
[48] Pasha L. Hsieh, 'The Discipline of International Law in Republican China and Contemporary Taiwan,' *Washington University Global Studies Law Review* 14 (2015), 105.
[49] Wellington Koo, *The Status of Aliens in China* (New York: Columbia University, 1912).
[50] Stephen G. Craft, *Wellington Koo and the Emergence of Modern China*, (Lexington: University Press of Kentucky, 2004), 7.
[51] N.A., 'Class Day at Yale,' *New York Daily Tribune*, 23 June 1903, 5.
[52] Liu Baodong刘宝东, *Chu shan wei bi zai shan qing: wang chonghui* 出山未比在山清:王宠惠 (Stepping out from the mountains without seeing any clearer: Wang Chonghui) (Beijing: Tuanjie chubanshe, 2010), 209.

they were naturally keen to take an active role in the UNWCC's work and legal discussions.[53] The decision to push for a sub-commission in China also showed the government's strong ambition to not only be involved in the Allied deliberations about war crimes on an international level, but to take up a leading position on the matter.

There was, however, a clear discrepancy between China's abstract commitment to the international policy of handling war criminals and the reality of the legal system in war-torn China. Despite previous promises that a large number of war crimes cases had already been prepared by the Chinese government, the delegates of the new sub-commission were soon dissatisfied with the lack of progress. In the fifth meeting of the commission in March 1945, the Australian delegate was dismayed by the fact that the sub-commission had yet to handle its first case.[54] The British ambassador Seymour blamed the Chinese government for the inefficiency of the commission and the American delegate Brigg was 'of the opinion that the situation may have to be taken up with the Generalissimo' to bring about any improvement at all.[55] The representatives' strategy to exert pressure on the government was effective. Giving in to foreign criticism and pressure, the Chinese Ministry of Foreign Affairs notified the sub-commission on 7 June 1945 that the institutions responsible for war crimes investigations in China would be reorganized.[56] Eventually, a new 'Commission on War Criminals'[57] was established, which was from then on responsible for all questions concerning war crimes in China.[58] The unsatisfactory results

---

[53] For details on the positions taken by the Chinese delegates see: Anja Bihler, 'Late Republican China and the Development of International Criminal Law: China's Role in the United Nations War Crimes Commission in London and Chungking,' in *Historical Origins of International Criminal Law: Volume 1*, Morten Bergsmo et al. (eds.) (Brussels: Torkel Opsahl Academic EPublisher, 2014), 507–40.

[54] Far Eastern and Pacific Sub-Commission, Minutes of the Fifth Meeting of the Far Eastern and Pacific Sub-Commission of the United Nations for Crimes Commission, 16 March 1945, http://www.legal-tools.org/doc/3494b3/. Accessed 25 May 2015.

[55] The Chargé in China (Briggs) to the Secretary of State, 20 April 1945, in *Foreign Relations of the United States: Diplomatic Papers, 1945. The Far East, China* (Washington: U.S. Government Printing Office, 1969), 96–7.

[56] Far Eastern and Pacific Sub-Commission, Minutes of the Sixth Meeting of the Far Eastern and Pacific Sub-Commission of the United Nations War Crimes Commission, 8 June 1945, Chungking. http://www.legal-tools.org/doc/941c34/. Accessed 25 May 2015.

[57] Zhanzheng zuifan chuli weiyuanhui 战争罪犯处理委员会 (Commission on War Criminals).

[58] Iko Toshiya 伊香俊哉, 'Zhongguo guomin zhengfu dui riben zhanfan de chuzhi fangzhen 中国国民政府对日本战犯的处置方针' (The Chinese Nationalist Government's Policy for

achieved by the sub-commission in Chongqing were due to a combination of practical problems encountered during the war crimes investigations[59] and the fact that bringing Japanese war crimes suspects to trial was not a priority for the government at the time.[60]

Chinese War Crimes Program

Three days of celebration marked the official end of extraterritoriality in 1943 as a momentous event that was immediately declared a diplomatic victory for the Nationalist Chinese government.[61] The 'relinquishment of the unequal treaties,' Chiang Kai-shek wrote in 'China's Destiny' was a 'preliminary step in the success of the Nationalist Revolution.'[62] In reality, however, several mechanisms established during the pre-1943 period survived into the postwar era. Shortly after the abolition of extraterritoriality the US government initiated new negotiations concerning a partial extraterritoriality for members of the American armed forces stationed in China. Eventually, the Sino–American Military Service Agreement granted the military authorities of the USA exclusive jurisdiction over criminal offenses committed by members of the American armed forces.[63] In addition, the USA requested permission to try Japanese war

---

Dealing with Japanese War Criminals), *Nanjing datusha shi yanjiu*, 4 (2012), 91. The commission took up its work on 6 December 1945.

[59] Compare: Song Zhiyong 宋志勇, 'Zhanhou chuqi zhongguo de duiri zhengce yu zhanfan shenpan 战后初期中国的对日政策与战犯审判' (China's early post-war strategy towards Japan and the trial of war criminals), *Nankai xuebao* 4 (2001): 44.

[60] From the US perspective the Chinese war crimes effort suffered from preoccupation with other problems while the USA had given the prosecution of war criminals priority in the Chinese theater. Compare: US National Archives (NARA), RG 153/180/12, From: Ram. T. Maddocks, Major General USA, To: Mr. Monnett B. Davis, American Consul General, Shanghai, 25 April 1946. 'The United States effort in war crimes in China has succeeded well. On the other hand, preoccupation with other problems and the unavailability of trained personnel had handicapped the Chinese effort.' NARA, RG 153/180/12, letter, From: Headquarter United States Forces China Theater To: Commanding Generals, Commanding Officers, and all United States Military Personnel in the China Theater, undated. 'The prosecution of War Criminals has been given top priority in the China Theater.'

[61] Quincy Wright, 'The End of Extraterritoriality in China,' *The American Journal of International Law* 37, 2 (1943): 288.

[62] Philip Jaffe, *China's Destiny and Chinese Economic Theory: With Notes and Commentary by Philip Jaffe* (New York, NY: Roy Publishers, 1947), 155.

[63] Hong Zhang, *America Perceived: The Making of Chinese Images of the United States, 1945–1953* (Westport, CT: Greenwood Press, 2002), 35.

criminals on the territory of the Republic of China in cases where the victims of war crimes were American citizens. Eventually, a military commission in Shanghai tried 12 cases involving 73 accused from January 1946 onwards.[64]

Similarly, the tradition of sending and receiving foreign legal advisers to the Republic of China continued after the end of extraterritoriality. Worried about the future protection of American economic and business interests and in preparation for the negotiations of a new Sino–American Commercial Treaty[65] the US State Department asked Milton J. Helmick, former judge at the United States Court for China,[66] to make recommendations on how the judicial administration in China could be improved. In October 1945, the Minister of Justice Xie Guansheng, equally sought out American legal advice and invited Roscoe Pound, his former teacher and dean of Harvard Law, school to China.[67] In the same vein, the USA also began to advise the Chinese government and military on how to deal with Japanese war crimes suspects.

They clearly communicated their expectation by calling on the Chinese to fulfil their obligation as an Ally and implement a common war crimes policy in China. On 4 December 1945 General Wedemeyer sent a communication to Chiang Kai-shek stating that: 'In accordance with the developing plans throughout the world for the trial of these criminals, it is imperative that your government and my Headquarters concur in a common policy which will bring about a speedy trial and firm punishment of such other war criminals as have offended against your people and the nationals of my country.'[68] Dissatisfied with the slow progress the USA 'strongly urged that the program for the prosecution of war criminals by the Chinese government be expedited

---

[64] Wolfgang Form, 'Charging Waterboarding As a War Crime: U.S. War Crime Trials in the Far East after World War II,' *Chapman Journal of Criminal Justice* 2, 1 (2011):257.
[65] For a discussion of this treaty see: M. E. Orlean, 'The Sino-American Commercial Treaty of 1946,' *The Far Eastern Quarterly* 7 (1948), 354–67.
[66] Effectively, the court stopped functioning after the start of the Pacific War in December 1941.
[67] Jedidiah J. Kroncke, 'Roscoe Pound in China: A lost Precedent for the Liabilities of American Legal Exceptionalism,' *Brooklyn Journal of International Law* 38 (2012): 18. Pound accepted the position and visited China in the summer of 1946 and again from 1947 to 1948.
[68] Quoted in: NARA 153/180/12 (293), From Edward H. Young, Colonel JAGD, Staff Judge Advocate Headquarters United States Army Forces, China to Col Jeremiah J. O'Connor, Hq, USAF, China, 1 May 1946.

contemporaneously with the trials to be conducted by the U.S. Forces in this theater.'[69] Major Willis A. West of the judge advocate's office was selected to act as an advisor to the Chinese government to formulate a strategy 'for the apprehension and trial of Japanese war criminals.'[70] In a report on his work he found it 'quite surprising' that the Chinese had 'some very definite ideas and plans in mind at the time of the first conference.'[71] A similar phenomenon can be observed in the case of war crimes trials on the Philippines, where the government of the newly independent republic continued the war crimes program initiated by the USA. Because of the lack of local experience and the necessary resources the 'USA reserved the right to take control of the prosecutions should the Philippine authorities fail.'[72] Using the threat to withdraw the new-found sovereignty and authority the USA continued to exert control over the war crimes proceedings.[73] In her recently published study of the trials in the Philippines, Yuma Totani points out that 'the Philippine court [...] took far greater care than its American predecessors in ensuring that the accused had a fair opportunity to make his case in the courtroom,'[74] while British and American courts faced criticism for denying the accused the 'due-process protection that their own servicemen were entitled to under their respective military justice systems.'[75]

---

[69] NARA, RG 153/180/12, Edward H. Young, Colonel JAGD, Staff Judge Advocate Headquarters United States Army Forces, China to Col Jeremiah J. O'Connor, Hq, USAF, China, 1 May 1946.
[70] NARA, RG 153/180/12, Memorandum, Ray T. Maddocks Major General, G.S.C, Chief of Staff To the National Military Council, Chinese Government, 15 November 1945.
[71] NARA, RG 153/180/12, Willis A. West To Colonel Edward H. Young, Theater Judge Advocate, United States Forces, China Theater, 20 October 1945.
[72] Wolfgang Form, 'Colonization and Post-Colonization justice – U.S. and Philippine war crimes trials after WWII in Manila.'
[73] Ibid.
[74] Yuma Totani, *Justice in Asia and the Pacific Region, 1945–1952* (Cambridge: Cambridge University Press, 2015), 181. The quote refers to the trial of Lieutenant General Kuroda Shigenori, army officer who commanded the 14th army between May 1943 and September 1944. According to the author the Kuruda case was the 'centerpiece of the Philippine trials.'
[75] Ibid., 180.

Drafting of Chinese Legislation

During preparations for the war crimes trials the Chinese were presented with the challenge of drafting suitable new legislation. The 'War Crimes Trials Regulation'[76] was first issued on 24 October 1946[77] and became the main law governing the war crimes trials in the Republic of China. By looking at the first articles of the regulation, two main features immediately become apparent. First, both in structure as well as in content the Chinese national legislation closely followed the international legislation drafted by the European Allies for the International Military Tribunal (IMT) in Nuremberg and, second, international law was given priority over Chinese national penal law.

Article 1 specifies international law as the primary source of law to be applied by the military courts. Only if international law was inapplicable were judges given the right to apply the regulation or, if necessary, the Chinese Criminal Code. This was unusual; most other Allied nations conducting class B and C war crimes trials relied on national legislation as the primary source of law. Legislation drafted earlier in 1945 had initially envisioned the application of the Chinese Criminal Law for the Armed Forces, which was a harsh military law prescribing the death penalty for a variety of offenses. Some Chinese scholars have interpreted the decision to switch from the application of military law to international law as an attempt to align the trials with the Chinese Nationalist government's strategy of 'leniency' towards Japanese war criminals.[78] This explanation, however, fails to account for the fact that instead of applying regular Chinese criminal law the drafters preferred the application of international law and custom.

During the First Sino–Japanese War, Japan attempted to prove that the country had already reached the desired standard of 'civilization' by meticulously adhering to the rules of war.[79] To try members of the Japanese forces by using the same international treaties not only served to unmask

---

[76] Zhanzheng zuifan shenpan tiaoli 战争罪犯审判条例 (War Crimes Trials Regulation). Full original text in Chinese reprinted in: Hu Jurong 胡菊蓉, Nanjing datusha shiliaoji – nanjing shenpan 南京大屠杀史料集-南京审判 (Collection of Historical Materials on the Nanjing Massacre- the Nanjing Trial), vol. 24, (Nanjing: Jiangsu renmin chubanshe, 2006), 33.
[77] A revised version, modifying articles 25 and 32, was promulgated on 15 July 1947.
[78] Compare: Song Zhiyong 宋志勇, 'Zhanhou chuqi zhongguo de duiri zhengce yu zhanfan shenpan 战后初期中国的对日政策与战犯审判' (China's early postwar strategy towards Japan and the trial of war criminals), *Nankai xuebao* 4 (2001): 46.
[79] Douglas Howland, 'Japan's Civilized War: International Law as Diplomacy in the Sino-Japanese War (1894–1895),' *Journal of the History of International Law* 9 (2007): 179.

Japanese atrocities in the Second Sino–Japanese War but also provided China with the opportunity to proclaim her own adherence to the laws of war and international law more generally.[80] At the same time, it was a way to avoid the need to rely on national Chinese criminal law, which had always been a focal point of Western criticism. Skepticism towards the Chinese, or what was more generally perceived as the 'oriental legal system,' was also present among the members of the UNWCC.[81] During his time as a member of the London International Assembly, Marcel de Baer, for instance, remarked that 'the Chinese law does not seem to coincide with Occidental ideas' on the subject of war crimes. He therefore concluded that it was 'not desirable that war criminals should be dealt with according to municipal law.'[82] This exemplifies what Teemu Ruskola has recently termed legal orientalism, the Western inclination to either outright deny the existence of Chinese law or to assume its inferiority.[83]

While the regulations clearly requested the judges to apply international law and custom, different courts showed varying levels of enthusiasm in using it. While the courts in Beijing and Taipei almost exclusively relied on the Chinese Criminal Code, the courts in Jinan, Xuzhou, Nanjing and Shanghai routinely referred to the 1907 Hague Convention on Respecting the Laws and Customs of War on Land.[84] A noticeable increase in the use of international legislation occurred in cases that were considered to be of international importance and interest. In the judgment of Tanaka Hisakazu the court referred to no less than five international treaties and nine legal regulations altogether.[85] whereas no reference to international

---

[80] Gong, *The Standard of 'Civilization' in International Society*, 18.

[81] Report of Commission II (later Commission I) On The Trial of War Criminals: Question 1 – Will Adequate Punishment of All War Criminals Be Procurable by the Application of the Penal Code of Each Nation Concerned, May 1942, TNA, TS 26/873.

[82] Ibid. On The Trial of War Criminals: Question 2 – Concerning the Criminals in Respect of Whom the Municipal Law Provides Means of Punishment, Is It Desirable That Any or All of Them Should Be Dealt with According to That Law?

[83] Teemu Ruskola, *Legal Orientalism – China, the United States, and Modern Law* (Cambridge, MA: Harvard University Press, 2013).

[84] Gong, *The Standard of 'Civilization' in International Society*, 70. The author argues that The Hague Conferences epitomized an early consensus of the foremost 'civilized' nations of what they considered to be international law.

[85] Case of Tanaka Hisakazu, 17 October 1946, Judgement by the Military Court of War Crime Justice of the National Government Chairman's Canton Local Headquarters. On File with the author.

legislation at all was made in other cases of the same court. The military court in Nanking referred to four international conventions in the judgment of Sakai Takashi, another high-profile case that was later reported in the UNWCC war crimes trials reports in English translation.[86] The heavy reliance on international law quite clearly caused difficulties for the trial program because of a severe shortage of qualified judges to interpret and apply international treaties and customary law.[87]

Another striking feature of the regulation was the fact that the wording of its central parts was strongly influenced by the laws drafted for the IMT in Nuremberg. This is evident in the wording of article 2, which contains the most important substantive part of the law: the definition of war crimes. In structure it closely follows article 6 of the charter of the IMT, covering crimes against peace and conventional war crimes as well as crimes against humanity. The definition of aggression in the Chinese regulation is a direct translation of article 6 (a) of the IMT Charter.[88] That Chinese national war crimes legislation contains the count of crimes against peace, or aggression, is in itself also noteworthy. In the UNWCC, Chinese representatives had already strongly supported the idea that waging a war of aggression constituted a crime under international law.[89] This demonstrates the significance the Chinese attached to the question of aggressive warfare. After the Japanese invasion of Manchuria, Wellington Koo had already argued before the League of Nations that Japanese

---

[86] Case of Sakai Takashi, 29 August 1946, Chinese War Crimes Military Tribunal of the Ministry of National Defence, reprinted in: The United Nations War Crimes Commission, *Law Reports of Trials of War Criminals,* vol. 14 (London: His Majesty's Stationery Office, 1949), 1–7.
[87] Compare Li Rong 李荣, 'Guomin Zhengfu shenpan qinhua rijun zhanfan luelun 国民政府审判侵华日军战犯略论' (Brief discussion of the Nationalist government's trial of war criminals of the invading Japanese forces), *Kangri zhanzheng yanjiu* 3 (1995): 143.
[88] IMT Article 6 (a): 'The following acts, or any of them, are crimes coming within the jurisdiction of the Tribunal for which there shall be individual responsibility: (a) Crimes against peace: namely, planning, preparation, initiation or waging of a war of aggression, or a war in violation of international treaties, agreements or assurances, or participation in a common plan or conspiracy for the accomplishment of any of the foregoing.' Full text available at: http://avalon.law.yale.edu/imt/imtconst.asp. Accessed 25 May 2015.
[89] United Nations War Crimes Commission, Minutes of Thirty-Fifth Meeting Held on 10 October 1944, Report on Whether Preparation and Launching a War Can Be Considered a War Crime, http://www.legal-tools.org/doc/daeb97/. Accessed 25 May 2015.

actions amounted to an act of aggression.[90] Dr. Wang Chonghui, who was the acting minister of foreign affairs when full-scale war broke out in 1937,[91] had hoped to garner support from the international community by drawing attention to Japanese aggression in China.[92]

In addition to aggression, article 2 of the Chinese Regulation also contained a definition of conventional war crimes, which was again strongly modelled after the Nuremberg Charter. The general definition is supported by a number of examples. Here, the Chinese relied on a list of war crimes originally drafted during the Paris Peace Conference in 1919,[93] which they slightly rearranged and expanded. The UNWCC had recommended the so called Versailles list to its members as a way of categorizing war crimes.[94] The Dutch, the Australians and the Chinese, however, decided to incorporate the list directly as part of their war crimes legislation.[95] While international law experts and diplomats were familiar with this list, ordinary Chinese judges could not be expected to independently apply the new concept of war crimes with any degree of precision and reliability. In order to facilitate the work of the bench, the judges were

---

[90] The Lytton Report in 1932 had not contained an outright condemnation of Japan but recognised the special nature of Japanese rights in Manchuria instead Thomas W. Burkman, *Japan and the League of Nations: Empire and World Order, 1914–1938* (Honolulu: University of Hawaii Press, 2008), 207.

[91] Liu, *Chu shan wei bi zai shan qing: wang chonghui*, 209.

[92] Ibid., 225.

[93] The list was drafted by the 'Commission on the Responsibility of the Authors of the War and on Enforcement of Penalties' composed of 15 members: two from the United States, the British Empire, France, Italy and Japan, plus five additional representatives. Reprinted in: *Violation of the Laws and Customs of War – Reports of Majority and Dissenting Reports of American and Japanese Members of the Commission of Responsibilities Conference of Paris 1919*, (Oxford: Clarendon Press, 1919), 17–8.

[94] National Archive Taiwan (NAT), File 020-010117-0021-0035, UNWCC Progress Report adopted by the Commission on 19 September 1944. 'The Commission further decided however that it would be convention for the purposes of its own work to adopt the list of war crimes prepared by the Responsibilities Commission of the Paris Peace Conference 1919 so that the National Offices might know the various headings under which war crimes can be grouped.'

[95] For the Australian legislation see: The United Nations War Crimes Commission, *The Law Reports of Trials of War Criminals* vol. 5 (London: his Majesty's Stationery Office, 1948), 95–6.
For the Dutch Legislation see: The United Nations War Crimes Commission, *The Law Reports of Trials of War Criminals* vol. 11 (London: his Majesty's Stationery Office, 1949), 93–5.

provided with concrete suggestions how to address the crimes listed by using the Chinese Criminal Code, with which all judges were familiar.[96]

Article 2(3) of the regulation contains a definition of crimes against humanity. Under the Nuremberg charter, crimes against humanity were only prosecutable if they were perpetrated in connection with either aggression or conventional war crimes.[97] This so-called 'war nexus' allowed the court to prosecute for crimes committed against a country's own nationals without calling into question the general concept of national sovereignty. The Chinese solution to this problem was to restrict crimes against humanity to crimes committed against citizens of the Republic of China. In 1944, Dr. Liang had already taken this position in the UNWCC, arguing for a strict definition of war crimes excluding atrocities committed by a government against its own citizens.[98] The most unusual part of the Chinese definition of crimes against humanity is the description of two additional methods by which the crime might be committed: the production, use and consumption of drugs and the attempt to stupefy the population. Anyone using these methods with the intention of enslaving, crippling or annihilating the Chinese nation was considered guilty of crimes against humanity under article 2(3). To incorporate drug related offenses into the definition of crimes against humanity was an unusual step only taken by the Republic of China. The opium question was of great importance for China's national history and self-understanding as a nation, unlike for the Western Allies. Following the First and Second Opium Wars, the trade and consumption of opium was inextricably linked to both the idea of Western domination and weakening of the Chinese nation. During the Second Sino–Japanese War, the Japanese government used the narcotics business to finance the war effort in China.[99] The narcotics trade now exemplified Japanese, not Western, imperial ambitions in China. This led the media in China to conclude that Japan was 'waging another "Opium

---

[96] Reprinted in: Hu Jurong 胡菊蓉, *Nanjing datusha shiliaoji – nanjing shenpan*南京大屠杀史料集-南京审判 *(Collection of Historical Materials on the Nanjing Massacre- the Nanjing Trial)*, vol. 24, (Nanjing: Jiangsu renmin chubanshe, 2006), 24–7.

[97] Kai Ambos, *Treatise on International Criminal Law: vol. 2 The Crimes and Sentencing* (Oxford: Oxford University Press, 2014), 50–51.

[98] Wenwei Lai, 'Forgiven and Forgotten: The Republic of China in the United War Crimes Commission,' *Columbia Journal of Asian Law* 25 (2012): 319.

[99] Hong Lu and Terance Miethe and Bin Liang, *China's Drug Practices and Policies – Regulating Controlled Substances in a Global Context* (Farnham: Ashgate Publishing, 2009), 64.

War" with the Chinese nation.'[100] In a message from Chiang Kai-shek to the people of Japan on 7 July 1939, he insisted that the Japanese were forcing the inhabitants of occupied territories to consume drugs in order to, 'paralyze and weaken the minds of (the) people' and 'render them incapable of saving themselves from foreign domination.'[101] Convinced that the Japanese involvement in the opium trade constituted a grave offense under international law, the Chinese members of the international prosecution team at the IMTFE also attempted to introduce the matter to the court in Tokyo.[102] After presenting evidence on the Nanjing massacre as well as ordinary war crimes,[103] Xiang Zhejun, a member of the Chinese delegation, continued to argue 'that the Japanese promotion of narcotics trade constituted a crime against the Chinese people.'[104]

As a second addition to the international concept of crimes against humanity, the Chinese legislation considered those war criminals who intended to enslave, cripple or annihilate the Chinese Nation by 'stupefying the mind and controlling the thought of its nationals.' This seemingly enigmatic expression was equally a result of the Chinese experience with Japanese colonialism and describes Japanese education programs in the occupied areas and Manchukuo. The goal of these programs, the Chinese claimed, was to 'anesthetize the people' and turn the inhabitants of the occupied areas into 'obedient subjects' of the empire.[105] 'Enslaving education' has since become a standard term in Chinese scholarship to describe Japanese sponsored education,[106] which is routinely understood as a form

---

[100] C. Y. W. Meng 'Japan's Opium War on China,' *The China Weekly Review*, 20 July 1940.
[101] The Chinese Ministry of Information, *The Collected Wartime Messages of Generalissimo Chiang Kai-shek, 1937–1945*, vol. 1 (1937–1940) (New York, NY: The John Day Company, 1946), 277.
[102] See Neil Boister, 'Punishing Japan's Opium War-making' in China: The Relationship between Transnational Crime and Aggression at the Tokyo Tribunal,' in Y. Tanaka, T. McCormack and G. Simpson, eds., *Beyond Victor's Justice? The Tokyo War Crimes Trial Revisited*, (Leiden: Martinus Nijhoff Publishers, 2011), 323–50.
[103] Yuma Totani, *The Tokyo War Crimes Trial: The Pursuit of Justice in the Wake of World War II* (Cambridge, MA: Harvard University Press, 2008), 152.
[104] Ibid., 154. For more details on evidence presented at the IMTFE and the judicial response please refer to Chap. 2 of this volume: Neil Boister 'Colonialism, Anti-Colonialism and Neo-Colonialism in China: The Opium Question at the Tokyo War Crimes Tribunal.'
[105] N.A., 'Huabei de nuhua jiaoyu 华北的奴化教育,' (North China's Enslaving Education) *Shenbao*, 24 March 1938.
[106] Guo Guiru 郭贵儒, 'Huabei lunxianqu riwei nuhua jiaoyu shulun 华北沦陷区日伪奴化教育述论' (A Discussion about the Enslaving Education under the Japanese Authorities in the Occupied Areas in North China) *Journal of Hebei Normal University* 28 (2005): 125.

of 'ruthless cultural invasion' aiming to turn the younger generation into willing tools to control China from within.[107]

PROCEDURAL STANDARDS

Western criticism had not only targeted the content of Chinese legislation but also the working of Chinese courts and procedural standards applied. The first case of an American national tried in a Chinese court after the end of extraterritoriality had already turned into a diplomatic *éclat*. The defendant, who was involved in a road accident, was found guilty of unintentional homicide by negligence.[108] Hurley, the American ambassador to China, remarked that it was 'unfortunate that verdict should be so glaringly unjust in first trial of American citizen in Chinese court since abolition of extraterritoriality.' This exemplifies, he continued, the 'shortcomings of Chinese judicial system' whose procedural safeguards in the criminal law system were not on par with the Western system.[109]

The procedural standards of the Chinese military courts for war criminals were equally determined by the newly drafted War Crimes Trials Regulation. Under the regulation, the Japanese were granted all the basic rights of defendants in non-military criminal trials: within ten days of judgment the defendant was entitled to apply for a review of the decision; oral arguments and the reading of the judgment were to be conducted in open court; trials were open to the general public and in some cases to journalists as well as foreign observers. Three out of five members of the bench, including the presiding judge, were judges from the regular civil court system; only two were selected from the ranks of the military judges. These basic regulations were, if necessary, supplemented by the Criminal Procedure Law of the Republic of China. This reflects a commitment to a certain minimum standard of procedural justice.

---

[107] Su Mingfei苏明飞 and Yu Shouhai于守海, 'Lun riben qinhua shiqi de nuhua jiaoyu 论日本侵华时期的奴化教育' (Discussing the Enslaving Education during the Time of the Japanese Invasion), *Journal of Shenyang Normal University (Social Science Edition)* 29 (2005): 133.

[108] Telegram, 20 December 1944, The appointed Ambassador in China (Hurley) to the Secretary of State, reprinted in: United States Department of State, *Foreign relations of the United States: Diplomatic Papers, 1945. The Far East, China 7* (Washington: U.S. Government Printing Office, 1969), 1450.

[109] Ibid., 1451.

The decision to uphold procedural standards that were unusually high for the time were motivated by the desire to avoid negative commentary from the Western Allies. The discussion surrounding the right to a defense lawyer for Japanese defendants may serve as a concrete example to demonstrate how far-reaching and influential such considerations really were. During the drafting process of the War Crimes Trials Regulation three options were being deliberated: (1) the Japanese should not be given any defense counsel, (2) the Japanese should have the right to choose a defense counsel of Japanese or any other nationality, (3) the defendants should have the right to choose a Chinese defense lawyer or the military court would appoint a defense lawyer for the defendant. The second option contravened national legislation that only allowed lawyers qualified and registered in China to appear in court. The first option was abandoned because of fear such a decision would incite unwanted 'international criticism.'[110]

Besides the question of procedural fairness, another feature of Chinese trials was equally threatening to damage the new and civilized legal face of the Republic: public executions of those found guilty. The case of Yonemura Harochi and Shimota Jiro on trial in Shanghai will serve to illustrate this point. The two defendants, who were known as the 'Wolf of Changshu' and the 'Tiger of Jiangyin,' were sentenced to death by a Chinese military court in Shanghai. On 17 June 1947 the two defendants were put on open trucks and paraded through the city for the onlooking Chinese crowd. The execution was caught on film and international media reported widely on the incident with detailed descriptions and sometimes graphic pictures.[111] The American journal *Life*, for instance, carried several pictures of the parade and the execution, including an image of the two executed men lying on the ground covered in blood.[112] The accompanying text describes how the parading and execution turned into a 'wild, roaring carnival.'[113] An elderly Chinese spectator is quoted as saying: 'The foreigners will see this and face is lost.'[114] The Nationalist government apparently came to the same conclusion and was highly dissatisfied with the impression

---

[110] NAT, File, 001-103022-0001-024, Ministry of Judicial Administration, 4 December 1945.
[111] See for instance: N.A., 'Japanese War Criminals Paraded to Their Death in China,' *New York Times*, 22 June 1947; N.A., 'Shanghai Execution,' *Life*, 14 July 1947, 34–35; N.A., 'Mob Applauds Execution,' *The Sydney Morning Herald* 19 June 1947, 3; N.A., 'Paraded Before They Were Shot,' *The Singapore Free Press*, 18 June 1947, 8.
[112] N.A., 'Shanghai Execution,' *Life*, 14 July, 34–35.
[113] Ibid., 35.
[114] Ibid.

the public executions created abroad of the Chinese justice system.[115] The Chinese newspaper *Shenbao* reported that there had been rumors that the Ministry of Defense had removed the president of the war crimes court in Shanghai from office because of negative foreign media coverage. While claiming that these rumors were unsubstantiated, the paper went on to state that the Ministry of Defense had prohibited all courts from parading war criminals sentenced to death through the streets. The reason for this, so the paper said, was the attempt to 'guarantee humanity and justice' as well as to 'protect the dignity of International Law.'[116]

Conclusion

The foregoing chapter discusses the Chinese war crimes program from the broader perspective of decolonization by focusing on the legacy of extraterritoriality in the Republic of China. It is suggested that for a complete evaluation of the history of extraterritoriality in China the time frame should be extended beyond the year 1943 to include the trials of Japanese war criminals in 1946. The period following the end of extraterritoriality in 1943 might either be interpreted as a period of de-imperialization or as the beginning of a period of more informal legal imperialism in China. To take the war crimes trials as a case study allows for a better understanding of the transition process to legal sovereignty that took place after 1943. By analyzing the trials from the overall perspective of decolonization it becomes possible to understand features of the trials that would otherwise seem like an anomaly. As the first opportunity to try a larger number of foreigners in Chinese courts, the war crimes trials possessed an added significance not only for showcasing the newly gained legal sovereignty but also for proving China's adherence to abstract ideals of justice and fairness. The trials were an opportunity to showcase a 'civilized' Chinese legal system capable of conducting trials in compliance with the internationally accepted standards of the time.

---

[115] Kushner, *Men to Devils, Devils to Men*, 162.
[116] N.A. "Chufa zhanfan bu zai baofu 处罚战犯不在报复" (To punish war criminals without taking revenge), *Shenbao*, 1 July 1947.

CHAPTER 6

The Burma Trials of Japanese War Criminals, 1946–1947

Robert Cribb

In the aftermath of the Second World War the victorious Allies launched a program of war crimes trials which prosecuted members of the Axis armed forces in Asia and Europe on charges of war crimes, crimes against humanity and crimes against peace. Around 10,000 Axis personnel—slightly more in Asia than in Europe—were charged in what remains by far the most ambitious international attempt to implement transitional justice that the world has yet seen. The intention of the trials was to take revenge on men who had committed atrocities against Allied military and civilians and against the inhabitants of occupied territories. The Allied planners wanted to avoid the impression that they were punishing whole nations; the strong element of collective national punishment that characterized the Versailles settlement after the First World War was widely seen as having created resentments that had led to the rise of Hitler and thus to the outbreak of the Second World War.[1] The trials therefore were

[1] Norman A. Graebner; Edward M. Bennett, *The Versailles Treaty and its legacy: the failure of the Wilsonian vision* (New York, NY Cambridge University Press, 2011): 107–123.

R. Cribb (✉)
Australian National University, Canberra, Australia

© The Author(s) 2016
K. von Lingen (ed.), *War Crimes Trials in the Wake of Decolonization and Cold War in Asia, 1945–1956*,
DOI 10.1007/978-3-319-42987-8_6

constructed as a holding to account of individuals for their own actions during the war and the proceedings were carefully managed to replicate as far as possible the rules of procedure and evidence that characterized the civil criminal courts of the prosecuting powers.

This legal intention, however, was nested within a complex of other considerations which varied sharply from region to region. The geopolitical context of Nazi imperialism was very different from that of Japanese or Italian expansion. Within the territory incorporated in each of the wartime empires, the invaders had very different ways of dealing with local institutions and political aspirations. Japan's empire had encompassed long-standing colonies in Taiwan and Korea, a client state in Manchukuo, a complex array of allies, fellow-travellers and opportunists in China, a formal ally in Thailand and a diverse array of former Western colonial territories in Asia and the Pacific. Economically, culturally and in terms of political experience, these regions were all very different. The meaning that attached to war crimes trials, therefore, varied widely across this vast region. The judges, prosecutors, defendants and victims who stood literally and metaphorically in court were there not just to seek or to be brought to reckoning for acts of cruelty that had been carried out by Japanese military men and their associates over the preceding years. They also had in mind the kind of world that could be shaped in the postwar era.

From March 1946 until November 1947, British authorities in Burma conducted 40 war crimes trials indicting 136 former members of the Japanese armed forces. The trials, conducted under a Royal Warrant that authorized military commanders to prosecute Japanese military personnel and employees for breaches of the laws and customs of war,[2] were part of a larger British war crimes trials effort in Southeast Asia. This effort was set in turn in a vast operation engaging Australia, China, France, the Netherlands Indies, the Philippines and the USA. This operation prosecuted some 5700 persons, most of them military personnel from the Imperial Japanese Army and Navy. Approximately 4500 were found guilty and received sentences ranging from brief prison terms to death.[3] The trials

---

[2] The Royal Warrant was a form of sovereign prerogative which did not require legislation for validity. A. P. V. Rogers, 'War crimes trials under the Royal Warrant: British practice 1945–1949,' *International and Comparative Law Quarterly* 39 no. 4 (Oct. 1990): 780–800.

[3] The standard account of these trials is Philip R. Piccigallo, *The Japanese on Trial: Allied War Crimes Operations in the East, 1945–1951* (Austin, TX: University of Texas Press, 1979). For more recent analysis, see Sandra Wilson, 'After the Trials: Class B and C Japanese War Criminals and the Post-War World,' *Japanese Studies*, 31 no 2 (2011): 141–149 and Sandra

were founded legally in national legislation and regulations, but they took place politically under the umbrella of postwar collaboration among the Allies. Accordingly, there was a massive exchange of criminal intelligence, of suspects or witnesses, and even of court personnel (judges and prosecutors) among the different jurisdictions. Just as the broad political aims of the peace were different for the different powers, so the imperatives of the war crimes trials process varied substantially even within national jurisdictions. Burma's program to try accused Japanese war criminals is no more typical of the whole than is that of any other region, but its experience illustrates the complex and sometimes contradictory political pressures that intersected in the war crimes trials process in Asia.

Burma had been conquered by Britain in three stages during the nineteenth century and was initially incorporated into the British Indian Empire. In 1937, following Burmese agitation, the region was separated from India as a colony in its own right with a high degree of internal self-government, including its own prime minister, Ba Maw. Burma, however, remained part of the British Empire and British economic interests were not threatened. In January 1942, the Japanese army invaded Burma as part of its general aim to seize control of Southeast Asia. Burma had specific importance to Japan as a source of oil. Strategically, moreover, it offered the possibility of cutting a major supply line between British India and the beleaguered Guomindang government of China in Chongqing. By May 1942, all but a few northern parts of the colony were in Japanese hands. In November 1944, Britain launched a counter-attack which succeeded in recovering most of the colony by May 1945.[4] Like the Philippines, thus, Burma was largely in the hands of Allied troops before the Japanese surrender in August 1945. Also like the Philippines, moreover, the former colony was devastated. As a result of bombing, shelling and scorched earth policies on both sides, a great part of infrastructure that had made the colony rich in the pre-war era now lay in ruins.

The greatest challenge faced by Britain in Burma was not the formidable task of economic reconstruction but rather the construction of a new political format. Both in Burma and in neighboring India, powerful

---

Wilson, Robert Cribb, Beatrice Trefalt and Dean Aszkielowicz, *Japanese War Criminals: The Politics of Justice After the Second World War* (New York, NY: Columbia University Press, 2017).

[4] Louis Allen, *Burma, the longest war, 1941–45* (London: J.M. Dent, 1984); Christopher Bayly and Tim Harper, *Forgotten armies: Britain's Asian empire & the war with Japan* (London: Penguin, 2004): 156–207, 394–404, 427–445.

nationalist movements had created a strong sense of historical momentum towards independence. This sense of momentum had been strengthened by the experiences of the war. When Japanese forces entered Burma in late 1941, they were accompanied by a small force of Burmese called the Burma Independence Army (BIA). This army was the joint initiative of a Japanese Army officer, Colonel Suzuki Keiji, and the so-called 30 Thakins, radical Burmese nationalists who saw Japan as the only force capable of removing Britain from their country. In August 1943, Japan granted formal independence to the State of Burma, placing it on the same international level as Thailand and Manchukuo and recruiting the pre-war prime minister Ba Maw as Adipadi (head of state). Elements of the BIA became the Burma National Army (BNA) under loose Japanese supervision. Headed by Aung San, the BNA grew to around 11,000 in size by early 1945 when it turned on its Japanese sponsors and, renamed the Patriotic Burmese Forces, formed a loose alliance with the British forces then engaged in their reconquest of Burma. Its role was sufficient to earn it a place in the Allied victory parade in Rangoon in June 1945. Thereafter, it was a strong presence in the countryside and a key asset for Aung San's political movement, the Anti-Fascist People's Freedom League, in its efforts to browbeat the British into announcing a program for prompt decolonization.[5]

Britain's postwar strategy in Burma was a daring version of the approach adopted by all the colonial powers in the region except Portugal and Australia: to engage with local national aspirations to whatever extent was needed to isolate radical forces that had taken advantage of the Japanese intervention to strengthen their political positions. Aung San was radical, but he was a man with whom the British believed they could do business. The two sides moved quickly to an understanding that Burma would become independent before long. At the same time, there was a pressing need to restore law and order in the colony. The Japanese retreat had led to extensive disorder and banditry (known locally as *dacoity*). Restoring civic order was necessary both as a prerequisite for economic recovery and in order to create an environment in which the 'moderate' elements of society would be able to function and prosper.

The war crimes trials of Japanese were a small piece in the jigsaw puzzle of British strategy in Burma. They fitted into that strategy in four ways.

---

[5] Joyce C. Lebra, *Japanese-Trained Armies in Southeast Asia: Independence and Volunteer Forces in World War II* (Hong Kong: Heinemann, 1977), 46–56.

First, they were embedded in the colonial responsibility that the British still claimed in the colony, despite their developing plans for withdrawal. There is little sign that British authorities hoped the trials would win them support, but they were probably conscious that failing to prosecute war criminals would leave them open to rebuke, given that trials were taking place in Europe and elsewhere in Southeast Asia. Second, the trials had a role to play in discrediting those in the Burmese elite—men such as Ba Maw—who had remained close to the Japanese, and anti-British—until the very end. Political circumstances made it impossible for such men to be tried for collaboration, but the brutal actions of Japanese troops and guards, made public knowledge by means of the trials, could still work to stain and compromise all those who had benefited from the Japanese interlude. Third, the trials offered a reassurance to the metropolitan British public that the transition to independence in Burma was not a second capitulation to Japan, despite Japanese wartime sponsorship of Burmese independence. And fourth, the trials had the potential to provide a small impediment to the restoration of Japan's important economic position in pre-war Burma by reminding the Burmese public of Japanese brutalities. Although the very first war crimes trial in Burma appears to have been selected to impress the Burmese public with the return of British justice, the later trials, conducted with increasing urgency in the lead-up to Burma's independence in January 1948, seem to have had different motives.

Preparations for the trial of war criminals in Burma had begun during the war, but were barely advanced by the time of the Japanese surrender in August 1945. In October 1944 the United Nations War Crimes Commission (UNWCC) had approved a proposal that the supreme commanders in each Allied theater should have the authority to set up their own military tribunals alongside eventual national courts, 'as an expeditious means of trying war criminals.'[6] In the war against Japan, this ruling meant that the task of preparing to prosecute war criminals devolved to three separate authorities The South East Asia Command (SEAC), which was largely British (and British Indian), was headed by Lord Louis Mountbatten, with its headquarters in Kandy in Ceylon (now Sri Lanka). Its territorial responsibilities for most of the war comprised only Burma, the Malay Peninsula and Sumatra. In an Allied division of responsibilities,

---

[6] United Nations War Crimes Commission, *History of the United Nations War Crimes Commission and the development of the laws of war* (London: HMSO, 1948), 450.

the rest of mainland Southeast Asia had been allocated to the China Theater while island Southeast Asia was under the South West Pacific Area (SWPA), headed by the US General Douglas MacArthur. Immediately upon the Japanese surrender on 15 August 1945, however, the Allies undertook a major reorganization of territorial responsibilities, in which the SWPA was dissolved and its responsibilities in island Southeast Asia, except the Philippines, were transferred to SEAC, which also took responsibility for Thailand and southern Indochina (Map 6.1). The mandate of SEAC in Southeast Asia was to accept the Japanese surrender and to prepare for the restoration of civil authority. Everywhere in the SEAC region, except in Thailand, this civil authority was colonial: British, Dutch, French and Portuguese. Much has been written about the challenging circumstances that SEAC faced in dealing with other colonial powers and local nationalist movements in the territories for which it was now responsible.[7] These circumstances obliged SEAC to concentrate its attentions on the new regions. Although Burma was formally part of SEAC until the dissolution of the command in December 1946, the British Military Administration there was relatively autonomous and continued only until 31 January 1946, before giving way to the civilian Government of Burma under the pre-war governor, Sir Reginald Dorman-Smith.[8]

US and Australian authorities had made major efforts to begin collecting testimony and other evidence that might lead to future prosecutions but SEAC, seriously pressed for resources, relied initially on lists prepared by the Far Eastern and Pacific Sub-Commission of the UNWCC, based in Chongqing. These lists contained mainly brief statements of atrocities that had been committed in China. SEAC did not generate its own list of suspects until September 1945. This initial list, however, indicated clearly that there would be work for war crimes investigators in Burma. The list referred to 152 incidents. Most of them took place in Burma or on the Thailand–Burma Railway, but a few were recorded from further

---

[7] Peter Dennis, *Troubled days of peace: Mountbatten and South East Asia Command, 1945–46* (New York, NY: St. Martin's Press, 1987); Richard McMillan, *The British occupation of Indonesia 1945–1946: Britain, the Netherlands and the Indonesian revolution* (London: Routledge, 2005); David G. Marr, *Vietnam 1945: the quest for power* (Berkeley: University of California Press, 1995).

[8] The transfer to civilian authority took place in stages, commencing on 1 November 1945. See F. S. V. Donnison, *British military administration in the Far East 1943–46* (London: HMSO, 1956), 125–26.

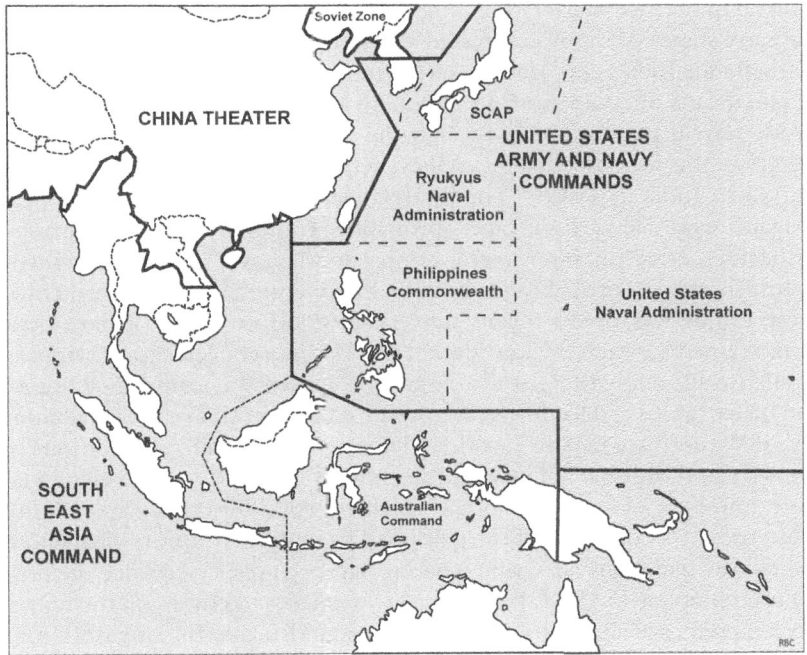

Map 6.1 Allied military command areas in Asia and the Pacific, 15 August 1945

afield—Malaya, Java, even China. Sometimes the list simply specified 'maltreatment of PW [prisoner of war]'; many of the perpetrators were 'U/I [unidentified]'(Map 6.2).[9]

Grievous maltreatment of military and civilian detainees and brutal reaction to real and presumed resistance on the part of indigenous populations constituted the majority of crimes for which Japanese military personnel were charged in the aftermath of the war. The first of these categories of crime, however, was less salient in Burma than in other parts of Southeast Asia and the Pacific. The tactical reality of the islands and peninsulas that comprised the rest of SEAC's territory was that retreat was

---
[9] The National Archives (UK) (hereafter TNA LONDON), WO 208/3899, 'S.E.A.C. Theatre list of suspects,' list no. 1, 21 September 1945.

difficult in the face of overwhelming forces or in the aftermath of defeat. In the early stages of the war defeated Western forces in the Philippines, the Netherlands Indies and Malaya were often trapped because of the absence of safe means of evacuation. In Burma by contrast, the land border made steady retreat possible, even though the terrain was difficult. It was estimated at the time that half a million refugees managed to escape from Burma to India in 1942.[10] For the relatively small number of European civilians who failed to escape—probably around 200[11]—the Japanese authorities establish internment camps in Maymyo, Kalaw and Tavoy. A British report, probably from early 1946, commented, 'Treatment in these camps was by no means universally good but only on rare occasions seemed to reach the low level of the German concentration camps.'[12] Similarly, although there was a large prisoner of war camp in Rangoon and other camps at Moulmein, Mandalay and Myitkyina, the overall number of Western soldiers in Japanese detention was small.[13] Conditions on the Thailand–Burma Railway had been appalling and had involved very large numbers of forced laborers—perhaps 300,000 Asians and 60,000 Westerners[14] – but much of the work had been done from the Thai end of the railway and many surviving workers had been dispersed once the project was complete in 1943. Relatively few witnesses to crimes on the railway were therefore available to the investigators in Burma. Investigators compiled a list of Burmese laborers from Myaungmya in the Burma Delta who had been discharged from service on the railway, but the individuals were

---

[10] Michael D. Leigh, *The Evacuation of Civilians from Burma: Analysing the 1942 Colonial Disaster* (London: Bloomsbury, 2014), 23.
[11] Karl Hack and Kevin Blackburn, 'Japanese-occupied Asia from 1941 to 1945: one occupier, many captivities and memories,' in Karl Hack and Kevin Blackburn, eds., *Forgotten Captives in Japanese-Occupied Asia* (London: Routledge, 2008), 5.
[12] Burma Office Records, British Library (hereafter BOR), IOR/M/4/3043: Japanese War criminals – miscellaneous, ALFSEA, 'War crimes: Summary of investigations in 1945' [n.d.]. See also Bernice Archer, *The Internment of Western Civilians under the Japanese 1941–1945: A Patchwork of Internment* (London: Routledge, 2005).
[13] On conditions in Rangoon and Moulmein jails, see K. P. MacKenzie, *Operation Rangoon Jail* (London: Christopher Johnson, 1954). US investigators undertook a separate investigation of the killings of downed American flyers in northern Burma. See BOR, IOR/M/4/3043: Japanese War criminals – miscellaneous, ALFSEA, 'War crimes: Summary of investigations in 1945' [n.d.].
[14] Van Waterford, *Prisoners of the Japanese in World War II: statistical history, personal narratives, and memorials concerning POWs in camps and on hellships, civilian internees, Asian slave laborers, and others captured in the Pacific Theater* (Jefferson, NC: McFarland, 1994), 236.

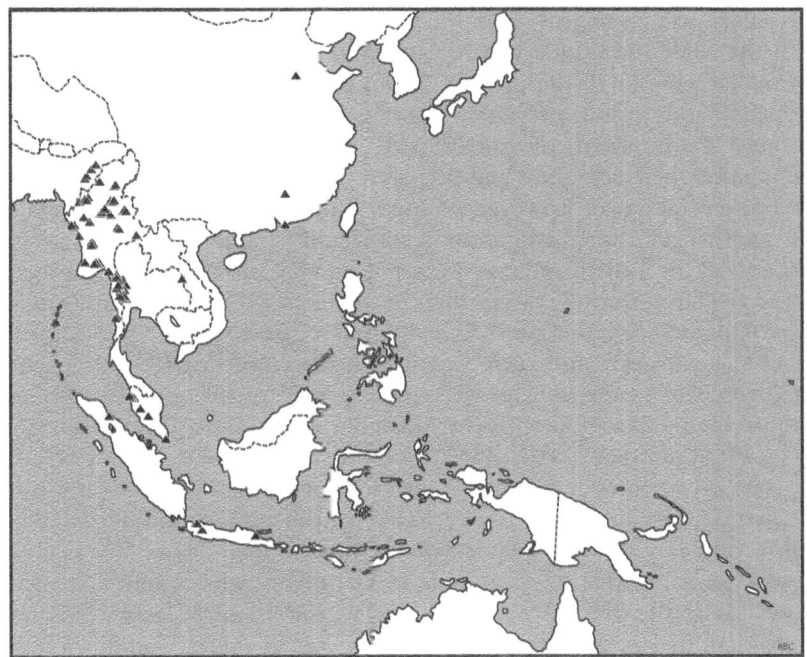

Map 6.2 First SEAC suspect list, September 1945: location of reported offenses (Constructed from data in WO 208/3899; some unidentified locations omitted)

hard to find and, when located, had to be questioned in Burmese using an interpreter.[15] For these reasons, and because better facilities were available in Bangkok and Singapore, the vast majority of the Thailand–Burma Railway trials took place in Singapore. There were also reports of the massacre of Asian laborers at Hsipaw (Thibaw) in the Shan States in January 1945 as Chinese troops approached,[16] but this region was remote and evidence was difficult to collect, and so no trials took place for that event.

The first step in preparing for prosecutions was the collection of evidence. In most of the SEAC territories, this task was undertaken by

---

[15] National Archives of Myanmar (hereafter NAM) accession no. 91 file 4M-4, 11/13 War Crimes Investigation Team, Rangoon to District Superintendent of Police, Myaungmya 28 February 1947.
[16] Werner Gruhl, *Imperial Japan's World War Two: 1931–1945* (New Brunswick: Transaction Publishers, 2007), 92.

specialized war crimes investigation teams. The first of these teams moved with the SEAC Headquarters to Singapore in September 1945, leaving Burma largely out of the picture. These teams gathered testimony from former prisoners and internees, visited crime scenes, identified suspects amongst the hundreds of thousands of Japanese military personnel, recommended their detention and prepared the evidence for subsequent trials. For several weeks, however, no investigation teams were dispatched to Burma. Instead, the investigation of suspected Japanese war criminals was carried out by British military personnel under the delegated authority of the civilian governor, rather than by virtue of the military authority of the commander-in-chief of SEAC, as was the case elsewhere in Southeast Asia.[17] The investigation task was in the hands of district officers, the regional civilian officials who were the lynchpin of the colonial administration, in collaboration with the intelligence section of the British 12th Army Headquarters.[18] The officials were instructed on 13 July 1945: 'It is proposed to compile a list of War Crimes with the object of punishing the perpetrators later [...]. It is realised that the compilation of such a list will not be easy but every endeavour should be made to obtain as complete a list as possible.'[19] As a guide to identifying what might constitute a war crime, the officials were provided with a list of 32 acts which had been identified as war crimes in 1919 by the so-called Commission on Responsibilities, formed as part of the Versailles Peace Process.[20] This list

---

[17] The British in Southeast Asia conducted trials under Royal Warrant which gave quasi-judicial authority to the local military commander. See R. John Pritchard, 'The Parameters of Justice: The Evolution of British Civil and Military Perspectives on War Crimes Trials and their Legal Context (1942–1956),' in John Carey, William V. Dunlap and R. John Pritchard, eds., *International Humanitarian Law: Origins, Challenges and Prospects* vol. 3 (Leiden: Brill, 2006), 283–289, 293–295 [277–326]; A. P. V. Rogers, 'War Crimes Trials under the Royal Warrant: British Practice 1945–1949,' *International and Comparative Law Quarterly* 39 no. 4 (Oct. 1990): 788–789 [780–800].

[18] BOR, IOR/M/4/3038, Draft letter to H. G. Wilkie, Chief Secretary to Govt of Burma, 31 October 1945, 184; IOR/M/4/3038, Chief Secretary of the Govt of Burma to L.B. Walsh Atkins (Burma Office) 21 December 1945, 170; NAM accession no. 541 file 4M-8 War Crimes, 'Memorandum of a meeting held in the Office of the Chief Secretary to the Government of Burma at 11 a.m. on Monday, the 28 November 1945'.

[19] NAM Accession no. 328, file C-8 War Crimes, Deputy Chief of Police, Intelligence, to All SCAOs 13 July 1945.

[20] UNWCC, *History of the United Nations War Crimes Commission*, 34–35. The 32 acts identified as war crimes were: Murders and massacres; systematic terrorism; Putting hostages to death; Torture of civilians; Deliberate starvation of civilians; Rape; Abduction of girls and women for the purpose of enforced prostitution; Deportation of civilians; Internment of

had never been endorsed by international treaty but it was adopted by the UNWCC during the Second World War as a starting point for identifying crimes that might be prosecuted. The officers were told to submit their reports by 1 November 1945.[21] Members of the Burmese public were invited in public announcements to make statements to the investigators in order to hasten the identification of suspects.[22] There is some evidence that the Burmese nationalist leaders were keen to have Japanese perpetrators of war crimes prosecuted. On 29 September 1945, the Central Committee of the Anti-Fascist People's Freedom League (AFPFL), the main nationalist organization, passed a motion calling on the colonial government to appoint a 'War Criminals Inquiry Commission to take action and charge Japanese soldiers and military police who killed and tortured Burmese during the war.' There is no evidence, however, that the nationalist leaders followed up on this motion.[23]

It appears that the early reports compiled by District Officers rarely provided sufficient reliable information to become the basis for trials. Even apparently solid leads could fail to result in prosecutions. Japanese forces were reported to have killed 20 people in the town of Hlaingbwe,

---

civilians under inhuman conditions; Forced laborr of civilians in connection with the military operations of the enemy; Usurpation of sovereignty during military occupation; Compulsory enlistment of soldiers among the inhabitants of occupied territory; Attempts to denationalize the inhabitants of occupied territory; Pillage; Confiscation of property; Exaction of illegitimate or of exorbitant contributions and requisitions; Debasement of currency, and issue of spurious currency; Imposition of collective penalties; Wanton devastation and destruction of property; Deliberate bombardment of undefended places; Wanton destruction of religious, charitable, educational and historic buildings and monuments; Destruction of merchant ships and passenger vessels without warning and without provision for the safety of passengers and crew; Destruction of fishing boats and of relief ships; Deliberate bombardment of hospitals; Attack on and destruction of hospital ships; Breach of other rules relating to the Red Cross; Use of deleterious and asphyxiating gases; Use of explosive or expanding bullets, and other inhuman appliances; Directions to give no quarter; Ill-treatment of wounded and prisoners of war; Employment of prisoners of war on unauthorized works; Misuse of flags of truce; Poisoning of wells.

[21] NAM Accession no. 328, file C-8 War Crimes, Deputy Chief of Police, Intelligence, to All SCAOs 13 July 1945.

[22] NAM accession no. 541 file 4M-8 War Crimes, HQ 12th Army, SEAC, to 17 Ind Div, 19 Ind Div, North Burma Area, South Burma Dist, 551 Sub Area, 8 December 1945.

[23] Item 8, Fifth Meeting Notes, Central Committee, AFPFL, 29 September 1945, held at No. 8 Churchill Rd, *AFPFL Central Working Committee Meeting Minutes, 27/8/41 [i.e. 45] to 24/8/46* [in Burmese] (Myanma Khit Press, Yangon, 2014), 18–19. I am grateful to Nick Cheesman for drawing my attention to this material and for translating it for me.

in the Karen Hills east of Moulmein in June and July 1945. Operatives of the British Special Forces unit Force 136 had been operating in the area behind Japanese lines and had made contact with local villages for information and supplies. The investigation units identified individual Japanese soldiers accused of involvement in the killings and in beatings, but none of them was brought to trial.[24] The named perpetrator of the murders of 23 people suspected of sympathies with the Allies in the Chin Hills was similarly never brought to trial.[25]

The first SEAC investigation team in Burma began its work only in December 1945.[26] The task was daunting. In the rest of SEAC, the investigation teams had access to a vast number of witnesses: former prisoners of war and internees were questioned as they left their camps or as they passed through Singapore and other centers, generating a rich, if chaotic, body of evidence. They produced voluminous lists of incidents and suspects which they gradually narrowed down to detainees for whom there was enough evidence to embark upon prosecution. By contrast, the prisoners of war and internees who had been held in Burma during the occupation had mostly been liberated and repatriated before the end of the war and before the commencement of serious war crimes investigations. At the height of the investigations in the rest of Southeast Asia, newly released prisoners and internees filled in tens of thousands of so-called 'Q-forms' in which they set out details of their experience that might provide evidence for war crimes trials. These forms then provided the basis for follow-up interviews and the taking of affidavits. In Burma, however, the collection of information was less systematic and less structured, often in the hands of officials who had little knowledge of legal procedure. The testimonies they collected therefore were often useless as evidence in court and sometimes were too vague to allow further investigation.[27] The intelligence teams in Burma had access to the voluminous reports produced by SEAC Headquarters in Singapore, but

---

[24] NAM accession no. 145 file no C_2A Jap atrocities 1946, Det 602 F.S. Sec. 63 Ind Inf Bde to HQ 17 Ind Div. 15 January 1946.
[25] NAM accession no. 9 file J.W.C., Assistant Superintendent, Falam, Chin Hills to Deputy Commissioner, Chin Hills, Falam, 22 October 1945.
[26] BOR, IOR/M/4/3038, G.R. Bardshaw, WO, to Walsh Atkins BO, 14 January 1946, 168.
[27] IOR/M/4/3043: Japanese War criminals – miscellaneous, ALFSEA, 'War crimes: Summary of investigations in 1945' [n.d.]; National Archives of Myanmar, accession no. 494 file J-R Office of the Deputy Commissioner, Naga Hills District: Japs Reparation, OC War

relatively little was relevant to Burmese cases. Investigators complained that the material was too sparse and unspecific to identify suspects. With a tone of complaint, they commented that they might be looking for a suspect described only as 'A Japanese about 5'4" in height, with sallow complexion and spectacles.'[28] The annual monsoon, difficult terrain and the destruction of infrastructure as a result of the war also hampered the collection of evidence.[29] So did the fact of the enormous casualty rate amongst Japanese forces in Burma. SEAC investigators maintained a card file in which they recorded the deaths of those whom they might otherwise have sought to indict.[30]

Both the rhetoric which surrounded the launching of the war crimes trials program in Europe and the logic of the long lists of suspects that each of the Allied commands produced alongside those of the UNWCC pointed to a comprehensive trial program. The determination not to indict enemy nations as a whole brought with it the implication that perpetrators had to be systematically identified and prosecuted. The aim of comprehensiveness, however, was undermined not just by practical difficulties but also by practical decisions that proved to have major consequences. Two decisions were especially important.

First, the British authorities decided not to prosecute Burmese who had aligned themselves with the Japanese. This decision encompassed not just potential trials for treason but also instances of direct engagement in atrocities. It contrasted with Allied prosecution of collaboration in other parts of Southeast Asia[31] and with the decision that Koreans and Taiwanese who had been part of the Japanese Imperial forces should be liable to prosecution, even if they were in ethnically segregated units. This decision, as Lawson has persuasively argued, was rooted in the practical problem presented by the Burmese leader, Aung San, in the form of evidence that he had personally killed a British-appointed village headman in

---

Crimes Investigation Team No 2 to Sub Area Comdr, H.Q. North Burma Area, SEAC, 21 May 1946.

[28] IOR/M/4/3043: Japanese War criminals – miscellaneous, ALFSEA, 'War crimes: Summary of investigations in 1945' [n.c.].

[29] IOR/M/4/3038, Extract from report of Major P. J. H. Pope n.d. [July 1946], 95.

[30] Card index in TNA LONDON WO 357/1.

[31] David Joel Steinberg, *Philippine Collaboration in World War II* (Ann Arbor, MI: University of Michigan Press, 1967); Han Ming Guang, 'Collaboration during the Japanese Occupation: Issues and Problems focusing on the Chinese Community' (BA Hons thesis: National University of Singapore, 2010).

1942.[32] Not only were many British planners, including Mountbatten as SEAC commander, reluctant to see Aung San removed as a negotiating partner, but they also feared an intensification of violence if the popular leader was arrested. In India, the prosecution of a small number of lower-ranked Indians who had fought on the side of the Japanese in Subhas Chandra Bose's Indian National Army had prompted riots.[33] The prospects for such violence were even greater in Burma.[34] After an agonized discussion, the British authorities finally issued an act under which the governor's assent was required before any court could consider a criminal case relating to the wartime period.[35] This stop-gap measure was followed in 1947 by the War-time Crimes (Exemption) Act, which formally exempted atrocities committed by Burmese from prosecution.[36] Nothing in the 1946 or 1947 acts directly affected Japanese suspects, but the issue gave British investigators reason to soften the principle of comprehensiveness and to focus instead on two categories of crimes which were less likely to generate political complications: the torture and killing of local residents by the Japanese military police (Kempeitai) and the ill-treatment of prisoners of war, downed Allied fliers and British special forces operating behind Japanese lines.[37]

The second major compromise of the principle of comprehensiveness was the practice of accepting the defense of superior orders from those suspected of war crimes. In its long deliberations towards laying a firm legal basis for postwar trials, the UNWCC had stated firmly that those who had committed war crimes could not escape a guilty verdict simply

---

[32] Konrad Mitchell Lawson, 'Wartime Atrocities and the Politics of Treason in the Ruins of the Japanese Empire, 1937–1953,' (PhD diss., Harvard University, 2012), 155.

[33] Maybritt Jill Alpes, 'The Congress and the INA Trials, 1945–50: A Contest over the Perception of 'Nationalist' Politics,' *Studies in History* 23, no. 1 (2007): 135–158. L. C. Green, "The Indian National Army Trials," *The Modern Law Review* 11, no. 1 (1948): 47–69.

[34] Lawson, 'Wartime Atrocities and the Politics of Treason,' 157–158.

[35] Lawson, 'Wartime Atrocities and the Politics of Treason,' 160–162.

[36] NAM accession no. 235, Governor's Executive Council 1946, file 44G46 (4), 44th Weekly Meeting – Wednesday the 30 October 1946; NAM accession no, 281 File 49G46(8), 49th Weekly Meeting – Wednesday the 4 December 1946, War-Time Crimes (Exemption) Bill, 1946; NAM accession no. 71 file 13-A(2), Government of Burma, Judicial Department to all Deputy Commissioner, 15 January 1947; NAM accession no. 71 file 13-A(2), War-Time Crimes (Exemption) Act 1946 (Burma Act no XLVII of 1946), published in *Burma Gazette Extraordinary* 19 December 1946.

[37] For an example, see the documents in TNA London in WO 325/63.

because they had been following orders.[38] Western powers had changed their military manuals during the war to remove the possibility of this plea, too.[39] Nonetheless, war crimes teams in Burma routinely ignored the lowest ranks in their investigations. Standard procedure in British investigations required the automatic detention of prison and camp staff along with members of the Kempeitai.[40] The jails in Rangoon and Moulmein, however, housing those over whom a shadow of suspicion had fallen, were largely inhabited by non-commissioned officers and junior officers, a majority of them from the Kempeitai. In other words, the investigations and trials focused not on the lowest ranks who had simply done what they were told, but rather on military personnel whose rank gave them responsibility to think and plan and who might therefore have been expected to know better.

As in other parts of Southeast Asia, the British authorities attributed most massacres to the members of the Japanese military police, Kempeitai, and they took especial care to detain all Kempeitai members whom they could track down.[41] By December 1945, some 350 members of the Kempeitai, described as 'the Japanese Gestapo,' were being held in Rangoon while their past actions were investigated.[42] In May 1946, a visiting delegate from the International Red Cross reported that the British in Burma held in detention approximately 70,000 Japanese surrendered personnel and 778 prisoners of war.[43] By this time, only 171 were identified as [suspected]

---

[38] UNWCC, *History of the United Nations War Crimes Commission*, 38.

[39] Alan M. Wilner, 'Superior orders as a defense to violations of international criminal law', *Maryland Law Review* 26 no. 2 (1966), 127–142. See also Gary D. Solis, 'Obedience of orders and the law of war: judicial application in American forums' *American University International Law Review* 15 no. 2 (1999): 481–526.

[40] BOR, IOR/M/4/3043: Japanese War criminals – miscellaneous, ALFSEA, 'War crimes: Summary of investigations in 1945' [n.d.].

[41] BOR, IOR/M/4/3043: Japanese War criminals – miscellaneous, ALFSEA, 'War crimes: Summary of investigations in 1945' [n.d.].

[42] BOR, IOR/M/4/3038 Japanese War Criminals: Trials in Burma, Far East Burma 2, 4 December 1945, 179.

[43] See NAM Accession no. 17 file 373 D(EA) 46 Box 1, 'Report by the Committee of the International Red Cross in Geneva on JSP (Japanese) and P of W Camps in Burma' [May 1946], 15–3 (18). The distinction between Japanese Surrendered Personnel (JSPs) and prisoners of war was a legal one adopted by the Allies at the conclusion of the Second World War. Prisoners of war (that is, Japanese troops captured before the end of hostilities) were protected by the Geneva Conventions which required, amongst other things, that they be repatriated as soon as practicable after the end of fighting. Throughout Southeast Asia, however, the British soon realized that Japanese military personnel formed a valuable source of disci-

'war criminals.' Half a year later, in December 1946, surrendered personnel still numbered 35,000 and only 458 suspects were being held.[44] Prior to trial, suspects were held in what was known as 110 P.W. [Prisoner of War] Cage, inside Rangoon Jail. Despite this ominous terminology, some accounts suggest that suspected war criminals were probably more comfortable there than they might have been in the crowded tent camp set up for surrendered Japanese troops in Ahlone Park on the edge of the city.[45]

It is possible, too, that British prosecution policy in Burma was influenced by the ideas of Alan Gledhill, legal scholar and justice of the high court in Burma, which he later expressed in a reflective paper on Japanese war crimes that was published in 1949. Gledhill paid careful attention to each of the grounds on which the Japanese military authorities in Burma might have been convicted of war crimes, concluding on issue after issue that Japanese behavior had remained within the rather broad limits set by British military law. Assessing the harshness of the Japanese army towards those it perceived as supporting the British, for instance, he noted:

> The Defence of Burma Act and Rules, and similar products of the legislatures of belligerents, made a statutory crime of almost every act remotely conducive to the advantage of the enemy's war effort, and the commander of military forces occupying enemy territory cannot be expected to be milder than the de jure government.[46]

Gledhill also argued that Mountbatten, in assuming authority over the British administration of Burma on 1 January 1944, chose not to invoke a formal martial law regulation, but asserted military authority on the basis of common law which recognized the unspecified justification of military necessity.[47]

---

plined labor. As Japanese surrendered personnel, they had no right to repatriation and could be used as an unpaid labor force for as long as it suited the Allies. See Stephen Connor, 'Side-stepping Geneva: Japanese Troops under British Control, 1945-7,' *Journal of Contemporary History* 45 no. 2 (2010): 389–405.

[44] NAM Accession no. 29, file 150 D(EA) 47, 'Japanese Surrendered Personnel and Prisoners of War visited between 30 November and 9 December 1946 by Mr. H. Frei, delegate of the International Committee of the Red Cross in India.'

[45] On Ahlone, see Aida Yūji, *Prisoner of the British: a Japanese soldier's experience in Burma*, trans. Hide Ishiguro and Louis Allen (London: Cresset Press, 1966), 23–29.

[46] Alan Gledhill, 'Some aspects of the operation of international and military law in Burma, 1941–1945,' *Modern Law Review* 12 (1939), 197 [191–204].

[47] Gledhill, 'Some aspects', 201–02.

Although there was some consideration of holding war crimes trials under the authority of the Government of Burma, it was decided in December 1945 to keep the process in line with the remainder of SEAC territory and to establish war crimes courts under the authority of SEAC.[48] In all their jurisdictions, the Allies were keen to commence trials early and with a notorious case. The first US trial was of General Yamashita Tomoyuki, commander of Japanese forces in the Philippines at the time of the Rape of Manila. The first Australian trial was of a Japanese accused of cannibalism.[49] The first British war crimes trial in Rangoon, which opened in March 1946, prosecuted 13 Japanese soldiers and their commander, Major Ichikawa Seigi, on charges of carrying out at massacre at Kalagon, a predominantly Muslim village near Moulmein.[50] An estimated 600 villagers were killed on 7 July 1945 because some of them had collaborated with British special forces operating in the region behind Japanese lines.[51] Defending counsel in the trials was Lt-Col. A. M. Sturrock (Royal Artillery), in peacetime a Scottish solicitor; the prosecutor was Capt. A. J. T. Collier, a London-born Cambridge graduate. The judge was Lt-Col. R. C. Laming, a barrister from the Judge Advocate General's office in British India, himself a former prisoner of war on the Thailand–Burma Railway. All these personnel were provided by the war crimes investigation team.

Kalagon had been troublesome for the Japanese by virtue of British paratrooper operations and the depredations of bandits. At this time, Japanese troops were especially suspicious of Muslims, because of their presumed connections with the Muslims of British India.[52] The Japanese unit on

---

[48] BOR, IOR/M/4/3038, Chief Secretary of the Govt of Burma to L. B. Walsh Atkins (Burma Office) 21 December 1945, 170; BOR, IOR/M/4/3038, C in C ALFEA to WO, 8 February 1946, 163; NAM accession no. 4 file 103 D(EA)46 Trial of War Criminals, HQ Burma Command, SEAC to HQ South Burma Area, 23 February 1946.

[49] Dean Aszkielowicz, 'After the Surrender: Australia and the Japanese Class B and C war criminals, 1945–1958,' (PhD Thesis, Murdoch University, 2012), 162–64.

[50] See TNA LONDON WO 235/961, Trial of Ichikawa Seigi and thirteen others, Rangoon, 1946.

[51] BOR, IOR/M/4/3038, 'Jap War Criminals to stand trial in Rangoon,' *Rangoon Liberator* 17 February 1946, 156. The monsoon season had begun the day after Rangoon fell to British forces, thereby greatly slowing military operations. The area around Moulmein was gradually conquered over the following weeks.

[52] In some witness testimonies, the villagers are described as 'Indians,' but this identification was not made by the British authorities and it is possible that the witnesses assumed the victims were not Burmese simply because they were not Buddhist.

this occasion consisted of both regular army and Kempeitai personnel, under the command of Major Ichikawa. On the afternoon of 7 July 1945, the Japanese soldiers rounded up all the men of the village and confined them to the mosque, where interrogations began. Some of the men were taken to a separate building for further interrogation by Kempeitai staff. Out of these interrogations came confirmation that the village had indeed assisted British commando forces. Ichikawa then ordered that all members of the village be killed. Men, women and children were tied together in groups of —four to ten, taken from the village, blindfolded, bayonetted and thrown down nearby wells. The killing was done hastily and some of the victims survived to become witnesses in the subsequent war crimes trial of Ichikawa and his men. After the massacre, the troops burnt the village and took with them ten women survivors who, they said, had agreed to act as 'spies' but who were probably intended for enforced military prostitution as so-called 'comfort women.'[53] The court found ten of the 14 guilty, acquitting the other four on the grounds that their participation in the killings had not been proven. Five of the guilty, including Ichikawa, were sentenced to death and the remainder to terms ranging from four to 12 years.[54]

Evidence from the Kalagon trial was later introduced at the International Military Tribunal for the Far East (IMTFE, better known as the Tokyo Trials) in the trial of General Kimura Heitarō. Kimura had been commander of the Japanese forces in Burma from August 1944 until the final repatriation of Japanese forces in September 1946. He was tried for the Kalagon massacre under the principle of command responsibility. This principle, the converse of superior orders, held commanding officers responsible for conduct of soldiers under their command, where those officers had either issued general instructions leading to atrocities or had failed to take sufficient steps to prevent their troops from committing atrocities.[55] Kimura

---

[53] TNA LONDON WO 235/961, Trial of Ichikawa Seigi and thirteen others, Rangoon, 1946. Yuma Totani, *Justice in Asia and the Pacific region, 1945–1952: Allied war crimes prosecutions* (New York, NY: Cambridge University Press, 2014), 138.

[54] For a detailed study of this trial, see Totani, *Justice in Asia and the Pacific region, 1945–1952*, 129–155.

[55] This principle had been applied with great strictness in the US trial of General Yamashita Tomoyuki for the Rape of Manila. See Richard L. Lael, *The Yamashita precedent* (Wilmington, DE.: Scholarly Resources, 1982), 7–8, 13, 82–83, 86, 97, 137–138; A. Frank Reel, *The Case of General Yamashita* (Chicago, IL: University of Chicago Press, 1949); Guénaël Mettraux, *The law of command responsibility* (Oxford: Oxford University Press, 2009), 6–8; Allan

was also charged with responsibility for assigning Allied prisoners of war to the Thailand–Burma railway; construction work had been completed by the time he arrived in Burma, but Allied prisoners of war and internees continued to be deployed there to maintain the railway and to repair damage caused by Allied air raids. He was also charged with ordering the murder of downed fliers and in his capacity as vice-minister of war (1941–44). He was found guilty of seven charges, condemned to death and hanged on 23 December 1948.[56]

In choosing the Kalagon massacre for the first war crimes trial, the British authorities evidently had a Burmese audience in mind. They commonly believed that trials would help both to restore the battered prestige of Western authority and to encourage local people to withhold support from those who had collaborated with the Japanese occupation.[57] Having failed to defend their colonial territories adequately against the Japanese, the colonial authorities grasped at every opportunity both to demonstrate that they had recovered their authority and to show that they understood the role of the state in prosecuting those who had vexed society. By the time the court assembled to judge the Kalagon events, however, the immediate political urgency to prosecute Japanese war crimes had diminished. Civilian rule had been restored and a rapid transition to Burmese independence, if not assured, was already likely. Moreover, the Muslim identity of the Kalagon victims made them less effective as a propaganda tool in a colony where religious tensions were strong and in which the Buddhist majority often regarded Muslims as a fifth column for British and Indian interests.[58] Four of the next five trials held immediately after the Kalagon trial, moreover, prosecuted crimes against Allied prisoners of war, suggesting that the British regarded the Kalagon case as providing

---

A. Ryan, *Yamashita's Ghost: War Crimes, MacArthur's Justice, and Command Accountability* (Lawrence, KS: University Press of Kansas, 2012).

[56] See Yuma Totani, *The Tokyo War Crimes Trials: The Pursuit of Justice in the Wake of World War Two*, (Cambridge, MA.: Harvard University Asia Center, 2008), 167–168, 186; Neil Boister and Robert Cryer, *The Tokyo International Military Tribunal: A Reappraisal*, (New York, NY: Oxford University Press, 2008), 56. The judgment of the IMTFE also specified massacres at: Shanywa, Tharrawaddy, Ongun and Ebaing in Burma between May and July 1945.

[57] See for instance BOR, IOR/M/4/3043: Japanese War criminals – miscellaneous, SACSEA to ALFSEA 13 March 1946.

[58] On colonial era tensions between Muslims and the Buddhist majority, see Michael Adas, *The Burma Delta: economic development and social change on an Asian rice frontier, 1852–1941* (Madison, WI: University of Wisconsin Press, 2011), 206–207.

some legitimacy for a focus on cases involving their own people. The demonstration effect of the trials in Burma was further diminished by the fact that they were held in just two centers. By contrast, British authorities in Malaya held trials as far as possible in the locations where the offenses had been committed, setting up makeshift courtrooms in small towns such as Raub and Teluk Anson and larger centers such as Taiping, Ipoh and Kota Bahru. Although this practice certainly had some symbolic intent—trying the suspects in the place where they had committed their crimes—it also had the more prosaic value of removing the need for witnesses to be paid to travel to another center to provide evidence. The decision to hold trials in Burma in only two locations was probably a consequence of the difficulty of obtaining courtroom space in the war-ravaged country, as well as the high degree of insecurity outside the major centers. In these circumstances, witnesses were brought to the trial centers to provide testimony.

Altogether British authorities in Burma conducted 40 war crimes trials indicting 136 former members of the Japanese armed forces (Map 6.3). Six trials were held in the northern town of Maymyo (a former British hill station above Mandalay, today known as Pyin U Lwin), the remainder in Rangoon. Given the intensity of the war in Burma, the total number of defendants was a relatively small proportion of the 920 Japanese prosecuted in 360 British trials in Asia.[59] The count of 439 suspects awaiting investigation in Rangoon Jail in December 1946 was also low by SEAC standards.[60] Fourteen defendants were acquitted. Of those found guilty, 38 were sentenced to death, though 13 of these sentences were commuted to prison terms and one was not carried out because the convicted man escaped. The remainder of the defendants were sentenced to prison terms ranging from one month to life. All sentences were subject to confirmation by the commanding officer, who took legal advice on the quality of the proceedings and considered any mitigating circumstances that

---

[59] Piccigallo, *The Japanese on trial*, 120. The precise number of trials, defendants and courts is surprisingly difficult to determine, partly because of uncertainties in the record, partly because of anomalous cases such as defendants who were tried twice on different or the same charges.
[60] NAM Accession no. 29, file 150 D(EA) 47, 'Japanese Surrendered Personnel and Prisoners of War visited between 30 November and 9 December 1946 by Mr. H. Frei, delegate of the International Committee of the Red Cross in India.'

THE BURMA TRIALS OF JAPANESE WAR CRIMINALS, 1946–1947 137

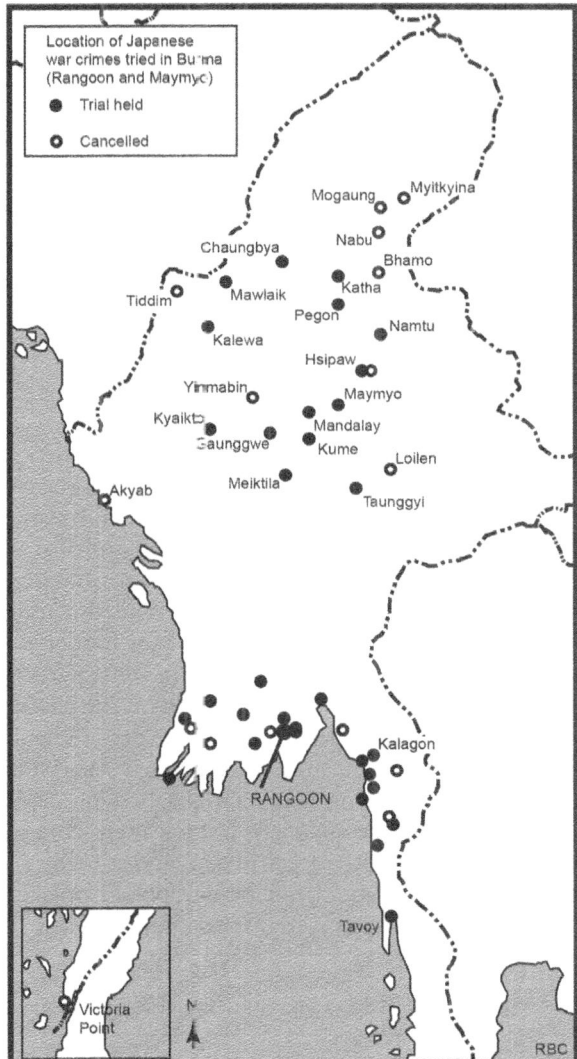

Map 6.3 Location of atrocities prosecuted or planned for prosecution in war crimes trials in Burma (Compiled from TNA LONDON, WO sources. All trials took place in Rangoon or Maymyo)

might have been identified. Three sentences were not confirmed during this process; in effect, though not in law, these men were acquitted.

With the exception of the trial of Yamawaki Hifumi in August–September 1947 for crimes against Indian prisoners of war,[61] the remaining trials involved accusations of atrocities against local residents. Many of these trials focused on the bad treatment of residents of Burma who had been detained by the Kempeitai on suspicion of sabotage, espionage or other forms of disloyalty. The largest trial arraigned 18 Kempeitai defendants in Rangoon from 11 August to 4 September 1947 on charges of murdering Burmese civilians in Moulmein jail.[62] A smaller number of trials focused on atrocities committed, like the Kalagon killings, in the context of counter-insurgency. Most such trials, however, were of just a few Japanese soldiers—from one to four—with a correspondingly small number of victims.

In the early months of 1946, the trial program proceeded in a leisurely fashion. There was little overlap between trials and sometimes weeks passed without any trial being in session. In early 1947, however, the British Prime Minister Clement Attlee and the Burmese nationalist leader U Nu reached a firm agreement that Burma would become independent in the short term.[63] As plans developed for the transfer, British trial authorities increased the pace of prosecutions, with as many as four trials being held concurrently. Although there was a perception in some parts of the Allied trial system that sentences became more lenient with the passage of time,[64] there does not seem to be any such slackening off in the Burma case. Rather, the looming date for Burmese independence galvanized the war crimes teams into action, making sure that the best prepared and most notorious cases were brought to trial. The last few men sentenced to death were transported to Outram Road jail in Singapore to be hanged, presumably because procedures could not be completed quickly enough in Rangoon. Some 19 planned trials were cancelled, apparently because they

---

[61] TNA LONDON, WO 235/948, Trial of Yamawaki Hifumi, Rangoon, August–September 1947.
[62] TNA LONDON WO 235/1064, Trial of Kume Matao and seventeen others, Rangoon, August–September 1947. See also Synopsis of British cases, UNWCC Archive, PURL: https://www.legal-tools.org/doc/4de1f0/ (last access).
[63] Richard Butwell, *U Nu of Burma* (Stanford: Stanford University Press, 1963), 94.
[64] TNA LONDON, DO 35/2937, Creech Jones to Shinwell, 31 August 1949 1949.

Table 6.1 Span and intensity of the British trial program in Burma

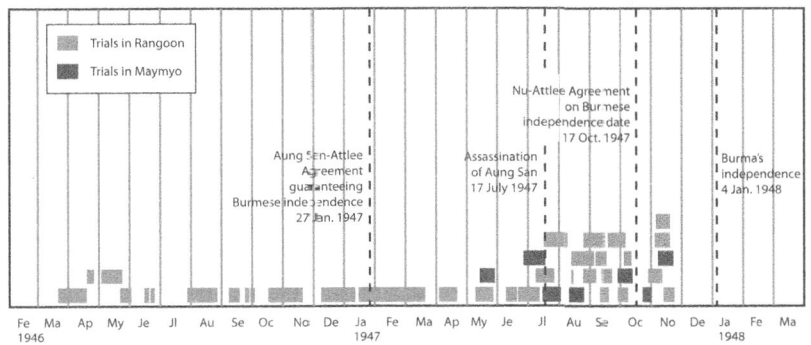

Calculated from trial data in TNA LONDON, WO 235

could not be completed before the handover to independent Burma on 4 January 1948 (Table 6.1).

The intensity of this late effort to bring trials to completion is hard to reconcile with the imperatives of re-establishing colonialism. It suggests more than anything else a determination on the part of the war crimes prosecutors to complete their job, however irrelevant it may have been to the immediate political circumstances. It is possible that the prosecutors had in mind a metropolitan audience which would have been displeased to see Burma achieving independence so soon after the allegedly puppet independence that Japan had bestowed upon it. But for the British public the political developments in Burma were overshadowed by the much more dramatic transition to independence in India that had occurred in August 1947 and it is unlikely that British policy-makers paid significant attention to domestic public opinion. If there was a broader political consideration at work, it is likely to have been a desire to taint Japan with the memory of war crimes in order to hinder Japan's postwar return to the Burmese economy. In the 1930s, Japan's economic penetration of Burma had become a significant threat to British interests,[65] and the British authorities after the war were keen to place limits on Japan's return. In particular, they ruled that all

---

[65] Thanyarat Apiwong and Yoshihiro Bamba, 'The Role of the Japanese in Myanmar: Economic relations between Japan and Myanmar in historical perspective,' *Shiga University Bulletin of the Faculty of Education Humanities and Social Sciences* [滋賀大学教育学部紀要 人文科学・社会科学], 59 (2009): 9–23.

Table 6.2 Verdicts and sentences by month, 1946–1947

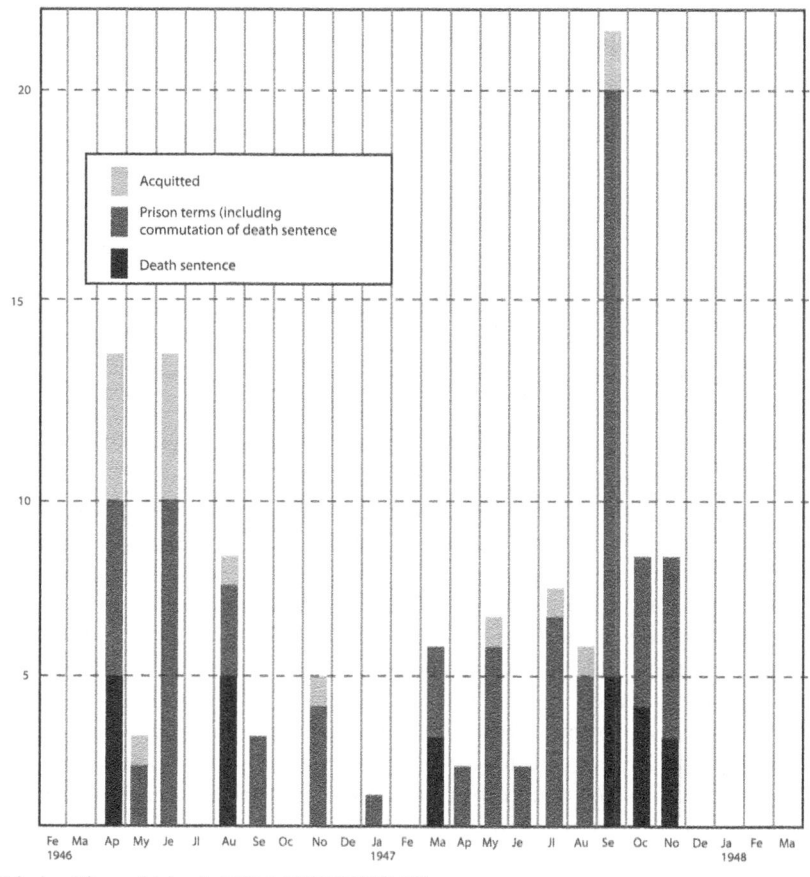

Calculated from trial data in TNA LONDON WO 235

Japanese should be repatriated from Burma, regardless of their former residential status (Table 6.2).[66]

The question of what would happen to convicted war criminals after sentencing had been raised within SEAC as early as February 1946. The British War Office expressed the view that war criminals would normally

---

[66] See discussion in NAM Accession no. 167 file 45HSB47; NAM Accession no. 39 file 32FAD(s)47 Responsibility for Japanese deserters and other Japanese nationals

serve their sentences in the country where they were convicted, especially if they had committed their crimes against the people of that country.[67] In February 1947, the judge advocate general in London determined that, upon conviction, war criminals would cease to be members of the Japanese armed forces and instead would be considered civil subjects of the prison regulations of the country where they had been tried.[68] With the cessation of war crimes trials in Burma in November 1947, this ruling left some 85 Japanese in Rangoon jail as subjects of the colonial Government of Burma which was now scheduled to surrender power to an independent Burma in January 1948. The British military authorities immediately warned London that they doubted the Burma government would accept this responsibility.[69] In September 1947 the governor of Burma pleaded lack of prison space as grounds for suggesting the transfer of convicted war criminals to Singapore which, he noted, had already received prisoners from other jurisdictions. But other correspondence suggested a political reason: the new authorities feared that the prospects for good relations with Japan would be hampered if independent Burma continued to detain Japanese war criminals. There was a strong likelihood, some British officials believed, that the convicted criminals would be released immediately by the newly independent government.[70] British officials then approached the American occupation authorities in Japan with the suggestion that Japanese war criminals convicted in Burma should be transferred to Japan for incarceration prior to the planned independence of Burma on 4 January 1948. The Americans, however, rejected this suggestion out of hand.[71] An increasingly frantic exchange of correspondence between British officials ensued, until it was agreed that the 57 war criminals convicted of crimes against Burmese could remain in Rangoon jail, while the remaining 28 were transferred into the cramped prison system of British Malaya.[72]

---

[67] BOR, IOR/M/4/3038, WO to ALFSEA 4 February 1946, 165.
[68] BOR, IOR/M/4/3038, Judge Advocate General, London, 'Treatment of Japanese War Crimes Convicts,' 11 February 1947, 80.
[69] BOR, IOR/M/4/3038, SEALF to WO 15 March 1947, 75.
[70] BOR, IOR/M/4/3038, Governor of Burma to Secretary of State for Burma, 20 September 1947, 63; BOR, IOR/M/4/3038, W. L. to Morley 6 October 1947, 59; BOR, IOR/M/4/3038, D.W. Brampton (PA/VAG) to WO 21 November 1947, 34.
[71] BOR, IOR/M/4/3038, FARELF to WO 3 November 1947, 49.
[72] See the extensive correspondence in BOR, IOR/M/4/3038 and NAM Accession no. 39 file 32FAD(s)47 Responsibility for Japanese deserters and other Japanese nationals, Govt of Burma, Judicial Dept, Memorandum, 'Japanese War Crime Convicts sentences to imprisonment' 31 December 1947.

The program of war crimes trials which followed the Second World War in Asia was intended to combine an appetite for vengeance on the part of the victorious Allies with principles of justice and aspirations for promoting democracy. The trials, however, took place in an era of strong and contested national and ideological identities. The trials of individual perpetrators were bound up with struggles over the future of vast regions of the world. They intersected not only the emerging Cold War struggle between communism and capitalism, but also with the struggle over the future of empire, especially in the Asian regions that had been conquered or touched by Japan. When the wartime allies brought Japanese war criminals to trial, they intended primarily to punish the perpetrators of grievous atrocities against Asians and Westerners. In addition, however, they hoped to bring other shades into the dock: Japan itself and its possible ambitions to restore its position in the region and all those locals whose anti-Westernism had led them to work with Japan. Yet the trials were a double-edged sword for the colonial powers. There was little real political credit to be had in Southeast Asia from the considerable expense of prosecuting Japanese. The cool selective dispensation of immunity from prosecution for transparently political reasons, too, undermined the purported universality of the trials process, even though it worked in favor of local elites. In the end, the political purpose of the trials was limited.

CHAPTER 7

Colonization and Postcolonial Justice: US and Philippine War Crimes Trials in Manila After the Second World War

Wolfgang Form

With the recognition by the USA of the independence of the Philippines on 4 July 1946,[1] the new government was confronted with the task of bringing the Japanese perpetrators of war crimes to justice. In view of the fact that the war had claimed the lives of more than a million civilians, postwar justice was a political endeavour of the utmost seriousness. Although Japanese propaganda had portrayed the occupation as a step towards decolonization, the reality had been one of mass murder, rape and destruction by the Japanese military. Among their crimes was the Manila

---

[1] However, in 1962, "'the Establishment of the Philippine Republic by the Revolutionary Government under General Emilio Aguinaldo' of June 12, 1898, was declared a national holiday. See http://www.bibingka.com/phg/documents/jun12.htm (last accessed 1 October 2014).

W. Form (✉)
Marburg University, Marburg, Germany

© The Author(s) 2016
K. von Lingen (ed.), *War Crimes Trials in the Wake of Decolonization and Cold War in Asia, 1945–1956*,
DOI 10.1007/978-3-319-42987-8_7

Massacre of February 1945, in which the Japanese turned the capital city into a veritable 'killing field' in which over 14,000 civilians perished.[2]

AMERICAN TRIALS

The American prosecution of Japanese war crimes in the Philippines was just the latest step in the erection of a global network of prosecution which spanned the course of several years.[3] The earliest steps were taken at meetings in London in 1941 and 1942 in which governments-in-exile and the 'Big Three' allied states agreed that war crimes committed by their enemies would not go unpunished. Additionally, the entrance of the USA into the war had a significant influence on international transitional justice endeavours. In October 1943, the Moscow Declaration marked the agreement of the Big Three on the territorial principle with regard to the prosecution of war crimes.[4] At the same time, the United Nations War Crimes Commission (UNWCC) was established to investigate war crimes around the world. Finally, in 1945, the Yalta and Potsdam Conferences laid the foundation for the postwar organization of both Europe and Asia.

Shortly after the end of military operations by US and Philippine forces, intensive preparations began for the trials of war criminals. The Military Commissions (MC) established in the Philippines in 1944 by Admiral Nimitz served as a reference.[5] 'The fundamental principle of the plan is that the prosecution of Japanese war criminals should be concentrated

---

[2] See R. Connaughton, J. Pimlott and D. Anderson, *The Battle for Manila* (London: Bloomsbury Publishing, 1995).

[3] For war crimes in general see Excerpts of the Report by the Commission on the responsibility of the Authors of war (1919), NA (National Archives Records Administration) RG (Record Group) 331, SCAP 1855 – folder 115.

[4] Moscow Declaration: 'Accordingly the aforesaid three Allied Powers, speaking in the interests of the 32 United Nations, hereby solemnly declare and give full warning of their declaration as follows: At the time of the granting of any armistice to any Government which may be set up in Germany, those German officers and men and members of the Nazi party who have been responsible for or have taken a consenting part in the [...] atrocities, massacres and executions will be sent back to the countries in which their abominable deeds were done in order that they may be judged and punished according to the laws of these liberated countries and of the Free Governments which will be erected therein.' See http://www.google.de/url?sa=t&rct=j&q=&esrc=s&source=web&cd=2&ved=0CC0QFjAB&url=http%3A%2F%2Fwww.un.org%2Fen%2Fga%2Fpresident%2F65%2Fissues%2Fmoscow_declaration_en.pdf&ei=EXlkVZX_KO3B7AaOsoL4CQ&usg=AFQjCNHBiyAz1EJaOGqrYHhX0Rykkqtf1Q&bvm=bv.93990622,d.ZGU.

[5] For example the case of Samuel T. Shinohara. NA film series C-72, reel 2, picture no 505 ff.

in the hands of the Supreme Allied Commander [...]. Such centralization [...] would assure the success of the prosecutions of Japanese war criminals by securing prompt prosecution [...], and the application of the established precedents of military command, military law, and international criminal law."[6] Cooperation with both domestic and international war crimes agencies, such as the UNWCC and the Philippine National War Crimes Office, was expressly envisaged.[7] On 9 June 1945 the War Crimes Investigating Detachment was established in Manila. This office was charged with advising the SCAP (Supreme Commander for the Allied Powers) and supervising the prosecution of war criminals.[8] The function of the section was to: (1) investigate war crimes, (2) collect and record evidence pertaining thereto, (3) prepare all such cases of alleged war crimes to be tried, (4) establish and maintain a central registry of war criminals and suspects, (5) make recommendations pertaining to their apprehension and trial and (6) to recommend establishing military commissions for the trial of Japanese (and other) war criminals accused of violation of the laws or customs of war (including rules and procedures).[9]

One of the first steps was to find out the locations of Japanese prisoner of war (POW) camps and create lists of potential war criminals in the Philippines. Early investigations were carried out in very confused circumstances. Units of the Japanese Army and Navy were still in the process of demobilization, and 'normal' channels for gathering information had to be reorganized after the end of the war. In mid-September 1945, President Truman ordered that a legal framework for sentencing Japanese war criminals should be created in line with the regulations in Europe.[10] At the same time, a preliminary conference was held on 14 September 1945 in Manila, during which a group of military experts discussed ongoing plans for prosecuting war atrocities in the Asia Pacific region. The chair, Major General Marshall, stated that 'the first thing to do is to bring

---

[6] NA RG 331, SCAP 2003 – folder War Crimes Regulation, Memo for Col. Carter 3 September 1945.
[7] Ibid., Memo for Supreme Allied Commander (SAC) 3 September 1945.
[8] Trials of "B" and "C" war criminals prepared in the Legal Section, General Headquarters, Supreme Commander for the Allied Powers, NA RG 331, SCAP 3676 – folder Class B and C War Criminals, 42–3.
[9] Ibid.
[10] NA RG 331, SCAP 2003 – folder War Crimes Regulations, top secret memo 16 September 1945.

to justice those war criminals who are on the higher levels.'[11] General Marshall wanted the first trial to be that of Yamashita.[12] 'In his case the charges should indicate that he failed to exercise proper control over his troops; that he permitted the sacking of Manila [...].'[13]

The 'Regulation Governing Trials of War Criminals' of 24 September 1945 provided the foundation for the legal prosecution of Japanese war crimes by the US military in the Pacific.[14] MCs were established as judicial bodies subordinate to the commander-in-chief.[15] Until 1945 they were a little-used measure for prosecuting crimes outside of regular court-martials by the American military prosecutors (Judge Advocate General— JAG), who had no jurisdiction over war crimes committed by the enemy. It was not a regular court and not part of the judicial system, although organized by it.[16] Accordingly, different judicial regulations would have to be applied on a case-by-case basis.

---

[11] NA RG 331, SCAP 155 – folder War Crimes Conferences, Report of the preliminary War Crimes Conference September 14, 1945, Manila, 3.

[12] Frank A. Reel, *The Case of General Yamashita* (Chicago: The University of Chicago Press, 1949).

[13] Ibid.

[14] Ordinance September 24, 1945. This regulation and later amendments to it are regularly enclosed with case documents. See, for example, the case from 20 December 1945. NA RG 331, SCAP 1552. See also UNWCC Misc.-Series no. 41, 19 August 1946; NA RG 153, Entry 145/230 – folder 150-14.

[15] Military commissions were unknown prior to the US–Mexican War (1846–1948) and were not mentioned in the article of war prior the 1916 revision. See Erika Myers, 'Conquering Peace: Military Commissions as a Lawfare Strategy in the Mexican War,' *American Journal of Criminal Law* 32,2: 201–40. United States Army and Navy Manual on War Crimes; NA RG 153, Entry 135/82. Thomas C. Marmon, Joseph C. Cooper and William P. Goodman, Military Commissions (Charlottesville, VA: The Judge Advocate General's School, 1953); William Winthrop, *Military Law and Precedents* (Washington, DC: Government Printing Office, 1920): 832–3. 'Military commissions derive their authority from Articles I and II of the Constitution. Article I, Section 8, grants to Congress the powers: To provide for the common defence (clause 1) and to define and punish piracies on the high seas, and offenses against the Law of Nations; To declare War, grant letters of Marque and Reprisal, and make Rules concerning Captures on Land and Water; To raise and support Armies; To provide and maintain a Navy; To make Rules for the Government and Regulation of the land and naval Forces. (clauses 10-14). Article II confers on the President the executive Power. (Section 1) and makes him the Commander in Chief of the Army and Navy. (Section 2).' American Bar Association Talks Force on Terrorism and the Law Report and Recommendation on Military Commission, 4 January 2002.

[16] Ex Parte Vallandigham, U.S. Supreme Court Volume 68 (1863): 243.

Theoretically, the MC would be staffed by multinational personnel if the victims were citizens of other Allied nations.[17] The MCs had jurisdiction over all persons, units and organizations in all areas occupied by US forces in the Pacific. They were responsible for the prosecution of a wide variety of crimes: the murder, torture or ill-treatment of POWs, hostages and civilians on land and on the high seas; forced labor; plunder and wanton destruction of inhabited areas; waging a war of aggression; murder, extermination, enslavement, deportation or other inhumane acts committed against any civilian population, or persecution on political, racial, national or religious grounds; and conspiracy or planning to commit any of the aforementioned offenses, irrespective of local laws. 'Leaders, organizers, instigators, accessories participating in the formulation or execution of any such common plan or conspiracy will be held responsible for all acts performed by any person in execution of that plan or conspiracy.'[18]

The possibilities for criminal prosecution were therefore manifold. The wide mandate of the MCs recalled the Control Council Law Number 10, which was enacted in the four zones of occupation in Germany on 20 December 1945. However, there was one essential difference: the regulation of 24 September made no distinction between war crimes, crimes against humanity and crimes of aggression (including conspiracy). As a result, the MCs had wider jurisdiction than their counterparts in Europe which could prosecute Nazi crimes[19] but not crimes against humanity or crimes

---

[17] This was envisaged by the other Allies. However, the USA remained an exception. Regarding this see as one of the few cases the trial of Soemu Toyoda in Toyko on 29 October 1948; NA Mikrofilm M-1729. The Netherlands, Australia and Great Britain, in contrast, invited judges of other Allies to join their tribunals. See, for example, 'Great Britain in Kuala Lumpur' (26 August 1946), S.B. Sahabya, Australien; The National Archive Kew, London (TNA), RG WO 235/888. Dutch East India in Batavia (today Jakarta – 6 September 1946), J. F. Hartmann, Great Britain; NIOD (Nederlands Instituut voor Oorlogsdocumentatie), Amsterdam Collection 400, Inventar 381 – Kenichi Sone. Australia in Rabaul (17 June 1946), Lee Chee Yoong, China; Australian National Archive Canberra (NAC), RG A-471/81033.

[18] Section 5 Ordinance 24 September 1945 See, for example, the case from 20 December 1945. NA RG 331, SCAP 1552. See also United Nations War Crimes Commission (UNWCC) Misc.-Series no. 41, 19 August 1946; NA RG 153, Entry 145/230 – folder 150-14.

[19] See United States Law and practice concerning trials of war criminals by Military Commissions, Military Government Courts and Military Tribunals. Law Reports of Trials of War Criminals. Selected and prepared by the United Nations War Crimes Commission, vol. III (London: Her Majesty's Stationary Office, 1948): 103–5.

of aggression.[20] The fundamental problem lay in the different definitions of war crimes in Europe and the Asia Pacific region. In Europe, only violations of the laws or customs of war were regularly on the docket. Unlike in the Asia Pacific area, there was no formulation regarding other criminal offenses.[21]

At the beginning of December 1945, General MacArthur[22] restructured the guidelines and reduced the crimes into three clear categories: aggressive warfare, violations of the laws or customs of war and atrocities against civilians. The temporal jurisdiction of the MC did not follow a strict framework: 'The offense need not have been committed after a particular date to render the responsible party or parties subject to arrest, but in general should have been committed since or in the period immediately preceding the Mukden incident of September 18, 1931.'[23] In this instance, the regulations also differed from those in Europe, which were strictly limited to the period of declared warfare with the Western Allies (from September 1939 and from the German declaration of war on the USA on 11 December 1941).

Investigations were conducted by the JAG Corps of the US military. As one might imagine, the inclusion of the war crimes trial program vastly increased the JAG workload. As a result, extra personnel had to be recruited for the War Crimes Sub-Section, which had been established in November 1945.[24] Both prosecution and defense lawyers appointed by the JAG required additional legal training, since most had no experience in this field. Extant documents from the Philippines demonstrate that

---

[20] Here it is exclusively about the activities of the MC and not the so-called Nuremberg Military Tribunals (NMT), which were not MCs and were established on the legal basis of Control Council Law No. 10. See Kim C. Priemel and Alexa Stiller (eds.), *Reassessing the Nuremberg Military Tribunals: Transitional Justice, Trial Narratives, and Historiography* (New York, NY: Berghahn Books, 2012). Trials of War Criminals before the Nuremberg Military Tribunals, vol. 1–15, (Washington, DC: U.S. Government Printing Office, 1949).

[21] This does not go into any further detail regarding the American regulations in China. See Regulations Governing the Trial of War Criminals in the China Theatre, issued by Command of Lieut. General Wedemeyer on 21 January 1947. UNWCC Misc-Series no. 51; NA RG 153, Entry 145/229 – folder 150-14.

[22] Douglas MacArthur (26 January 1880–5 April 1964) was an American five-star general and Field Marshal of the Philippine Army.

[23] Article I, para. 2, no. 2, Regulations Governing the Trials of Accused War Criminals 5 December 1945 (Regulation December 1945).

[24] NA RG 331, SCAP 2002 – folder military commission, Memo from Col. Ashton M. Haynes, 21 November 1945: 1.

this training took place.[25] For example: 'War Crimes Office Indoctrination Course Interrogation of Witnesses and Suspects,' 'Outlines of Investigation Methods and Techniques'[26] and 'Suggestions to Investigators of War Crimes.'

The USA approached the crimes before the MCs in the Philippines (and elsewhere in the Pacific) differently than in Europe. What set the two areas of jurisdiction apart? In the case of the Philippines the crimes had occurred on the territory of what had technically been an American colony. By contrast, crimes in Europe had taken place on Allied or German territory. The principle was also valid for other regions such as Guam which today remains an unincorporated territory of the USA.[27]

Despite all of the differences between Europe and the Asia Pacific region, officials in the Pacific kept abreast of legal developments in the West and tried to achieve a certain legal parity.[28] 'The peoples of the United Nations are unlikely to see or understand any valid reason why the militarists of Japan should be treated any more leniently than those of Germany.'[29] In particular, Robert Jackson was an advocate of a prosecution strategy based on war of aggression.[30] A memo from 3 September 1945 confirms this: 'We fear that published limitations of the Far East prosecutions to offenses strictly definable as war crimes, not expressly inclusive of the planning or preparation for war, waging of aggressive war, persecution of racial or national minorities, etc., would lead many to conclude that a "soft" policy is to be applied to Japan.'[31] It appears likely, as we will see, that the Americans would take this approach as a guideline for the war crimes trials program in the Asia Pacific region.

---

[25] Ibid., Memos from Comdr. George H. Brereton – probably end of 1945.
[26] Ibid.
[27] See Werner Gruhl, *Imperial Japan's World War Two, 1931–1945* (New Brunswick: Transaction Publishers, 2007), 101–5.
[28] The political structures in liberated Japan were, in comparison to Germany, different. The establishment of a control council was considered unimportant as the Allies were represented by Supreme Commander for the Allied Powers; NA RG 331, SCAP 2003, See Memo: Draft plan for trial of war criminals in the Far East (1 September 1945), 1.
[29] NA RG 331, SCAP 2003 – folder War Crimes Regulation, Memo to Col. Carpenter, subject: Definition of war crimes, 3 September 1945, 5.
[30] Robert Houghwout Jackson was United States Solicitor General (1938–40), United States Attorney General (1940–41) and an associate justice of the United States Supreme Court (1941–54). He was also the chief United States prosecutor at the Nuremberg Trials.
[31] NA RG 331, SCAP 2003 – folder War Crimes Regulation, Memo to Col. Carpenter, subject: Definition of war crimes, 3 September 1945, 5.

Beyond that the JAG seemed doubtful about whether they would really need the criminal offense of 'crimes against humanity.' It was assumed that crimes which had been committed during the war would be interpreted simply as war crimes ('strictly known as war crimes'[32]). The fact that Japan did not commit crimes against its own civilians on a scale similar to that of the Germans may have played a role. However, the regulations of 24 September and 5 December 1945 took this into account: class C cases applied to violence against 'any civilian population.'

For this reason, cases involving the so-called 'comfort women system' (organized forced prostitution by the Japanese army) would theoretically have been open to prosecution.[33] There is proof of such crimes in the Philippines[34]: 'The appalling acts of sexual violence perpetrated by the Japanese army in Shanxi Province in North China and the Philippines during the last phase of the war can be regarded as representative of this pattern. There [...] confined, and repeatedly raped women. Japanese troops frequently forced village leaders to provide them with women. In other words, sexual violence against women at comfort stations took place].'[35] Regardless, no American MC in Manila (or any Philippine court) initiated proceedings regarding forced prostitution. There is one documented prosecution of forced prostitution in Guam, that of Samuel T. Shinohara from 27 August 1945.[36] He was initially sentenced to death, but the confirming officer reduced the sentence to 15 years hard labor. However, the defendant was not a Japanese citizen and his offense classified as one of collaboration, not war crimes.[37] Shinohara, a citizen of Guam, was accused of treason, theft, bodily harm and forced

---

[32] NA RG 331, SCAP 2003, Memo: Draft plan for trial of war criminals in the Far East (1 September 1945), 2.

[33] See Hirofumi Hayashi, 'The Japanese military "comfort women" issue and the San Francisco System,' in: Kimie Hara (ed.), *The San Francisco System and its Legacies. Continuation, Transformation and Historical Reconciliation in the Asia-Pacific* (Florence, KY: Routledge, 2015), 162–82 (163–5).

[34] Maria Rosa Henson, *Comfort Women. A Filipina's Story and Slavery under the Japanese Military* (Manila: Rowman & Littlefield Publishers, 1999).

[35] Ibid., 173.

[36] NA film series C-72, reel 2 (picture no. 505 ff).

[37] There were MC cases due to war crimes in Guam after the Second World War. The report by the Commission on War Crimes for Guam in Section 2. NA RG 59, Entry ZZ 1005/3 – folder 8 gives an introductory description of which crimes had occurred on the islands. See also Jeanie M. Welch, 'Without a Hangman, Without a Rope: Navy War Crimes Trials After World War II,' *International Journal of Naval History* 1, 1 (April 2002).

prostitution.[38] Although a failure to prosecute forced prostitution is evident, the reasons for this have not been satisfactorily clarified.

The preceding outline of the legal basis for the trials gives only a formal indication of the legal practice. What kinds of crimes did the prosecuting authorities actually bring before the courts? The MCs were responsible for so-called 'B' and 'C' war crimes trials. Under class B one finds conventional war crimes (violation of the laws or customs of war). In contrast, class C crimes fell under the area of crimes against humanity, which were not explicitly mentioned as such in the regulations from 24 September to 5 December 1945.[39]

The Charges

An analysis of the charges shows that the full range of potential charges was not applied when it came to the classification of crimes. The following set of charges is typical: 'Tomoyuki Yamashita, General Imperial Japanese Army, between 9 October 1944 and 2 September 1945, at Manila and at other places in the Philippine Islands, while commander of armed forces of Japan **at war with the United States of America and its allies**, unlawfully disregarded and failed to discharge his duty as commander to control the operations of the members of his command, permitting them to commit brutal atrocities and other high crimes against people of the United States and of its allies and dependencies, particularly the Philippines, and he, General Tomoyuki Yamashita, **thereby violated the laws of war**.'[40]

In the trial of Yamashita, one of the most important to take place at the tribunal in Manila,[41] the crimes occurred during the period after the

---

[38] 'Taking a female for the purpose of prostitution. Specification 1: In that Samuel T. Shinohara, an inhabitant and resident of Guam, and subject to the Military Government thereof, did, within the Island of Guam, in and about the month of February 1942, unlawfully take one Alfonsina Flores, a female person, for the purpose of prostitution, procuring her consent thereto by misrepresentation; the United States during said period being at war with Japan. Specification 2: In that Sameal T. Shinohara [...] in or about the month of February 1942, unlawfully take one Nocholasa P. Mendiola, a female person against her will and without her consent, for the purpose of prostitution; the United States during said period at war with Japan.' NA RG 59, Entry ZZ 1005/3 – folder 8.

[39] See Barak Kushner, *Men to Devils, Devils to Men: Japanese War Crimes and Chinese Justice* (Boston: Harvard University Press, 2015), 7.

[40] UNWCC Law reports vol. IV, 1–95; NA microfilm M-1727, roll 29-34.

[41] Memo by A. Frank Reel and Courtney Whitney. See Military Legal Resources (Library of Congress): http://www.loc.gov/rr/frd/Military_Law/pdf/Yamashita.pdf (last accessed 21 October 2014).

USA declared war on Japan. This was often the case in indictments. In a sample consisting of more than 75 % of all the MC trials held in the Philippines, none involved war crimes occurred before the attack on Pearl Harbor.[42] MC cases—not just in the Philippines—can be divided into six main groups: command responsibility trials; POW camp trials; atrocities against airmen atrocities cases; trials of the Japanese military police, the Kempeitai; violation of the right to a fair trial; and atrocities against the civilian population (murder, ill-treatment, rape etc.).[43]

The US cases in Manila dealt with crimes against POWs and the civilian population. An internal overview shows that in addition to more than 35,000 POWs, there were more than 90,000 civilian victims of war crimes.[44] The majority of them were murdered, tortured, starved and neglected or died as a result of other mistreatment.[45] By May 1946, the JAG had investigated more than 7600 Japanese nationals being held prisoner in the Philippines.[46] There were more cases with civilian victims (about 57 %), than non-civilians, which makes sense in the case of the Philippines as the Japanese occupation's violence did not just manifest itself in the treatment of POWs but also in the day-to-day life of non-combatants. This was in complete contrast to Japan, where during the war few civilians from enemy states lived.

More than one-third of the Japanese defendants were low and mid-ranking officers (lieutenant to major). In many cases they were in the command interface between the high command and the lower ranks. About a quarter of the war criminals were amongst the lower ranks (non-commissioned officers) and about as many were rank-and-file. US war crimes trials policy in the Philippines was clearly aimed at mid-level commanders who were accused of command responsibility[47] rather

---

[42] Database ICWC, Marburg.

[43] NA RG 331, SCAP 3676 – folder Class B and C War Criminals (243 pages), See Trials of "B" and "C" war criminals prepared in the Legal Section, General Headquarters, Supreme Commander for the Allied Powers. Database ICWC, Marburg.

[44] NA RG 331, SCAP 2004 – folder Filipinos died, Handwritten list 'War Crimes Victims' (without date, probably mid 1946).

[45] Ibid., 2 July 1946.

[46] NA RG 331, SCAP 2005 – folder Monthly Summation, 8 May 1946, 11.

[47] See memo Responsibility Military Commanders and Staff for War Crimes Committed by Subordinates November 20, 1945, NA RG 331, SCAP 1853 – folder 2-B. See Hans Kelsen, 'Collective and Individual Responsibility in International Law with Particular Regard to the Punishment of War Criminals,' *California Law Review* 31 (1943), 530–571. Georg Schwarzenberger, 'War Crimes and the problem of an international criminal court,' *Czechoslovak Yearbook of International Law* (1942), 67–88.

than direct perpetrators.[48] In the monthly reports, many such cases were described. For example: 'Kiyoshi Nishikawa [...] The accused war charged with having violated the law of war, by wrongfully and unlawfully permitting members of his command to kill, attempt to kill or brutally mistreat or torture about 16 Filipino civilians during 1943.'[49] These often included cases against former members of the Kempeitai.[50]

Cases involving POWs were mainly related to the camps O'Donnell, Cabanatuan, Davao, Bilibid Hospital and Nichols Field.[51] Two group of war criminals can be discerned: (1) camp guard and/or minor ranks and (2) commanding ranks from sergeant to generals/admirals. The specifics of the first group were direct participation. A typical example was the trial of Kin Ryu Rin, a civilian guard at Cabanatuan POW camp No. 1 (Luzon, Philippines). He was accused of shooting and killing an American POW while on duty as a tower guard. The accused testified that the POW was trying to escape when shot, but witnesses gave evidence that the victim was working in a garden at the time he was shot. Kin Ryu Rin was sentenced to death.[52] Examples from the second group are General Yamashita, Lieutenant General Takeshi Kono[53] and General Lieutenant Homma.[54] But lower officers' ranks could also be tried for command responsibility. Major Saito, commander of the so-called 'Tiger Unit,' was accused of 'wilfully and unlawfully disregard[ing] and fail[ing] to discharge his duties as such commanding officer to control the operations of the members of his command, permitting them to commit brutal atrocities and other high crimes against the people of the United States of America, its allies and

---

[48] Database ICWC, Marburg.
[49] NA RG 331, SCAP 2005, Judgment 3 October 1946 (death by hanging). Monthly Summation No 13 – Statistics and Reports, October 1946, 16.
[50] For example the case of Michinori Nakamura et al. All accused were members of the Kempeitai stationed at Sangking (Celebes) and charged with the murder of American POWs by bayoneting and/or striking them with swords. NA RG 331, SCAP 1580.
[51] NA RG 331, SCAP 1270, History, 1.
[52] NA RG 331, SCAP 1561, judgment 20 April 1946.
[53] NA RG 331, SCAP 1563, judged to death 1 May 1946.
[54] Transcript of the proceeding of the US MC in Manila, Philippine Islands, in the trial of Masaharu Homma on war crimes charges. Commander of Japanese forces in the Philippines from December 1941 to August 1942, Homma was charged with firing on a flag of surrender and bombing Manila after it was declared an open city and with all of the abuses committed by Japanese forces against Allied military and civilian personnel during his period of command. NA RG 153 Entry 177/1-5. See Aubrey Saint Kenworthy, *The Tiger of Malaya: The story of General Tomoyuki Yamashita and "Death March" General Masaharu Homma* (New York, NY: Exposition Press, 1951).

dependencies, particularly the Philippines, and [...] thereby violat[ing] the laws of war.'55 The chain of command was identified in several trials. An MC sentenced Lieutenant General Hikotaro Tajima to death on 1 February 1946.56 One of his subordinates, Mitsuji Tanaka, was prosecuted for 'ordering and participating in killing of four American aviators' (life imprisonment). His subordinates were, in turn, sentenced to long periods of internment.57 The disparity in sentencing between the top to the bottom of the chain of command is significant.

A high number of MCs were concerned with crimes against the civilian population of the Philippines and national minorities (mainly Chinese). In a sample of just under 70 (of about 100) cases there are 40 cases that pertain exclusively to civilian victims. In comparison with other American war crimes trial programs (in the first place Yokohama) this is a notably high number.58 In this instance the colonial status of the Philippines surely played a role. Crimes against civilians were evidently considered an attack on a victim group which was protected under American law.

An exception which has already been mentioned were the victims of forced prostitution ('comfort women'59). They were not the focus of JAG investigations, in contrast to cases of rape during the Japanese occupation. In at least 15 American MCs, Japanese defendants were prosecuted for offenses including rape.60 This finding is also indicated in the Philippine cases (see below). Further trials of incidents of rape took place in the Dutch East Indies,

---

55 NA RG 331, SCAP 1555, judgment 19 January 1946 – death by hanging.
56 Ibid.
57 NA RG 331, SCAP 1560, 7 May 1946.
58 Database ICWC, Marburg.
59 See Sarah C. Soh, *The Comfort Women. Sexual Violence and Postcolonial Memory in Korea and Japan* (Chicago: The University Chicago Press, 2009).
60 (1) UNWCC Law Reports vol. 4, 1–96, 12 December 1945 (Tomoyuki Yamashita). (2) NA RG 331, SCAP1553, 20 December 1945 (Tosimitsu Miyagi et al.). (3) 11 February 1946 (Masaharu Homma), NA RG 153 Entry A1 145/136-144, NA RG 153 Entry A1-177/1-5, NA RG 331, SCAP 1671-1672. (4) NA RG 331, SCAP 1558, 15 March 1946 (Tetsuo Naito); (5) NA RG 331, SCAP 1570, 27 March 1946 (Jiro Mizoguchi et al.); (6) 10 April 1946 (Seiichi Onishi et al.), NA RG 331, SCAP 1559. (7) NA RG 331, SCAP 1562, 3 June 1946 (Miko Taneichi et al.). (8) NA RG 331, SCAP 1564, 1 July 1946 (Tadashi Yoshida et al.). (9) NA RG 331, SCAP 1559, 11 November 1946 (Bunji Kanto et al.). (10) NA RG 331, SCAP 1576, 1 January 1947 (Masakazu Yamaguchi et al.). (11) NA RG 331, SCAP 1579, 2 February 1947 (Naoki Hamasaki). (12) NA RG 331, SCAP 1579, 27 February 1947 (Yasuo Hiroshi et al.). (13) NA RG 331, SCAP 1580, 10 March 1947 (Yokio Ogo et al.). (14) NA RG 331, SCAP 1585, 13 March 1947 (Masami Fujimoto). (15) NA RG 331, SCAP 1585, 4 April 1947 (Hisamitsu Imamura et al.).

in Saigon (Indochina), China and Australia.[61] After 1945 the JAG examined at least another 78 relevant crimes in the Philippines.[62] Not one of them led to prosecution. The reasons included failure to identify the perpetrator,[63] failure to identify the victim,[64] lack of witnesses[65] and insufficient evidence.[66]

In case B-72, for example, preliminary investigations were taken on the basis of a witness statement: 'In this station, we had a pair of twenty-power binoculars. One day I was looking through the binoculars and saw a Filipino woman tied to a tree. She apparently had been stripped and I saw a number of Japanese rape her.'[67] Evidence in addition to this statement could not be found and the file was closed: 'It is recommended that no investigation be made of the [...] case for the following reasons: (1) Only data are statement of 2nd Lt. Anthony Bujinowski that through binoculars, he saw a woman raped by the Japanese. (2) Name of victim unknown. Perpetrators unknown. No data given. (3) Recommend that case be closed. December 8, 1945.'[68] The fact that preliminary investigations were undertaken was remarkable, given how vague the witness statement was. There is a slew of similar cases, which in hindsight raises questions about the motivation for the JAG's activities. To return to the connection to forced prostitution: in cases of organized crimes, inquiries did not always follow by order of the authorities—unlike the case of individual atrocities which happened outside of the 'comfort station' system. In those cases it was obviously enough to have heard of a criminal offense liable to public prosecution. As it is to be assumed that the US investigating authorities had knowledge of the military brothels, one could expect that they would have investigated, on a large scale, those who were operating and organizing the comfort stations.[69]

An initial screening of the American investigation documents on the Philippines (SCAP/JAG) showed only one that led to preliminary proceedings in cases of forced prostitution. Witnesses reported systematic

---

[61] Database ICWC, Marburg. For China: only about 25 % of the cases are accessible. See China collection, ICWC Database Legal Tools (ICC) – folder China.
[62] References of rape as war crimes are to be found at Philippines cases. See NA RG 331, SCAP 993-1134 und 1927–2002.
[63] E.g. NA RG 331, SCAP 1066, Case F-25.
[64] E.g. NA RG 331, SCAP 1065, Case E-3.
[65] E.g. ibid., Case E-8.
[66] E.g. ibid., Case D-86.
[67] NA RG 331, SCAP 1062, Case B-72 Rape of Filipino woman.
[68] Ibid.
[69] Maria Rosa Henson, Comfort Women, see *supra note* 30.

inquiries about prostitutes in Cabadbaran (Mindanao) in September 1944. Five prostitutes known to the police were traced and taken to local barracks. A witness reported: 'Two or three of these girls were badly hurt as the result of sexual abuse. They escaped after a short time, and the incident was reported directly to me by the girls involved.'[70] Despite evidence of the use of force and forced prostitution the proceedings were stopped. For the employees of the Investigating Section, the five women were prostitutes and as a result were not considered victims of force: They 'carried out their trade during the Japanese occupation and later when the Americans liberated the area.'[71] The investigating officers clearly did not consider prostitutes to also have the right to protection. The fact that five women had fled the Japanese barracks was not given any further attention. Their 'immoral way of life' obviously outweighed the violence against them, which in turn led to the perpetrators being considered innocent.

Sentences

An overview shows that the sentences that were handed down in Manila differed greatly from those in other regions where war crimes trials were being held by the USA. From the beginning of their work in the Philippines to September 1946, 65 of 136 accused (47 %) were sentenced to death. By the end of their task, 213 men had been brought before the court.[72] By comparison, the MC in Yokohama sentenced on average 7.5 % of all of the accused to death. The high number of life sentences (over 20 %) issued in Manila is remarkable. In this instance there are also no equivalent findings in the Yokohama trials (the number is almost identical to the number of death sentences at just under 7.5 %). As a result, the number of death sentences in Manila was clearly above the American average worldwide—14 %[73]—or 11 % in the Asia Pacific region. In comparison to other countries in the region, the USA tops the league in this regard: Australia

---

[70] NA RG 331, SCAP 1069, Case K-80. Forced prostitution of five Philippine girls. Testimony of Ernest Edward McClish, Lt. Col., taken at Okmulgee, Oklahoma on 7 June 1945.
[71] NA RG 331, SCAP 1069 – Case K-80, 22 March 1946.
[72] NA RG 331, SCAP 2005 – folder Monthly Summation, 19 April 1946 – Statistics and Reports, 22-3; summary of the results of war crimes trials in the Philippines from the first trial through 20 April 1947. See also Robert R. Piccigallo, *The Japanese on Trial: Allied War Crimes Operations in the East* (Austin, TX: University of Texas Press, 1979), 67.
[73] Database ICWC, Marburg.

Table 7.1 US war crimes trials in the Philippines, September 1945–April 1947

Trials	Convictions	Death sentences	Executed (20 April 1947)
213	195	92	46

Source: NA RG 331, SCAP 2005, Monthly summation no. 19 (April 1946), statistics and reports, 22–3

19 %, the Netherlands 23 %, France 26 % and Great Britain 30 %.[74] The values listed here do not relate to the number of death sentences actually carried out. A slew of sentences were either commuted to prison terms by Commander MacArthur or subject to pardon later. By the end of the American war crimes trials program on the Philippines[75] (April 1947) 46 of 92 death sentences had been carried out (see Table 7.1).

In cases which were not completed before the end of April 1947, the accused appeared in Yokohama, Japan before the MC[76] or were passed on to Philippine authorities. One of the first transports of 59 suspected war criminals from Luzon Prisoner Camp No. 1 (Philippines) to Sugamo in Tokyo, Japan took place in June 1947.[77] In the same transport 42 war criminals, who had been sentenced by the USA in Manila, were taken to Japan.[78] The centralization of the trials in Yokohama was more effective and economical.[79] It is significant that the trials continued to be conducted by SCAP, Prosecution Division Philippine.[80] In all of the cases tried in Yokohama where the scene of the crime was the Philippines, the victims were exclusively POWs; the US prosecuting authorities did not prosecute crimes against Filipino civilians (Table 7.2).

---

[74] Ibid.
[75] For Legal Section Manila staff see NA RG 331, SCAP 1262-A – folder Manila Roster. See also NA RG 153 Entry 146/9, Statistics of US War Crimes Trials in All Theaters as of 30 September 1948.
[76] The first case was United States of America v. Kazutana Aihara et al. NA microfilm M-1112 reel 2. In general, see Annex A (20 March 1947) Check Sheet, General Headquarters SCAP, Legal Branch to Chief of Staff, 6 May 1947; NA RG 331, SCAP 1434 – folder War Crimes Trials Program.
[77] NA RG 331, SCAP 2002 – folder War Crimes Execution, Transferred the following named Japanese War Criminals Suspects to Sugamo Prison, Tokyo, Japan for trial. 27 June 1947.
[78] Ibid.
[79] NA RG 331, SCAP 1434 – folder War Crimes Trials Program, Letter from 3 April 1947, Annex A.
[80] NA RG 331, SCAP 1270 – SCAP Philippines Prosecution Division.

Table 7.2 American trials in Yokohama – crime scene: the Philippines – victims: POWs

Akutsu, Toshi	Capas Bridge (Luzon)	9 Sept. 1947
Okubo, Matsuo	Davao Penal Colony	9 Sept. 1947
Iwataka, Kenji et al.	Nichols Airfield (Bataan)	6 Nov. 1947
Mori, Shigeji	Commander Cabantuan POW Camp	7 Nov. 1947
Takasaki, Iku	Davao Penal Colony	12 Dec. 1947
Maeda, Kazuo	Davao Penal Colony	2 Jan. 1948
Okamoto, Hitoshi et al.	Cabanatum POW Camp	30 Jan. 1948
Fukunaga, Kiyozo	Pikit, Cotabato (Mindanao)	16 April 1948
Morimoto, Iichiro	Commander-In-Chief of all Philippine Island POW Camps	23 April 1948
Iwasaki, Masutaro	San Jose (Mindoro)	19 May 1948
Kawane, Yoshikata et al.	Death March (Bataan)	29 June 1948
Shiomi, Tasashige	San Jose (Mindoro)	12 Feb. 1948
Tsuneyoshi, Yoshio	Camp O'Donnell	19 July 1949

Source: NA film series M-1112 reel 2, 3, 4, and 5

Piccigallo[81] affirmed that trials in the Philippines and the Pacific islands (for example, Guam) followed legal standards—in particular concerning the translation of documents, affidavits or simultaneous translations (Japanese or English). However, in his conclusions he refers exclusively to American sources and passages from the law reports of the UNWCC.[82] Without going into greater detail, the contrasting assessment by the Japanese side would be worth evaluating—at least from the perspective of a fair trial or with regard to defense strategies.

Philippine Trials

Following American guidelines, the Philippines should only have prosecuted crimes against their own population: 'At the outset of the war crimes program [...] it was contemplated that after independence the Philippines Government would desire to participate in the trials of those Japanese suspected of having committed atrocities against residents' of the Philippine Islands. As will appear hereinafter the Philippine Government expressed

---

[81] Piccigallo, The Japanese on Trial (see *supra* note 74), 91ff.
[82] Ibid., 94; UNWCC Law Report vol. 15, 193f.

its willingness to assume this responsibility.'[83] In the few Philippine trials concerning US citizens, victims from other countries were consistently involved[84]—civilians were regularly found amongst them.[85]

In July 1947, the government of the Philippines established a war crimes trial program for Japanese war criminals.[86] The first plans and consultations between the USA as the former colonial power and the Philippine government had taken place in 1946.[87] Accordingly, during that spring all of the investigations and cases that had not been completed by the Americans were to be entrusted to the Philippine authorities. At that time about 350 suspected Japanese war criminals were incarcerated in Luzon POW Camp No. 1 (Canlubang, Laguna), and 100 trials were expected in all.[88] Conversely, that means the Americans had already completed a significant part of the investigative work. 'In order to meet the established dead-line we may have to bring some of the cases to Japan [...]. Therefore, you better make a survey of your cases and those in which the Filipinos are primarily involved, and which are notorious cases, should be put on a priority list.'[89]

---

[83] NA RG 331, SCAP 1434, War Crimes Trials Program, Check Sheet, General Headquarters SCAP, Legal Branch to Chief of Staff, 6 May 1947. The cases against the anti-Japanese resistance movement, Hukbalahap, on the Philippines which struggled against both the Japanese occupation as well as the colonial ruling structure, are not further thematized here. They played a significant role in the recapture of the Philippines and fought on the side of the USA. However, MacArthur had the leaders of the Hukbalahap incarcerated following combat operations. See Inglis T. Moore, 'The Hukbalahap in the Philippines,' *Australian Outlook* 1/2 (1947): 24–31; Alberto M. Bautista, *The Hukbalahap Movement in the Philippines, 1942–1952* (Manila: University of California Press, 1952); Lawrence M. Greenberg, *The Hukbalahap Insurrection. A case Study of a Successful Anti-Insurgency Operation in the Philippines, 1946–1955* (Washington, DC: United States Center of Military History, 2005).

[84] See cases Haruda et al. (NA RG 331, SCAP 1690), Mazusaki (NA RG 331, SCAP 1691), Takana (NA RG 331, SCAP 1694), Yokoyama (NA RG 331, SCAP 1698-1699), Kuroda (RG 331, SCAP 1699-1701) & Koike (NA RG 331, SCAP 1704).

[85] As of summer 1947, all of the trials which had been transferred to Yokohama bar one (trial of Kawane, Yoshikata – see Table 7.1, NA microfilm M-1112, reel 5, case 304 – Bataan Death March), concerned themselves with crimes relating to non-Filipino POWs.

[86] So-called collaboration trials are not dealt with in the following. They had already taken place in 1946. See amongst other the trial of Bishop Cesar Marie Guerrero in Manila from June 7, 1946. A 'Peoples Court' sentenced him for high treason. UNWCC War Crimes News Digest No. 14; Australian National Archive Canberra (NAC) RG A-2937/319. See David Joel Steinberg, *Philippine Collaboration in World War II* (Ann Arbor, MI, 1967); Hitoshi Nagai, *The Philippines B&C Class War Crimes Trials* (Tokyo: Kodansha, 2013).

[87] NA RG 331, SCAP 1270 – folder History, 1.

[88] NA RG 331, SCAP 1434 – folder War Crimes Trials Philippines, Check Sheet, General Headquarters SCAP, Legal Branch to Chief of Staff, 6 May 1947.

[89] NA RG 331, SCAP 1262, Carpenter Papers, Letter 15 November 1946.

As a result of a month of discussion between the US War Crimes Branch and Philippine officials, President Roxas committed his government to the holding of war crimes trials. He indicated that his government did not have the resources to continue the program and requested both logistical and financial assistance from the USA. The US Army was prepared to lend a large amount of their equipment,[90] local personnel and buildings. The assistance included supervision of the accused and their transfer from prison to the court. The Japanese government provided translators and lawyers for the defense.[91] Without the financial and logistic support of the USA, the Philippine government would not have been able to undertake the trials of Japanese war criminals. A look at the case documents (charge sheets, case records etc.) clearly shows that only the letterhead had changed. Aside from that, the Philippine format is identical to that of the JAG including the layout of forms and minutes.[92]

The USA reserved the right to take control of the prosecutions should the Philippine authorities fail. They argued that the islands had, after all, been American territory during the Second World War. Additionally, they had to keep their word as given in their consent to the Potsdam Declaration. In the event that the trials, which had yet to be heard, failed, they wanted to be able to conduct them in Yokohama instead.[93] But this was not the only reason why the USA continued to maintain a legal section in Manila following the end of their war crimes trials program.[94] This way, the Philippine prosecutors felt that they were permanently under pressure. The Philippines–Ryukyus Command (PHILRYCOM)[95] hung

---

[90] For a list in detail see NA RG 331, SCAP 1434 – folder War Crimes Trials Program, Annex C.

[91] Ibid. folder War Crimes Trials Program, Check Sheet, General Headquarters SCAP, Legal Branch to Chief of Staff, 6 May 1947. As early as spring 1947 there were discussions regarding financial compensation from Japan for the expenses accrued within the framework of the War Crimes Trials Program. All of the demands were to be regulated following a peace treaty. See Nagai, *The Philippine B&C Class War Crimes Trials* (*see supra* note 84), 55–56.

[92] Ibid., Annex C.

[93] Ibid., Check Sheet, General Headquarters SCAP, Legal Branch to Chief of Staff, 6 May 1947.

[94] There was an exchange of correspondence regarding the planned dissolution of Manila's legal section in December 1948; Ibid. folder War Crimes Trials Philippines.

[95] David J. Obermiller, The United States Military Occupation of Okinawa: Politicizing and Contesting Okinawan Identity, 1945–1955 (Iowa: ProQuest, 2006), 84ff. NA RG 331, SCAP 3176. Arnold F. Fisch, Military Government in the Ryukyu Islands, 1945–1950 (Washington, DC: U.S. Government Printing Office, 1988).

like a sword of Damocles over the trials, as it received a copy of all of the case documents.[96] This allowed the former colonial power to continue their rule partially, if indirectly, via the threat that it would, if necessary, complete the pending trials in Yokohama. This may have been one of the reasons why the court cases were so fastidiously prepared and executed.[97] Even in relatively simple trials the case documents contain many hundreds of pages.[98]

The Japanese defendants criticized the American plans to permit the Philippine government to take responsibility for the prosecutions. In April 1947, General Shizuo Yokoyama, for example, wrote to PHILRYCOM with a request to be tried by a US MC. He argued that, from his perspective, a trial in the Philippines would be unfair for 'emotional and mercenary reasons.'[99] Additionally, the JAG had much more experience conducting such trials. However, the criticism must be questioned as it ignores the fact that in about half of its sentences the US MCs imposed the death penalty—in particular for generals (see the cases of Yamashita and Homma). This line of argument was ineffective as the number of death sentences in the Philippine trials was practically the same as those held by the USA.

Jurisdiction

On 29 July 1947, President Manual Roxas enacted the legal basis of the Philippine War Crimes Trials Program in Executive Order No. 68 ('Establishment a National War Crimes Office and Prescribing Rules and Regulations Governing the Trial of Accused War Criminals').[100] A War Crimes Office which was to prepare the trials was established under the administration of the Philippine Army JAG. The preamble to the order declared that only Japanese war criminals should be prosecuted there

---

[96] They are found in NA RG 331, SCAP 1688-1709 & 1728-1729.
[97] See Yuma Totani, *Justice in Asia and the Pacific Region, 1945–1952: Allied War Crimes Prosecutions* (New York, NY: Cambridge University Press, 2015), 55.
[98] See for example the case of Hideo Tanaka et al. (579 pages) or the case of Katsuyoshi Taninaka (699 pages). NA RG 331, SCAP 1694. Here exemplarily the charges in the final case listed: 'fully order, direct and permit member of the Imperial Japanese Army under his command, to kill Niceto Sanchez, Antonie Tumalon and Demaso Advincula, all unarmed, non-combatant Filipino civilians, in violation of the laws and customs of war.'
[99] NA RG 331, SCAP 1434 – folder War Crimes Trials Program, Annex D, Letter from 10 April 1947. See further Letter from 25 April 1947 to 15 June 1947; ibid. TAB E.
[100] All of the case documents include a copy of Order 68. See *inter alia* NA RG 331, SCAP 1729.

and that their crimes must have been committed in the Philippines after December 1941. MCs modeled on the American example were intended as judicial bodies that would, in each individual case, be opened by the president or a person authorized by him (art. III/a). The jurisdictions of the MC (art. II b 1–3), with the exception of a few details, were borrowed directly from the American regulations of 5 December 1945.[101] As with the trials under the US MCs, only war crimes could be brought before the court (art. II 1 b 2, Executive Order No. 68). On the one hand this led to broadly comparable results in sentencing in the American and Philippine trials,[102] but on the other it meant that the Philippines could not be expected to have an independent postcolonial war crimes policy. It was, as the formalities already show, a direct continuation of American criminal law. Certainly it is correct to say that the Philippines had the possibility to conduct its own trials.[103] Nevertheless: 'To have their own trials' does not indicate anything about their demarcation from previous trials per se—above all because Filipinos contributed to them.[104] It was a complex mix of colonial dependence, partial participation and independent, national decision-making authority.

Trials

The official Philippine statistics show that in total 72 trials were held.[105] SCAP received reports on all of the trials. However, only 71 cases can be found in those documents.[106] Whether a script was lost or whether the statistics show discrepancies can only be resolved by making a comparison with the documents in the Philippine National Archive.[107] Altogether there

---

[101] In art. II b 1 war of aggression is not referred to literally and in art. II b 3 the pronoun: **any** (civil population) is missing. But because *population* is used in the plural, one can speak of a similarly worded regulation.

[102] The question of criminal procedure and the legal position of witnesses or the rights of the accused is beyond the scope of this chapter.

[103] Sharon W. Chamberlain, *Justice and Reconciliation: Post-war Philippine Trials of Japanese War Criminals in History and Memory* (Ann Arbor, MI: ProQuest LLC, 2010), 47.

[104] Chamberlain, Philippine Trials of Japanese War Criminals (*see supra note* 101, 51).

[105] Guillermo S. Santos, Report on the War Crimes Program of the Philippines, in: *Philippine Armed Forces Journal*, Vol. IV, 2 (Jan.–Feb. 1951): 27; Piccigallo, The Japanese on Trial (see *supra note* 70, 197); Chamberlain, Philippine Trials of Japanese War Criminals (see *supra note* 105), Appendix 1, 235–48.

[106] See NA RG 331, SCAP 1688-1709 & 1728-1729.

[107] Only case documents from the National Archive have been used for this article.

is information on 168 accused. In 16 instances the sentence is unknown; they appear in the charges but not under the rubric of 'sentences.' One accused died during his trial.[108] As a result there is an adjusted total of 151 accused. This corresponds with the statistics of the Philippine JAG from 1951.[109]

Japanese war criminals were to be taken to Sugamo prison in Japan to serve their sentences. The US Army agreed to the transfer, but this did not apply to every case. Only the death penalty was to be enforced in the Philippines.[110]

The first trial took place in Manila on 1 August 1947.[111] The majority of the trials are dated 1948. According to the original plans the war crimes trials program should have ended on 30 June 1949.[112] The last MC concluded, due to pressure from the Americans who no longer wished to support it,[113] on 28 December 1949.[114] The high-ranking Japanese accused were almost all prosecuted for command responsibility—a clear parallel with the American trials. So, amongst others, the commander of the garrison in Manila, Lieutenant General Shizuo Yokoyama, who in addition to the 35,000 civilians killed under his command, was accused of rape through his subordinates: Charge: 'That Shizuo Yokoyama [...] **while a state of war existed between the United States of America, its allies and dependencies, including the Philippines**, and Japan, did, wrongfully and unlawfully, disregard and fail to discharge his duties as commander to control the operations of Japanese Armed Forces under his command, directing and permitting them to commit brutal atrocities, and other high crimes against unarmed, non-combatant civilians, and to wantonly burn and destroy, without military justification, public and private properties, in violation of the laws and customs of war. [...] Specifications 24: [...] did, wrongfully and unlawfully, direct and permit

---

[108] NA RG 331, SCAP 1705, Tatsumosuke Ueda (Hajime Ainoda et al.).
[109] Guillermo S. Santos (*see supra note* 103). Chamberlain presents 155 accused (*see supra note* 101), 70. It was not possible to clarify the differences.
[110] NA RG 331, SCAP 1434 – folder War Crimes Trials Program, Check Sheet, General Headquarters SCAP, Legal Branch to Chief of Staff, 6 May 1947.
[111] NA RG 331, SCAP 1729, People of the Philippines v. Chushiro Kudo.
[112] NA RG 331, SCAP 1434 – folder War Crimes Trials Program, Memo: Responsibility and Custody of War Criminals and Witnesses, 5 April 1948, TAB A.
[113] Ibid., TAB E, Letter 4 December 1948 (Reduction in Force, Legal Section, Manila Branch).
[114] NA RG 331, SCAP 1707, 10 years imprisonment at hard labor, People of the Philippines v. Kensichi Masuoka.

members of the Imperial Japanese Armed Forces under his command, on or about 3 February 1945 [...] rape and thereafter to brutally kill, Pilar Campos, an unarmed, noncombatant civilian, in violation of the laws and customs of war.'[115] This charge is remarkable in that in the first instance war crimes are referred to during the war between the USA and Japan, secondly against the allies and finally against the colonies of the USA, to which the Philippines belonged. As a result, it followed that Philippine responsibility for its war crimes trials program was always defined by its US colonial background.

Civilian victims were the only victims in 68 of 71 cases—not only Philippine nationals, but also three Chinese[116] and Spanish[117] citizens respectively. Three indictments were issued for war crimes against American and Philippine POWs.[118] This finding confirms the division of labor at the beginning of the Philippine war crimes trials program to only bring war crimes against Filipino victims before the MCs. However, the characterization of 'division of labor' can be understood as an American stipulation. The Philippine government did not really have a choice. Even after its formal independence the Philippines was still at times in its colonial shackles.

MC trials were structured in four main groups: command responsibility trials, Kempeitai trials, atrocities against civilians, and other notorious cases like cannibalism.[119] Aside from the latter crimes, trial categories show a clear parallel to comparable cases before US MCs.[120] Although the USA processed additional types of trials, this was, above all, due to the absence of crimes against POWs. The prosecution structure of both programs was also similar (see Table 7.3): the majority of the trials concerned

---

[115] NA RG 331, SCAP 1698-1699, 8 November 1948. For more rape atrocities see Specification 35, 42, 43, 47 and 51.

[116] NA RG 331, SCAP 1695, 16 December 1948 (Noburo Tsuneoka). NA RG 331, SCAP 1694, 3 September 1948 (Hideo Tanaka et al.).

[117] NA RG 331, SCAP 1690, 27 November 1948 (Hideichi Nakamura et al.).

[118] (1) NA RG 331, SCAP 1695, 16 December 1948 (Noburo Tsuneoka); (2) NA RG 331, SCAP 1694, 3 September 1948 (Hideo Tanaka et al.); (3) NA RG 331, SCAP 1691, 29 July 1948 (Hideichi Matsuzaki).

[119] See exhibit no. 388, US v. Tomoyuki Yamashita (13 September 1945), para 2: Cannibalism, 14ff. NA RG 331, SCAP 1699.

[120] Data base ICWC, Marburg. See Nagai, *The Philippine B&C Class War Crimes Trials* (see *supra note* 84), 86.

Table 7.3 Sentences Philippines MC

	Total	A	D	L	P	O	U
I. General	6	–	2	2	2	–	–
II. Officer							
Col. – Major	13	1	7	3	2	–	–
Captain – Lieutenant	56	7	36	7	4	1	1
	33.3 %		64.3 %				
III. Non-commissioned officer	40	2	16	10	10	–	2
	23.8 %		40.0 %				
IV. Private	45	1	16	8	6	4	10
	26.8 %		35.6 %				
V. Combatants							
Interpreter	1	–	–	1	–	–	–
Japanese Volunteer Army	4	1	1	–	2	–	–
VI. Civilian	3		1		2		
Total	168	12	79	31	28	5	13

Source: Data base ICWC, Marburg. *A* acquittal, *D* death penalty, *L* lifelong imprisonment, *P* imprisonment, *O* other, *U* unknown

mid-ranking officers. There are no significant differences in the sentences: the percentage of death sentences is almost identical and the number of life sentences does not show any significant difference.

In the Philippine trials sexual violence against women was also prosecuted on a similar scale (USA = 15/92 [15.5 %]; Philippines = 10/72 [13.9 %]). Three types of trials can be identified: individual acts[121]; multiple rapes[122]; and command responsibility of subordinates for rape.[123] All of the cases concerned Filipino women. 'In that Hideichi NAKAMURA, Sadeo KANEDA, members of the Imperial Japanese Army, did, in the month of October, 1944 […] at or near the Medellin-Bogo Sugar Central, Cebu Province, Philippines, wrongfully and unlawfully permit and participate in the rape, intimidation, and imprisonment for the purpose of sexual intercourse, of Carmon Yap, a Filipino civilian.'[124] Here too, like in comparable trials before US MCs, no victims of forced prostitution are to be found despite the fact that such crimes were noted.

---

[121] E.g. NA RG 331, SCAP 1707, 25 March 1949 (Takao Fujimoto).
[122] E.g. NA RG 331, SCAP 1690, 27 November 1948 (Hideichi Nakamura et al.).
[123] E.g. NA RG 331, SCAP 1698, 1 November 1948 (Shizuo Yokoyama).
[124] E.g. NA RG 331, SCAP 1690, 27 November 1948 (Hideichi Nakamura et al.).

Conclusion

The USA developed and structured guidelines for the implementation of MCs on Philippine territory. The Philippine government adapted not only the legal basis but also consistently oriented itself to the sentencing of the former colonial power. It developed prosecution strategies and shaped definitions of perpetrators and severity of sentencing. The latter was markedly above the regional and global average, differing greatly from other areas where war crimes trials were being held under American aegis. In many respects, the US and Philippine trials in Manila were comparable in terms of severity of sentencing, types of sentences and, in part, victim groups. The same applies to the fact that sexual violence against women was only prosecuted in the case of rape—although both jurisdictions had the ability to prosecute forced prostitution.

In the Philippine press of the era, the war crimes trials program was depicted as a test of national fairness and the practice of rule of law.[125] A detailed comparison may show that sentences for similar crimes varied slightly,[126] but overall it is evident that there were no significant differences between the US and Philippine trials.

---

[125] Chamberlain, *Justice in Asia and the Pacific Region* (see *supra note* 101), 92–3. Yuma Totani, Justice in Asia and the Pacific Region argued similar (see *supra note* 99), 54–5.

[126] E.g. Totani's comparative study on Yamashita/Homma cases vs Kuroda (see *supra note* 95), 21–55.

CHAPTER 8

Justice and Decolonization: War Crimes on Trial in Saigon, 1946–1950

Ann-Sophie Schoepfel

INTRODUCTION

'The Japanese aggression of 9 March 1945, which aimed at permanently abolishing French sovereignty over Indochina,[1] was committed with absolute disregard for the law of nations' declared French prosecutor Gratien Gardon in late 1947 at the military court of Saigon.[2] Gardon was accusing Japan not only of war crimes but also of suppressing the French colonial presence in Southeast Asia. This declaration demonstrated that the Japanese coup d'état on 9 March 1945 had far-reaching political implications for France. Japan had indeed dismantled the French colonial administration in Indochina. Moreover, during the war, Nationalist China and the USA had been determined to prevent the recommencement of French

---

[1] Indochina was a French federation established at the end of the nineteenth century from the three Vietnamese regions, Tonkin (North), Annam (Central) and Cochinchina (South), as well as Cambodia and Laos.
[2] Dépôt Central des Archives de la Justice Militaire (DCAJM), French Permanent Military Tribunal in Saigon, The Case of Tomitake YAMANE, Indictment Act, 15 December 1947.

A.-S. Schoepfel (✉)
Heidelberg University, Heidelberg, Germany

rule there.³ As a result, revolutionary groups filled the power vacuum in Indochina immediately after the Japanese capitulation on 15 August 1945.⁴ The Viet Minh, the nationalist communist party founded by Ho Chi Minh in 1941 in Vietnam, declared independence on 2 September 1945.⁵

In the fallout from the Second World War, France wished to regain its power and to become a player on the international scene.⁶ The inter-Allied effort to prosecute war crimes in Europe and in Asia constituted a valuable opportunity to announce the 'return' of the French to the international stage. Although France first focused on offenses committed in Europe by Nazi Germany,⁷ it was admitted in 1945 as an Allied nation to judge Japanese war criminals at the International Military Tribunal for the Far East (IMTFE) in Tokyo and at the Saigon Military Court.

Between 1946 and 1950, the French Military Tribunal in Saigon heard 39 cases of Japanese war crimes.⁸ The pursuit of justice in Saigon was entangled in the struggle for decolonization. France therefore had to rely on a transnational network for the coordination of war crimes prosecution in Asia and to adapt its war crimes trials policy to local circumstances.

The French political and legal approach to war criminals in Asia differed from that employed in Europe. The fact that they took place during the struggle for decolonization had decisive implications on the conduct of the trials.⁹ This historical study will address just how decolonization affected the trials, which remains one of the most complex issues in the postwar interaction between France and Southeast Asia.

---

³ Gary H. Hess, "Franklin Roosevelt and Indochina", *The Journal of American History* 59, 2 (1972): 353–68.
⁴ David G. Marr, *Vietnam 1945: The Quest for Power* (Berkeley: University of California Press, 1995), 347–540.
⁵ Vietnamese Declaration of Independence, 1945, available at http://www.fordham.edu/halsall/mod/1945vietnam.html (last accessed at 25 January 2014).
⁶ Bent Boel, 'France's Role in the World in 1945, Back to the Future?' in Joachim Lund, Per Øhrgaard, ed., *Return to Normalcy Or a New Beginning: Concepts and Expectations for a Postwar Europe around 1945* (Copenhagen: Narayana Press, 2008), 85.
⁷ Henry Rousso, 'L'Épuration. Die politische Säuberung in Frankreich,' in Klaus-Dietmar Henke and Hans Woller, eds., *Politische Säuberung in Europa: die Abrechnung mit Faschismus und Kollaboration nach dem Zweiten Weltkrieg* (München: Deutscher Taschenbuch Verlag, 1991), 214–26.
⁸ DCAJM, French Permanent Military Tribunal in Saigon, 1946, 1947, 1948, 1949, 1950.
⁹ In contrast to the European scene, East Asian war crimes policy was characterized by national trials conducted by transnational legal authorities, most of them with thinly veiled colonial interests.

Writing in 1979, Philip R. Piccigallo argued that the Allies influenced the French legal approach to Japanese war crimes despite significant procedural, statutory and interpretative differences between French and other Allied nations' war crimes regulations.[10] In 2011, Chizuru Namba showed that the French involvement in the Tokyo and the Saigon Trials constituted the French 'return' to the international stage in the Far East after 1945.[11] According to Beatrice Trefalt, the French war crimes trials policy in Asia aimed at rehabilitating France in Asia; it reinforced the French position amongst the victorious Allied nations, and it supported its right to govern Indochina.[12] In 2014, this author argued that the prosecution of Japanese war crimes was part of a French national state-building process.[13]

The purpose of this chapter is to analyze the colonial dimension of the application of military justice to war crimes in Indochina in the struggle for decolonization. The first section focuses on power relations. It looks at how the French prosecution of Japanese war crimes fit into the larger context of Allied war crimes policy by analyzing the French records of the Departments of Justice, Foreign Affairs and the Colonial Office.[14] The second section focuses on the proceedings and the implementation of sentences based on the first analysis of the Saigon trials papers.[15]

Transnational Strategies in Pursuit of Justice

In the aftermath of the Second World War, major changes in international relations had shifted the focus of Allied efforts towards investigating, prosecuting as well as judging Japanese war criminals. The Japanese surrender

---

[10] Philip R. Piccigallo, *The Japanese on Trial. Allied war crimes operations in the East, 1945–1951* (Austin, TX: University of Texas Press, 1979), 201–8.
[11] Chizuru Namba, 'La France face aux procès de Saigon et de Tokyo,' *Outre-mers, Revue d'histoire* 380–381 (2013): 313–31.
[12] Beatrice Trefalt, 'Japanese War Crimes in Indochina and the French Pursuit of Justice: Local and International Constraints,' *Journal of Contemporary History* Vol. 49 (4) (2014): 727–42.
[13] Ann-Sophie Schoepfel, 'The War Court as a Form of State Building: The French Prosecution of Japanese War Crimes at the Saigon and Tokyo Trials,' in: Morten Bergsmo, Cheah Wui Ling and YI Ping, eds., *Historical Origins of International Criminal Law: Volume 2* (Brussels: Torkel Opsahl Academic EPublisher, 2014), 119–42.
[14] These records are located at the Archives Nationales (AN) in Paris, the Archives du Ministère des Affaires Etrangères (AMAE) in Courneuve-Aubervilliers and in Nantes, the Archives de la France d'Outre-Mer (ANOM) in Aix-en-Provence, and at the Service Historique de la Défense in Vincennes (SHD).
[15] The trial transcripts are located at the DCAJM in Le Blanc, and at the Japanese National Archives in Tokyo.

led to major political, social and cultural transformations in Southeast Asia: new political groups struggled for independence in Indonesia, in Burma, in the Malay Peninsula and in Indochina.[16] The pursuit of justice at the Saigon Military Tribunal must be viewed in the transnational context of Allied war crimes trials in Asia.

The War Crimes Ordinance of 28 August 1944

The French War Crimes Ordinance created during the Second World War was the legal point of departure for the French government in Allied war crimes trials. On 28 August 1944, the Provisional Government of the French Republic—the interim government that ruled France from 1944 to 1946[17]—then located in Algiers, issued an ordinance concerning the prosecution of war criminals.[18] This decree was the result of long reflection among anti-collaborationist jurists such as René Cassin.[19] These jurists took an active part in the creation of Allied war crimes policy.[20]

In May 1944, the French Committee of National Liberation urged French legal experts to think about the 'most effective way to punish collective crimes committed by Nazi Germany and Japan.'[21] One of the key ideas was that French Resistance fighters would hold a central role in the prosecution of war criminals. Commissioner for Justice François de Menthon suggested that war criminals should be punished in military tribunals composed primarily of Resistance members, replacing the military

---

[16] Paul H. Kratoska, 'Dimensions of Decolonization,' in: Marc Frey. Ronald W. Pruessen, Tai Yong Tan, eds., *The Transformation of Southeast Asia* (New York: Routledge, 2015), 3–22.

[17] On 9 December 1941, the French government-in-exile, led by General Charles de Gaulle, declared war on Japan and called on Indochina to resist. In December 1943, it decided to release Indochina from the Japanese and to restore the rights of France in Indochina and the republican legality.

[18] Ordonnance du août 1944 relative à la répression des crimes de guerre, 28 August 1944, Journal Officiel (Algiers), 30 August 1944, 780. ('Ordonnance du 28 août'); see also United Nations War Crimes Commission, 'French Law Concerning Trials of War Criminals by Military Tribunals and by Military Government Courts in the French Zone of Germany,' available at http://www.legal-tools.org/doc/198950/ (last accessed at 11 February 2015).

[19] Mario Bettati, *Droit d'ingérence (Le): Mutation de l'ordre international* (Paris: Editions Odiles Jacob, 1996), 40.

[20] Claudia Moisel, *Frankreich und die deutschen Kriegsverbrecher, Politik und Praxis der Strafverfolgung nach dem Zweiten Weltkrieg* (Göttingen: Wallstein Verlag, 2004), 41–62.

[21] AN, BB-30/1785, Note sur la répression des crimes de guerre, 22 May 1944.

elite in France who had collaborated with the Axis Powers during the Second World War.²²

According to a memorandum issued by Cassin, legal procedure would be a determining factor in the quality of the prosecution of war crimes: 'if the national tribunals were not to be a travesty of justice, they would be furnished with all the relevant documentation and information concerning the cases.' Moreover, it was 'essential' that the 'proceedings were public and that the accused had the right to choose their own counsel for defense.'²³ He argued that the primary reference for the prosecution of war crimes in France should be French criminal procedure, namely the Penal Code and the Code of Military Justice.²⁴

Both Menthon and Cassin's ideas on the prosecution of war criminals were taken into account in the War Crimes Ordinance. On the one hand, Menthon suggested war crimes should be prosecuted in permanent military tribunals consisting of five military judges, the majority of whom were to be selected 'among officers, non-commissioned officers and other ranks belonging to the French Forces of the Interior or a Resistance Group' according to Article 5 of the War Crimes Ordinance.²⁵ Article 14 of the Code of Military Justice stated that the President of the Tribunal should be a civil magistrate.²⁶ On the other hand, as Cassin had recommended, French criminal procedure was to be the main frame of reference for the prosecution of war crimes.²⁷

According to the historian Claudia Moisel, two vital factors influenced the composition of the ordinance of 28 August 1944.²⁸ Firstly, the democratic branch of the resistance movement, guided by Christian values, issued the War Crimes Ordinance. Secondly, the interim government

---

²² Ibid.
²³ TNA, TS 26/873, René Cassin, Notes of violations of the laws and customs of war perpetrated by the German since September 1939, p. 47.
²⁴ These legal codes were established in the *longue durée*. The guiding principles of the Penal Code and the Code of Military Justice referred to the legal codification of criminal acts and punishment after the French Revolution and under Napoleon at the beginning of the nineteenth century, and their evolution under the positivist school in the 1880s and after the First World War. See F. Debove, F. Falletti, E. Dupic, *Précis de droit pénal et de procédure pénale* (Presses Universitaires de France, 2013), pp. 23–30.
²⁵ War Crimes Ordinance, Journal Officiel (Algiers), 30 August 1944, p. 780.
²⁶ Ibid.
²⁷ Ibid.
²⁸ Claudia Moisel, *Frankreich und die deutschen Kriegsverbrecher, Politik und Praxis der Strafverfolgung nach dem Zweiten Weltkrieg*, 70.

refused to hold the prosecution of war crimes in civilian courts and opted for military courts instead, since it held that violations of the rules of war concerned military justice.[29] This decision was taken against the background of European debate about how to punish war criminals. Indeed, a few months later after the publication of the French Ordinance of 28 August 1944, the British War Cabinet decided that 'war crimes committed against British subjects or in British territory should be dealt with by military courts set up to try them in Germany.'[30]

The guidelines of French criminal law to prosecute war criminals were influenced by the wartime divide of French society between the supporters of the Petain's Vichy regime and the French Resistance. They demonstrated the wish of France to return to its democratic and republican tradition by establishing fair procedures with the ordinance of 28 August 1944 and with French criminal law.

Prosecuting Japanese War Crimes in the Midst of Conflict

Following the Second World War in Indochina, the provisional government of the French Republic was confronted with the urgent need to reform the foundations of the French colonial empire. In Indochina, it wanted to devolve more power to local authorities within the framework of a new Indochinese Federation under French trusteeship. But France struggled with its own legacy as a colonial power, since the Viet Minh were increasingly winning over the Vietnamese with their vision of full independence.

The provisional government initiated discussions with the Viet Minh to find an acceptable compromise. But after several months of negotiations, the two parties were unable to reach agreement. On 19 December 1946, fighting broke out in Vietnam, although French colonial authorities were still not aware of the risk that the Viet Minh represented.[31] The Colonial Office thought that it was just a local revolt similar to those which had already occurred in Indochina in the 1920s and early 1930s.

But France was getting bogged down in Vietnam in a *guerre qui ne dit pas son nom*—a war in everything but name. The French government of

---

[29] AN, BB 30/1785, Note of Surdon to De Menthon, 29.6.1944.
[30] National Archives (London), War Cabinet 131, CAB65/44.
[31] Marguerite Guyon de Chemilly, *Asie du Sud-Est: la décolonisation britannique et française : étude comparative* (Paris: L'Harmattan, 2010), 102.

the Fourth Republic created in October 1946 did not recognize the state of war and continued to believe that the struggle for independence was fleeting. It agreed to grant more autonomy to Cambodia, Laos and to the Vietnamese state created in 1949 under French tutelage. But this was not enough. The conflict between the French and the Viet Minh ended in 1954 in Dien Bien Phu with the demise of the French colonial era in Southeast Asia.

The First Indochina War (1946–1954) had its roots in the Pacific War, since the weakening of the French colonial power during the Japanese occupation strengthened the authority of local elites and incited nationalism. French Indochina during the Second World War represented a unique chapter in colonial history. It was the only colony where Japan permitted the Western colonial administration to continue functioning.[32] In Malaysia, Burma, Indonesia, the Philippines, Hong Kong and Singapore, members of the so-called Greater East Asia Co-prosperity Sphere, Japan replaced the Western colonial administration with its own.

After the French defeat in Europe in June 1940, Japan reached two agreements with Vichy France in September 1940 and July 1941 relating to the stationing of troops in North and South Indochina. Japan aimed to build a solid basis for military operations in Southeast Asia. Disagreements remained between the Japanese elite: the Sambosho (Headquarters) wished to invade Indochina for strategic reasons, while the Gaimusho (Foreign Ministry) advocated a neutral Indochina under French guidance.

In the shadow of the Empire of the Rising Sun, Vichy France promoted its 'National Revolution' in Indochina. The National Revolution was the official ideological name of Petain's program established in July 1940. This program was characterized by its anti-parliamentarism, rejection of the constitutional separation of powers, personality cult, promotion of traditional values and rejection of modernity.[33] From July 1940 to March 1945, Jean Decoux, the Governor-General of French Indochina, remained loyal to Petain's regime. He sought to portray Petain as a Confucius—the best of the Western and Eastern traditions.[34] The confrontation of the

---

[32] David Chandler, 'Legacies of World War II in Indochina,' in David Koh Wee Hock, ed., *Legacies of World War II in South and East Asia* (Singapore: Institute of South East Asian Studies, 2007), 24.
[33] Jacques Cantier, Eric T. Jennings, *L'Empire colonial sous Vichy* (Paris: Editions Odile Jacob, 2004), 14.
[34] Eric T. Jennings, *Vichy in the Tropics: Petain's National Revolution in Madagascar, Guadeloupe and Indochina* (Stanford, CA: Stanford University Press, 2004), 127.

Japanese and French colonial ideologies resulted in the reinforcement of the struggle for decolonization in Indochina.[35]

On 9 March 1945, Japan abruptly placed French colonial personnel under arrest in Indochina. After two days of resistance, 37,000 French were taken prisoner: 22,000 civilians (men, women and children) were placed under house arrest in mini-ghettos in Hanoi Haiphong, Nam Dinh, Vinh, Hue, Nha Trang, Dalat, Saigon and Phnom Penh; 7000 soldiers and 2000 civil servants were interned in disciplinary camps, such as those of Pakson in Laos, of Hoa Binh in North Vietnam; 5000 soldiers and 900 French Resistance fighters were deported to camps with especially harsh conditions.[36]

After the announcement of the Japanese capitulation on 15 August 1945, the Viet Minh launched a revolution against the French colonial rule four days later. Against this backdrop, the French Ministry of Foreign Affairs and the Colonial Office both agreed on the importance of the creation of a new legal and colonial framework and of the prosecution of Japanese war crimes not only for the French 'prestige in the Far East'[37] but also for 'the beneficial effect' on the Indochinese population.[38] The French state-builders had to develop a national strategy in Indochina to restore the confidence of the

---

[35] On the French 'cohabitation' with Japan during the Second World War, see: Chizuru Namba, *Français et Japonais en Indochine (1940–1945): Colonisation, propagande et rivalité culturelle* (Paris: Éditions Karthala, 2012). On the French National Revolution, see: Sebastien Verney, *L'Indochine sous Vichy. Entre Révolution nationale, collaboration et identités nationales 1940–1945* (Paris: Riveneuve éditions, 2012), 315–411; Eric T. Jennings, *Vichy in the Tropics: Petain's National Revolution in Madagascar, Guadeloupe and Indochina*, 130–162; See also this book about the Greater East Asian Prosperity Sphere: John W. Dower, *War Without Mercy: Race and Power in the Pacific War* (New York, NY: Pantheon, 1986).

[36] In 1951, France officially classified as deportation camps the prison cells of the Shell Property, the Central House and the Security Prison in Hanoi, the Security Prison of the Henri Rivière School and the Civil Prison in Haiphong, the Municipal Prison in Nam Dinh, the Civil Prison and the Chamber of Commerce in Saigon, the Security Prison in Vinh and the cells of the Japanese Gendarmerie, the Security Prison and the Central Prison in Phnom Penh. See: Ralph B. Smith, 'The Japanese Period in Indochina and the Coup of 9 March 1945,' *Journal of Southeast Asian Studies* Vol. 9 No. 2 (1978): 268–301; Pierre Jautée, 'Les Camps Japonais en Indochine pendant la Seconde Guerre Mondiale.' *Mémoires Vivantes – Bulletin de la Fondation pour la Mémoire de la Déportation* 4 (2007); Kiyoko Kurusu Nitz, 'Japanese Military Policy Towards French Indochina during the Second World War: The Road to the Meigo Sakusen (9 March 1945).' *Journal of Southeast Asian Studies* Vol.14 No. 2 (1983): 328–53.

[37] ANOM, INF 1364, Report to the Secretary-General of the Indochinese Comittee, 30 October 1945.

[38] AMAE, Asie Océanie, Généralités 161, Report to the Conference Secretariat, Direction d'Asie Océanie, 24 September 1945.

Indochinese population in the French government, since the Japanese invasion of French Indochina had undermined French authority.

The investigation of war crimes was part of a comprehensive recovery strategy for the French colonial empire.[39] This approach was very much in line with other colonial retrenchment strategies in Southeast Asia. In British colonies, for example, war crimes trials were thought to present a good opportunity to impress upon the local population that Britain had enough power to protect and govern its empire. According to the historian Hayashi Hirofumi, 'it is clear that the British authorities saw the war crimes trials from the viewpoint of recovering British prestige in Southeast and East Asia in order to re-build her empire.'[40]

France had to demonstrate that it could prosecute war crimes. In November 1945, representatives of the Ministries of Foreign Affairs, of Justice and the Colonial Office held a meeting to create a war crimes national investigation program in Indochina.[41] The Colonial Office established an ad hoc organization in Indochina, the Federal War Crimes Office (in French: *Service Fédéral des Crimes de Guerre*).[42] The minister of foreign affairs gave clear instructions from the United Nations War Crimes Commission (UNWCC) to make strategic decisions in the best interests of the Allies. The Colonial Office protected French interests in the investigation of Japanese war crimes. The War Crimes Section in Saigon worked closely with the War Crimes Research Service in Paris and was responsible for conducting investigations in Indochina.[43]

France was faced with rebuilding its power structure in Indochina and removing criminals and collaborators from office. The new colonial authorities wished to distance themselves from the policy of Jean Decoux,[44] the wartime pro-Vichy governor-general of French Indochina. The new French government of General Charles de Gaulle regarded him

---

[39] Schoepfel (2014), 127.
[40] Hirofumi Hayashi, "British War Crimes Trials of Japanese", in *Nature-People-Society: Science and the Humanities* 31 (2001).
[41] AN, BB30 / 1791, Minutes of the meeting of 15 November 1945 of war crimes investigation in Indochina.
[42] CAOM, AFFPOL 3438, Note of the Director of Political Affairs in Indochina on the investigation and prosecution of war crimes in Indochina, 6 December 1945.
[43] CAOM, AFFPOL 3438, Letter of Amiral d'Argenlieu to the General Secretary of the Indochina Committee, 13 December 1945; AMAE, Asie Océanie, Généralités 161, Note for the General Secretary of the Indochina Committee, 30 October 1945.
[44] Amiral Thierry d' Argenlieu, *Chronique d'Indochine, 1945–1947* (Paris: Editions Albin Michel, 1985), 32–33.

as a Japanese collaborator.⁴⁵ Many key responsible persons of the former colonial administration were tried and the wave of official trials led to confusion and division within the French community in Indochina.⁴⁶

In Saigon, the prosecution of Japanese war criminals took place simultaneously with the prosecution of Vietnamese independence activists, as well as Chinese and French wartime collaborators as part of the French legal purge.⁴⁷ In 1947, the Saigon Military Court prosecuted 92 Japanese war criminals and charged 493 defendants with collaboration: 473 were Vietnamese, 13 French, and seven Chinese.⁴⁸

The ongoing war with the Viet Minh was reflected in legal measures the French government adopted regulating the prosecution of Japanese war crimes in Indochina.⁴⁹ A common theme in French investigations was the belief that thousands of Japanese soldiers had joined the Viet Minh after the Japanese defeat. According to the prosecution, the collaboration between the Japanese and the Viet Minh was very strong during the Indochina War. Avoidance of prosecution for war crimes might be a factor in the collusion of Japanese soldiers with the Viet Minh.⁵⁰ The French government decided therefore to offer immunity from prosecution to convince Japanese soldiers to surrender.⁵¹ However, relatively few Japanese war criminals took advantage of this offer.⁵²

---

⁴⁵ Amiral Jean Decoux, *A la barre de l'Indochine: histoire de mon Gouvernement Général, 1940–1945* (Paris: Soukha Editions, 2013), 389–92.

⁴⁶ Frédéric Turpin, *De Gaulle, les gaullistes et l'Indochine: 1940–1956* (Paris: Les Indes Savantes, 2005), 135.

⁴⁷ The French Permanent Military Tribunal in Saigon tried Vietnamese and French collaborators. For example: on 13 August 1946, the Vietnamese Ho Van Minh was sentenced to lifetime forced labor for 'participating in an attempt to demoralize the Army or the Nation,' with the object of weakening national defense. During the Second World War, Ho Van Minh had denounced some French citizens supporting the Allies, see: French Permanent Military Tribunal in Saigon, The Case of Ho Van Minh, Judgment, 13 August 1946. In 1946, the first French citizen to be sentenced was Emile Eychenne, an entrepreneur born in Indochina. Eychenne was charged with 'attacks on the state security – friendly and inconvenient agreements with Japanese,' because he had supported the Japanese after March 1945, See: DCAJM, French Permanent Military Tribunal in Saigon, The Case of Emile Eychenne, Judgment, 18 September 1946.

⁴⁸ DCAJM, Proceedings of the French Permanent Military Tribunal in Saigon, 1947.

⁴⁹ Schoepfel (2014), 140.

⁵⁰ ANOM, HCI. 57.198, Report on the Japanese and Viet Minh collaboration, 30 May 1947.

⁵¹ SHD, 10H1044, Information Note for the High Commissioner, Commander-in-Chief of the armed forces in the Far East, 28 August 1948.

⁵² Trefalt (2014), 737–8.

Against this troubling background, the prosecution of Japanese war crimes carried great significance for the French recovery from the war. It commemorated French Resistance fighters and brought some measure of solace to victims' families. However, Paris refused to provide assistance and redress for the French victims of Japanese war crimes committed in Indochina between 9 March 1945 and 15 August 1945. The historian Pierre Jautée has explained that these victims had to wait several years before they could obtain the status of deportees.[53]

The Role of the United Nations War Crimes Commission

The UNWCC played an important role in dealing with the challenges encountered in Indochina by the French authorities. Before the Second World War had ended, the Allied governments had begun investigating war crimes committed in countries occupied by Japan. On 13 January 1942, delegates of the Free French National Committee signed the Inter-Allied Declaration on Punishment for War Crimes, better known as the St James's Declaration, establishing the UNWCC in London. Under the aegis of the Allied powers, the UNWCC was to investigate and obtain evidence of war crimes. Seventeen countries took part, including Free France, Belgium, the USA, Norway, Great Britain, Australia, New Zealand, Canada, China, India, Greece, South Africa, the Netherlands, Poland, Yugoslavia and Luxembourg. Even if special attention was devoted to Japanese war crimes, priority was given to Nazi war crimes cases.

To facilitate investigations in the Pacific theater of war, an UNWCC Sub-Commission was created in May 1944 in the Chinese capital of Chungking to pursue Japanese war crimes. Representatives from the French government-in-exile possessed only limited powers in Chungking because of the ambiguity regarding the legality of the ongoing collaboration between Vichy and Japan in Indochina.[54] At the sub-commission, six different jurists successively represented France from 29 November 1944 to 4 April 1947: Achille Clarac, Jean Daridan, M. de Montousse, Jean

---

[53] French victims of Japanese war crimes committed in Indochina between 9 March 1945 and 15 August 1945 only obtained in 1951 the same status as the French government accorded to deported people and the victims of the Nazi concentration camps. See: Jautée, 'Les Camps Japonais en Indochine pendant la Seconde Guerre Mondiale,' 8.

[54] Cherif Bassiouni, *Introduction to International Criminal Law* (Leiden: Martinus Nijhoff, 2012), 549.

Brethes, Eric Pelin and Michel Bertin.⁵⁵ The constant changes meant that the French staff could not participate as substantially as at the UNWCC's London headquarters.

In February 1945, the sub-commission had requested member countries to collect information on war crimes and to establish a clear list of war criminals following a list compiled by Australia.⁵⁶ The investigation of war crimes in Indochina concerned the interests of all players in Southeast Asia since Japan was holding Allied prisoners of war (POWs) in Indochina. In early 1945, for example, Alan Mansfield, the Australian delegate at the UNWCC, was expecting the French to send him a list of war criminals involved in persecuting Australian POWs.⁵⁷

The French delegate at the UNWCC in London at the time, André Gros, saw the need for speedy action. Even before the surrender, he urged the French Ministry of Foreign Affairs to gather evidence about Japanese war crimes in Indochina.⁵⁸ Other countries had already started to compile a list of Japanese war crimes in early 1945. The French director of the War Crimes Unit wrote on 9 January 1945: 'I do not doubt that war crimes have been committed in Indochina.'⁵⁹ But, because France had to face structural, judicial and administrative difficulties in Indochina, it could not provide valuable information on Japanese war crimes before reconquering the country.⁶⁰ Only after the Japanese coup d'état on 9 March 1945 did the investigation of war crimes became a political priority.

Once France re-established its sovereignty over Indochina in early 1946, it was finally granted permission on behalf of the Allies to 'bring war criminals to justice.' It established a list of war criminals and handed it to the USA 'to demonstrate the French will' to participate in the Allied

---

⁵⁵ United Nations War Crimes Commission, Far Eastern and Pacific Sub-Commission, Minutes Nos. 1–38, S-1804-0005-15835 (http://www.legal-tools.org/en/go-to-database/ltfolder/0_28557/#results) (Last accessed: 24 January 2015).
⁵⁶ Hiroshi (2001), 24–25.
⁵⁷ ANOM, INF 1364, Letter of the Minister of Foreign Affairs to the Secretary-General of the Inter-ministerial committee on Indochina, 22 January 1946.
⁵⁸ AN, BB30 / 1791, Lettrer of André Gros to the Minister of Justice, François de Menthon, 26 March 1945.
⁵⁹ AN, BB30 1791, Letter of Colonel Chauveau, Director of the War Crimes Office to the Director of the Indochina Office, Colonial Office, 9 January 1945.
⁶⁰ France still tried to re-establish its sovereignty and to weaken the Indochinese people's fight for independence. The French government involved in the war crimes prosecution faced indeed a twofold challenge: past collaboration with Japan, and pressure coming from decolonization movements.

investigation program 'that would have repercussions at the international level.'[61] After 1946, France paid close attention to the work currently being undertaken by the UNWCC.[62] On the one hand, France wanted to show with its legal engagements that it was a victorious nation too. On the other, it aimed at sending a message to the world that it had emerged from the war as a new republican power, capable of protecting Indochina and re-establishing its colonial authority in a new way that guaranteed the autonomy of the Indochinese peoples.[63]

Nevertheless, France played a minor role in the pursuit of justice in Asia, which belonged to an international movement dedicated to judging Japanese war crimes under the umbrella of the UNWCC. It consisted of a multi-layered system of commissions—the UNWCC Far Eastern Sub-Commission in Chungking, the War Crimes Branch of the Allied Headquarters under MacArthur in Yokohama and the South East Asian Command in Singapore—from which France was isolated because its difficult economic situation made it hard to participate effectively.[64]

The UNWCC exercised a moral influence on governments to compel cooperation in the pursuit of accused war crimes at the IMTFE, known as the Tokyo Trial, and in other domestic trials. The IMTFE was convened in Tokyo from 1946 to 1948 to prosecute 28 Japanese military and political leaders, charged with class A war crimes.[65] At the same time, about 5700

---

[61] ANOM, AFFPOL 3438, Letter of the Colonial Office Minister, De Langlade, to the High Commissioner of Indochina, 24 January 1946.

[62] Schoepfel (2014), 127–30.

[63] Paul H. Kratoska, South East Asia, Colonial History: Independence through revolutionary war (New York, NY: Routledge, 2001), 370.

[64] The prosecution of Japanese war criminals had three different legal categories: (1) 'class A' crimes were reserved for those who had committed a crime against peace; (2) 'class B' crimes were reserved for those who committed conventional war crimes; (3) 'Class C' crimes were reserved for those who committed 'crimes against humanity.' See: no author, 'Report by the State-War-Navy Coordinating Subcommittee for the Far East.' *Foreign Relations of the United States* 4 (1945): 926–36.

[65] US General Douglas MacArthur, the Supreme Commander for the Allied Powers (SCAP) in Japan, appointed an international panel of 11 judges from Australia, Canada, China, India, the Netherlands, New Zealand, the Philippines, the United Kingdom, the USA, the Soviet Union and France. About the Tokyo Trial see: Neil Boister and Robert Cryer, *The Tokyo International Military Tribunal: a reappraisal* (Oxford: Oxford Univ. Press, 2008), Madoka Futamura, *War crimes tribunals and transitional justice: the Tokyo trial and the Nuremberg legacy* (London: Routledge, 2008); Richard H. Minear, *Victor's Justice: the Tokyo War Crimes Trial* (Tokyo: Tuttle, 1984); Yuma Totani, *The Tokyo War Crimes Trials: The Pursuit of Justice in World War II* (Cambridge, MA, Harvard East Asian monographs, 2009).

Table 8.1 Allied class B and C trials in Asia

	Number of cases	Number of accused
France	39	228
Philippines	72	169
Australia	294	949
Great Britain	330	978
Netherlands	448	1038
USA	456	1453
China	605	883
Total	2244	5698

Source: Hayashi Hiroshi, p. 5

Japanese nationals were charged with class B and C crimes in 51 different locations.[66] France conducted fewer Japanese war trials than any other major Allied powers in Asia, as Table 8.1 shows.[67]

Even though the UNWCC helped France join the transnational network for the coordination of war crimes prosecution in Asia, French involvement remained limited in Southeast Asia.

Investigating War Crimes: China, Great Britain and the USA

After the Japanese capitulation on 15 August 1945, Indochina became a pawn in a power struggle. The pursuit of Japanese war crimes constituted a strategic element in the pursuit of national interests. On behalf of the Allies, Nationalist China occupied Indochina above the 16th parallel, and the British occupied it below the 16th parallel.[68] Great Britain and China started to collate information on war crimes. In North Indochina, Nationalist China did not recognize France as an ally and questioned the authority of the French government to pursue war crimes trials. Chinese authorities viewed France as an illegitimate colonial power in Indochina.[69]

---

[66] Barak Kushner, "Paws of Empire", in Adam Clulow, ed., *Statecraft and Spectacle in East Asia, Studies in Taiwan-Japan relations* (New York, NY: Routledge, 2013), 116.
[67] Hayashi Hiroshi, *Sabakareta sensô hanzai*, (Tokyo: Iwanamishoten, 1998), 5.
[68] At the Potsdam Conference in July 1945, Allied chiefs of staff decided to temporarily partition Vietnam at the 16th parallel until the arrival of the French troops in Indochina: British forces would take the surrender of Japanese forces in Saigon for the southern half of Indochina, Chinese troops in the northern half. See: David G. Marr, *Vietnam 1945: The Quest for Power*, 241–96.
[69] ANOM, INF 1364, Letter of J. Meyrier, French ambassador in China to the Foreign Affairs Minister, 5 February 1947.

In early 1946, China sent about 400 Japanese suspected of war crimes back to Japan without even informing the French government.[70] Also, in May 1946, upon the evacuation of Chinese troops from Indochina, Chinese commanders transported 160 Japanese suspected of war crimes against Chinese nationals to Guangzhou.[71]

According to Piccigallo, Franco-Allied cooperation took place mainly in British-supervised theaters.[72] The British authorities in Singapore saw war crimes trials as a platform to earn credit in the eyes of the decolonization movement in Southeast Asia.[73] British officers led investigating teams in South Indochina. They arrested about 650 Japanese suspects of war crimes before January 1946 and sent the results of their investigations to the War Crimes Registry in Singapore, where the Allied Land Forces South East Asia (ALFSEA) led the prosecution of Japanese war crimes in the region.[74] After 1946, Great Britain continued to collaborate intensively with France in the investigation of war crimes in order to help France to re-establish its standing as political power in the region.

A high degree of cooperation in the investigation, arrest, detention and transfer of war crimes suspects was required to ensure the Allied prosecution of Japanese war criminals. But coordination was lacking among all actors in Indochina in 1945 and 1946.[75] In late 1945, the US military was involved in the process of investigation in Indochina without having informed the French authorities. This mistrust was reflected in the fact that the French authorities interrogated suspected Japanese war criminals in 1946 just to get more information about the American hunt for war criminals in Indochina.[76]

---

[70] AN, BB30 / 1791, Letter of the Federal Justice Commissioner to the Minister of Justice, 13 June 1946.
[71] ANOM, INF 1364, Letter of J. Meyrier, French ambassador in China to the Foreign Affairs Minister, 5 February 1947.
[72] Philip R. Piccigallo, *The Japanese on Trial. Allied war crimes operations in the East, 1945–1951*, 205.
[73] Peter Dennis, *Troubled Days of Peace: Mountbatten and Southeast Asia Command, 1945–1946* (Manchester : Manchester University Press, 1987), 11–2.
[74] Iwakawa Takashi, *Kodokuno tsuchito narutomo : BC kyû senpan saiban* (Tokyo: Kôdansha, 1995), 400.
[75] DCAJM, French Permanent Military Tribunal in Saigon, *The Case of the Kempetai in Saigon*, Judgment 26, Note of the investigating judge at the Permanent Military Tribunal in Saigon.
[76] DCAJM, French Permanent Military Tribunal in Saigon, *The Case of the Kempetai in Saigon*, Judgment 26, Letter of the former chief of the Military Police Section in Indochina, S. Yoshioka, to the investigating judge at the Permanent Military Tribunal in Saigon, 28 December 1947.

The onset of the Cold War marked a qualitative shift in relations between France and the USA in Indochina. After 1947, the USA strongly supported France in its fight against the Viet Minh and the collaboration between France and the USA became less strained in Southeast Asia. In early 1947, the US military mission in Japan helped Captain Gabrillagues, the French representative from the War Crimes Section in Saigon, to send 52 Japanese suspects of war crimes back from Japan to trial in Saigon.[77] French military authorities assisted also US war crimes teams in regions under their control. But the difficulty of investigating war crimes in Indochina resulted in only four prosecutions by US authorities involving the executions of 11 American pilots by the Japanese.[78]

France actively cooperated with the British and American military authorities in East Asia. But the unfavorable background for France in Asia limited the results of war crimes investigations.

The Saigon Military Tribunal: A Criminal Court with Political Implications

Because the Japanese had put an end to the French colonial presence in *l'Indochine*, the 'Pearl of the French Empire,' the French prosecution of Japanese war crimes held special significance. The prosecutions took place in Saigon, in a climate of political and social strife, violence and a thirst for revenge and retribution from the French side. The Saigon Military Tribunal sought to speak the 'truth' about the Second World War; it used its institutional power to create an 'official version' of the past. The analysis of the structure and the internal dynamic of the Saigon court clearly show its political implications.[79]

Overview

The prosecution of war crimes in Saigon was limited by international political pressure.[80] Of the 228 defendants at the Court of Saigon, 68 were condemned to death (37 in absentia), 26 to hard labor for life (four in

---

[77] AMAE, Asie, Indochine 130, Note of the French Mission in Japan on the arrest of Japanese war criminals, 21 February 1947.
[78] Philip R. Piccigallo, *The Japanese on Trial. Allied war crimes operations in the East, 1945–1951*, 206.
[79] Schoepfel (2014), 136.
[80] Trefalt (2014), 732.

Table 8.2 Number of convictions, death sentences and acquittals

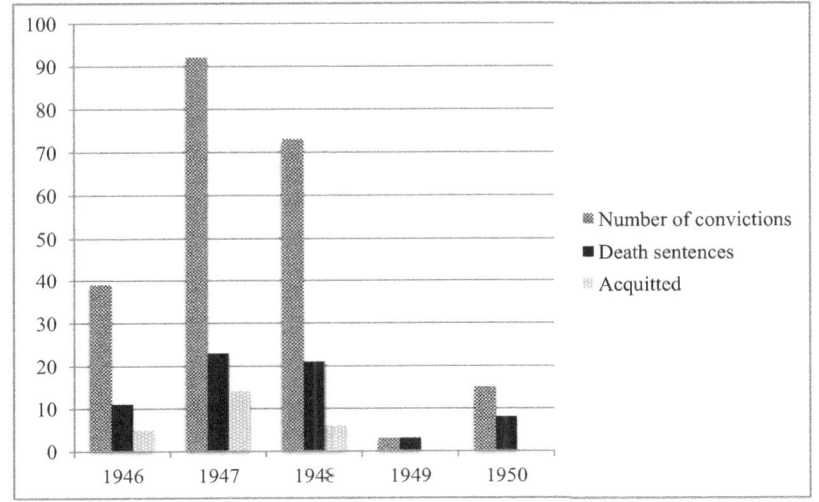

Source: Schoepfel based on DCAJM

This chart was designed by the author using the proceedings of the French Permanent Military Tribunal in Saigon from 1946 to 1950. These proceedings are located at the DCAJM and at the International Research and Documentation Centre for War Crimes Trials (ICWC). See: DCAJM, Proceedings of the French Permanent Military Tribunal in Saigon, 1946, 1947, 1948, 1949, 1950; ICWC/Bestand Le Blanc/Crimes de guerre japonais – tribunal militaire de Saigon

absentia), 62 to a hard labor term (two in absentia), and 40 to a penalty of less than five years of imprisonment, while 26 were acquitted (Table 8.2).[81]

Table 8.2 shows that there are two clearly different phases in the prosecution of war crimes in Saigon. From 1946 to 1948, there were an increasing number of convictions. After 1949, the number of convictions decreased, and at the same time acquittals also decreased. The reason could be that the more serious cases, which resulted in clear convictions, needed longer investigation and came to court only after some preparation.[82]

After 1949, France was losing the war in Indochina. On 8 March 1949, France made belated and ineffective offers of limited independence to three 'associated states' within the French Union: Vietnam, Cambodia and Laos.

---

[81] Dépôt Central des Archives de la Justice Militaire (DCAJM), French Permanent Military Tribunal in Saigon, 1946, 1947, 1948, 1949, 1950.

[82] DCAJM, French Permanent Military Tribunal in Saigon, *The Case of the Langson Massacre*, Judgment, 25 January 1950.

Table 8.3 Locations of Japanese war crimes in Indochina

Cochinchina	67	28.8 %
Tonkin	60	25.8 %
Cambodia	52	22.3 %
Annam (Center of Vietnam)	32	13.7 %
Laos	22	9.4 %
Total	233	100 %

Source: Schoepfel based on DCAJM

This chart was designed by the author using the proceedings of the French Permanent Military Tribunal in Saigon from 1946 to 1950. These proceedings are located at the DCAJM and at ICWC. See: DCAJM, Proceedings of the French Permanent Military Tribunal in Saigon, 1946, 1947, 1948, 1949, 1950; ICWC/Bestand Le Blanc/ Crimes de guerre japonais – tribunal militaire de Saigon

In October 1949, the victory of Mao Tse Tung over Chiang Kai-shek gave a powerful ally to the Viet Minh. In this respect, the French government adopted a new war crimes trials policy in Asia in accordance with the Cold War and the perception of Japan as a new powerful ally in Asia.[83] After 1949, many Japanese war criminals had their sentences commuted.[84]

The Statute of the Saigon Permanent Military Tribunal

The prosecution of Japanese and German war criminals relied on the same legislation. Persons liable to prosecution were:

> Enemy nationals or agents not of French nationality who are serving the enemy administration [...] and who are guilty of crimes or offenses committed since the beginning of hostilities; either in France or in territories under the authority of France, or against a French national, or a person under the French protection [...] or against the property of any natural persons enumerated above, and against any French corporate bodies.[85]

Punishable offenses included:

1. The illegal recruitment of armed forces, [...]
2. Criminal association [...] organisations or agencies engaged in systematic terrorism; [...]

---

[83] Trefalt (2014), 738–39.
[84] DCAJM, French Permanent Military Tribunal in Saigon, 1946, 1947, 1948, 1949, 1950.
[85] Ordinance of 28 August 1944, art. 1.

3. Poisoning [...]
4. Premeditated murder [...] shall include killing as a form of reprisal; [...]
5. Illegal restraint [...] shall include forced labour of civilians
6. Illegal restraint [...] shall include the employment on war work of prisoners of war or conscripted civilians;
7. Illegal restraint [...] shall include the employment of prisoners of war or civilians in order to protect the enemy;
8. Pillage [...][86]

However, there were problems defining the exact beginning of the French–Japanese War, which had proceeded in stages:

1. When the colonial administration of French Indochina was bequeathed to the Vichy French government, it ceded the control of Hanoi and Saigon in 1940 to Japan.
2. In 1941, Japan extended its control over the whole of French Indochina.
3. In March 1945, the Japanese imprisoned the Vichy French and took direct control of Vietnam until the Allies defeated them in August.

The federal councillor at the Office of Legal Affairs, Albert Torel, underlined his views that the Japanese had engaged in military operations against French troops from March 1945 onwards, and therefore the date should be considered as a starting point. His suggestion was accepted at the Legal Office and the Political Office of the High Commission in Saigon. War crimes to be tried in Saigon were then restricted to the period between 9 March 1945 and 15 August 1945.[87]

Composition of the Court and Procedure

The war crimes prosecution took place in an open session at the Saigon Military Court. The Code of Criminal Procedure laid out the judicial procedure to be followed for the war crimes prosecution. Proceedings were opened and directed by the president, who was responsible for the proper conduct of the hearing. The prosecutor had to read the indictment act in front of the court. After reading the indictment, the president

---

[86] Ordinance of 28 August 1944, art. 2.
[87] ANOM, INDO HCI ConsPol 153, Note of Albert Torel.

asked questions to the parties, witnesses and those in the know, in order to clear ambiguities and shed light on the subject. The prosecution and defense then presented their arguments. If necessary, the court could ask for further investigation or reconsideration, and the trial was postponed and rescheduled.[88] At the end of the hearing, the court issued a judgment. The public hearing could take place over a number of days but, more often, a case normally lasted about half a day.

'Nolle prosequi'

In Saigon, the examining judge often decided to voluntarily discontinue criminal charges before the trial began.[89] The entry of a *nolle prosequi*[90] was not an acquittal, but the Japanese suspected of war crimes were liberated.

The apprehension of Japanese war crimes was difficult because of the delay in the disarmament of Japanese troops, the Viet Minh fight for independence and the insecurity in particular regions.[91] France did not control certain cities or regions in Indochina and could not have access to these areas, and carry out war crimes investigations there. In June 1946, the War Crimes Section in Indochina had finally identified 933 Japanese war crimes suspects.[92] The General Directorate for Studies and Research and local authorities collected evidence from intelligence reports and interrogations. After the investigation, the French authority sent a file document to the UNWCC. The selection of evidence for Japanese war crimes was easier in urban environments. Table 8.4 shows that most of the crimes were identified in Cochinchina (South Vietnam), Tonkin (North Vietnam) and in Cambodia.[93]

---

[88] For example, the trial against Taketsubo for murder and rape was sent back to court four times because the defendant claimed that his name was not Taketsubo but Taketsugi. See: French Permanent Military Tribunal in Saigon, *The Judgment of Taketsubo*, Judgment 498, 31 August 1948.

[89] DCAJM, French Permanent Military Tribunal in Saigon, *The Case of the Langson Massacre*, Record of the proceedings, 25 January 1950.

[90] The *nolle prosequi* represents the traditional power of the Attorney General to stop proceedings.

[91] ANOM, AFFPOL 3439, Letter of the French prosecutor Robert Oneto to the Minister of the Foreign Affairs, 28 January 1947.

[92] AN, BB30 / 1791, Letter of the Federal Justice Commissioner to the Minister of Justice, 13 June 1946.

[93] DCAJM, Proceedings of the French Permanent Military Tribunal in Saigon, 1946, 1947, 1948, 1949, 1950.

Table 8.4 Charges against class B and C war criminals

Sequestration with torture	167	65.7 %
Complicity in murder	21	8.3 %
Intentional assault and battery	14	5.5 %
Spoliation	12	4.7 %
Murder	10	3.9 %
Plundering	10	3.9 %
Illegal recruitment of POWs or French protected	6	2.4 %
Ill-treatment and brutality against POWs	5	2 %
Complicity in assault and battery	5	2 %
Complicity in plundering	4	1.6 %
Total	254	100 %

Source: Schoepfel based on DCAJM

This chart was designed by the author using the proceedings of the French Permanent Military Tribunal in Saigon from 1946 to 1950. These proceedings are located at the DCAJM and at ICWC. See: DCAJM, Proceedings of the French Permanent Military Tribunal in Saigon, 1946, 1947, 1948, 1949, 1950; ICWC/Bestand Le Blanc/Crimes de guerre japonais – tribunal militaire de Saigon

The investigation files were forwarded to Saigon to start proceedings. An investigating judge processed the complaint. He questioned witnesses, interrogated suspects and ordered further investigations. His role was not to prosecute the accused, but rather to gather facts. A Saigon newspaper commented about the interrogation of Japanese war crimes that: 'Great dexterity is required to obtain information from the Japanese, who seem to be afflicted with amnesia.'[94]

The examining judge had to decide if there was a valid case against Japanese suspected of war crimes or not. For example, on 22 July 1948, the examining judge, Clevenot, decided to voluntarily discontinue criminal charges against Ichiro Miyoshi on charges of rape and sequestration with torture and pillage, although the defendant took moral responsibility for his crimes. Evidence was too weak to carry the burden of proof. Therefore, Clevenot had to decide that the charges against Ichiro Miyoshi were regulated only by 'Moral Law,' meaning that his crimes were socially unacceptable and immoral but that it was impossible for the judge to condemn them. Clevenot regretted that the legislation on war crimes was very contentious.[95]

---

[94] *Journal de Saigon*, 9 Mai 1946.
[95] Archives du Comité International de la Croix Rouge (Geneva), B AG G.7/IX 2. Criminels de Guerre Généralités 1945–1950.

Charges of War Crimes

The Saigon Military Tribunal tried mainly defendants accused of committing crimes against the Resistance networks supporting the Allies at the end of the Second World War. The Japanese wanted to stop and 'break up [...] the enemy intelligence network' in Indochina. They arrested many French Resistance fighters and 'resorted to torture with the aim of extracting information.'[96]

Despite a high number of identified war crimes, Japanese war criminals were convicted of only 254 charges.[97] Table 8.4 shows that the majority of them were convicted for sequestration with torture.

In an affidavit, the Japanese colonel T. Kodo submitted many detailed reports for the Saigon Military Court on Japanese war crimes committed against French citizens in Indochina.[98] In his view, the Japanese arrested French nationals only when they had legitimate grounds to suspect them of espionage and the use of torture was justified to extract information.[99]

According to a first analysis of the indictments and the judgments obtained by the author, the civilians represented the largest group of victims (58 %), followed by soldiers (16 %), prisoners of war (12 %), companies (8 %) and American prisoners of war and aviators (6 %). The majority of civilian victims of war recognized before the Saigon Tribunal were French (70 %).

Among the civilian victims, women constituted only a seventh of the victims. They were the victims of murder (37.5 %), rape (25 %), sequestration followed by torture (25 %), plunder and robbery (12.5 %).[100] To illustrate the prosecution of sexual violence, here is an example: a Japanese captain was tried because he had captured two French sisters (one was only 14 years old) in March 1945, and allowed his troops to rape them

---

[96] DCJAM, French Permanent Military Tribunal in Saigon, *The Case of the Kempetai in Saigon*, Judgment 26, Letter of the former chief of the Military Police Section in Indochina, S. Yoshioka, to the investigating judge at the Permanent Military Tribunal in Saigon, 28 December 1947.

[97] DCAJM, Proceedings of the French Permanent Military Tribunal in Saigon, 1946, 1947, 1948, 1949, 1950.

[98] DCAJM, French Permanent Military Tribunal in Saigon, *The Case of the Kempetai in Saigon*, Judgment 26, Note of Colonel T. Kodo, about the arrest of French resistance members, 9 October 1946.

[99] Ibid.

[100] DCAJM, Proceedings of the French Permanent Military Tribunal in Saigon, 1946, 1947, 1948, 1949, 1950.

Table 8.5 Overview of the Japanese defendants

Servicemen	210	92 %
Civilian	15	6.6 %
Unknown	3	1.4 %
Total	218	100 %

Source: Schoepfel based on DCAJM

This chart was designed by the author using the proceedings of the French Permanent Military Tribunal in Saigon from 1946 to 1950. These proceedings are located at the DCAJM and at ICWC. See: DCAJM, Proceedings of the French Permanent Military Tribunal in Saigon, 1946, 1947, 1948, 1949, 1950; ICWC/Bestand Le Blanc/Crimes de guerre japonais – tribunal militaire de Saigon

over a period of seven weeks before killing them in May 1945.[101] He was subsequently sentenced to death.

Japanese Defendants

Japanese defendants at the Saigon Military Tribunal can be defined as those incarcerated because of political crimes committed against French resistance fighters from 9 March 1945 to 15 August 1945. Table 8.5 shows that 92 % of the defendants were servicemen.

Most of the Japanese defendants were warrant officers (63 %). A few were junior officers (19 %), privates (15 %) and senior officers (3 %). Colonel was the highest rank of defendants tried (Table 8.6).

Of the accused, 155 or 68 % of the total defendants belonged to the Kempeitai, the military police of the Imperial Japanese Army.[102] Detention centers and military camps were placed under the direction of the Kempeitai. The Kempeitai was often compared with the Nazi Gestapo at the Saigon Military Court, insofar as their methods of inquiry were comparable to those of the Gestapo.[103]

The three most important trials against the Kempeitai were held between October 1946 and April 1948. The Saigon Military Court

---

[101] Archives Nationales du Japon, *Saigon saiban shiryô* (Fonds du procès de Saigon), n° 11.
[102] DCAJM, Proceedings of the French Permanent Military Tribunal in Saigon, 1946, 1947, 1948, 1949, 1950.
[103] Jautée, 'Les Camps Japonais en Indochine pendant la Seconde Guerre Mondiale,' 4.

Table 8.6 Defendants by rank

	Rank	Number tried	Percentage
Senior Officers	Colonel	6	2.9
	Lieutenant-Colonel	1	0.5
Junior Commissioned Officers	Major	9	4.3
	Captain	17	8.1
	Lieutenant	6	2.9
	2nd Lieutenant	10	4.8
Warrant Officers	Adjutant	28	13.3
	Sergeant-Major	9	4.3
	Staff Sergeant	17	8.1
	Sergeant	48	22.9
	Master Corporal	6	2.9
	Corporal	33	15.7
Privates	Private first class	4	1.9
	Private	17	8.1
Total		210	100

Source: Schoepfel based on DCAJM

This chart was designed by the author using the proceedings of the French Permanent Military Tribunal in Saigon from 1946 to 1950. These proceedings are located at the DCAJM and at ICWC. See: DCAJM, Proceedings of the French Permanent Military Tribunal in Saigon, 1946, 1947, 1948, 1949, 1950; ICWC/Bestand Le Blanc/Crimes de guerre japonais – tribunal militaire de Saigon

judged the Kempeitai jointly under the charge of sequestration with torture in three trials: 27 former members of the Phnom Penh Kempeitai in a trial on 19 November 1946, 49 former members of the Saigon Kempeitai on 14 February 1947, and 37 former members of the Hanoi Kempeitai on 5 April 1948.

Defense

Japanese War criminals could choose their own attorneys, and of course a few of them wanted to be defended only by Japanese lawyers. The Allies conducted trials in collaboration with a small group of Japanese lawyers they had chosen and whom they trusted. These Japanese lawyers were appointed in many different trials in Southeast Asia, in Saigon, Shanghai and Singapore for example.[104] If Japanese war criminals refused to choose

---

[104] DCAJM, French Permanent Military Tribunal in Saigon, *The Case of the Langson Massacre*, Plaidoirie générale, 25 January 1950.

JUSTICE AND DECOLONIZATION: WAR CRIMES ON TRIAL IN SAIGON, 1946-1950   191

their own attorneys, the examining judge appointed a French defense counsel for them. The translation into Japanese was to be made by a sworn translator from the country.[105]

In Saigon, the War Crimes Section had established a particular defense strategy for the Japanese defendants to help them to defend themselves against the French indictment. Mitigating circumstances included family status, military career, position during the war, civilian profession, education, religion, stay abroad, knowledge of foreign languages, associations with a political party, previous punishment, good treatment of French nationals, reaction to the indictment.[106] The majority of the accused emphasized the fact that they had protected the French from the Vietnamese.[107] One example is Kanai Tetsuo, a Kempeitai officer, who was accused of sequestration with torture. In his statement before court, he underlined first that during his work from February 1943 to March 1945 with French authorities, the French very much appreciated him, and secondly that he protected the French population from Viet Minh's acts of terrorism after 9 March 1945.[108] Kanai Tetsuo was tried but his assistance to the French population was accepted as a mitigating factor for the final judgment.

Verdicts and Implementation of Sentences

Military tribunals reached all decisions by majority vote.[109] Upon a conviction, French military tribunals awarded a wide range of punishments under the Penal Code: death, penal servitude for life; deportation; penal servitude for a term; detention and confinement.[110] Before issuing a sentence, tribunals considered any possible extenuating circumstances. Under the Code of Military Justice, an accused, once convicted, could register an appeal within 24 hours of the time of judgment. Review of such petitions

---

[105] French Code of Criminal Procedure, Article 594.
[106] DCJAM, French Permanent Military Tribunal in Saigon, *The Case of the Kempetai in Saigon*, Judgment 26. Defense rights.
[107] DCJAM, French Permanent Military Tribunal in Saigon, *The Case of the Kempetai in Saigon*, Judgment 26. Defense rights.
[108] DCJAM, French Permanent Military Tribunal in Saigon, *The Case of the Kempetai in Saigon*, Judgment 26. Defense rights of Kanai Tetsuo.
[109] Code of Military Justice, Article 222.
[110] Penal Code, Article 7.

Table 8.7 Number of convictions given by sentence

Death	68	29.8 %
Hard labor for life	26	11.4 %
>15 years of hard labor	17	7.5 %
10–15 years of hard labor	28	12.3 %
5–10 years of hard labor	17	7.5 %
<5 years' imprisonment	40	17.5 %
Acquitted	26	11.4 %
Others	6	2.6 %
Total	228	100 %

Source: Schoepfel based on DCAJM

This chart was designed by the author using the proceedings of the French Permanent Military Tribunal in Saigon from 1946 to 1950. These proceedings are located at the DCAJM and at ICWC. See: DCAJM, Proceedings of the French Permanent Military Tribunal in Saigon, 1946, 1947, 1948, 1949, 1950; ICWC/Bestand Le Blanc/Crimes de guerre japonais – tribunal militaire de Saigon

by a Military Appeal Tribunal followed. The court concentrated exclusively on determining whether the decision pronounced thereby constituted a correct application of the law.

In Asia, about 920 accused of war crimes were convicted to death sentence.[111] In Saigon, the death penalty was the most frequently imposed sanction (29.8 %), as Table 8.7 shows in the number of convictions by sentence.

Japanese war criminals were held at either at Chi Hoa prison in Saigon, or at the island penitentiary of Poulo Condore in Vietnam. The last executions took place in May 1951.[112] In May 1950, class B and C war criminals came under American jurisdiction at Sugamo Prison in Tokyo. After the Japanese return to sovereignty in April 1952, the government of Japan took custody of them, although war criminals' sentences could only be modified with the approval of the French government.[113] By that time, most of the Japanese war criminals had already been released or their sentences had been reduced.[114]

---

[111] Gavan Daws, *Prisoners of the Japanese: POWs of World War II in the Pacific* (New York, NY: William Morrow and Company, 1994), 370.
[112] SHD, H10 H6039. Executions Poulo Condore 1950–51.
[113] San Francisco Peace Treaty, Art. 11.
[114] Trefalt (2014), 740–741.

Conclusion

In the aftermath of the Second World War, the Allied war crimes trials had to address a new global issue in Southeast Asia: the struggle for decolonization. At the Saigon Military Court, the French prosecution of Japanese war crimes was entangled in the Viet Minh fight for independence.

War crimes prosecution offered significant advantages for the new French government. Firstly, they highlighted the fact that France was accepted as an ally in the transnational network for the coordination of war crimes prosecution in Asia. Secondly, it was a way for France to reassert its sovereignty over Indochina after 1946. Thirdly, it helped create an official version of the Second World War, stressing the fact that there were many French victims of the Japanese violence who had supported the Allies during the war. It was thus no impartial justice. The pursuit of justice at the Saigon Military Court had strengthened French national prestige in the Far East.

Against the backdrop of fighting with the Viet Minh and Cold War tensions, war crimes trials represented a secondary priority for France in its attempt to regain power in Asia. The first priority was the restoration of the French rule of law in Indochina and the prosecution of suspected collaborators as part of the legal purge. From 1946 to 1948, war crimes trials seemed to facilitate the consolidation of French power. After 1949, the numbers and correspondence show that the trials lost importance in the political spectrum. Given that other Allies such as the Dutch and British had already ended their war crimes prosecutions, this is not surprising, but it underlines the ongoing political and military struggle in which France found itself in Indochina.

The Viet Minh fight for independence affected the outcome of the war crimes trials in Indochina. Despite the French efforts to create a fair justice system, the Saigon Military Court also had to deal with the ambiguity of the new colonial authorities. The war crimes definition had been restricted to offenses committed by the Japanese against the French Resistance fighters between March and August 1945. Moreover, the French Colonial Office had to adapt the scope of war crimes prosecution to local circumstances. The difficulties in the investigation, arrest, detention and transfer of Japanese war criminals in the struggle for decolonization limited the number of convictions. Even though France had identified 933 Japanese war crimes suspects in 1946, many cases were dismissed due to insufficient evidence. About 20 % of the 228 Japanese defendants at the Court of Saigon were condemned in abstentia. France thus convicted fewer Japanese war criminals than any other major Allied power.

Acknowledgements The author would like to thank Dr. Beatrice Trefalt and Dr. Kerstin von Lingen for their constructive comments.

CHAPTER 9

Netherlands East Indies' War Crimes Trials in the Face of Decolonization

Lisette Schouten

After the conclusion of the Second World War, the Dutch convened war crimes trials in both the Netherlands and in the Netherlands East Indies (NEI). These trials were, however, mounted in very different circumstances, and drew on different bodies of law. While peace had been re-established in the Netherlands, the Netherlands Indies war crimes trials took place within the framework of decolonization and the Indonesian Republic's postwar struggle for independence.

More than in the European theater, the trials held in the Netherlands Indies were part of a larger Allied trial program. When the war drew to a close, it had been agreed among the Allies that, like in Europe, they would follow standardized procedures for the investigation and adjudication of war crimes in Asia, with the United Nations War Crimes Commission (UNWCC) as the coordinating body.[1] However, shortly after Japan's surrender, South East Asia Command was still awaiting the final Allied

---

[1] Representatives of the Allied governments gathered in the London International Assembly, the International Commission for Penal Reform and Development, and the United Nations War Crimes Commission (UNWCC) to discuss legal methods for dealing with atrocities. The Netherlands government-in-exile in London played an active and

L. Schouten (✉)
Heidelberg University, Heidelberg, Germany

decision on arrangements for dealing with war criminals. In October 1945, Lord Admiral Louis Mountbatten, Commander-in-Chief of Allied Land Forces South East Asia (ALFSEA), therefore assumed responsibility for the investigation, preparation and trial of 'minor' Japanese war crimes in Southeast Asia.[2] The trials themselves, however, would be based on national legislations and procedures.

In order to collate information on war crimes and the identity and location of suspected war criminals a War Crimes Registry was set up in Singapore. Seventeen investigation teams, led by British officers, were created and the results of their investigations were sent to the registry.[3] At ALFSEA headquarters in Singapore, a liaison section was set up by the Dutch (along with the Australians, Americans and French) where in December 1945 two former Dutch prisoners of war, Mr. B. Damen and Mr. J. Ph. Mullemeister, were appointed as liaison officers.[4]

During the war, Dutch intelligence operations had mostly been unsuccessful, leaving the Indies authorities in the dark about the general situation

---

determined role, through their representatives, Dr. J. M. de Moor and Dr. M.W. Mouton, in these early international efforts.

[2] Although official ratification of these arrangements never took place, they were later implicitly accepted by the Netherlands Indies government. Institute for War, Holocaust and Genocide Studies (NIOD), collection 400, inventarisnummer (inv. no.) 1926, 'Voorlopige informatie van het Departement van Justitie te Batavia over de berechting van oorlogsmisdadigers' (20 February 1946), 15.

[3] Four of these seventeen War Crimes Investigation Teams (WCIT), were stationed in the Netherlands Indies and placed under a British war crimes coordinating officer at HQ AFNEI. While the teams were led by British officers, Dutch staff was added. Teams 1, 2 and 3 were stationed on Java, with WCIT 1 and 3 positioned around Batavia while WCIT 2 worked in the surroundings of Surabaya. WCIT 4, with Captain N. D. J. Read-Collins as C.O. was stationed on Sumatra and had its base in Medan. Teams 2 and 3 were dissolved in the beginning of 1946 and when the British withdrew from the Netherlands Indies in November 1946 their tasks were transferred to the military prosecutors of the temporary courts-martial. The registry became part of the War Crimes (Coordination) Section in May 1946.

NIOD, collection 400, inv. no. 4526, J. Ph. Mullemeister, 'Verslag van de werkzaamheden der Nederlandse Liaison Sectie voor oorlogsmisdaden te Singapore over het tijdvak December 1945 tot December 1947' (Singapore, December 1947), 8–12. Bart van Poelgeest, *Japanse besognes: Nederland en Japan 1945–1975* (Den Haag: SDU Uitgevers, 1999), 91–2.

Zahar mentions eighteen SEAC war crime investigation teams. Alexander Zahar, 'Trial Procedure at the British Military Courts, Hong Kong, 1946–1948,' in Suzannah Linton, ed., *Hong Kong's war crimes trials* (Oxford: Oxford University Press, 2013), 35.

[4] Mullemeister, 'Verslag van de werkzaamheden,' 2, 5.

in large parts of the Netherlands East Indies.[5] Yet, through interrogations of those who had been able to flee from the archipelago, the Netherlands Forces Intelligence Service (NEFIS) was able to gather some sparse information on collaboration with and atrocities committed by the Japanese.[6] Additionally, while the main islands of Java and Sumatra were still under control of the Japanese military administration at the time of Japan's surrender,[7] Allied forces—often accompanied by Netherlands Indies Civil Administration (NICA) detachments—had reoccupied Hollandia, Biak, Morotai, Tarakan and Balikpapan.[8] With the help of the Allies, these NICA detachments, together with advance parties from NEFIS, started to collect and gain access to data concerning the Japanese occupation.[9] Although their efforts were hampered by a lack of personnel, dossiers were prepared and through a decree issued in June 1945 (*Staatsblad van Nederlandsch-Indië* (Statute Book of the Netherlands Indies) 1945 no. 112) the foundations for the trial of Japanese war criminals were laid even before Japan's capitulation.[10]

When, shortly after the ending of hostilities, more and more information about the wartime situation started to flow in, the countless atrocities

---

[5] The intelligence operations of the Netherlands Forces Intelligence Service (NEFIS) on Java and those of the Anglo Dutch Country Section (ADCS) on Sumatra had been a fiasco and also MacArthur had failed to collect any intelligence. Petra M. H. Groen, *Marsroutes en dwaalsporen: het Nederlands militair-strategische beleid in Indonesië 1945–1950* (Den Haag: SDU Uitgevers, 1991), 18 and Andrew Roadnight, 'Sleeping with the Enemy: Britain, Japanese Troops and the Netherlands East Indies, 1945–1946,' *History* 87 (2002): 248. Stanley Woodburn Kirby, *The war against Japan*, 5 vols. (London: HMSO, 1969), vol. 5, The Surrender of Japan, 311 (hereafter Woodburn Kirby, *Surrender*). Jaap de Moor, *Generaal Spoor: Triomf en Tragiek van een Legercommandant* (Amsterdam: Boom, 2011), 163–4. See also Johannes J. Nortier, *Acties in de Archipel*, (Franeker: Uitgeverij T. Wever bv, 1985).

[6] De Moor, *Generaal Spoor*, 139.

[7] During the war, Sumatra was placed under control of the 25th Army, Java and Madura were under the 16th Army, while Borneo and eastern Indonesia were controlled by the Navy 2nd South Fleet. The Japanese established a military administration on Java and Sumatra and naval civil administration on the outer islands.

[8] Elly Touwen-Bouwsma, 'Van Banzai tot Bersiap,' in *Tussen banzai en bersiap: de afwikkeling van de Tweede Wereldoorlog in Nederlands-Indië*, Elly Touwen-Bouwsma and Petra Groen, eds. (Den Haag: SDU Uitgevers, 1996), 10–1. Govert C. Zijlmans, *Eindstrijd en ondergang van de Indische Bestuursdienst: Het Corps Binnenlands Bestuur op Java, 1945–1950* (Amsterdam: Bataafsche Leeuw, 1985), 28–32.

[9] De Moor, *Generaal Spoor*, 148. The Dutch also benefitted from the efforts of British and Australian war crimes investigation teams who also collated information on war crimes and the identity and location of suspected war criminals in the NEI.

[10] Van Poelgeest, *Japanse besognes*, 88–9.

committed against its population motivated the Indies' government to pursue and punish those responsible for the committed crimes. On 11 September 1945 a *Regeringsbureau tot Nasporing van Oorlogsmisdrijven* (Government Bureau for the Investigation of War Crimes) was established in Brisbane,[11] while a second Regeringsbureau was later set up in The Hague to interrogate those persons who had already been repatriated to the Netherlands.[12] Despite the unremitting efforts of its officers, the investigation efforts were plagued by time constrains—as many of the Dutch victims were being repatriated back to the Netherlands—as well as unqualified and insufficient personnel. Work was also hampered by the unavailability of photos to establish a positive identification of the suspects, the repatriation of Japanese troops and the fact that many of the Japanese suspects were interned far from the location of the crimes committed.[13]

Meanwhile, the number of accusations brought forward in Singapore was so excessive that in January 1946 another team was founded: the Netherlands War Crimes Investigation Team (NWCIT) led by Captain J. G. Benders.[14] The NWCIT examined war crimes committed by the Japanese, Koreans and Formosans within the Netherlands Indies as well as war crimes committed against Dutch nationals elsewhere in the Pacific theater. By February 1946, their investigations had been extended to cover war crimes committed by (Indonesian) independence fighters, collaborators with the Japanese or Indonesian independence

---

[11] NIOD, collection 400, inv. no. 1905, 'Uittreksel uit het register der besluiten van den Lieutenant-Gouverneur Generaal van Nederlandsch-Indië' (Brisbane, 11 September 1945). The Bureau was initially established in Brisbane but relocated to Batavia.

[12] On August 1, 1946 a Sub-Bureau Nederland tot Nasporing van Oorlogsmisdaden was founded at the Commissariaat voor Indische Zaken. Between August 1946 and March 1948, 447 interrogation reports were made. Members of the sub-bureau were the aforementioned reserve Captain Benders (until April 1947), W. Th. Spier, and C. S. Sant, who all had been part of the war crimes investigations teams in Medan and Singapore. A. Mieremet became head of the sub-bureau, assisted in his activities by several secretaries.

NIOD, collection 400, inv. no. 486, A. Mieremet, 'Verslag over de werkzaamheden van het Subbureau Nederland van het Regeringsbureau tot Nasporing van Oorlogsmisdaden' (1948).

[13] NIOD, collection 400, inv. no. 650, 'Gecertificeerd verslag Nefis Balikpapan oorlogsmisdaden 1946'. Robert Cribb, 'Avoiding clemency: the trial and transfer of Japanese war criminals in Indonesia, 1946–1949,' *Japanese Studies* 31 (2011): 160–1.

[14] Around 1000 persons had been interrogated under oath, when the NWCIT of Captain Benders was dissolved in May 1946. Mullemeister, 'Verslag van de werkzaamheden,' 19–20.

movement and Europeans with proscribed political affiliations during and after the war.¹⁵

Temporary Courts-Martial

In the meantime, it had been decided between ALFSEA headquarters and the Netherlands Indies attorney-general in December 1945 that the cases with predominantly Dutch victims would be allocated to the Netherlands Indies authorities without interference from Singapore. The attorney-general subsequently assigned each case to one of the *temporaire krijgsraden* (temporary courts-martial) of which there were eventually 23, 12 of them dealing with war crimes cases. The courts were not just convened to hear cases against the Japanese accused of war crimes. They also, often in the same composition but on different legal grounds, dealt with cases against European, Eurasian and Indonesian collaborators; Indonesian independence fighters; and Royal Netherlands Indies Army (KNIL) soldiers who had committed 'excesses' during the struggle for independence.¹⁶

Each court-martial consisted of a president and two members, assisted by a legal secretary, who were either serving officers or civilians given a military rank under the state of emergency that had been in place since May 1940.¹⁷ As there was a lack of qualified staff, many of the judges worked at both the courts-martial and the civilian courts. The prosecutors were usually civilians, and like the judges, often served in several capacities—for example, some of them also functioned as the court secretary or had previously be employed as investigators and interrogators.¹⁸ Most of

---

¹⁵ NIOD, collection 400, inv. no. 442, J. G. Benders, 'Rapport uitgebracht ingevolge mondelinge opdracht van den heer Procureur-Generaal Generaal Professor Mr. Jonkers' (8 March 1946).

¹⁶ Jan Bank (Introduction), *De excessen nota: Nota betreffende het archievenonderzoek naar gegevens omtrent excessen in Indonesië begaan door Nederlandse militairen in de periode 1945–1950* (Den Haag: SDU Uitgevers, 1995), Annex 8, 2.

¹⁷ Levinus F. de Groot, *Berechting Japanse oorlogsmisdadigers in Nederlands-Indië 1946–1949: Temporaire Krijgsraad Batavia*, 2 vols. (Den Bosch: Art & Research, 1990), vol. 1, 18.

¹⁸ NIOD, collection 400, inv. no. 5325, Christoffel van den Berg, 'Verslag werkzaamheden' (Batavia, 19 February 1949).

the personnel involved had a Dutch or Eurasian background, only a handful of Indonesians participated in the trials.[19]

The defendants were mostly represented by Japanese lawyers who had traveled from Japan to the Netherlands Indies or by officers from the Japanese military still present in the Netherlands Indies.[20] If the accused believed that the president or the members might not be suitable judges in their case, they were allowed to challenge them on grounds of lack of impartiality.[21] And even if there was no right for appeal, the defendants had the option to summit petitions for mercy.[22]

The reasoned verdicts were subject to a confirmation (a so-called *fiat executie*) by the commanding general of the area concerned. In those cases in which the death penalty had been given the commanding officer had to refer the verdict to the lieutenant governor-general for decision as to whether pardon should be granted. If contact with the lt-governor-general was for some reason impossible, the commanding officer was authorized to give the fiat of execution in his own responsibility.

In most cases, a conformation of the sentence was indeed given by the local commanders. Yet, when the commanding officer repudiated the trial's outcome, the case was referred back to the court for re-examination.

---

[19] Iris Heidebrink, 'Military Tribunals in the Netherlands East Indies,' in ed. Peter Post et al., *The Encyclopedia of Indonesia in the Pacific War* (Leiden: Brill, 2009), 414.

[20] The defendants had to right to choose their defense counsel; otherwise, one was assigned to them by the court. The Japanese lawyers were often assisted by Dutch-, Malay- or English-speaking interrogators.

[21] During interrogations, some of the suspects had not been treated according to the established rules and the judges were frequently presented with unreliable witnesses and unsafe evidence during trial. Additionally, many of the jurists involved had first-hand experience with Japanese atrocities; either as POW or as civilian prisoners. A situation that in certain cases led to biased justice, as acknowledged by former Batavian Judge L. F. de Groot.
De Groot, *Berechting Japanse oorlogsmisdadigers in Nederlands-Indië 1946–1949*, 376. Nationaal Archief, Den Haag, inventarisnummer. 2, nummer toegang 2.21.281.31, Collectie 584 L.F. de Groot, 1946–1991, Draft of an untitled article by P. Schumacher on L. F. de Groot (September 1989), annexed to letter from P. Schumacher to De Groot (19 September 1989), 4. Levinus F. de Groot, 'De rechtspraak inzake oorlogsmisdrijven in Nederlands-Indië (1947–1949),' *Militair Rechtelijk Tijdschrift* 78 (1985): 86. Charles van der Sloot, a former investigation officer in Morotai and substitute judge-advocate at the temporary court-martial in Makassar, acknowledged that hatred for the Japanese influenced the legal decision-making of the court. Interview with Charles van der Sloot, 13 November 2014, on file with author.

[22] United Nations War Crimes Commission, *Law reports of trials of war criminals*, 15 vols. (London: HMSO, 1947–1949), vol. 11, 109–110.

If the court decided to uphold its verdict and the commanding officer still refused to give his fiat, the case was again referred back to the lt-governor-general. If he found himself in agreement with the court, instruction was given to the commanding officer to grant the 'fiat of execution.' In the event that the lt-governor-general agreed with the commanding general, the case was referred to the *Hoog Militair Gerechtshof van Nederlands-Indië* (Supreme Military Court for the Netherlands Indies) for the final decision.[23] In most cases referred to the Supreme Military Court, the accused was given a substantially higher penalty.[24]

The largest number of trials were held in the two main cities on Java and Sumatra, before the temporary courts-martial of Batavia and Medan. These courts dealt not only with the highest profile cases, but also with the greatest number of prisoner of war (POW) and civilian internment camp cases. The other temporary courts-martial, located in the so-called outer islands, were generally more occupied with cases in which the indigenous population had been the victim. In the 61 cases of the temporary court-martial in Hollandia for example, all but four victims had been either of Indonesian or Chinese nationality.[25]

The Legal Basis of the Trials

By December 1945, the Netherlands Indies had already selected around 200 Japanese suspects for trial, while dozens had been arrested.[26] After a novel legal framework for the courts was completed in June 1946, the first war crimes trial was held before the court martial in Batavia in August 1946.[27]

Although the NEI had a civil law jurisdiction, the definition of 'war crime' in the Netherlands Indies, drew on international law sources.[28]

---

[23] UNWCC, *Law Reports*, vol. 11, 109.

[24] Van Poelgeest, *Japanse besognes*. 107.

[25] Most victims had been *heiho*, auxiliary soldiers that had been recruited by the Japanese army among the Indonesian population were trained under Japanese officers and integrated into the Japanese army.

[26] Philip R. Piccigallo, *The Japanese on Trial: Allied War Crimes Operations in the East, 1945–1951* (Austin, TX: University of Texas Press, 1979), 178–9.

[27] This was the trial of Captain Sōmei Kenichi, former commander of the women's camp Cideng. The temporary court-martial in Batavia had been established on 31 December 1945. Between March 1946 and August 1946 it had primarily tried collaboration cases. De Groot, *Berechting Japanse oorlogsmisdadigers in Nederlands-Indië 1946–1949*, vol. 1, 21.

[28] However, in practice the 'definition of war crimes degree' did not replace but merely augmented the already existing penal code. Unlike the Netherlands, where the majority of

Staatsblad (Statute Book of the Netherlands Indies) no. 44 of 1946, known as the 'Definition of War Crimes Decree,' stated that war crimes were 'acts which constitute a violation of the laws and usages of war committed in time of war by subjects of an enemy power or by foreigners in the service of the enemy.'[29]

There are several reasons why the Dutch looked at the 'laws and customs of war' for prosecutable offenses and not the existing NEI penal code. Firstly, the NEI criminal statute had not given sufficient provision for the criminalization of various war crimes, as they were committed during the Pacific War. There existed in the NEI penal code, for example, no statute that covered 'imposition of collective punishment,' 'misuse of the white flag' or 'employment of prisoners of war on unauthorised works.'[30] By adopting offenses from the laws and customs of war, extra flexibility was given to the prosecutors.[31] In addition, the adoption of customary law gave the possibility to address the systematic and widespread nature of the crimes committed, especially of those by the Kempeitai and Tokkeitai, Japan's military police and special naval police.[32] Finally, as the investigation of war crimes was very much an Allied effort, the Dutch—by adopting this approach to war crimes—were able to synchronize their war

---

general provisions of the penal code and the code of military justice were made applicable for the adjudication of war crimes, the general principles and rules of the Netherlands East Indies Penal Code were valid in the sphere of war crimes, as long as they did not depart from the Special War Crimes Legislation. To further enable the inclusion of sufficient provision for the sort of war crimes committed during the Asia Pacific war, several articles were suspended, including article 1 of the Indies Penal Code which described the rule *Nullum crimen, nulla poena sine lege*. UNWCC, *Law Reports*, vol. 11, 91–2. *Staatsblad van Nederlandsch-Indië* 1946 no. 45.

[29] *Staatsblad van Nederlandsch-Indië* 1946 no. 44.

[30] No. 15031. Rechtswezen. Oorlogsmisdrijven. 'Toelichting op de ontworpen wetgeving inzake oorlogsmisdrijven' (also known as *Bijblad op het Staatsblad van Nederlandsch-Indië* 15031), 36–37.

[31] 'The reference to the "laws and usages of war" was at the same time a reference to the international treaties and conventions or agreements which contain the rules concerning these laws and usages and was the formal basis on which some of the Temporary Courts Martial applied relevant provisions of The Hague regulations and the Geneva Convention.' Case of Tanabe Koshiro, Temporary Courts Martial Makassar in UNWCC, *Law Reports*, vol. 11, 3.

[32] About one-third of the 1056 defendants before the TCMs were members of the Kempeitai, the army's military police, or the Tokkeitai, its naval equivalent. Lou de Jong, *Het Koninkrijk der Nederlanden in de Tweede Wereldoorlog, 1939–1945*, 14 vols. (Leiden: Martinus Nijhoff, 1988), vol. 12, 2, 896.

crimes prosecutions and case-building with those of the USA, UK and Australia.[33]

The definition of war crimes was followed by an *exempli causa* list of offenses drawn from the *Paris Peace Conference's Commission of Responsibilities of the Authors of the War and on Enforcement of Penalties* of 1919, and amplified by the UNWCC in 1944.[34] The Netherlands Indies, however, decided to add five additional crimes that had been committed repeatedly and on a large scale to this existing list. Four of these crimes were primarily designed to address offense that had been committed by the Japanese during the war.[35] The fifth offense, 'commission contrary to the conditions of a truce, of hostile acts or the incitement thereto, and the furnishing of others with information, the opportunity or the means for that purpose,' was unmistakably designed to deal with actions taken after the end of the war.[36]

Rules of Procedure and Evidence

The rules of procedure of the temporary courts-martial were set out in the 'War Crimes Penal Procedure Decree' (*Staatsblad* 1946 no. 47) which was designed to supplement the Revised Judicial Procedures of the Army (Herziene Rechtspleging bij de Landmacht).[37] The rules of evidence were

---

[33] Fred L. Borch, 'In the Name of the Queen: Military Trials of Japanese War Criminals in the Netherlands East Indies (1946–1949),' *Journal of Military History* 79 (2015): 101–2.

[34] One report from a Dutch meeting of departmental heads stated: 'Some doubt was expressed on whether one should consider the crimes [enumerated] to be war crimes, as the Allies have also committed such acts. However, since the United Nations War Crimes Commission has laid down this list of war crimes, it seemed better to maintain them.' Nationaal Archief, Den Haag, Algemene Secretarie van de Nederlands-Indische Regering en de daarbij gedeponeerde Archieven, nummer toegang 2.10.14, inventarisnummer 2289, 'Kort verslag van de vergadering van den Raad van Departementen hoofden, gehouden op Woensdag 29 Mei 1946 ten Paleize Koningsplein,' 3.

[35] The four added crimes were: ill-treatment of interned civilians or prisoners, carrying out of or causing execution to be carried out in an inhuman way, refusal of aid or prevention of aid being given to shipwrecked persons, and intentional withholding of medical supplies from civilians.

[36] In the years that the war crimes trials in the Netherlands East Indies took place Japan and the Netherlands were technically still in a state of war. Peace between the countries was officially signed in 1952.

[37] Revised Judicial Procedures of the Army of 29 August 1945, laid down in *Staatsblad van Nederlandsch-Indië* 1945 no. 112, and revised by *Staatsblad van Nederlandsch-Indië* 1945 no. 126.

especially pertinent to the war crimes trials. They stated that the judge might recognize as evidence 'all documents produced at the sitting and all statements wherever made,' ascribing to them 'such conclusive strength as he thinks they may possess, if, in his opinion, the particular circumstances under which the war crime was committed or in which a piece of evidence would have to be furnished, would form an obstacle to the further production of evidence or would result in an inadmissible delay in the termination of the case, should this further evidence have to be produced.'[38] In certain cases defendants thus received punishments based on limited evidence. For example, Corporal Mizuo Katsuno who had deserted from the Japanese army and joined the Indonesian Lasykar Rakjat (People's Militia),[39] an organization carrying out opposition against the NEI government, received a heavy prison sentence primarily based on his admission made during the preliminary investigation, which he revoked in court.[40]

OUTCOME OF THE TRIALS

In the few available studies on the administration of justice against the Japanese, different statistics can be found regarding the number of defendants, cases and judgments delivered. The figures stated below have been extracted from the database at the International Research and Documentation Centre for War Crimes Trials (Marburg); from materials at the NIOD Institute for War, Holocaust and Genocide Studies (Amsterdam); the Dutch National Archives (The Hague); and the US National Archives and Records Administration (Maryland).[41]

Around 1050 Japanese soldiers, sailors, civilians and affiliated defendants in about 450 trials would eventually be prosecuted before Netherlands Indies courts between August 1946 and early 1949.

---

[38] 'Rechtspleging Oorlogsmisdrijven,' *Staatsblad van Nederlandsch-Indië* 1946 no. 47, 5–6; and UNWCC, *Law reports*, vol. 11, 108.

[39] Lasykar Rakyat was the Indonesian translation of Giyūgun (volunteer army), the local equivalent of the PETA (The PETA, Pembela Tanah Air, was a locally based volunteer army, officered by Indonesians) in Sumatra. From late 1945 onwards the word *lasykar* was generally applied to armed groups not belonging to the official republican forces. Robert Cribb, *Gangsters and Revolutionaries: The Jakarta People's Militia and the Indonesian Revolution 1945–1949* (Singapore: Equinox Publishing, 2009), 71.

[40] 'Netherlands Trial Report No. 18 (Sentence against Mizuo Katsuno),' (original translation) available via http://www.legal-tools.org/doc/2bf8e6/

[41] Research is however still in progress and the final numbers might slightly vary.

Death	248	24,4%
Life	36	3,5%
< 5 years	211	20,7%
>5-10 years	247	24,3%
>10-15 years	166	16,3%
<15-20 years	109	10,7%

Fig. 9.1 Number of convictions given by sentence (Numbers compiled by author)

Of this total number of defendants, 14 persons stood trial in more than one court or were sentenced before the same court on different charges.[42] All in all there were 1017 convictions and nearly a quarter of those convicted received the death penalty while others received prison sentences.

Article 4 of the 'War Crimes Penal Law Decree' had restricted the punishments which the courts were allowed to impose in the case of war crimes and read as follows: 'He who has been guilty of a war crime shall be punished with the death penalty, or imprisonment for life, or imprisonment for not less than 1 day, and not more than 20 years.'[43] It was left to the discretion of the courts to decide which of these punishments was to be imposed in each case. Forty-two times a defendant was acquitted, while ten defendants could not be adjudicated as they had either committed suicide, died before the trial commenced or because the court declared itself incompetent to try the case (Fig. 9.1).[44]

---

[42] *Staatsblad van Nederlandsch-Indië* 1946 no. 45, article 7 stated: 'In the case that a person after a conviction for war crimes is once more found guilty of a war crime committed before the previous sentencing, this former conviction will be taken into account in the sense that besides a death penalty no other penalty may be imposed, besides a life sentence no temporary prison term can be imposed, and in the event of temporary imprisonment the joint duration of the sentences should not exceed twenty years.'

[43] *Staatsblad van Nederlandsch-Indië* 1946 no. 45.

[44] See for example the trial against Miwa Keijiro et al. In this case the court-martial in Batavia declared itself incompetent because the alleged victims were of Siamese and not of Dutch nationality. NIOD, collection 400, inv. no. 379.

Death	4	5,8%
Life	-	-
< 5 years	16	23,2%
>5-10 years	30	43,5%
>10-15 years	15	21,7%
<15-20 years	3	4,3%

Fig. 9.2 Korean defendants by sentence (Numbers compiled by author)

Most of the defendants, 93 %, were of Japanese nationality, the remaining 7 % mainly originated from Japan's colonies in Taiwan and Korea. Of the Korean defendants, who as members of the Noguchi Unit had largely functioned as guards for Allied POW and civilian internment camps, four out of 69 or almost 6 % were given the death sentence while the majority received a prison sentence between five and ten years. Whereas recent scholarship has pointed to the allegedly 'unfair' treatment of Korean camp guards, portraying them as victims of both Japanese and Allied policy,[45] these numbers show that in the case of the Netherlands Indies, the Korean suspects were not given the heaviest sentences (Fig. 9.2).

About one third of the total defendants belonged to the Kempeitai and its equivalent the Tokkeitai.[46] Defendants belonging to these two special forces were often charged for crimes that had been committed within the

---

[45] Utsumi Aiko, 'Korean "imperial soldiers": remembering colonialism and crimes against Allied POWs,' in *Perilous memories: the Asia-Pacific war(s)*, ed. Takashi Fujitani et al. (Durham: Duke University Press, 2001), 212.

[46] In cases where the courts relied on concepts of conspiracy and membership of a criminal organization rather than on more straightforward attributions of personal liability, this could often be explained by the difficulties they encountered when collecting evidence against individual members of the Kempeitai, and the Tokkeitai. "'Much knowledge had been obtained about the Kempeitai; the conclusion had been drawn that it would be extremely difficult, if not impossible, to gather enough evidence against individual officers; the names of the perpetrators were often unknown to the victims and it was uncertain if they would

Death	76	24,6%
Life	12	3,9%
Acquitted	6	1,9%
< 5 years	55	17,8%
>5-10 years	61	19,7%
>10-15 years	51	16,5%
<15-20 years	48	15,5%

Fig. 9.3 Kempeitai and Tokkeitai defendants by sentence (Numbers compiled by author)

framework of Kempeitai or Tokkeitai employment. In their verdicts references are frequently made to the systematic nature of the crimes and methodology used by both the organizations: 'which method was also in vogue with the Kempeitai, and even with the Japanese civil police as the Court Martial has found when trying other cases, and which, as is generally known, formed also the well-tied method of the German Gestapo and Russian G.P.U.'[47] It seems, however, that in most of the trials the courts tried to establish the individual responsibility of each of the defendants and to impose sentences accordingly.

To increase the probability of detection of war criminals, ALFSEA Legal Section had labeled certain wartime enemy staff presumed guilty; their members were then treated to automatic arrests. Further investigation was subsequently performed to either confirm their guilt or absolve them of the allegations. Staff of Japanese POW and internment camps as well as all Kempeitai and Tokkeitai fell into the 'presumed guilt' category.[48] One might therefore expect severer punishment for this particular

---

recognize them during a confrontation.' De Jong, *Het Koninkrijk der Nederlanden*, vol. 12, 892.

[47] 'Case No. 79 (Trial of Shigeki Motomura and 15 Others),' 13 (original translation) available via http://www.legal-tools.org/doc/952e93/

[48] A. Zahar, 'Trial Procedure at the British Military Courts,' 34.

Rank	Total number tried	Death	Life	Acquittal
Senior Officers (Lieutenant-Colonel and above)	45	18	-	6
Junior Officers (Lieutenant, Captain, Major)	218	62	9	2
Non Commissioned Officers and Warrant Officers	508	101	18	17
Privates	32	6	1	-
Total	**803**	**187**	**28**	**25**

Fig. 9.4 Accused by rank and sentence (Numbers compiled by author, not included are those with unknown ranks, civilians or militarized civilians)

group of defendants. The outcome of the Kempeitai and Tokkeitai trials (Fig. 9.3) however seems to reflect the general figures given in Fig. 9.1.[49]

Examination of the Fig. 9.4 shows that while senior officers received the relatively harshest punishment, non-commissioned officers and warrant officers were targeted in largest numbers, while the lowest ranks seem to have been mostly passed by. It was thus precisely the lower ranks, those officers who exercised direct and individual command over their subordinates, who paid the price.

---

[49] The Kempeitai and Tokkeitai were for example especially targeted during investigations by the Australians. Australian War Memorial, 619/7/52, 'Intelligence tasks,' 2, annexed to 'Report on operational and administrative activities HQ Morotai Force' (15 August 1945–31 December 1945).

At the time when the special war crimes legislation was designed, the Indies authorities held the belief that both higher and lower ranks should be held accountable for their crimes, due to the nature of and circumstances surrounding the committed atrocities.[50] Hence, they did not accept that a war crime committed in the course of carrying out an official order might be considered to be a mitigating circumstance. However, they were faced by an impediment to the prosecution of the Japanese in the form of article 51 of the penal code which specified that 'a subordinate is not punishable for a crime committed in the execution of the official order issued by the competent authority.'[51] Although the authorities were aware of other approaches taken—article 8 of the Nuremberg Charter for example removed the superior orders plea as an absolute defense, but allowed its consideration in mitigation of punishment—they deliberately decided against following this line. Acknowledging that the Japanese approach to obedience was different than those of the Dutch, the Indies legislature decided to keep the issue of superior order completely outside the law and instead of an amendment of article 51, suspended (in article 1(3) of *Staatsblad* 1946 no. 45) the complete article from the code. It was left to the discretion of the judge whether or not to remove a defendant's liability for punishment.[52]

It can be read in the verdicts of the trials of lower rank defendants that, although the crimes committed had been atrocious, the court ruled that persons involved had often 'simply followed orders' or 'did not know

---

[50] During the war, various international organizations, including the UNWCC, had discussed the plea of superior orders. The members of the UNWCC unanimously agreed that in principle the mere fact of having acted in obedience to superior orders did not of itself relieve a person who has committed a war crime from responsibility. It decided, however, not to lay down any principles or rules for the guidance of the national courts due to the fact that most countries already had established legal rules on the subject, that these rules varied considerably, and that national courts could decide what weight to attach to a plea of superior orders in each separate case. UNWCC, *History of the United Nations War Crimes Commission and the development of the laws of war* (London: HMSO, 1948), 274–281. Dr. Yuen-Li Liang, 'Report on the plea of obedience to superior orders,' UNWWC (28 August 1944), 1, 2, available via http://www.legal-tools.org/doc/1e39d7/.

[51] UNWCC, *Law reports*, vol. 11, 99.

[52] UNWCC, *Law reports*, vol. 11, 99. International Military Tribunal, *Trial of the major war criminals before the International Military Tribunal*, 'The Blue Series,' 42 vols. (Nuremberg: IMT, 1947–1949), Charter, vol. 1, 12. No. 15031. Rechtswezen. Oorlogsmisdrijven. 'Toelichting op de ontworpen wetgeving inzake oorlogsmisdrijven' (also known as *Bijblad op het Staatsblad van Nederlandsch-Indië* 15031), 46–7.

better.' In other cases the command structure of the Japanese army was considered to be a mitigating circumstance.[53] It thus seems that in spite of the war crimes legislation, the temporary courts were receptive to the plea of superior order.

Postwar Justice in Times of Turmoil

As mentioned above, little was known about the developments in the Netherlands Indies when the Japanese capitulated. Rumors about a growing and strengthening nationalist movement were disregarded and Indies representatives generally believed that the Indonesian population had remained loyal and would welcome them as liberators from Japanese rule.[54] It was thought that eventual unrest would be limited to skirmishes with those Japanese troops who would disobey Allied orders and continue fighting.[55]

Yet, the Allied forces responsible for the reoccupation of the Indies soon found out that the Dutch had misjudged the situation completely. When an advance party of British South East Asia Command (SEAC) officers finally set foot in Java on 8 September 1945 they were surprised to find that not only the Republik Indonesia (RI) had been proclaimed, it had also quickly gained control of vital areas on Java and was functioning

---

[53] Also in the case of command responsibility it was generally left to the courts to decide if an accused could be held accountable for the deeds of his subordinates. The liability of superiors could be found in the Netherlands Indies penal code; 'as perpetrators of a punishable act (the following) shall be punished: those who commit the act, cause it to be committed, or are accessories to it.' The term 'cause it to be committed' clearly covered the case of a superior giving orders upon which a crime is perpetrated. However, in the sphere of war crimes, it was thought advisable to introduce specific rules for cases in which superiors were involved other than by issuing express orders. This would, for example, be the case if persons in authority had neglected to undertake measures which would have prevented or reduced the possibilities for a subordinate to perpetrate a crime, or if they should have tolerated such crimes to be committed; 'He whose subordinate has committed a war crime shall be equally punishable for that war crime, if he has tolerated its commission by his subordinate whilst knowing, or at least must have reasonably supposed, that it was being or would be committed.' If the court decided that the superior had taken the necessary measures to prevent a particular war crime or the perpetration of war crimes by his subordinates, the superior should be acquitted. UNWCC, *Law reports*, vol. 11, 100. 'No. 15031. Rechtswezen,' 48.

[54] Woodburn Kirby, *Surrender*, 311. De Moor, *Generaal Spoor*, 163–8.

[55] De Moor, *Generaal Spoor*, 153–6. Wim van den Doel, *Afscheid van Indië: de val van het Nederlandse imperium in Azië* (Amsterdam: Prometheus, 2001), 81–2.

administratively.[56] Whereas nearly three and half years of Japanese occupation had devastated the country and bereaved its population[57] the Indonesian nationalist movement had, at the same time, grown in strength as the Japanese provided them with (military) training, expertise and weapons. When Japan surrendered, the two most prominent nationalist leaders took advantage of the sudden interregnum; two days after Japan's capitulation Sukarno and Hatta declared the Indonesian Republic.

During the war, the Netherlands East Indies fell under General MacArthur's South West Pacific Area (SWPA) command. However, on the same day as Japan's capitulation, jurisdiction over the Netherlands Indies transferred from MacArthur's SWPA to Lord Louis Mountbatten's SEAC.[58] In his area of command, Lord Mountbatten was given the duty to disarm and evacuate Japanese forces, rescue and repatriate prisoners

---

[56] Christopher Thorne, *Allies of a Kind. The United States, Britain, and the war against Japan, 1941–1945* (New York, NY: Oxford University Press: 1978), 681–2.

[57] During the Japanese occupation a large part of the European population and a significant part of the Eurasian population disappeared in internment camps. Thirteen per cent of the civilian internees would die in these camps. Meanwhile a fifth of prisoners of war—many of whom were used by the Japanese as forced labor elsewhere—perished in their camps, on the Siam–Burma Railway and in Japan's mines and shipyards.

The Japanese compelled as many as 4.1 million Indonesian laborers to work as so-called *rōmusha* or labor soldiers. From Java alone, around 300,000 Indonesians were sent to work elsewhere; it is thought that around three quarters of this group died from exhaustion, starvation and disease. The Japanese Army and Navy also recruited some 80,000 local auxiliary soldiers, the so-called *heiho*, from the ranks of the disbanded Royal Netherlands Indies Army (KNIL) and from among Indonesian youth, and coerced thousands of Indonesian women into serving as the so-called 'comfort women.'

E. Touwen-Bouwsma, 'Japanese minority policy: the Eurasians on Java and the dilemma of ethnic loyalty,' *Bijdragen tot de Taal-, Land- en Volkenkunde* 152 (1996): 560. L. de Jong, *Het Koninkrijk der Nederlanden*, vol. 12, 625, 753. K. Maekawa, 'The *heiho* during the Japanese occupation of Indonesia,' in P. H. Kratoska, ed., *Asian labor in the wartime Japanese Empire: unknown histories* (Armonk: M. E. Sharpe, 2005), 189–191. P. H. Kratoska, 'Labour mobilization in Japan and the Japanese Empire,' in Kratoska, *Asian labor in the wartime Japanese Empire*, 20. H. Hovinga, 'End of a forgotten drama: the reception and repatriation of *rōmusha* after the Japanese capitulation,' in Kratoska, *Asian labor in the wartime Japanese Empire*, 213–215. Y. Tanaka, *Japan's comfort women: sexual slavery and prostitution during World War II and the US occupation* (London: Routledge, 2002), 82.

[58] When command over the NEI was transferred to SEAC, Australian forces had already occupied parts of the outer islands of the NEI (outer islands: Borneo, Celebes, western New Guinea and the string of islands running eastwards of Java (except Bali and Lombok)). It was agreed between Mountbatten and Blamey that SEAC eventually would take over command from the Australian forces (except for Timor and Dutch New Guinea) Woodburn Kirby, *Surrender*, 224–31, 353.

of war and internees and maintain law and order.⁵⁹ The Netherlands Indies were unable to contribute much to the SEAC forces, as the war had drained their military and economic resources. Most of their troops had been interned in POW camps, leaving only a handful of brigades in Australia ready for action. In order to reassert Dutch authority, the NEI thus had to rely on its British, American and Australian allies.

With SEAC resources already severely strained before the command transfer, Mountbatten was now responsible for an extra 500,000 square miles of territory and 80 million people.⁶⁰ As the landing of the first troops on Java was planned for the last week of September 1945, Mountbatten had no other choice but to 'instruct the Japanese [...] to maintain order in the areas for which they had been responsible up to the termination of hostilities.'⁶¹ He ordered them to halt all political activities in the areas they still occupied and to maintain the civil administration and status quo.⁶² While Mountbatten had hoped this would be a temporary measure,

---

⁵⁹ Richard McMillan, *The British occupation of Indonesia 1945–1946. Britain, the Netherlands and the Indonesian Revolution* (Taylor & Francis e-Library, 2006), 2.

⁶⁰ The complete command area consisted of 1.5 million square miles, containing more than 128 million people. Woodburn Kirby, *Surrender*, 230 and Roadnight, 'Sleeping with the Enemy,' 248.

⁶¹ Roadnight, 'Sleeping with the Enemy,' 249. Petra Groen, *Marsroutes en dwaalsporen*, 21.

⁶² Roadnight, 'Sleeping with the Enemy,' 249.

The morning after Japan's capitulation, awaiting official confirmation of the surrender, the top of the Japanese military administration and the headquarters of the Japanese 16th Army on Java held a meeting to discuss and decide on how to proceed. While Allied contact with the Japanese Supreme Commander of the Southern General Army Terauchi Hisakazu had yet to be established—this happened only on 20 August—and thus no orders had been received, those present decided to comply with the imperial broadcast. A 'sincere' attitude towards the Allies was adopted, while the 'interests of Japan and the protection of the Japanese' were to serve as guidelines for further decisions. Swift repatriation of the Japanese troops was paramount and Allied accusations of non-obedience had to be avoided at all costs. Official efforts to 'guide' the Indonesians to independence were therefore halted and the PETA and *heiho* forces disbanded and disarmed, leaving the question of Indonesian independence an issue between Indonesia and the Netherlands. Several days later, on 21 August, the 16th Japanese Army ordered preparations for confinement to areas were its troops would be able to live self-sufficiently for at least half a year. To maintain law and order, detachments would be left in the cities. Japanese women and children were sent to hospitals in the mountains while other civilians were told to stay at their posts.

Kenichi Goto, 'Caught in the Middle: Japanese Attitudes toward Indonesian Independence in 1945,' *Journal of Southeast Asian Studies* 27 (1996): 40. Willem Remmelink, 'The Emergence of the New Situation: The Japanese Army on Java after the Surrender,' *Militaire Spectator* 147 (1978): 52–4. Anthony Reid and Akira Ōki, eds., *The Japanese Experience in*

limited till the arrival of the first Allied troops, the unexpected political developments in the Indies quickly made it clear that it would be impossible for ALFSEA to maintain law and order without the deployment of the surrendered Japanese troops.[63]

During the first month after the declaration of independence, the situation in Java and Sumatra remained relatively calm.[64] Yet, soon after the arrival of the first Recovery of Allied Prisoners of War and Internees (RAPWI) teams and Allied troops—who were accompanied by the Dutch colonial administration represented by NICA[65]—the situation on the two main islands quickly deteriorated.[66] From mid-September onwards attacks by *pemudas*—youngsters who mostly had been members of Japanese youth organizations—on Japanese troops and Dutch (European and Eurasian) citizens became more frequent.[67] In the following weeks, the Indonesian revolutionary movement turned on the control of Japanese arms and fierce battles broke out between the Allied forces, the Japanese and the nationalists.[68] During the Bersiap that lasted from October 1945 until early spring 1946, numerous atrocities were committed by independence fighters.[69] Especially on Java, vicious attacks on Europeans, Eurasians and Indonesian

---

Indonesia: Selected Memoirs of 1942–1945 (Athens, OH: Ohio University, Center for International Studies, Center for Southeast Asian Studies, 1986): 217–8. Van Poelgeest, *Japanse besognes*, 142.

[63] Roadnight, 'Sleeping with the Enemy,' 252.

[64] Herman Bussemaker, *Bersiap! Opstand in het paradijs: de Bersiap-periode op Java en Sumatra 1945–1946* (Zutphen: Walburg Pers, 2005), 16–7.

[65] The Netherlands Indies Civil Administration later changed its name to AMACAB (Allied Military Administration – Civil Affairs Branch) in January 1946 on Java and Sumatra. Zijlmans, *Eindstrijd en ondergang*, 37.

[66] Woodburn Kirby, *Surrender*, 356–7. The situation in the outer islands was however different; notwithstanding opposition in certain areas the Dutch authorities were more successful in reconsolidating Dutch rule and a governmental apparatus was fairly quickly restored.

[67] Bussemaker, *Bersiap!*, 15–7.

[68] Han Bing Siong, 'The Indonesian Need of Arms after the Proclamation of Independence,' *Bijdragen Tot de Taal-, Land- en Volkenkunde* (2001): 799–830. Shigeru Sato, 'The PETA,' in Peter Post et al., eds., *The Encyclopedia of Indonesia in the Pacific War* (Leiden: Brill, 2009), 143–4. Van Poelgeest, *Japanse besognes*, 35–42. Benedict R. O'G Anderson, *Java in a Time of Revolution: Occupation and Resistance, 1944–1946* (Ithaca, NY: Cornell University Press, 1972), 129–131.

[69] During the Bersiap around 75,000 Dutch nationals, mostly Indo-Europeans who had managed to stay outside the Japanese camps during the war, were interned by the Indonesian authorities. The living conditions in these camps, generally located in Republican-held territory on Java and Madoera, varied greatly. Historians disagree on the reasoning behind this internment policy, see for example Bussemaker, *Bersiap!* and Mary C. van Delden, 'De

minorities regarded as being pro-Dutch such as the Christian Ambonese and Menadonese, left thousands missing or dead.[70] From October 1945 until mid-1946, Japanese surrendered personnel (JSP) in the Netherlands Indies performed military duties alongside Allied forces, not only protecting ex-POWs and civil internees against Indonesian nationalist forces and extremists,[71] but also those SEAC forces that were responsible for the disarmament of the Japanese.[72]

After law and order was restored in those areas under Allied control, the Dutch gradually took over from the British, until formal colonial authority over the Netherlands Indies reverted to the Dutch in November 1946. Over the next three years, the Dutch embarked on several brutal military campaigns to prevent the consolidation of the Indonesian Republic. Despite this, they were not able to re-establish their former authority over large parts of the archipelago, and were eventually obliged to acknowledge Indonesian sovereignty on 27 December 1949.

Meanwhile, most of the most of the Japanese troops—around 170,000 Japanese in the outer islands, 70,000 Japanese in Sumatra and just under 70,000 Japanese in Java—had confined themselves in camps located all over the archipelago.[73] The majority of these camps, which were mainly self-sufficient, were located in remote areas.[74] Although they fell

---

republikeinse kampen in Nederlands-Indië, oktober 1945 – mei 1947. Orde in de Chaos? (PhD Diss., Universiteit Nijmegen, 2007).

[70] Bussemaker, *Bersiap!*, 11, 342.

[71] On Java alone between 8000 and 10,500 JSP served alongside SEAC forces. In Sumatra, JSP were generally deployed for financial and political reasons and less for the maintenance of law and order as was the case on Java. Roadnight, 'Sleeping with the Enemy,' 251–261.

[72] Han Bing Siong, 'The Secret of Major Kido: The Battle of Semarang, 15–19 October 1945,' *Bijdragen tot de Taal-, Land- en Volkenkunde* 152 (1996): 382. Roadnight, 'Sleeping with the Enemy,' 249. Also Stephen Connor, 'Side-Stepping Geneva: Japanese Troops under British Control, 1945–7,' *Journal of Contemporary History* 45 (2010): 400. Van Poelgeest, *Japanse besognes*, 36–8.

[73] Bart van Poelgeest, 'Figuranten op het Indische toneel. De Japanners in Nederlands-Indie 1946–1949,' Elly Touwen-Bouwsma and Petra Groen, eds., *Tussen Banzai en Bersiap. De afwikkeling van de Tweede Wereldoorlog in Nederlands-Indië* (Den Haag: SDU Uitgevers, 1996), 95–6.

[74] Responsibility for the disarmament and repatriation of the Japanese was assigned to Lord Mountbatten's SEAC. The Netherlands Indies government as well as the families of the Japanese troops and the Japanese government pressured SEAC for a speedy repatriation. However, as shipping availability was scarce, it took months before the first Japanese troops left Indonesia and it would eventually take years before all the Japanese were brought back

under authority of SEAC, the camps were hardly ever guarded by the Allies—much to the mortification of the Indies authorities, who considered the Japanese to be a threat to the restoration of Dutch authority and wanted to keep contact between the local population and the interned Japanese to a minimum.⁷⁵

After Japan's surrender, the Japanese military generally maintained discipline among its troops, as most of the Japanese abided by their emperor's wishes and cooperated with the Allies.⁷⁶ Yet, there were also some

---

to their homeland. Whereas the repatriation of the troops in Sumatra and the outer islands went swiftly once sufficient shipping was provided, on Java there existed a complicating factor as around 30,000 JSP had confined themselves in areas administered by the RI. Cooperation with the republican authorities was thus needed for the effective repatriation and disarmament of these particular JSPs. When the repatriation of Japanese through actions 'Puff' and 'Nippoff' came to an end in October 1946, around 17,000 Japanese stayed behind in Indonesia, of which 13,500 performed labor for the Netherlands Indies government. Van Poelgeest, 'Figuranten,' 96, 100.

⁷⁵ Van Poelgeest, 'Figuranten,' 96–8. 'Minister voor algemene oorlogvoering van het koninkrijk (Schermerhorn) aan regeringsvertegenwoordigers bij combined chiefs of staff te Washington' (2 December 1945), in Simon van der Wal, ed., *Officiële Bescheiden betreffende de Nederlands-Indonesische Betrekkingen 1945–1950* (hereafter *NIB*), 20 vols. (Den Haag, Martinus Nijhoff, 1971), vol. 2. no. 138, 276. 'Lt. gouverneur-generaal (Van Mook) aan minister van overzeese gebiedsdelen (Logemann)' (29 November 1945), *NIB*, vol. 2, no. 107, 207–9. 'Overzicht van chief commanding officer Nica te Morotai (De Rooy) betreffende de algemene situatie in Borneo en de Grote Oost over de periode 21 t/m 30 november 1945,' *NIB*, vol. 2 no. 112, 230. 'Politiek verslag over Sumatra van gouverneur, chief commanding officer Amacab Sumatra (Spits) over de maand maart 1946,' *NIB*, vol. 4, no. 5, 25. 'Overzicht van chief commanding officer Nica te Morotai (De Rooy) betreffende de algemene situatie in Borneo en de Grote Oost over de periode 1 t/m 10 jan. 1946,' *NIB*, vol. 3, no. 45, 105.

⁷⁶ The number of Japanese casualties (in action, illness, suicide) on Java sustained by the Japanese from 15 August 1945 until the June 1946 surrender stands higher (1057) than the total number of casualties inflicted during the occupation of the island in 1942 (957, of which 255 were killed, 702 wounded). Remmelink, 'The Emergence of the New Situation,' 64. Goto, 'Caught in the Middle,' 42.

On Sumatra, the 25th Japanese Army lost at least 626 (in action, illness, suicide) after the surrender. Nationaal Archief, Den Haag, Netherland Forces Intelligence Service [NEFIS] en Centrale Militaire Inlichtingendienst [CMI] in Nederlands-Indië, No 109/ Geh., Gegevens uit de Intelligence Summaries van de 26th Indian Division no. 46 and 52 (31 Augustus and 12 October 1946), inventarisnummer 2156, nummer toegang 2.10.62, 'Annex no. 1 to Dr. J.J. van de Velde, de Regeringscommissaris voor bestuursaangelegenheden voor Noord-Sumatra aan de directeur NEFIS' (Medan: 25 Augustus 1947).

individuals who took a different trajectory.[77] The sudden capitulation of their country deeply shocked the Japanese, leading to cases of demoralization, desertion or suicide.[78] Others disobeyed by seeking participation in the Indonesian independence movement or by simply 'disappearing' into Indonesian society. While the number of deserters was relatively low, with around 500 deserters on Sumatra and 700 on Java,[79] Japanese deserters and stragglers remained a thorn in the side of the Netherlands Indies authorities.[80] This was particularly so as at this point in time many Dutch, especially those residing in the Netherlands Indies, labelled the RI 'a Japanese puppet-government of the Quisling type.'[81] Disregarding and misinterpreting the strong popular support for Indonesian nationalism, they attributed its consolidation to the result of previous and ongoing machinations of the Japanese. The fact that much of the Japanese weaponry, either voluntarily of by force, had fallen in the hands of the Indonesian military or in paramilitary hands only reinforced their ideas.[82] As Spoor, the newly appointed army commander and former director of the NEFIS explained the situation in Borneo and the 'Great East'[83] in April 1946: 'Just as in Java, the Japanese still present on these islands are a

---

[77] Han Bing Siong, 'Captain Huyer and the Massive Japanese Arms Transfer in East Java in October 1945,' *Bijdragen tot de Taal-, Land en Volkenkunde* 159 (2003): 311–3.

[78] NL-HaNA, inv.nr. 2156, NEFIS en CMI, 2.10.62.

The responsible Japanese officers had been instructed by the Allies to prevent desertion and bring deserters to justice. Japanese deserters who were caught and arrested by the Allies were transferred to the competent Japanese military command, which had them judged by a court-martial. Van Poelgeest, 'Figuranten,' 98. Goto, 'Caught in the Middle,' 42.

[79] Van Poelgeest, *Japanse Besognes*, 84 Sato, 'The PETA,' 143–4. Goto (1996) based on Miyamoto Shizuō (*Jawa Shusen Shori-Ki* [An Account of the Disposition of the End of the War in Java] (Tokyo: Jawa Shusen Shori-Ki Kanko-Kai, 1973)) mentions 277 deserters on Java. Unfortunately no numbers for the outer islands are available.

[80] 'Overzicht van chief commanding officer Nica te Morotai (De Rooy) betreffende de algemene situatie in de Grote Oost en Borneo over de periode 10 t/m 20 jan. 1946,' *NIB*, vol. 3 no. 93, 176–7. 'Overzicht van chief commanding officer Nica (De Rooy) betreffende de algemene situatie in Borneo en de Grote Oost over de periode 16 maart-1 april 1946,' *NIB*, vol. 4, no. 7, 31.

[81] 'Memorandum on the situation in Java (Netherlands East Indies) ingediend bij de Britse minister van buitenlandse zaken (Bevin), 29 September 1945,' *NIB*, vol. 1, no. 116, 188. Robert Cribb, 'Avoiding clemency,' 158–9.

[82] Van Poelgeest, *Japanse besognes*, 35, 84. Frances Gouda and Thijs Brocades Zaalberg, *American Visions of the Netherlands East Indies/Indonesia US Foreign Policy and Indonesian Nationalism, 1920–1949* (Amsterdam: Amsterdam University Press, 2002), 174.

[83] The 'Great East' (*Groote Oost*), was an administrative entity of the Netherlands East Indies between 1938 and 1946. It comprised all the islands to the east of Borneo (Celebes,

major problem. As long as the Japanese have not been evacuated from the Netherlands East Indies, it will not be able to full restore law and order, because also in these outer regions, one finds Japanese, either directly or indirectly, engaged in possible resistance attempts over and over again.'[84] In reality the number of Japanese that joined the Indonesian forces for ideological reasons most probably did not exceeded 200, and over the course of the next years the authorities' belief in a purported linkage between the Japanese and the RI slowly faded.[85] However, stories about looting, stealing, deserted and roving JSP continued to be covered in the media, with the Japanese portrayed as the instigators of unrest, leaders of Indonesian mobs or as instructors of the Indonesian nationalist forces.[86]

Furthermore, the issue of deserters and feared Japanese support for the independence movement probably influenced the drafters of the war crimes legislation as 'breaking the terms of the armistice' was added to the already existing 'Versailles list.'[87] Between February 1947 and September 1948, the clause that criminalized breaking the terms of the armistice was invoked in at least five cases and against 13 defendants.[88] In eight cases the defendant was convicted for 'commission of hostilities contrary to the terms of an armistice', while two others were convicted for incit-

---

the Moluccas and West New Guinea with their offshore islands) and of Java (the Lesser Sunda islands). The capital was Macassar on Celebes.

[84] 'Nota van de legercommandant (Spoor), 2 april 1946. Appreciatie van de militaire situatie in Nederlandsch-Indië op 1 April 1946,' *NIB*, vol. 4, no. 14, 46.

[85] Van Poelgeest, *Japanse besognes*. 67–76. Sato, 'The PETA,' 144, Bussemaker, *Bersiap!*, 309.

[86] For newspaper articles see for example: 'Japanse Deserteurs,' *Het Dagblad*, 11 August 1947, 2. 'De Bloem der Rep. Strijdkrachten,' *De Locomotief.* Samarangsch handels- en advertentie-blad, 29 October 1947, 1. 'Japans bendehoofd gevat,' *Het Nieuws. Algemeen Dagblad*, 28 May 1948, 1. 'Japanners stonden aan hoofd van Terroristen,' *Het Dagblad*, 28 October 1948, 2.

[87] The importance addressed to the issue of Japanese deserters by the Indies authorities—especially the army and intelligence service—is reflected in the fact that the topic was placed on the agenda during the talks and negotiations that were held between the Netherlands Indies authorities and the Republic Indonesia in 1947–1948. Until the second police action (19 December 1948–5 January 1949) the Dutch used these negotiations to apprehend the Japanese war criminals still at large in republican territory. Van Poelgeest, *Japanse besognes*, 85–7, 111.

[88] The number of four defendants as mentioned by Piccigallo and De Jong is thus incorrect. Philip R. Piccigallo, *The Japanese on Trial: Allied War Crimes Operations in the East, 1945–1951* (Austin, TX: University of Texas Press, 1979), 183. De Jong, *Het Koninkrijk der Nederlanden*, 893.

ing hostile acts contrary to the conditions of a truce. The three other suspects were indicted for the same crimes but acquitted or eventually sentenced for another crime. The trials took place in Macassar (Sulawesi), Medan (Sumatra) and in Tandjong Pinang (Riau Archipelago) and with the exception of the case of Prosecutor v. MIZUO Katsuno, the crimes had been committed in the first months after the Japanese surrender. Most of the defendants were younger lower and middle rank officers, which corresponds with the overview given in Fig. 9.4.[89]

Yet, while a number of Japanese chose to contribute to the Indonesian cause by joining the Indonesian nationalists, other Japanese soldiers fought with the Allies against the Indonesians nationalists in order to protect the European and Indo-European population. When they were subsequently charged for war crimes committed during Japanese occupation of the NEI, their defense counsel tried to take advantage of this fact as a mitigating circumstance. Unlike in French Indo-China, where the postwar acts of Japanese were taken into consideration during the war crime trials, the Indies' temporary courts-martial were unresponsive to the defense pleas, denying the Japanese any leniency when deciding on punishments. The refusal of the courts-martial to take their support during the Allied operations into account heavily disappointed and infuriated the Japanese standing trial. As a result, the courts' ruling led in some cases to even greater unwanted consequences.[90] For example, Captain Wada Kunishige and several of his men who had received death sentences by the Batavian Court in September 1948 broke out of Cipinang prison after their conviction.[91]

---

[89] The defendants who deserted were mostly privates or low ranking officers, which can be explained by the fact that these ranks had often great belief in the cause of the Greater East Asia War and had regularly been in touch with Indonesian officers and men participating in the PETA. Goto, 'Caught in the Middle,' 38.

[90] De Groot, *Berechting Japanse Oorlogsmisdadigers*, 374–5

[91] Han Bing Siong states that Wada Kunishige and his men broke out of prison because the Dutch military courts refused to take their actions in Semarang into account. However, the break-out of Cipinang prison Bing Siong refers to, in which—according to Vice-Admiral Shibata—most of the escaped were members of the Semarang Kempeitai, dates from 27 March 1947. Almost a year before the Semarang Kempeitai verdict was pronounced (March 1948; Kunishige was not a defendant is this trial), and half a year before the verdict was pronounced in the trial of the Djember and Bandoeng Kempetai (September 1948, in which Kunishige was convicted). The mass escape from Cipinang mentioned by de Groot and Han Bin Siong also took place before the Batavian Kempeitai trial in which the same defense argument was used. However, it could well be that earlier trial outcomes of the courts-martial or the living conditions in Cipinang prison influenced the decision of the inmates to escape.

Whilst some of the convicts joined the Indonesian nationalists, Kunishige found refuge with a Chinese family instead.[92]

Conclusion

After the war, the myriad cruelties and atrocities committed against its Asian and European population proved to be a strong incentive for the Netherlands East Indies government to pursue and punish the Japanese and affiliated defendants for the crimes committed. The war crimes trials were considered by the Dutch as a moral obligation to the victims of the Japanese repression and served as reparation of not only the private but also the public damage caused by the Japanese. Four years of investigation, interrogations and trials proceedings resulted in the conviction of more than 1000 accused.

The fact that the war crimes trials were established in the midst of this period of great political unrest influenced the justice process and brought particular problems of legitimacy in its wake. As the Dutch were motivated to re-establish a cordial relationship between themselves and their colonial subjects and claimed to be the proper and legitimate government of Indonesia, the trials illustrated a stable society based on justice and the rule of law. By demonstrating that all parties—European and Asian alike—had suffered under Japanese occupation, the Dutch positively contrasted their 'benign' colonial rule to that of the 'criminal' colonial rule of the outgoing Japanese. However, the fact that Dutch and KNIL forces—while trying to prevent the consolidation of the Indonesian Republic—committed atrocities during their military campaigns not dissimilar to those ascribed to the Japanese defendants undermined the credibility of the trial process.[93]

In addition, the trials were a way to bring into disrepute those Indonesian nationalist groups who during the war had been pro-Japanese but for political reasons could not be prosecuted. As the Indies authorities kept emphasizing the linkage between the Japanese and the RI, their ideas were

---

According to De Groot and Siong, Wada escaped several times from Cipinang and was eventually shot when found by patrol. Siong, 'The Secret of Major Kido,' 407 and De Groot, *Berechting Japanse oorlogsmisdadigers*, 64, 374–7.

[92] Han Bing Siong, 'Captain Huyer,' 311 and De Groot, *Berechting Japanse Oorlogsmisdadigers*, 62–4, 377.

[93] See Larissa van den Herik, 'Addressing "colonial crimes" through reparations? Adjudicating Dutch atrocities committed in Indonesia,' *Journal of International Criminal Justice* 10 (2012): 693–705.

concretized by the prosecution policy of the temporary courts-martial, which not only convicted the Japanese from the former occupation forces, but also the Indonesian nationalists and those who had thrown in their lot with them. Yet, while the Netherlands Indies government attempted to portray the RI as a puppet of the Japanese military administration, its own reliance on the Japanese troops for law and order during the Bersiap discredited this argument. It highlighted that despite trying and punishing Japanese war criminals, the Dutch were unable to effectively settle their wartime account with Japan.

CHAPTER 10

Australia's Pursuit of the Taiwanese and Korean 'Japanese' War Criminals

Dean Aszkielowicz

Soon after the surrender of Japanese forces around the Asia Pacific region in August 1945, the victorious Allies arrested thousands of Japanese soldiers, sailors and civilians on war crimes charges. Twenty-five senior Japanese officials were convicted as 'class A' war criminals for offences related to the planning, initiating or waging of aggressive war at the International Military Tribunal for the Far East, a multinational tribunal held in Tokyo between 1946 and 1948.[1] Roughly 5700 other Japanese of lower ranks in the military or in civilian roles associated with the Japanese war effort were prosecuted as 'class B' and 'class C' war criminals. The offences prosecuted in these trials ranged from, at the lower end, slapping, beating or mistreating a prisoner, to cases of murder and cannibalism,

---

[1] For details of the Tokyo trials see Timothy Maga, *Judgment at Tokyo: The Japanese War Crimes Trials* (Lexington: University Press of Kentucky, 2001); Yuma Totani, *The Tokyo War Crimes Trials: The Pursuit of Justice in the Wake of World War Two* (Cambridge, MA: Harvard University Press, 2008); Richard Minear, *Victor's Justice: The Tokyo War Crimes Trial* (Tokyo: Charles E. Tuttle, 1971); Neil Boister and Robert Cryer, *The Tokyo International Military Tribunal: A Reappraisal* (New York, NY: Oxford University Press, 2008).

D. Aszkielowicz (✉)
Murdoch University, Perth, Australia

and to the question of the guilt of Japanese commanders for failure to prevent war crimes being perpetrated by soldiers under their command. Class B and class C prosecutions were conducted by seven Allied countries, the USA, the UK, the Netherlands, France, China, the Philippines and Australia, between September 1945 and April 1951. The prosecuting countries acted in loose cooperation with each other, but the class B and C trials were conducted according to each country's own war crimes laws and procedures. Trials were held at venues around the Pacific and in parts of Asia, usually at locations where Japanese forces had surrendered. Convicted prisoners were either executed or held at, or near, the place of their trial before being returned to Japan from 1949 onwards to complete their sentences in Sugamo Prison, Tokyo. They were eventually all released by 1958, even if their original terms of imprisonment had not expired.

A number of the Japanese suspects who faced Allied courts were not ethnically Japanese, but were former colonial subjects of Korean or Taiwanese (Formosan) origin who had served in the Japanese military. Japan had colonized Taiwan in 1895 and Korea in 1910. When Japan surrendered, it immediately lost control of all of its colonial possessions, not just those acquired after war began with the Western powers in 1941. Though Taiwan and Korea were thus freed from Japanese rule, 319 former colonial subjects were convicted as war criminals by the Allies in the class B and C prosecutions.[2] The view among all of the Western Allies was that at the time of their offences the war criminals had been Japanese and therefore they should be tried as Japanese subjects. In representations to the Allied governments, Taiwanese and Korean officials disagreed with this position and, moreover, they indicated their governments considered the prisoners to be victims of Japanese imperialist expansion, caught in circumstances beyond their control and therefore due some special consideration when it came to the judgment of their alleged offences.

In this chapter I analyze the discussions among the Australian, Korean, Nationalist Chinese and Japanese governments about the 110 Korean and Taiwanese 'Japanese' war criminals who were convicted in Australian war crimes courts. These discussions took place during a dynamic period in

---

[2] Utsumi Aiko, 'The Korean guards on the Burma–Thailand railway,' in Gavan McCormack and Hank Nelson, eds., *The Burma–Thailand railway* (St Leonards, NSW: Allen & Unwin, 1993), 134. Utsumi Aiko has written extensively in Japanese on Korean prisoners. Her major work on this subject is Utsumi Aiko, *Kimu wa naze sabakareta no ka: Chōsenjin BC-kyū senpan no kiseki* (Tokyo: Asahi Shinbun Shuppan, 2008). See also the chapter by Sandra Wilson in this volume.

Asian politics from the end of the Second World War to the late 1950s, an era marked by two powerful political and ideological forces: decolonization and the emergence of the Cold War. Australia's pursuit of Japanese war criminals was primarily a legal and military undertaking, but policy for war criminals was shaped by the government's overall policy for Japan and outlook on regional affairs. The Australian government's incarceration of Korean and Taiwanese prisoners, and the decision to treat them as Japanese nationals, were not particularly distinctive policies at the time: they accorded with the actions of the other Allies and seemed like natural choices under the circumstances of the early postwar period. I argue in this chapter, however, that Australia's dealings with Korean and Taiwanese war criminals drew the government and its approach to war criminals into the complex politics of decolonizing Asia in ways that were not foreseen in 1945.[3]

Australia prosecuted almost 1000 suspected Japanese war criminals between 1945 and 1951, including 98 of Taiwanese origin—more Taiwanese than were prosecuted by any of the other Allies—and 12 Koreans.[4] Trials were held around Asia and the Pacific, and in Darwin. The war criminals served their sentences in military compounds near where they were tried. Those still in custody were eventually moved to the Australian war criminals compound on Manus Island, in the Admiralty Islands, to the north of New Guinea, by the end of March 1949.[5] As early as 1947, the Nationalist Chinese government sought information on the Taiwanese war criminals and requested that Australia send them back to Taiwan from the military compounds they were being held in. This did not eventuate and instead, in 1953, the government sent all the war criminals it held from Manus to Sugamo Prison, Tokyo. Japan had made peace with the Allies in 1952, but article 11 of the San Francisco Peace Treaty bound Japan to keep the prisoners incarcerated until the country that convicted them allowed their release. On several occasions the Japanese government

---

[3] I have noted elsewhere the influence that the Cold War had on policy for war criminals: Dean Aszkielowicz, 'Changing Direction,' in Tim McCormack, Narrelle Morris, Georgina Fitzpatrick, eds., *The Australian Class B and C War Crimes Trials* (Leiden: Martinus Nijhoff, 2016); Dean Aszkielowicz, 'Repatriation and the Limits of Resolve: Japanese War Criminals in Australian Custody,' *Japanese Studies*, 31, (2011).
[4] Utsumi, *Chōsenjin BC-kyū senpan no kiseki*, 7. The exact number of Taiwanese prosecuted varies across different sources.
[5] As discussed later, this did not include around 60 war criminals who were convicted by Australian courts in Singapore and Hong Kong.

lobbied the Australians to release the Korean and Taiwanese prisoners on legal or humanitarian grounds and allow their return to their home countries. Neither line of argument swayed the Australian government, nor any other convicting government, and the Taiwanese and Korean prisoners did not receive any special clemency on the grounds of their ethnicity.

For legal and political reasons, the Australian government refused to acknowledge the prisoners as Korean and Taiwanese nationals. Most of the Korean and Taiwanese 'Japanese' war criminals convicted by Australia were evidently guilty of their crimes. In a legal sense, their ethnicity mattered very little during their prosecution, as war crimes law did not limit the postwar trials to Japanese war criminals only. In the early 1950s, when the trials were over, the Australian government began to consider repatriation of convicted war criminals to serve out their sentences in Japan. It appeared possible, however, that once the Korean and Taiwanese prisoners were in Japan, they might be released; some Japanese lawyers believed that Japanese domestic law did not have the jurisdiction to incarcerate them, as they were now foreign nationals. The Australian government believed that its prosecutions had constituted an exercise of fair and necessary justice, and that the ultimate integrity of that process depended on ensuring convicted war criminals served their full sentences. Treating the Korean and Taiwanese prisoners as Japanese strengthened the legal position of the Australian government and closed off any potential for the prisoners to be released through technicalities under Japanese domestic law. Whilst the Korean and Taiwanese war criminals were in prison, former colonial subjects not facing war crimes charges had been liberated from Japanese oppression. This apparent contradiction led to a feeling of injustice on the part of the Korean and Taiwanese war criminals and those who worked on their behalf, who often felt they were victims rather than perpetrators of Japanese aggression. This line of argument did not sway the Australian authorities enough to secure release, but it did challenge the government's straightforward view of the Second World War as a conflict in which it was clear which countries were on the winning side and which were on the losing side.

The Australian government's handling of the prisoners is evidence of the balance it between two of its goals in foreign affairs after the war. The government's priority was the security of Australia from threats in the Pacific. It considered the best way to achieve security was by maintaining strong relations with its major allies, and, until the mid-1950s, by persisting in a tough stance on Japanese militarism. The government considered war criminals to have played a key part in the establishment and perpetuation of Japanese militarism, and thus maintained its resolve to punish war criminals thoroughly. The government, however, also sought to create or strengthen postwar ties with Asian countries, a number of which had recently become independent or were in the process of decolonization: Taiwan, Korea, Burma, the Philippines and India had rid themselves of their former colonial masters by 1948, while Indonesia was in the midst of independence struggles.[6] Thus, while respect for the sovereignty of Taiwan and Korea, and affirmation of their independence from their former colonial masters, sat happily within the government's approach to the region, lenient treatment of war criminals, on any grounds, did not. From the mid-1950s onwards, however, in the context of the escalating Cold War, the Australia became less concerned about Japanese militarism and war criminals. The possibility of releasing war criminals thus increased, as the Australian government sought to pursue good relations with Japan.[7]

The Australian government assumed a particularly determined stance on Japanese war criminals from the closing stages of the war until the early 1950s. Australia's pursuit of Japanese war criminals began in 1943 when Sir William Webb, who would later be appointed as president of the Tokyo War Crimes Trial, was commissioned by the government to undertake an investigation into alleged Japanese war crimes in New Guinea.[8] When Japanese units surrendered in 1945, Australian investigations gained further momentum and thousands of Japanese soldiers, including Taiwanese and Koreans, were arrested as war crimes suspects. As Australian prisoners of war (POWs) were liberated from Japanese camps, reports of atrocities committed by Japanese units during the war began to feature in the Australian press, especially during September 1945. Community sentiment and the mood of senior Australian government officials favored swift and comprehensive justice for war crimes committed by the Japanese.[9]

---

[6] Christopher Waters, 'War, Decolonisation and Post-war Security,' in David Goldsworthy, ed., *Facing North: A Century of Australian Engagement with Asia* (Melbourne: Melbourne University Press, 2001), 97–8, 121–5, 132–3.

[7] On the shift in relations between Japan and Australia see Alan Rix, *The Australia–Japan Political Alignment: 1952 to Present*, (London: Routledge, 1999), 1–12.

[8] National Archives of Australia (hereafter NAA), Canberra, A10943, 1580069, 'A Report on Japanese Atrocities and Breaches of the Rules of War' (1944).

[9] See for example the speeches of Herbert V. Evatt, *Australia in World Affairs* (Sydney: Angus & Robertson, 1946), 141–6. For press reaction see for example Rohan Rivett, 'War Correspondent Indicts Japanese POW Authorities,'"*The Argus*, 15 September 1945, 8. Rivett also produced a book, *Behind Bamboo* (Victoria: Angus & Robertson, 1946).

Moreover, bringing Japan to account for the war became a key element of Australian foreign policy after the war and a rallying point for Australian discourses that favored a cautious approach to Asia.

In October 1945, the Australian parliament passed the Australian War Crimes Act 1945, which created the legal framework for trials and prosecutions which began in November. In the first few months, trials were conducted at Wewak in New Guinea, on Morotai in the Netherlands Indies, and in Labuan and Rabaul in Borneo. These early prosecutions coincided with the first US prosecutions; Australian trials were thus at the forefront of the Allied prosecutions. In 1946 and 1947 Australian trials were also held in Darwin, Singapore and Hong Kong.[10] For the first 12 months, progress was steady. Australian prosecutions slowed in 1948 and stalled completely in 1949, however, as shortages of legal personnel and other logistical problems emerged.[11] Nevertheless, the Australian authorities were determined to continue prosecutions, even though other Allies soon began to wind down their efforts.

At the end of the war, Japan was viewed by all of the Allies as a former enemy that needed to be held to account for the war and to be removed as a threat to Pacific security.[12] To punish Japan and prevent its resurgence the country was subjected to the US-led Allied occupation from September 1945 until the San Francisco Peace Treaty was enacted in April 1952. From 1947 onwards, however, the Western democracies began to regard Japan as a possible ally in the Cold War and the occupation of Japan became less focused on punitive measures. The Australian government was slow to embrace this new direction for Japan, believing that security in the Cold War and potential economic advantages of a change in course should not come at the cost of reckoning with Japanese militarism.[13] By 1948–49, however, the government found it hard to find support from its

---

[10] A full list of sentences including those handed down at each venue is in NAA Melbourne, MP927/1, A336/1/29, 'Japanese War Criminals Charged Under the War Crimes Act 1945 by Australian Military Authorities 30 Nov 1945 to Apr 1951 Against Whom Findings and Sentences were Confirmed.'

[11] Caroline Pappas, 'Law and Politics: Australia's War Crimes Trials in the Pacific 1943–1961' (PhD diss., University of New South Wales, 2001), 59.

[12] 'Initial Post Surrender Policy for Japan 29 August 1945,' in Supreme Commander for the Allied Powers, Government Section, *Political Reorientation of Japan September 1945 to September* 1948, Vol. II (Connecticut: Greenwood Publishing Company, 1970), 423–6 and Peter Duus, *Modern Japan*, (Boston: Houghton Mifflin, 1998), 253–73.

[13] Richard Rosecrance, *Australian Diplomacy and Japan 1945–1951* (Victoria: Melbourne University Press, 1962), 103; Waters, 'War, Decolonisation and Post-war Security,' 118–21.

major allies for further punitive measures against Japan, and this included war crimes trials.

The Australian government selected a new trial venue at Manus Island and resumed prosecutions in June 1950.[14] Twenty-six further trials were held on Manus. Prosecutions ended in April 1951, bringing all Australian trials and in fact all Allied prosecutions of Japanese war criminals to a close. Those prosecuted on Manus were imprisoned in the Manus war criminals compound. They joined other Japanese prisoners who had been convicted by Australian courts elsewhere and had been moved to Manus by March 1949. All the convicted criminals were eligible for remission of sentence under Australian regulations, but not parole. They could only get off Manus Island if their sentences expired, after which they were returned to Japan as free men, or if they required extensive medical treatment, for which they needed to be transported to Japan. Fifty war criminals convicted by Australian courts in Singapore and Hong Kong did not go to Manus, but instead remained in prisons in Hong Kong and Singapore before being repatriated to Japan in 1951 along with prisoners convicted in British courts to serve out their time in Sugamo Prison.[15]

Diplomatic exchanges over the Korean and Taiwanese war criminals held by Australia occurred both during the occupation of Japan and after its conclusion in April 1952. The Nationalist Chinese government made sporadic representations to the Australian government on behalf of Taiwanese prisoners in the late 1940s, and the Korean government entered the discussion in the early 1950s. The first approach came in December 1947. The Nationalist Chinese government requested that Australia repatriate Taiwanese prisoners to Taiwan, simply on the grounds the prisoners were not Japanese.[16] During these exchanges Chinese officials made it clear they felt the nationality of the prisoners should make a major difference to how their crimes and incarceration were viewed, but their Australian counterparts disagreed. Despite the rigid Australian pol-

---

[14] NAA, Canberra, A1838, 551834. 'Memo to Department of External Territories,' (21 February 1950); Commonwealth of Australia, *Parliamentary Debates*, House of Representatives, Vol. 206, 24 February 1950, 'Prime Minister Menzies February Speech in Parliament,' 101–2; NAA, Canberra, 1334903 'Coalition Cabinet Agendum on Continuation of War Crimes Trials' (January 1950); Decimal 290-12-04-06, SCAP Legal Section, National Archives and Records Administration, Washington D.C. (hereafter NARA), RG331, Box 1435, 'Chief of Legal Section – Memo for Record' (February 1950).
[15] NAA, Canberra, A1838, 140817, 'Cabinet Agendum No. 347' (September 1952).
[16] NAA, Canberra, A1838, 140817, 'Cabinet Agendum No. 347 – Korean and Formosan Prisoners' (September 1952).

icy, the Chinese embassy in Canberra did receive some encouragement. In reply to the embassy's 1947 request, an Australian External Affairs official enquired whether, if there was to be repatriation, the Chinese government would ensure that sentences were carried out.[17] There was no indication that a transfer to Taiwan was likely, and the discussions were probably only exploratory. It seems that any small chance of returning the prisoners to Taiwan was extinguished when the Chinese embassy failed to reply to the request from External Affairs for details of potential supervision arrangements in Taiwan.[18]

In July 1951 the Chinese embassy in Canberra contacted the Australian government's Department of Territories and shortly after approached External Affairs for details of the Taiwanese prisoners' sentences and release dates. During the subsequent discussions, External Affairs pointed out to the Chinese embassy that requests for special consideration for the Taiwanese prisoners might be used by the Japanese government as a precedent for the release of other Japanese war criminals and that the issue of war crimes remained a sensitive one for the Australian people.[19] Chinese officials also directly approached the Australian Navy, which was supervising the prisoners on Manus Island, and requested the prisoners' release. This was an unusual channel through which to pursue the issue; it appears there may have been some confusion among Chinese officials and possibly even initially within some Australian government departments over which department had ultimate authority over the prisoners.[20] In November 1951, External Affairs confirmed that 74 Taiwanese prisoners remained on Manus Island.[21] A small number of prisoners had been released after serving their full terms, and three had died while in custody. Another, Toyoka Eijiro, was flown to Japan for medical treatment on 22 February 1948, and he later absconded from hospital.[22]

---

[17] NAA, Canberra, A1838, 273128, 'External Affairs letter' (24 March 1948).
[18] NAA, Canberra, A1838, 273128, 'External Affairs note Formosan war criminals at Manus' (12 November 1951).
[19] NAA, Canberra, A1838, 273128, 'External Affairs – Record of Conversation with Chinese Charge d'Affaires' (9 November 1951).
[20] NAA, Canberra, A1838, 273128, 'Protocol note external affairs' (12 November 1951). See also NAA, Canberra, A1838, 273128, 'Chinese Embassy request for Releases' (18 September 1951).
[21] 'External Affairs – Record of Conversation with Chinese Charge d'Affaires.'
[22] NAA, Canberra, A1838, 273128, 'Appendix A to 1951 letter updating previous correspondence from 1948' (12 September 1951).

Petitions from families and grassroots political groups in Japan on behalf of war criminals were common in the 1950s, and similar representations were made in Taiwan.[23] Such petitions provided ammunition to the Japanese and Nationalist Chinese governments in their efforts to pressure the Australian authorities. The Nationalist Chinese government informed External Affairs in November 1951 that it had received petitions from the families of war criminals, requesting their repatriation, and implied that the prisoners should be released.[24] In 1952, Japanese officials took similar diplomatic action and claimed that public pressure was forcing them to represent the war criminals' interests in discussions with the Australian government.[25] It seems the Nationalist Chinese and Japanese diplomats thought that linking the war criminals to domestic pressure might create a sense of urgency around the issue, or perhaps explain at least why they continued to request the Australian government review a matter that it felt was closed.

Information about conditions on Manus Island was scarce outside the Australian agencies responsible for the prison or the war criminals. People in Japan and Taiwan were left to speculate about how the prison operated. The motivation behind this speculation appears to be concern for the welfare of the prisoners, but also on occasion a desire to use the issue of prison conditions as a vehicle for political arguments about the war criminals' incarceration. In June 1951 British consular officials in Taiwan contacted the Australian Mission in Tokyo to inform officials there that a press campaign on behalf of Taiwanese war criminals had emerged in Taiwan. It appears the British consulate's chief interest in the matter was that the campaign had grown to include general anti-British sentiment, presumably because the campaign did not distinguish between British and Australian policy. After requesting a meeting with the agitators, the British consulate received a delegation from an organization called the Taiwan Youth Cultural Association, which was apparently active on behalf of the war criminals.[26] The delegation suggested British treatment, and,

---

[23] For release campaigns in Japan see Sandra Wilson, 'Prisoners in Sugamo and Their Campaign for Release, 1952–53,' *Japanese Studies* 31 (2011): 172–3.
[24] 'External Affairs – Record of Conversation with Chinese Charge d'Affaires.'
[25] NAA, Canberra, A1838, 140817, 'Memo from Japanese Foreign Minister to Australian Government' (10 July 1952).
[26] NAA, Canberra, 273128, 'British Consulate to Australian Mission Tokyo' (18 June 1951). See also NAA, Canberra, A1838, 273128, 'Article from Hsin Sheng Pao' (19 February 1952).

by extension, probably also Australian treatment, of war criminals had been harsher than that of the USA. Furthermore, the association recast the argument over the prisoners' nationality into a claim that they should receive better treatment than their Japanese counterparts while in prison, given that, they said, the Taiwanese prisoners had been pressed into service for the Japanese.[27] The delegation did not make any ground with the British or subsequently the Australians on these political points. The two governments could not be induced to believe that Taiwanese suffering under Japanese imperialism constituted an excuse for war crimes, or a reason for better treatment of those who had been convicted.

Aside from the public campaign, Chinese diplomats continued to press their Australian counterparts through official channels, despite having so far gained little ground. Mostly, Chinese officials insisted in their approaches to the Australian government that there was a difference between the Taiwanese prisoners and the ethnically Japanese war criminals, but, when it was advantageous to do so, diplomats were happy to draw on the parallels between their situations. The Chinese embassy asked the Australian government in March 1952 for remission of sentence for Taiwanese prisoners on the grounds that several significant Japanese war criminals had recently received clemency, though the embassy officials did not mention which released war criminals they were referring to in particular.[28]

Discussions about the Korean prisoners also took place within the US-led occupation of Japan. In June 1950, the Social Welfare Society for Residents of Great Korea in Japan contacted US occupation officials in Tokyo. The group had been created on 10 January 1949 with permission of the Public Welfare Ministry of the Japanese government. It ran two relief houses, and was committed to assisting in the education of Korean children, assisting Koreans living in Japan and creating jobs for them. The letter was a request for 50 Koreans to be released into the care of the organization, which was prepared to accept responsibility for their supervision.[29] Like all those who had requested the release of the war criminals to this point, the organization was unsuccessful. Around this

---

[27] 'British Consulate to Australian Mission Tokyo.'
[28] NAA Canberra, A1838, 273128, 'Chinese Embassy to External Affairs' (25 March 1952).
[29] RG331 SCAP Legal Section Law Division Parole Board Documents 1946–51, Chinese, Dutch and American Convictions to Parole Office memo, Box 1392, 'Cho Sung-Ki – SCAP Legal Section' (26 June 1950).

time, however, the politics of the occupation had begun to show the early signs of turning in favor of the war criminals, and, over the next few years, political developments in occupied Japan brought new hope to those who sought clemency for them.

Between 1949 and 1951, convicted war criminals held in Nationalist Chinese, Dutch and British prisons around Asia were repatriated to Sugamo Prison in Tokyo, where they joined the prisoners who had been convicted by US courts. Sugamo was under the control of the US-led occupation, specifically the US 8th Army, until April 1952, when the end of the occupation returned sovereignty to Japan and in the process transferred Sugamo to Japanese control. The end of the occupation did not, however, mean that Japan assumed control of the war criminals' sentences. Article 11 of the San Francisco Peace Treaty stipulated that decisions on the fate of convicted criminals remained the prerogative of the Allied governments that had prosecuted them, even after full sovereignty returned to Japan. Article 11 stated:

> Japan accepts the judgments of the International Military Tribunal for the Far East [the Class A trials] and of other Allied War Crimes Courts both within and outside Japan, and will carry out the sentences imposed thereby upon Japanese nationals imprisoned in Japan. The power to grant clemency, to reduce sentences and to parole with respect to such prisoners may not be exercised except on the decision of the Government or Governments which imposed the sentence in each instance, and on recommendation of Japan.[30]

Article 11 and the peace treaty changed the dynamic of the discussions about all war criminals, including those of disputed nationality. There was no legal apparatus or separate diplomatic agreement accompanying the treaty that compelled convicting countries to release prisoners or to repatriate those still held overseas to Japan. Japan had been restored to the community of nations, however, and the Japanese government view was that the time for punishment was coming to an end. Japanese diplomats began to pressure the convicting countries for more lenient terms on war criminals. The prosecuting countries' responses were mixed. The Nationalist Chinese, who had not signed the San Francisco Peace Treaty but had signed a separate treaty with Japan, responded to Japan's new

---

[30] 'Article 11, Treaty of Peace with Japan,' in John M. Maki, ed., *Conflict and Tension in the Far East: Key Documents, 1894–1960* (Seattle: University of Washington Press, 1961), 136–7.

status by releasing 88 Japanese war criminals convicted in their courts when the treaty came into effect in August 1952.[31] Actions such as this gave diplomats engaged in discussions with prosecuting countries, and the war criminals themselves, hope that political pressure could lead to widespread early release.

To some, it appeared that the peace treaty, specifically the wording of article 11, had also created a potential legal way of releasing Korean and Taiwanese prisoners. According to one reading, article 11 only required Japan to accept the sentences passed against prisoners who continued to be Japanese nationals. British officials initially were concerned that article 2 of the treaty, which provided for renunciation of Japanese interests in Taiwan and recognition of Korean independence, had removed the Japanese nationality of the prisoners, and thereby the Japanese had perhaps lost the right to hold Korean and Taiwanese prisoners.[32] The Japanese government raised the matter with the British in April 1952, suggesting the non-Japanese war criminals should be released.[33] After consideration, the British position was that the Japanese had 'got their international law wrong.' The Koreans and Taiwanese had not lost their Japanese nationality simply because they 'were racially connected with a transferred territory.' Furthermore, if the Korean or Chinese governments sought to confer their own nationality on the war criminals, they would become dual nationals, and under the treaty could still be held by the Japanese in Sugamo.[34] On 27 June 1952 the Foreign Office circulated the UK views to Washington and the Commonwealth countries, reiterating that the determining factor was that these men held Japanese nationality at the coming into force of the peace treaty.[35] The USA shared this view, though American officials argued that the important point was not the date of the treaty but the date that sentence was passed.[36] The effect, however, was the same: Korean and Taiwanese prisoners could still legally be held in Japan in this case.

The Allies were in agreement that the existing policy on the prisoners of disputed nationality was not invalidated by the treaty, but the complex

---

[31] NAA, Melbourne, MP729/8, 452817, 'Cabinet Agendum – Release of war criminals by Nationalist China' (20 August 1952).
[32] The National Archives of the UK (hereafter TNA), FO 371/99516, 'War Criminals of Nationality other than Japanese' (8 May 1952).
[33] TNA, FO371/99516, 'British Embassy letter' (28 April 1952).
[34] TNA, FO371/99516, 'Pilcher to Tokyo' (10 May 1952).
[35] TNA, FO371/99516, 'Foreign Office to Washington' (27 June 1952).
[36] TNA, FO371/99516, 'Washington to Foreign Office' (27 June 1952).

nature of the terms of imprisonment of the Koreans and Taiwanese was obvious. They were not Japanese, but were considered Japanese nationals in the treaty and they resided in a Japanese prison. Their sentences, however, were not under Japanese control. The legitimacy of this arrangement was tested not only in diplomatic discussions but also in the Japanese legal system. A case was brought before the Japanese courts in July 1952 on behalf of 30 prisoners of disputed nationality that tested the Japanese government's right to hold them. The Japanese government's legal counsel contended that the prisoners should be treated as Japanese nationals for the duration of their sentence, and the court case was ultimately unsuccessful from the point of view of the prisoners. The Allies' interpretation of the peace treaty for war criminals had held up in court.[37]

Though the Japanese legal counsel argued that the prisoners should retain their Japanese status for the duration of their sentence, other actions indicate the Japanese government did not want anything to do with these prisoners, who were now really foreign nationals. When Taiwanese and Korean soldiers were demobilized after the war they had not been treated as Japanese citizens by the Japanese government and were not considered eligible for military pensions or financial aid.[38] While the Japanese government had formally accepted the Allied position on the nationality of the prisoners, it simultaneously made representations for their release. In 1952, Japanese officials requested a pardon for 19 Koreans and Taiwanese held by the British and Australian governments and made similar overtures to the Dutch government.[39] Australia and the other Allies remained resolute in their stance, however, and Japanese requests were rebuffed.

Australian officials were in close internal discussion about potential repatriation of war criminals from Manus Island to Japan throughout late 1952 and early 1953. The negotiations were protracted, and one of the holdups was the Australian government's uncertainty over whether Japan could be relied upon to ensure that prisoners completed their sentences.

---

[37] NAA, Canberra, A1838, 140815, 'Cabinet Agendum No. 347 – Korean and Formosan Prisoners'; 'Cable from External Affairs to Australian Mission in Tokyo' (23 June 1952). See also Utsumi Aiko, 'Korean "Imperial Soldiers": Remembering Colonialism and Crimes Against Allied POWs,' Mie Kennedy, trans., in Takashi Fujitani, Geoffrey M. White, Lisa Yoneyama, eds., *Perilous Memories: The Asia-Pacific War(s)* (Durham: Duke University Press, 2001), 209.
[38] Utsumi, 'Korean "Imperial Soldiers",' 200.
[39] TNA, FO371/99516, 'Koreans and Formosans Sentenced as War Criminals' (31 July 1952); TNA, FO371/99516, 'British Embassy Tokyo' (11 August 1952).

This unease was partly based on lingering mistrust of Japan and a perception of ambiguity in the peace treaty, but it was also directly related to the Japanese requests for the release of Taiwanese and Korean prisoners, which suggested to some Australian officials that the Japanese government was not committed to the terms of article 11 of the peace treaty. Negotiations were still at a delicate point and the additional uncertainty was probably unwelcome for all parties. Repatriation from Manus to Japan did go ahead in August 1953, but only after the Australian government had received extra assurances from Japan that prisoners would not be released unless on the orders of Australian authorities.[40]

After the initial activity when the peace treaty was enacted, diplomatic representations concerning Korean and Taiwanese war criminals paused briefly, but discussions resumed between Korea and the UK near the end of 1953. Given the close relationship between Australia and the UK, the British view in these discussions was always relevant to Australia's position. On 27 November 1953, the Korean government asked the UK Foreign Office to consider offering clemency to the Koreans, while assuring the British that the Korean government did not question the original trial verdicts or the arrangements of the peace treaty. The UK government advised the Korean government that the 11 Korean men convicted in British courts and still in British custody were considered Japanese nationals and that they would not receive special consideration for clemency.[41] The Korean government then requested that the prisoners at least be repatriated to Korea. Britain declined this request also. Evidently, the issue had become slightly heated: after repeated Korean requests, a British official commented in May 1954 that he would let the Korean minister 'cool off' before again declining the latest request.[42] Despite the small number of Koreans in British custody by this time, their release was a sensitive matter because they had committed crimes in prisoner of war camps and British officials feared a backlash from former POWs who remained bitter about Korean guards.[43] The British felt there was no legal basis either in the war

---

[40] NAA, Canberra, A1838, 246874, 'External Affairs to Australian Embassy in Tokyo Regarding the Repatriation of War Criminals' (7 July 1953); NAA, Melbourne, MP729/8, 452815, 'Cabinet Minute Decision No. 731' (2 July 1953); NAA, Canberra, A1838, 140817, 'Cabinet Agendum No. 347' (September 1952).
[41] TNA, FO371/110514, 'Reply to Parliamentary question' (9 February 1954).
[42] TNA, FO371/110514, 'Clemency for Class B and C War Criminals: War criminals of the Korean race' (25 May 1954).
[43] TNA, FO371/110514, 'Note From Crowe' (7 May 1954).

crimes courts or the treaty to regard the prisoners differently from ethnic Japanese prisoners. In the official UK view, not only was their nationality irrelevant in legal terms, but it may in fact have lessened their chance of receiving clemency, given how the Korean camp guards were viewed by British POWs.

While the early representations from Taiwan appear to have been at least partly driven by public concern for war criminals' welfare, in Korea, public interest seems to have been moderate at best. The British legation in Seoul advised the Foreign Office in August 1954 that the issue had appeared in the press, but that interest was low outside state-controlled discourse.[44] It is uncertain what the Korean prisoners themselves thought. The Korean government seemed to indicate they were suffering discrimination in Sugamo, but one Korean who was due for release in 1954 refused to leave, since he did not want to face the hardships in the outside world.[45]

In 1954, the Korean government turned its attention to prisoners held by Australia. The government claimed not to challenge the legitimacy of the Australian view that war crimes proceedings had been lawful, nor did it claim the prisoners were not legitimate war criminals. Instead, Korean government overtures through the Australian embassy in Japan evoked images of young Korean men who had been pawns of Japanese imperialism. In many of the war crimes trials the accused had claimed they had committed their crimes under orders. None of the Allied governments considered the existence of orders from a superior to be a defense against guilt, but if a guilty war criminal had truly been acting under orders then the court could impose a lighter sentence.[46] In January 1954, Korean officials wrote to the Australian embassy in Tokyo and questioned the opportunity Korean soldiers had had to choose between observing international

---

[44] TNA, FO371/110514, 'Letter from Seoul Legation' (5 August 1954).
[45] TNA, FO371/110514, 'Press article and attached commentary' (30 December 1954).
[46] See Military Board (Australia), *Australian Edition of Manual of Military Law 1941 (Including Army Act and Rules of Procedure as Modified and Adapted by the Defence Act 1903–1939 and the Australian Military Regulations)*, (Canberra: Commonwealth Government Printer, 1941), 288; NARA, Decimal 290-15-15-05, SCAP Legal Section. Monographs, RG331, Box 3676, 'The Trial of Class B and C War Criminals (includes forward)' (19 May 1952); Phillip R. Piccigallo, *The Japanese on Trial: Allied War Crimes Operations in the Far East 1945–1952* (Austin, TX: University of Texas Press, 1979), 39; Sheldon Glueck, *War criminals: their prosecution and punishment* (New York, NY: Knopf, 1944), 140–2. See also the chapter by Sandra Wilson in this volume that shows the prosecuting countries did make significant allowances for the lowest ranking personnel in the Japanese forces outside the courtrooms.

law and following the orders of a superior officer. In their view, Korean soldiers had been pressed into service and were then immediately compelled by the Japanese to harbor hatred for the Western powers. They were placed at prisoner of war camps as the lowest ranking guards and were not given detailed information on the international laws of war. They then had to follow brutal orders. When they faced Allied war crimes proceedings, the Koreans were again left underprepared, as the trials were conducted in English with Japanese language assistance, but not Korean language assistance. The Korean government urged the Australian government to regard the Korean prisoners as 'the scapegoats of Japanese militarism.'[47] It was a provocative position that used Japanese imperialism to tie the situation of the war criminals to Australian sympathies, as fellow victims of Japan. Social and geopolitical factors from the period of Japanese colonization, however, were never likely to sway Australian views on war criminals convicted in Australian courts.

Ultimately, none of the early moves by Korean and Nationalist Chinese diplomats had much effect on any of the Western governments, especially Australia. Nor could the Japanese government persuade the Australian government that non-Japanese prisoners deserved special consideration. The Australian government felt it was in a sound legal position. During the discussions in the early 1950s, considerations of the law and of formal justice, and the still largely negative views of Japan in the Australian electorate, outweighed politics and diplomacy on most decisions about war criminals. Gradually, however, things began to change, and political imperatives became increasingly salient as the decade wore on.

The seeds of change had been sown in the peace treaty and in the subsequent awkward repatriation negotiations between the Japanese and Australian governments. A slow process had begun which eventually recast Japan as Australia's friend rather than adversary. The major turning point came in 1954, when the Australian government resolved to change its general policy on Japan. The Pacific War was no longer omnipresent in official Australian thinking. The government felt that, in the context of the Cold War, it had to do all that it could to pursue better relations with Japan. This resulted in a commitment in 1955 and 1956 to offer parole

---

[47] NAA, Melbourne, MT1131/1, 3250205, 'Korean Mission in Japan to Australian Mission' (28 January 1954). This perspective on the Korean prisoners is also explored in Yi Hak-Nae, 'The man between: a Korean guard looks back,' in Gavan McCormack and Hank Nelson, eds., *The Burma–Thailand railway* (St Leonards, NSW: Allen & Unwin, 1993), 120–6 and Utsumi, 'The Korean guards on the Burma-Thailand railway,' 127–38.

to war criminals and increase the rate at which they left prison. Ultimately, it was this political shift that brought about the release of the Korean and Taiwanese prisoners by altering the discourse surrounding all war criminals from a focus on justice to a focus on diplomacy.

Still, Australian policy on the ethnicity of the Korean and Taiwanese prisoners had to be resolved before their release, because of the complexities of releasing a non-Japanese prisoner under parole conditions in Japan. In July 1955 the East Asia Section of External Affairs prepared a paper on the Taiwanese and Korean prisoners. The paper noted that the Australian government was not legally compelled to act on requests from foreign governments for a change in policy on the prisoners, but in the opinion of External Affairs Australia's relations with Korea and Taiwan were being harmed by the current policy and, furthermore, there appeared to be humanitarian grounds for a softening of the government's stance. East Asia Section identified a range of courses of action, from outright release to supervised parole in Korea and Taiwan.[48] The Japanese government wanted Korean and Taiwanese prisoners to receive a general amnesty. In an indication that Australian officials were not yet prepared to forgo all of their rights over war criminals in order to secure better relations with Japan, however, External Affairs recommended that an amnesty not be granted and that instead the prisoners be allowed to serve out parole in their country of origin.[49] Parole in Korea or Taiwan was never arranged. When the Korean and Taiwanese prisoners did eventually receive clemency, it was on the same conditions as for Japanese prisoners, not as a special case as their governments desired. The last war criminals convicted by Australian courts were released on 28 June 1957.

In their diplomatic exchanges with the Korean, Chinese and Japanese governments, Australian officials showed little regard for the origins of war crimes in Japanese imperialist expansion. The bellicose rhetoric of early postwar Australian statesmen demonstrated that war crimes trials were part of a broader plan to bring Japan to account and to secure the Pacific from future Japanese ambition. When planning for war crimes justice, the Australian government clearly did not take into account the Japanese expansion of the late nineteenth and early twentieth centuries, when Taiwan and Korea were colonized. Regarding the prisoners as Japanese

---

[48] NAA, Melbourne, MP729/8, 444972, 'War criminals of Korean and Formosan origin' (25 July 1955).
[49] Ibid.

served the purpose of punishing the Japanese aggression of 1941–1945 but did not encompass the imperialist incursion into Taiwan and Korea that had landed these war criminals in Australian courts in the first place.

Australian officials did appear somewhat sensitive to the sovereign rights of the newly emerging Chinese and Korean governments. Although they continued to insist that the prisoners remained Japanese, officials recognized that they needed to deal with the war criminals' countries of origin as well as with Japan over their repatriation and release. Neither the Chinese nor the Korean government could guarantee, however, that paroled prisoners or transferred prisoners could serve their sentences fully in prisons in those countries. Had these assurances been forwarded it would have provided an interesting test of how far the Australian government felt it could trust the governments of Korea and Taiwan at that stage. The fate of war criminals was never an issue the Australian government took lightly and it felt for much of the late 1940s and early 1950s that it could not afford to take lenient steps on war criminals out of fear of public backlash. Even a small scale of clemency granted to a select group of prisoners had the potential to produce public hostility in the estimation of the government.

The manner of the eventual release of the war criminals highlights one final contradiction in the case of Korean and Taiwanese prisoners. Since 1947, the governments concerned had asked the Australian government to consider the political factors that had led to the men being in the Japanese military in the first place. Australian officials and those from other countries maintained that these factors were irrelevant and that crimes needed to be punished. The eventual release of prisoners did result from political considerations. But the operative factor was Japan, rather than any other Asian country. After 1954 the Australian government concluded that the benefits of good relations with Japan outweighed the need to keep war criminals in prison. Japan was restored to friendship with the Western democracies and the war criminals were released. By the mid-1950s the political situation in Asia and in Australia had changed to the point that diplomatic and economic imperatives were much more salient to the Australian government than reckoning for war crimes. Just as Japanese imperialist expansion meant that Koreans and Taiwanese ended up in war crimes courts in the first place, it was largely Japanese political and economic influence that resulted in their release.

CHAPTER 11

From Tokyo to Khabarovsk: Soviet War Crimes Trials in Asia as Cold War Battlefields

Valentyna Polunina

Despite the fact that the Soviet Union was not as heavily involved in the Pacific theater of the Second World War as the other Allies,[1] it was still very much interested in shaping postwar justice in Asia. From the first days of the Soviet state, its leaders were fully aware of the didactic, geopolitical and propaganda benefits of open political trials. At the beginning of the Cold War, war crimes tribunals were treated by the USSR as a tool for achieving their goals on the international stage. Japanese war crimes trials were 'made to fit into the overall national and foreign policy objectives of

---

[1] Further reading: Tsuyoshi Hasegawa, *Racing the Enemy: Stalin, Truman, and the Surrender of Japan* (Harvard, MA: Belknap Press, 2005), Boris N. Slavinskii, *The Japanese-Soviet Neutrality Pact: A Diplomatic History, 1941–1945* (City: Psychology Press, 2004), Prasenjit Duara, 'The New Imperialism and the Post-Colonial Developmental State: Manchukuo in comparative perspective,' in *Japan Focus* http://www.japanfocus.org/-Prasenjit-Duara/1715 (last accessed 10 March 2015).

V. Polunina (✉)
Heidelberg University, Heidelberg, Germany

© The Author(s) 2016
K. von Lingen (ed.), *War Crimes Trials in the Wake of Decolonization and Cold War in Asia, 1945–1956*,
DOI 10.1007/978-3-319-42987-8_11

each Allied country'[2] and the Soviet Union was no exception. It saw war crimes trials as politically staged events that had to reflect the Soviet official representation of the past.[3]

The Soviet Union's approach to war crimes prosecution in Asia differed from their approach in Europe. The trials of Nazi war criminals and their European collaborators were aimed primarily at bringing justice to the mainly Soviet victims, delivering retribution for the crimes, deterring the Nazi perpetrators from committing further crimes and the Soviet people from cooperating with the enemy. The Soviets also used the trials as a tool to demonstrate the advantages of the communist state system.

The Japanese war crimes trials, on the other hand, were a means of projecting Soviet influence in the Pacific Rim despite the late entrance of the Red Army into the war against Japan. The Soviet Union had not entered the Pacific War until 9 August 1945, when it invaded Manchuria and defeated the Japanese Kwantung Army.

Even after a less than positive experience at the International Military Tribunal (IMT) in Nuremberg and being shut out of the creation of the International Military Tribunal for the Far East (IMTFE), the Soviets still willingly participated in the prosecution of the Japanese political and military leaders in Tokyo. The Soviets considered the IMTFE—with its lukewarm finding of 'crimes against peace' against the Soviet Union, and its failure to address Japan's biological weapons program—inadequate. In order to correct this 'failure' and to address the crimes not properly considered at Tokyo, the so-called Khabarovsk Trial was held in the Soviet Far East in December 1949. The Japanese defendants were charged with aggressively 'manufacturing and employing bacteriological weapons' against the Soviet Union and China.[4] While earlier Soviet military courts in Europe were seen as an extension of the Nuremberg Tribunal,[5] the

---

[2] Philip R. Picigallo, *The Japanese on trial: Allied war crimes operations in the East, 1945–1951* (Austin, TX: University of Texas Press, 1979), xiii.

[3] See Prusin, in: Norman Goda, ed., Writing Retribution. Holocaust Justice and its Meaning (2016).

[4] *Materials on the trial of former servicemen of the Japanese Army charged with manufacturing and employing bacteriological weapons* (Moscow: Foreign Languages Publishing House, 1950), 7.

[5] According to Andreas Hilger, there were 38 Soviet trials of Germans in 1945, 245 in 1946, 841 in 1947, 2,432 in 1948, 15,145 in 1949 and 1,416 in 1950. (Andreas Hilger, 'Die Gerechtigkeit nehme ihren Lauf?': Die Bestrafung deutscher Kriegs- und Gewaltverbrecher in der Sowjetunion und der SBZ/DDR, in Norbert Frei, ed. *Transnationale*

Khabarovsk Trial was conceived as a corrective to the Tokyo Tribunal. The inability of the Soviets to influence the agenda of the American-directed IMTFE did not discourage them from planning a subsequent international tribunal: after reaching the verdict at Khabarovsk, the Soviet leadership insisted on establishing another international tribunal for trying Emperor Hirohito for his involvement in the Japanese biological warfare program.[6]

Although the Soviets had long experience with staging domestic trials, they found themselves frustrated when they attempted to monopolize the organization of multinational tribunals. The lack of well-trained and experienced staff combined with Moscow's attempts to control the Soviet delegation led to the fiasco of the Soviet performance in Nuremberg.[7] Nevertheless, the Soviet leadership surprisingly expressed their willingness to participate in the common prosecution of Japanese war criminals even though it clearly understood the leading role of the USA in the tribunal.[8] This unexpected willingness can be explained by the Soviet belief that ideological and geopolitical benefits of participation in an international war crimes tribunal exceeded the possible risks.

Set in an intricate context of decolonization and the Cold War, Soviet propaganda messages differed depending on their intended recipients—the Soviet public, prospective allies, or above all, the new chief adversary, the USA. The most important propaganda aims of the Soviets were to persuade the international community that the Soviet Union was the only power interested in delivering justice to the victims of Japanese occupation, preventing the spread of 'American imperialism' and re-militarization of Japan, and protecting its allies from attacks and new colonization. The main target of this anti-imperialist rhetoric was the newly created People's Republic of China, where it found fertile ground. Although

---

Vergangenheitspolitik. Der Umgang mit deutschen Kriegsverbrechern in Europa nach dem Zweiten Weltkrieg, (Göttingen: Wallstein Verlag, 2006), 182.

[6]'Nota Sovetskogo Pravitel'stva pravitel'stvam SSHA, Velikobritanii i Kitaia,' *Pravda*, 3 February 1950, 2.

[7]Francine Hirsch, 'The Soviets at Nuremberg: International Law, Propaganda, and the Making of the Postwar Order,' *American Historical Review* 2 (2008): 701–730.

[8]Moscow's response to George Kennan's invitation to participate in the International Military Tribunal for the Far East (IMTFE) revealed that despite their unfamiliarity with the IMTFE, the Soviets assured that their "'interest was more than formal,' and they wanted to know much more about the role of the USSR in the proposed trial. Philip R. Piccigallo, *The Japanese on trial: Allied war crimes operations in the East, 1945–1951* (Austin, TX: University of Texas Press, 1979), 145.

China was formally independent, its leaders considered it to be informally colonized and therefore needed to be liberated 'as part of the anti-imperial movement.'[9]

Even if the propaganda elements and didactic goals were also evident at the Western Allies' war crimes trials, the Soviet contribution to international war crimes tribunals was often criticized and dismissed as mere propaganda. The vague legal basis of the Soviet trials contributed to this negative image. Formally held according to Soviet laws and definitions of legality, Soviet trials had little in common with Western legal practices.

The Bolsheviks used political spectacles and rituals widely in their geopolitical and ideological encounters with enemies. The show trials of the 1920s and 1930s helped the Soviets internally legitimize their regime and broadcast their values internationally.[10]

Elements of political trials (показательный процесс)[11] became an integral part of the Soviet war crimes trials policy. Confessions or admissions of guilt by the accused often provided the sole basis for conviction. In some cases, the prosecution relied heavily on circumstantial evidence and the principle of 'the highest probability' or 'objective possibility' of an alleged fact. Detailed coaching of the defendants before the start of proceedings and a high degree of legal technicality remained the features of Soviet war crimes trials.

In the West, the Khabarovsk Trial was perceived to be yet another Stalinist affair modeled on the infamous Moscow purge trials of the 1930s. The fact that there was no prior announcement of the trial, that international observers were excluded and that there was a strong whiff of propaganda about the proceedings, made it easy to dismiss it as a mere show trial. But unlike the purge trials, the evidence presented at Khabarovsk was mostly real. Some scholars have convincingly argued that the testimonies there have subsequently been largely corroborated, either by documents discovered in archives, or by testimonies offered by former Japanese

---

[9] Prasenjit Duara, ed., *Decolonization. Perspectives from now and then* (London: Routledge, 2004), 2.
[10] See Elizabeth Wood, 'The Trial of Lenin: Legitimating the Revolution through Political Theater, 1920–23,' *Russian Review* 61 (2002): 235–48, Robert Argenbright, 'Marking NEP's Slippery Path: The Krasnoshchekov Show Trial,' *Russian Review* 61 (2002): 249–75, Michael Ellman, 'The Soviet 1937–1938 Provincial Show Trials Revisited,' *Europa-Asia Studies* 8 (2003): 1305–21.
[11] Manfred Zeidler, 'Der Minsker Kriegsverbrecherprozeß vom Januar 1946. Kritische Anmerkungen zu einem sowjetischen Schauprozeß gegen deutsche Kriegsgefangene,' *Vierteljahrshefte für Zeitgeschichte* 2 (2004): 216.

servicemen.¹² It was unnecessary for the Soviets to concoct evidence—the reality was horrendous enough.

Critical examination of archival materials indicates that it would be shortsighted to reject the findings of Soviet war crimes trials as typical Stalinist justice. This is particularly true with regard to the Khabarovsk Trial, which will be discussed in the following sections.

THE SOVIETS AT TOKYO

Soviet leaders had a generally ambivalent attitude towards the Tokyo Trial. On the one hand, they approved of its overall outcome. On the other hand, the setting of the trial, its conduct and some results were heavily criticized by the Soviets. The Soviet criticism was primarily focused on blaming the Western Allies, especially the USA, for exercising control over the tribunal in order to pursue their own political agenda.

It is evident that previous experience of participation in national and international trials was a crucial criterion for the Soviet leaders in making an important decision on the composition of the delegation. It is possible that they had learned a lesson from their first negative experience in Nuremberg, when they struggled to compete with the USA propaganda efforts and had difficulties influencing the agenda of the trial.¹³

The Soviet delegation was headed by the member of the board of the Ministry of Foreign Affairs of the USSR, Professor Sergey Golunsky. Golunsky participated in the Yalta and Potsdam conferences, where he worked as Stalin's consultant and interpreter. The Soviet judge at the Tokyo Tribunal was Major-General of Justice Ivan Zaryanov, a member of the Military Collegium of the Supreme Court of the USSR. A major inconvenience for the whole Soviet delegation was the fact that Zaryanov did not speak any foreign languages. The peculiarity of the Soviet legal system of the time that gave state prosecutors a leading role in trial proceedings impacted the effectiveness of the Soviet delegation. Soviet leaders, focusing on the prosecutor as the most important member of the delegation, hoped that Golunsky's previous experience and mastery of

---

¹² See Yudin, 'Research on humans,' 70–2; Nie, 'The West's dismissal,' 35, 37; Suzy Wang, 'Medicine-related war crimes trials and post-war politics and ethics' in J-BaoNie J-B et al., eds., *Japan's wartime medical atrocities: comparative inquiries in science, history, and ethics* (London: Routledge, 2010), 41; Peter Williams and David Wallace, *Unit 731*, 230.

¹³ Francine Hirsch, 'The Soviets at Nuremberg: International Law, Propaganda, and the Making of the Postwar Order,' *American Historical Review* 2 (2008): 703.

foreign languages would help him to establish contacts with other delegations and promote the interests of the USSR at the tribunal. However, the Soviets did not anticipate that the judges were expected to be at the head of the delegations and were quite surprised when, on arrival in Tokyo, they were faced with a completely different understanding of their role.[14]

As mentioned above, the major point of Soviet criticism was that all the states did not have equal control over the tribunal. In contrast to Nuremberg, where the judges elected their own court president, Tokyo's Court President, Australian William Webb, was appointed by General Douglas MacArthur, the American Supreme Commander for the Allied Power. Furthermore, in contrast to Nuremberg, where the participating Allies nominated their own chief prosecutors, Tokyo's sole chief prosecutor, American Joseph Keenan, was appointed by US President Harry Truman. The court's charter was written by American legal scholars, and the trial was conducted along 'Anglo-American' lines[15]—indeed, from the Soviet perspective, 'the most complicated and most conservative' character of the common law proceedings made it possible for the defence to 'deliberately protract' the trial.[16]

The Soviets were dissatisfied with the absence of representatives from the Soviet satellite, the Mongolian People's Republic, from among the prosecutors and judges. Mongolia had been the site of a Soviet and Mongolian clash with the Japanese Kwantung Army near the Khalkhin-gol River (or Nomonhan) in 1939, and so had a justifiable claim to membership of the court. (The British and Americans had decided to accept the membership of *their* satellite Asian states, India and the Philippines, on the grounds that the Indians had fought in the Allied forces, and the Filipinos had suffered occupation by the Japanese). But when the Soviets pushed Mongolia's claim, they met 'fierce resistance from the Anglo-American reactionary bloc,' on the grounds that Mongolia was not considered a member of the Allies' wartime alliance.[17]

Furthermore, to the dissatisfaction of the Soviet delegation in Tokyo, English and Japanese (but not Russian and French, as at Nuremberg) were designated as the working languages of the court. Although the Soviet

---

[14] Anatoliy Nikolaev, *Tokio: sud narodov. Po vospominaniiam uchastnika protsessa* (Moskva: Iuridicheskaia literatura, 1990), 48–9.
[15] Mark Raginskii and Solomon Rosenblit, *Mezhdunarodnii protsess glavnikh iaponskikh voennikh prestupnikov* (Moskva-Leningrad: Izdatel'stvo akademii nauk SSSR, 1950), 79.
[16] Ibid., 78.
[17] Mark Raginskii, *Militaristy na skam'e podsudimykh: po materialam Tokiiskogo I Khabarovskogo protsessov* (Moskva: Iuridicheskaia literatura, 1985), 42.

prosecutors had reserved in advance their right to disclose evidence in Russian, the predominance of English and other unequal arrangements 'secured American influence on the preparations and progress of the trial.'[18] Another criticism of the trial was that it failed to prosecute *all* the major Japanese war criminals. Although they did not raise the idea of trying the Japanese Emperor before or during the proceedings, they took issue with the Allies' failure to try leading members of the *zaibatsu*, Japan's huge financial and industrial conglomerates.

In general, when voicing their criticisms on the Tokyo trial, the Soviets focused on the more politicized issues, such as the Americans' selective approach to the defendants, their unequal, if not actively hostile, treatment of the USSR and attempts to control all the aspects of the trial. They were less interested in the Tribunal's many legal flaws, which set them apart from the dissenting judges from India, the Netherlands and France, who concentrated on the retrospective creation of the charges, the unsatisfactory interpretation of the facts and the misapplication of the law.

Anatoly Nikolaev, a member of the Soviet delegation's secretariat at Tokyo, was struggling to point out that the Japanese counsel shared their clients' outlook and beliefs.[19] Special attention was directed to the attorney Kiyose Ichiro, a former member of parliament, and Ikeda Shunkichi, a former deputy chief-of-staff of the Kwantung Army, who had defended his wartime superior, General Umezu Yoshijirō.[20]

According to the Soviet position, the accused were not only being protected by the defence counsel, but also by 'many high officials from the USA and England who [...] did not shun dirty slanders against the USSR and other nations.'[21] American officials, indeed, sought to undermine the Soviet case against Japan. To this end, senior American figures provided testimony to the defense showing that, contrary to the Soviets' arguments, the Japanese had avoided rather than provoked conflict with the Soviet Union, and that it was the Soviets, not the Japanese, who had violated the Neutrality Pact by attacking Manchuria in August 1945. Finally, the majority judgment itself was rather more equivocal about the question of Japanese aggression than the Soviets had hoped. It was silent on the subject of Japanese attacks on the Soviet Union, or the Soviets' justifications for breaching the Neutrality Pact.

---

[18] Mark Raginskii and Solomon Roseablit *Mezhdunarodnii protsess*, 49.
[19] Aanatoliy Nikolaev, *Tokio: sud narodov*, 61.
[20] Mark Raginskii *Militaristy*, 44.
[21] Ibid.

Khabarovsk Trial: A 'Hybrid' Show Trial

The Khabarovsk Trial took place in the Russian Far East in late December 1949, more than four years after the accused had been taken prisoner and about a year after the IMTFE had finished its work. The Soviets did not succeed in finding a reasonable explanation about why it was necessary to wait for so long before starting the trial proceedings and revealing the truth about the Japanese biological weapons (BW) program and human experiments related to it. The choice wreaked havoc with Soviet war crimes trials policy in the Far East and contributed to the negative perception of the trial in the West. This adverse image has changed little since then. As Philip R. Picigallo rightly pointed out, 'whatever comments may be found [about the Khabarovsk Trial], however, are negative in their appraisal.'[22]

Apart from its belatedness, the ideological nature of the Soviet bacteriological warfare trial was another important reason why its outcome was dismissed by Western scholars as 'Soviet propaganda' and forgotten for nearly 40 years. Even if the Khabarovsk Tribunal was held formally according to Soviet laws and definitions of legality, it was a classic show trial, but with one big difference from the notorious Stalin trials in the 1920s and– 1930s: the prosecution made efforts to collect facts about Japanese biological warfare crimes that proved to be mostly correct with time.

Significant geopolitical and ideological considerations led to the conducting of this 'hybrid' show trial. By combining elements of a show trial with truthful facts of Japanese medicine-related atrocities, the Soviet leadership strived to legitimize their propaganda tribunal. An internationally recognized war crimes trial would significantly ease the task of imposing the Soviet vision of postwar order in the Far East and to achieve some vital geopolitical goals in the emerging bipolar world—establishing a good relationship with the newborn People's Republic of China and opposing the growing influence of the USA in the Far East during the early days of the Cold War.

---

[22] Philip R. Picigallo, *The Japanese on trial: Allied war crimes operations in the East, 1945–1951* (Austin, TX: University of Texas Press, 1979), 156. More about the perception of the Khabarovsk Trial as a show trial in Valentyna Polunina, 'Soviet War Crimes Policy in the Far East: The Bacteriological Warfare Trial at Khabarovsk 1949' in Morten Bergsmo, CHEAH Wui Ling and YI Ping (eds.), *Historical Origins of International Criminal Law: Volume 2* (FICHL Publication Series No. 21, 2014), 539–560, Valentyna Polunina, 'The Khabarovsk Trial: the Soviet riposte to the Tokyo Tribunal,' in Kirsten Sellars (ed.), *Trials for International Crimes in Asia* (Cambridge University Press, 2016), 121–145.

The reasons behind the decision to conduct the trial in Khabarovsk are accurately described in a collective work of Soviet legal scholars Mark Raginskii, Solomon Rosenblit and Lev Smirnov[23]:

> to expose criminal preparations of bacteriological war by reactionary circles in the United States and to show that the use of bacteriological warfare, as well as other criminal means of mass extermination – nuclear and chemical weapons – was and still is an integral part of the aggressive plans of the imperialist states. At the same time [...] to highlight the leading role of the Soviet Union in the struggle for peace, for the prohibition of weapons of mass extermination.[24]

The trial in Khabarovsk was the only trial that was entirely dedicated to the Japanese wartime biological weapons program. Twelve defendants who served in medical units of the Kwantung Army stood trial for preparations towards bacteriological war and medical experiments on human beings 'punishable under Article I of the Decree of the Presidium of the Supreme Soviet of the USSR of 19 April 1943' (Ukaz 43), and were sentenced to labor camp internments ranging from two to 25 years. The group of defendants was extremely heterogeneous and included a very high-ranking figure, Yamada Otozō, former commander-in-chief of the Kwantung Army; three senior administrators; various mid-ranking managers, bacteriologists, physicians and veterinarians who were involved in the day-to-day running of the biological warfare sections; and two low-ranking soldiers, who had cultivated pathogens.

Charges against the defendants were derived from the aforementioned 1943 Presidium Decree, 'On measures of punishment for German-fascist criminals guilty of the murder and torture of Soviet civilians and Red Army prisoners of war; also for spies and traitors to the Motherland among Soviet citizens and their accomplices.'[25] The preamble targets 'German, Italian, Romanian, Hungarian and Finnish fascist monsters [...] as well as traitors among Soviet citizens,' while article 1 singles out 'German-fascist villains'

---

[23] Lev Smirnov served as a state prosecutor during the Khabarovsk Trial.
[24] Mark Raginskii, Solomon Rosenblit and Lev Smirnov, *Bakteriologicheskaia voina – prestupnoe orudie imperialisticheskoi agressii. Khabarovskii protsess iaponskikh voennykh prestupnikov* (Moscow: Izdatel'stvo Akademii nauk SSSR, 1950), 3.
[25] Decree of the Presidium of the Supreme Soviet of the USSR, 'O merakh nakazaniia dlia nemetsko-fashistskikh zlodeev, vinovnykh v ubiistvakh i istiazaniiakh sovetskogo grazhdanskogo naseleniia i plennykh krasnoarmeitsev, dlia shpionov, izmennikov rodiny iz chisla sovetskikh grazhdan i ikh posobnikov' (19 April 1943).

and the Soviet 'spies and traitors.'[26] In other words, this decree was thus originally designed to facilitate the trial and punishment of European war criminals and their local collaborators—not Japanese defendants. Moreover, because the decree was drafted several years prior to the Nuremberg and Tokyo Charters, it contained no specific reference to the substantive charges of 'crimes against peace,' crimes against humanity or war crimes, but instead relied on different formulations such as 'murder and torture of civilians and Red Army prisoners of war,' 'brutality' and 'atrocities.'[27]

The importance of this decree should not be underestimated, however: no fewer than 81,780 people accused of crimes committed during the war—of whom at least 25,209 were non-Soviets—were sentenced under its terms between 1943 and 1952.[28] The Soviets emphasized the significance of the decree: in their view, it was not only the first law on the punishment of war criminals issued by an Allied country, but also the first one that was actually applied in war crimes trials.[29]

But the full text of the decree was not publicly released during this period. Neither the accused nor their defense counsel knew what it contained. This raises the question: why did they use the decree as the basis for the Khabarovsk Trial when they might have used the Tokyo Charter? After all, the latter had the patina of international credibility, and may have seemed more appropriate for prosecuting Japanese defendants. It is possible that the Soviets rejected the Tokyo Charter because it was directed at 'major war criminals in the Far East'[30]—that is, leaders of Japan's government and armed forces—'charged with offenses which include Crimes against Peace.'[31] The Khabarovsk defendants, with the exception of Yamada Otozō, former Kwantung Army Commander-in-Chief, were either not senior enough, or their crimes did not encompass 'crimes

---

[26] Ibid.
[27] Decree of the Presidium of the Supreme Soviet of the USSR, 'O merakh nakazaniia dlia nemetsko-fashistskikh zlodeev, vinovnykh v ubiistvakh i istiazaniih sovetskogo grazhdanskogo naseleniia i plennykh krasnoarmeitsev, dlia shpionov, izmennikov rodiny iz chisla sovetskikh grazhdan i ikh posobnikov' (19 April 1943).
[28] Aleksandr Epifanov, '*Otvetstvennost' za voennye prestupleniia, sovershennye na teritorii SSSR v period Velikoi Otechestvennoi Voiny (istoriko-pravovoi aspekt)*' (PhD diss., 2001), 4.
[29] Mark Raginskii, Solomon Rosenblit and Lev Smirnov, *Bakteriologicheskaia voina*, 118.
[30] John Pritchard, ed., International Military Tribunal for the Far East, *The Tokyo major war crimes trial*, 124 vols. (Lewiston: Edwin Mellen Press, 1998), Amended Charter, vol. 2, 1.
[31] John Pritchard (ed.) International Military Tribunal for the Far East, *The Tokyo major war crimes trial*, 124 vols. (Lewiston: Edwin Mellen Press, 1998), Amended Charter, vol. 2, 2.

against peace.' Furthermore, the incorporation of the Tokyo Charter into domestic law would have been a cumbersome process, whereas the decree, which was already on hand, could provide a quick fix.

As Soviet lawyers pointed out, there was no chance that an international tribunal would be established to try Japanese medical crimes on the basis of already recognized standards due to the unwillingness of the USA. In that situation the Soviet authorities had to create their own tribunal and apply national law.[32]

Having made this decision, the question was how to apply the decree, which targeted just European fascists from Germany, Italy, Romania, Hungary and Finland and local Soviet collaborators to Japanese defendants.[33] The solution was to proceed by way of analogy: the Japanese had committed similar crimes, and were thus liable under the same decree. As Kruglov, Safonov and Gorshenin stated in their working party report to Stalin on 22 November 1949, 'although Japanese military are not mentioned in this Decree, their criminal activities are analogous to the crimes of the fascist German army.'[34] This concept of analogy was, of course, already well known in the Soviet legal system: article 16 of the 1926 Russian Criminal Code, which was widely replicated in the other republics, stated that if a socially dangerous action was not foreseen by the code, liability would be determined by the sections of it dealing with the most closely related crimes.[35] The propaganda purposes of the trial were evident even in the unusual choice of the trial site—a remote city in eastern Siberia. The location of the trial was not chosen by chance. First of all, it served as an obstacle to foreign observers and reporters attending the hearings in the officially 'open' trial. Furthermore, the location of the trial near the biggest human research laboratory just across the Soviet–Chinese border near the Manchurian city of Harbin had a symbolic meaning to the Chinese victims of biological weapons and their families. It also served as a sign of retribution, justice and deterrence to potential perpetrators from the enemy bloc. The Soviets wanted to emphasize their role as a liberator and as a new superpower that could guarantee security for their weaker

---

[32] Mark Raginskii, Solomon Rosenblit and Lev Smirnov, *Bakteriologicheskaia voina*, 116.
[33] Presidium Decree (19 April 1943).
[34] GARF, D 596, Op 1a, R 9492, 5270/k, 'Results of the investigation into criminal activities of nine persons among accused Japanese generals and officers serving in the anti-epidemic Detachment 731' (22 November 1949), 16. The decree was also applied by analogy to Austrian, Dutch and Belgian citizens (Epifanov, 53.)
[35] Article 16, *Criminal Code* of the Russian Soviet Federative Socialist Republic (1926).

allies, especially the new People's Republic of China. State Prosecutor Smirnov claimed in his speech that 'it was only the swift crushing blow of the Armed Forces of the Soviet Union that paralyzed the enemy and saved the world from the horrors of bacteriological warfare.'[36]

As a result, the world knew about the tribunal what the Soviet Union wanted it to know. The general public followed the progress of the Khabarovsk Trial only through official reports, carefully prepared and sanctioned by the highest Soviet leadership. It is remarkable that the local population was permitted to watch the trial: every day the court proceedings were witnessed by 1000–1600 people.[37] Those who could not get into the courtroom were listening to radio broadcasts outside of the House of the Officers where the proceedings took place.

Analysis of archival materials shows that Stalin and other Soviet leaders took a keen interest in the trial.[38] The decision to start the trial proceedings in Khabarovsk was made at the highest level. Under Stalin's chairmanship, the Soviet of Ministers of the USSR passed a special resolution on 8 October 1949 establishing the trial. A working group consisting of Sergei Kruglov, the Minister of Internal Affairs; Grigori Safonov, the Procurator-General; and Konstantin Gorshenin, the Minister of Justice, were in charge of the organization of the Khabarovsk Trial.[39] Several representatives of the Ministry of the Interior sent daily reports from the courtroom to Moscow. Moreover, four judges had to cover the trial proceedings in telegrams on each day of the trial.

The Soviet leaders had no reason to worry that the thoroughly prepared script of the trial would be interrupted by unpleasant surprises. Although

---

[36] *Materials*, 466.

[37] Sheldon H. Harris *Factories of death. Japanese biological warfare, 1932–45, and the American cover-up* (New York, NY: Routledge, 1994), 227.

[38] GARF, R 9492, Op 1a, F 596 'Otkrytyi sudebnyi protsess nad iaponskimi prestupnikami v g. Khabarovske 25-30/XII 949 goda.'

[39] It should be mentioned that creating special working groups was a common practice for organizing the most important war crimes tribunals in the Soviet Union. For example, a ministerial commission, consisting again of Sergei Kruglov, the head of the People's Secretariat for State Security (NKGB) Bogdan Kobulov, and the head of counterintelligence 'SMERSH' Viktor Abakumov was created by the Politburo of the Communist Party in November 1945 with the aim to establish and monitor eight war crimes trials against German perpetrators in the period from December 1945 to February 1946. As in the case of the Khabarovsk Trial, Stalin's closest circle consisting, among others, of Lavrentiy Beria and Vyacheslav Molotov were in charge of the overall progress of the trials and decided upon the persons to be tried, indictments and verdicts.

they were entitled to put questions to witnesses, experts and to each other, to make explanatory statements, and to call further witnesses and experts or call for other 'proofs and documents,' the defendants made little use of these rights and pleaded guilty to the charges against them. They willfully gave detailed descriptions of their crimes. This behavior in Khabarovsk contrasted with the behavior of other Japanese defendants brought to trial by other allied nations and made them 'the most cooperative and contented Japanese accused of all those tried after World War II.'[40] Even in their final pleas, the Japanese defendants kept expressing their repentance. One defendant, Kawashima, stated that 'the Soviet Union is a democratic country which cares for the welfare of the people and stands on guard for peace.'[41] Another, Hirazakura, went even further by assuring that 'Stern punishment of us [...] will be a warning and a lesson for those criminals who are now trying to prepare to conduct a second bacteriological war.'[42]

It should be kept in mind, that despite all the efforts, the attributes of a fair trial were applied along the rules which were valid in the Soviet Union and did not have much in common with Western legal practice. This was evident not only in the unusually cooperative behavior of the accused but also in the strategy of the defense lawyers. In line with the common practice in the Soviet Union, they did not attempt to prove the innocence of the accused, but simply tried to mitigate their guilt, emphasizing their contrition and willingness to cooperate. Even so, the defence counsel's role at Khabarovsk was hardly decorative or nominal, as some have claimed.[43] Like the prosecution, they had a crucial role to play in advancing the Soviet critique of the Tokyo Tribunal, and in particular, its American sponsors. This assumption is supported by the willingness of the Ministry of Internal Affairs to pay the 'qualified members of the Moscow City Bar Association' sent to Khabarovsk proper salaries since the Ministry of Justice did not have enough money in their budget and Konstantin Gorshenin, therefore, had to ask his colleague Sergei Kruglov to step in. The Soviets learned a lesson from Tokyo that defense lawyers can play an important role in supporting the 'plot' of the trial—in this case

---

[40] Philip R. Picigallo, *The Japanese on trial: Allied war crimes operations in the East, 1945–1951* (Austin, TX: University of Texas Press, 1979), 154.

[41] *Materials*, 515.

[42] *Materials*, 519.

[43] See for example, Boris G. Yudin, 'Research on humans at the Khabarovsk war crimes trial. A historical and ethical examination' in J-Bao Nie J-B et al., eds., *Japan's wartime medical atrocities: comparative inquiries in science, history, and ethics* (London: Routledge, 2010).

by accusing the Americans of cooperating with Japanese war criminals in retaliation for the refusal of the Americans to let the Soviets interrogate Japanese scientists.

The defense had already played a crucial role in the denunciation of the emperor and those responsible for Japan's biological warfare program, but they had one final contribution to make. The indictment had already specified four crimes relating to preparation for and execution of biological warfare. But the defense team and their clients *added* to the roster of crimes set out in the indictment. Two lawyers, A. V. Zveryev and V.P. Lukiantsev, conceded that their respective clients, Takahashi Takaatsu and Karasawa Tomio, had committed crimes against humanity.[44] And two of the accused, Kawashima Kiyoshi and Satō Shunji, themselves admitted that they had committed a crime against humanity.[45] The frequency of the references to this crime, which did not appear on the Khabarovsk charge-sheet (and only nominally on the Tokyo charge-sheet[46]) strongly suggests that the Soviets wished to establish a precedent for crimes against humanity charges because they were contemplating further allegations against senior Japanese figures—a suggestion that was borne out by subsequent events that will be elaborated in greater detail below.

We can now return to the propaganda nature of the trial and the unusual level of collaboration of the defendants. The unpublished interrogation reports and appeals of the accused to the court of cassation show that their behavior was not as perfect as it may seem. For example, one of the accused, Kajitsuka, complained that he did not 'agree with the Verdict of the War Tribunal.' His main complaint was that General Yamada 'did not have a direct connection to the investigative activities of Unit 731 and did not exercise active leadership. On the contrary, Yamada was an opponent of bacteriological warfare.'[47]

Apparently there were other reasons for the unusually cooperative behavior of the defendants besides the well-known methods to obtain confessions as a result of physical and/or emotional pressure on defendants. Although they were officially illegal, these 'methods for extracting confession were also a normative component of the Soviet police system before,

---

[44] *Materials*, 511.
[45] *Materials*, 516, 519.
[46] Kirsten Sellars *'Crimes against peace' and international law* (Cambridge: Cambridge University Press, 2013), 190.
[47] GARF, R 9492, Op 1a, F 595 'Perepiska po otkrytomu protsessu nad iaponskimi prestupnikami v gorode Khabarovske (18.11.1949–28.02.1950),' 44.

during, and after the Stalin era.'[48] Nevertheless, there are grounds to believe that the defendants agreed to cooperate in exchange for lenient sentences. According to the archival documents, it was decided long before the start of the proceedings that the Japanese defendants would not receive severe punishment.[49] It is likely that the prosecution team was trying to avoid the death penalty for the defendants in Khabarovsk by reaching the verdict before capital punishment was to be restored on 12 January 1950. But why was it so important for the Soviets not to impose the capital punishment? It seems that 'the unusually light sentences handed down at Khabarovsk were a form of barter'[50] for 'valuable' information on bacteriological weapons.

The tribunal, which pronounced the sentences on 30 December 1949, found all 12 defendants guilty. Four of the accused—the most senior figures—received 25 years in a labor camp, the highest possible imprisonment term, presupposed by the organizers of the trial.[51] The imprisonment terms had little to do with the decree from 19 April 1943. The decision to impose 25 years in a labor camp was made as a compromise between death penalty which they could not (or even did not want) to impose and the maximum of 20 years of hard labor which could be applied by the decree only to the local accomplices and was seen as too lenient for the most important Japanese war criminals (at least they were afraid that it would be seen as too lenient, which was not good for propaganda purposes).

The rest were sentenced to terms ranging from ten to 20 years, with the exception of the lowest-ranking defendants who were given three and two years.[52] One notable feature of the sentences was that while the prosecutors had demanded the harshest punishment available, the judges had leeway to hand down marginally lighter sentences than recommended. This was a break from the unstated but almost universally observed practice at the time in the Soviet Union. (At the 1943 Kharkov Nazi war crimes trial,

---

[48] Prusin, Alexander '"Fascist Criminals to the Gallows": The Holocaust and Soviet War Crimes Trials, December 1945–February 1946.' *Holocaust and Genocide Studies* 17,1 (2003): 17.

[49] GARF, R 9492, Op 1a, F 596 'Otkrytyi sudebnyi protsess nad iaponskimi prestupnikami v g. Khabarovske 25-30/XII 949 goda.'

[50] Boris G. Yudin, 'Research on humans at the Khabarovsk war crimes trial. A historical and ethical examination' in J-Bao Nie et al., eds., *Japan's wartime medical atrocities: comparative inquiries in science, history, and ethics* (London: Routledge, 2010), 69.

[51] *Materials on the trial of former service men of the Japanese Army charged with manufacturing and employing bacteriological weapons* (Moscow: Foreign Languages Publishing House, 1950), 534.

[52] *Materials*, 534–535.

for example, the prosecutors' demand that all four defendants be hanged was followed to the letter.)

Immediately after the proclamation of the verdict, the Soviets started to spread information about the Khabarovsk Trial and its findings. As early as 1950, selected materials of the trial, including testimonies of the accused, documentary evidence and the reports of Soviet experts were published in a book and translated into several major languages, including Chinese, Japanese and English. The Soviet press intensively reported from the courtroom. The central message of the propaganda was to praise the leading role of the Soviet Union in defeating Japan and rescuing the world from an inevitable bacteriological war. It should be noted that this message was intended not only for the Soviet citizens but even more directed at the international stage and for the future enemy in the incipient Cold War the USA, as well as an ally to come—the People's Republic of China (PRC).

The major Soviet newspapers such as *Pravda* and *Izvestiya* published the most important documents from the trial, including the verdict that appeared on their front pages on 1 January 1950, together with propagandistic caricatures and excerpts from the Chinese newspaper *People's Daily*. The popular illustrated magazine *Ogoniok* dedicated a whole issue to the new ally, the PRC, and featured among contributions about the political, cultural and economic life there an article on the Khabarovsk Trial entitled 'Warning to all those clamoring for a new war.' It condemned 'capitalist science,' which had become a 'servant of the imperialist traders of the nation's blood' and claimed that 'modern followers of the Nazis and the Japanese samurai, the Anglo-American contenders for world domination, would like to lull the conscience of peoples in order to erase from their memories the atrocities of World War II criminals.'[53] The authors did not forget to mention one of the most important propaganda messages of the Khabarovsk Trial: collaboration between American authorities and Japanese war criminals and the omission of the topic of biological warfare in Tokyo:

> The US imperialists in MacArthur's headquarters in Japan made a stand to protect Japanese war criminals responsible for the preparation and use of biological weapons. [...] One of the main organizers of preparing for bacteriological warfare, Lieutenant General Ishii Shiro, is on the loose in Tokyo, and MacArthur puts forward to leading government positions his former masters from the Japanese financial monopolies and the reactionary imperial bureaucracy.[54]

---

[53] *Ogoniok*, (8 January 1950), 9.
[54] *Ogoniok*, (8 January 1950), 9.

Another important propaganda aspect that emerged in the beginning of the Cold War related to the growing influence of the USA in the region and especially in Japan: the USA was accused in the Soviet press of the re-militarization of Japan and preparations for a new war for world domination:

> US imperialists more and more openly encourage revanchist elements and arrogant claims of the Japanese militarists for our Soviet land. The intercession of the American occupation authorities in Japan for Japanese war criminals, of course, is no accident. It speaks of 'kinship' between the Japanese 'ideologists' of bacteriological warfare and those overseas preparing a new world war.[55]

'American imperialism' was often described in this context as the next wave of colonialism in Asia, namely that 'the ruling clique in the USA that borrowed from Nazi Germany and imperial Japan the crazy idea about gaining dominance over the world' and tries to create a 'new order'—'the American way of life' that would mean 'enslavement of entire peoples by American imperialism and deprivation of political independence of all [nations] fallen into American servitude.'[56]

The PRC also contributed to the publicity, depicting the Khabarovsk trial as 'an expression of friendship of the Soviet people towards the Chinese people' and 'a warning to Anglo-American warmongers trying to use biological weapons to endanger peace in the Far East and throughout the world.'[57] The information about the American collaboration with Japanese war criminals and the demands for Emperor Hirohito's liability as a war criminal was reprinted as headlines from the Chinese press.[58]

At the same time, not a word was said about the fact that the trial in Khabarovsk was a complete surprise for the PRC leaders. Moreover, reports were silent on the reality that while Mao and his followers were aware of what was going on in the Japanese biological warfare camps in China, it was not until December 1950 that the Communist Party of China (CPC) called for the prosecution of Emperor Hirohito and his

---

[55] Ibid.
[56] Mark Raginskii, Solomon Rosenblit and Lev Smirnov, *Bakteriologicheskaia voina*, 9.
[57] Renmin Ribao (People's Daily), quoted in 'Chinese newspaper on the trial of former military of the Japanese Army,' *Pravda*, 1 January 1950, 4.
[58] Justin Jacobs, 'Preparing the People for Mass Clemency: The 1956 Japanese War Crimes Trials in Sehnyan and Taiyuan,' *The China Quarterly* 205 (2011): 160.

accomplices for waging germ warfare, after the Soviets had initiated the bacteriological warfare trial in Khabarovsk.[59] The reason why this potentially useful propagandistic issue was overlooked by the CPC might have been their focus on re-establishing their authority over the country or, as some scholars suggest, discouragement by 'the allies of the Kuomintang–Communist warring factions, the United States and the Soviet Union' from raising this issue, as they both had a keen interest in the Japanese biological warfare expertise and tried to avoid any public debate.[60]

Needless to say, both the Soviets and the Chinese used the trial to underline the close and amicable relationship between the two communist powers in the run-up to the signing of the Sino–Soviet Treaty of Friendship, Alliance and Mutual Assistance in February 1950.

Khabarovsk Trial as Communist Weapon in the Burgeoning Cold War

One of the most reasonable explanations for why the Soviets opted for 'belated justice' with the Khabarovsk Trial is connected to their inability to influence the agenda of the IMTFE in order to gain any geopolitical or propaganda benefits out of the tribunal. The Soviets were well aware of the fact that the most prominent Japanese scientists involved in the biological warfare program, including its longtime leader Ishii Shiro, were in the hands of the Americans, so they desperately tried to get access to these persons by negotiating with the American occupational authorities in Japan during the Tokyo Tribunal. The Soviets made repeated requests to Washington for permission to interrogate Ishii and other senior scientists. The Americans stalled, telling them that their requests were being considered.[61] There was a modicum of truth in this: the Americans did discuss this possibility, first, on the grounds that the Soviets would not gain 'any positive technical intelligence in the biological warfare field'[62]; and second, because American monitoring of 'the general trend of Soviet questioning

---

[59] Sheldon H. Harris *Factories of death. Japanese biological warfare, 1932–45, and the American cover-up* (New York: Routledge, 1994), 225.
[60] Ibid. 226.
[61] Peter Williams and David Wallace, *Unit 731: Japan's secret biological warfare in World War II* (New York, NY: Free Press, 1989), 187.
[62] See, for example, National Archives and Records Administration (NARA) IWG Reference Collection, Selected Documents on Japanese War Crimes and Japanese Biological Warfare, 1934–2006, RG 9999, Entry ZZ-106, Box 4, State-War-Navy Coordinating Subcommittee

might serve as a key to Soviet knowledge and activity in the biological warfare field.'[63] Eventually they decided against it, but they kept making promises, knowing that as long as Moscow thought it might be granted access to Ishii and the others, it had a strong motive for keeping silent about the Americans' amnesty-for-information deal, and for acceding to the exclusion of Japanese medical crimes from the Tokyo Tribunal's proceedings.

Eventually it seems the Soviets 'finally gave up hope of persuading the West to allow them access to Ishii and the other Japanese scientists.'[54] There was no chance that they would receive the missing second part of experimental data on bacteriological warfare, so there was no need to keep silent about the agreement between the Americans and the Japanese regarding medical war criminals. Moreover, the Soviet propaganda machine could benefit from bringing justice to 'Chinese patriots' and 'Soviet citizens,'[65] thereby establishing close contacts with the PRC and at the same time embarrassing the Americans.

Furthermore, the trial in Khabarovsk was a great opportunity to distract the public from the issue that several hundred thousand Japanese POWs were still being held captive in the Soviet Union almost four years after the war's end, a subject that reached its boiling point in 1949.

The Khabarovsk Trial was conceived as a corrective to the Tokyo Tribunal. This was confirmed by another event that took place on 1 February 1950, and which represented the culmination of the Khabarovsk project. That day, the Soviet Ambassador in Washington, Alexander Panyushkin, handed a diplomatic note to the US Secretary of State, Dean Acheson. This proposed the establishment of an international criminal court to try the Japanese emperor and four senior generals involved with the biological warfare program—Ishii Shiro, Kitano Masaji, Wakamatsu Yujiro and Kasahara Yukio.[66] These five men were, of course, the same individuals that the Americans continued to protect from prosecution. The note attracted a flurry of press attention, especially in the Soviet Union, China and Japan. But Acheson, ascribing devious Cold War motives to the Soviet Union, declined to reply.

---

for the Far East, 'Request of Russian prosecutor for permission to interrogate certain Japanese' (26 February 1947), 1.
[63] Ibid.
[64] Peter Williams and David Wallace, *Unit 731*, 230.
[65] *Materials*, 15–6.
[66] Nota Sovetskogo Pravitel'stva pravitel'stvam SSHA, Velikobritanii i Kitaia, Pravda (3 February 1950).

A peculiar response to the note from the Soviet Union by the USA was the publication on 7 March 1950 of circular letter number 5, which stated that all Japanese war criminals, serving their sentences could be released.[67] It provoked a note from the USSR to the USA on 11 May 1950, in which such intentions were condemned as an attempt to change or even reverse the decision of the International Military Tribunal in Tokyo, a gross violation of basic norms and principles of international law.[68] As in the previous case, the note was ignored by the Americans.

With the Khabarovsk Trial, Soviet and more generally communist propaganda discovered a useful tool: charges brought against the defendants in Khabarovsk—the planning of bacteriological war against the Soviet Union and other peaceful nations—proved to be a powerful propaganda weapon and were successfully used later during the Korean War (1950–1953). Drawing on the Soviet experience with the Khabarovsk Trial, North Korea and the PRC launched a full-scale campaign of biological and chemical warfare accusations against the USA that was supported by many left-wing and pacifist organizations throughout the world. Inevitably, the names of Ishii Shiro, Ishii, Kitano, Wakamatsu and the other biological warfare experts were destined to be connected to the Korean charges.[69] Ultimately, the Khabarovsk trial served its purpose, namely, to provide ammunition in the burgeoning Cold War.

Conclusion

A critical examination of the archival materials indicates that it would be incorrect to reduce the participation of the Soviet delegation at the Tokyo Tribunal only to propaganda objectives and reject the findings of the Khabarovsk Trial as an example of Stalinist justice. The Khabarovsk Trial needs a more thorough evaluation since it constitutes valuable historical evidence regarding Japan's biological warfare program and crimes associated with it. Moreover, a detailed study of this trial provides us with a better understanding of the Soviet war crimes trials policy during the early Cold War with regard to the Far East and the role of political context and propaganda in pursuing cross-national justice.

---

[67] Mark Raginskii, *Militaristy*, 46–7.
[68] Nota Sovetskogo Pravitel'stva pravitel'stvu SSHA, *Pravda*, 13 May 1950.
[69] Sheldon H. Harris *Factories of death. Japanese biological warfare, 1932–45, and the American cover-up* (New York, NY: Routledge, 1994), 230–1.

In contrast to the early Soviet war crimes trials, the Khabarovsk Trial is strong evidence of the professionalization of the Soviet justice system. The prosecution team in Khabarovsk put emphasis on the individual guilt of the defendants. It was not enough anymore to hold the accused responsible as a group; the criminal activities of individuals received more attention than, for example, at the Kharkov Trial (1943).

In addition, there were some noticeable changes in the rights of the accused in the postwar period. In 1943 Soviet criminal justice played a retributive rather than a correctional role, which was manifested in the severity of punishments. Back in 1943 it was difficult to imagine that the defendants would receive lighter sentences as demanded by the prosecutor. The idea of retribution did not play the role it had during the war. Japanese atrocities took place mainly on Chinese soil; the majority of the victims were not Soviet citizens, which resulted in a much lower level of patriotic rhetoric. This all meant that the 'cost' of lenient sentences was much lower and the Soviets could allow themselves to praise Khabarovsk as an act of justice and at the same time collaborate with the accused war criminals. The official justification for the leniency of the sentences was the fact that the Soviets had abolished capital punishment in May 1947 by the Presidium Decree, 'On the abolition of the death penalty.'[70] (This explains why the Soviet judge Ivan Zarianov was among the judges who voted against the executions at the Tokyo tribunal.[71])

With the Khabarovsk Trial, Soviet and more generally communist propaganda discovered a useful tool: the specter of bacteriological warfare proved to be a powerful propaganda weapon that was successfully used later during the Korean War (1950–53). Nevertheless, in a 'hybrid' show trial like the one at Khabarovsk it is important to remember that despite the flaws in the legal proceedings, the majority of the evidence presented in the courtroom was sound.

In the long run, the Soviet war crimes trials in Asia during the early Cold War were thus a combination of geopolitics and propaganda that were aimed at supporting the diplomatic efforts of the new Soviet superpower.

---

[70] Decree of the Presidium of the Supreme Soviet of the USSR, 'Ob otmene smertnoi kazni,' 26 May 1947 (Moscow: Gosudarstvennoe Izdatel'stvo iuridicheskoi literatury, 1950), reprinted verbatim in *Ugolovnyi kodeks RSFSR* (Moscow: Ripol Klassik, 2013), 140–11.
[71] Kirsten Sellars *'Crimes against peace' and international law* (Cambridge: Cambridge University Press, 2013), 255.

They were meant to secure Soviet interests in the region while deterring the encroachment of the new archenemy—the USA.

Illustrations

1. General Yamada depicted as a 'fascist plague flea,' Izvestiya, 13 December 1949
2. 'The mysterious disappearance of General Ishii,' Izvestiya, 16 January 1950
3. 'Unfulfilled dreams of Samurai,' Ogoniok, 8 January 1950

CHAPTER 12

Resurrecting Defeat: International Propaganda and the Shenyang Trials of 1956

Adam Cathcart

In the People's Republic of China, the topic of Japanese war crimes trials never seems particularly far away. The International Military Tribunal for the Far East (Tokyo Trials) and the international meetings that preceded them are referenced with increasing regularity in Chinese academic discourse, even forming a cornerstone of popular culture and mass media.[1] The reconstruction of war crimes trials within Communist Party of China (CPC) mass communication was particularly evident on 3 July 2014, when Beijing rolled out a propaganda campaign whose centerpiece was the daily online publication of written testimonies or affidavits collected for the

---

[1] Bingbing Jia, 'The Legacy of the Tokyo Trial in China,' in: Yuki Tanaka, Tim McCormack, Gerry Simpson, eds., *Beyond Victor's Justice? The Tokyo War Crimes Trial Revisited* (Leiden: Martinus Nijhoff, 2011), 207–25.

A. Cathcart (✉)
Leeds University, Leeds, UK

tribunal of 45 war criminals in Shenyang and Taiyuan in 1956.[2] Affidavits had been collected from prisoners who, mostly, had spent four years of captivity in the Soviet Union, and then another four to six years of captivity in northeast China, primarily in Fushun, a hub industrial city of Shenyang best known for its massive coal deposits.[3] Released online daily for 45 days in summer 2014, the CPC's interpretation of the documents focused on the inhuman atrocities committed by the Japanese defendants during the War of Resistance (1937–1945). Rape, bacteriological weapons experimentation and random killings of defenseless civilians were regularly at the fore over the course of Beijing's information campaign, ostensibly meant to counteract Japanese war amnesia. Only secondary attention was paid in these releases to Manchukuo, the Japanese-sponsored puppet state in northeast Asia from 1931 to 1945, which had been another critical aspect of the trials. Instead, state television seemed more interested in reviving attention to the atrocities and the contrition expressed by the defendants at Shenyang. The information campaign was highlighted by the unveiling of a new exhibition of wax statues in Shenyang, depicting Japanese defendants bowing in grateful humiliation in the 1956 courtroom.[4] At a time when pressure was needed on Japan's Liberal Democratic Party and its leader, Japanese Prime Minister Abe Shinzo, it seemed clear that the Shenyang materials had proven to be the instrument of clear convenience. A press conference by Li Minghua, deputy director-general at China's Central Archives, made the matter rather clear.[5] While denunciations of key cultural figures in the "Hundred Flowers Campaign" later in 1956 or

---

[2] Bi Mingxin, 'Xinhua Insight: Japanese war criminal confessions renew Chinese anger,' *Xinhua Online*, 15 July 2014. http://news.xinhuanet.com/english/indepth/2014-07/15/c_133485556.htm (accessed 1 June 2015).

[3] Limin Teh, 'From Colonial Company Town to Industrial City: The South Manchuria Railway Company in Fushun, China,' in *Company Towns: Labor, Space, and Power Relations across Time and Continents*, Marcello Borges, ed. (New York: Palgrave Macmillan, 2012), 69–90.

[4] Liu Ce, 'War criminal trials recreated for exhibition,' *China Daily Europe*, 29 August 2014, 5; see also Anonymous, 'Zhongguo (Shengyang) shenpan Riben zhanfan fating jiuzhi chenlieguan shenpan xianchang quanbu fuyuan' ['Exhibition in China (Shenyang) recreates trial of Japanese war criminals in full'] '中国(沈阳)审判日本战犯法庭旧址陈列馆审判现场全部复原,' *Sohu*, 25 September 2014. http://roll.sohu.com/20140925/n404640820.shtml (accessed 1 June 2015).

[5] Michael Martina, 'China cites Japan wartime 'confessions' in propaganda push,' Reuters, 3 July 2014. http://www.reuters.com/article/2014/07/03/us-china-japan-idUSKBN0F-80M320140703 (accessed 1 June 2015).

of the much more ambitious 'Anti-Rightist Campaign' of 1957 are still very much wrapped in an archival shroud, the Shenyang Trials—or a very specific version of them—have now more or less emerged fully into the light of day with much state support. The documents from the Central Archives, however, were not entirely new: they were published in printed version in 2009, as part of stream of official documentation which has been opened to researchers or published since the 60th anniversary of the end of the War of Resistance in 2005.[6] And this documentary flood should interest historians, in part, because of the very contingent, and in some ways unlikely, fashion in which the Shenyang Trials came about.

During the International Military Tribunal for the Far East in Tokyo (1946–1948, hereafter Tokyo Trials), the CPC was rather busy with more immediate matters. In the summer of 1946, whilst Joseph B. Keenan and the International Prosecution Section was laying out its case in Tokyo, the CPC was locked in existential battle with Guomindang armies, the party's power base effectively exiled from any center of substantial Chinese population other than Harbin.[7] The Chinese public in cities like Shanghai were taking a keen interest in the trials, but even the communist cadre tasked with handling the party's foreign and urban underground affairs were besieged with more survivalist concerns, and paid the Tokyo Trials relatively little heed.[8] From the moment of the resumption of the Chinese civil war in August 1945, the CPC showed far more prevalent concern for Japan's possible 'militarist revival' and Guomindang's alleged impotence

---

[6] In 2009, the full handwritten confessions of the 45 Japanese defendants were published in ten huge volumes (including Chinese and Japanese versions) by the Central Archives Bureau. See *Riben qinHua zhanfan bigong* zhongyang dang'anguan chu li, zhongguo dang'anguan chubanshe, 2005 (hereafter Central Archives, *Written Confessions*).

[7] For a pessimistic prognosis for the CPC in Harbin, see G. A. Wallinger, Memorandum re: Burdett's Conversation in Mukden with Chang Kia-gnau, 1 January 1947, British National Archives, FO 371/63332.

[8] On 15 December 1945, the CPC's main organ, the *Jiefang Ribao* (Liberation Daily) called for swifter prosecutions to be brought by the Americans in Japan; see Barak Kushner, 'Chinese War Crimes Trials of Japanese, 1945–1956: A Historical Summary,' in *Historical Origins of International Criminal Law: Volume 2*, Morten Bergsmo, Cheah Wui Ling, and Yi Ping, eds. (Brussels: Torkel Opsahl Academic EPublisher, 2014), 253. The Shanghai press was more focused on Japanese elections and purges than the Trials themselves, although coverage of the beginning of the proceedings was substantial; see Adam Cathcart, 'Urban Chinese Perspectives on the U.S. Occupation of Japan, 1945–1947,' *Studies on Asia* Series II, Vol. 3, 2 (2006), 21–48.

in preventing such a revival.[9] Perhaps for obvious reasons, the CPC chose not to echo its War of Resistance-era (1937–1945) united front. There was no practical way or venue to bolster China's prosecution at Tokyo, such as providing evidence, as this might have been seen as overt support which might aid Chiang Kai-shek and the Republic of China in reinforcing their relatively high stature within Keenan's transformational matrix of the forces of 'civilization' responsible for exacting justice from Japanese defendants at Tokyo.[10] Indeed, as the Tokyo Trials drew to their conclusion in the shortening days of late 1948, the CPC was endeavoring to accomplish the utter destruction (or *fanshen/*'turning over') of the very Chinese Republic whose judge, Mei Ru'ao, was sitting on the bench of international judges in Tokyo.[11]

The difficult and churning reality of the Chinese civil war was referred to but seldom at the Tokyo proceedings themselves, apart from a handful of semi-desperate yet wholly unapologetic lines from the defense about wartime Japan's desire to prevent Asia from going communist.[12] Tojo Hideki's written affidavit at Tokyo contained the ominous prediction that 'certainly the China Incident II and the China Incident III' would follow from a communist victory in China in the aftermath of Japanese withdrawal.[13] Yet, even in his apocalyptic vision of an East Asia freed from Japanese influence, Tojo could not refer to Mao directly, nor did the former war minister seem to comprehend that various segments of Chinese public opinion might be cheer his death rather than laud his anti-communist zeal.[14] As for Mao Zedong,

---

[9] For CPC involvement in cities of the anti-Japanese movements of 1948, in which dissatisfaction with war crimes prosecutions played only a seemingly small part, see Hong Zhang, *America Perceived: The Making of Chinese Images of the United States, 1945–1953* (Westport, Connecticut: Praeger, 2002).

[10] John Dower, 'Victor's Justice, Loser's Justice,' in *Embracing Defeat: Japan in the Wake of World War II* (New York: Norton: 1999), 443–84.

[11] On Mei and his split Chinese cohort, see Kushner, 'Chinese War Crimes Trials of Japanese, 1945–1956,' 247–8.

[12] International Military Tribunal for the Far East (IMFFE), *The Tokyo Major War Crimes Trial: The Transcripts of the court proceedings of the International Military Tribunal for the Far East*, R. John Pritchard, ed., (Lewiston, NY: Edwin Mellen Press, 1998), 20,869 and 36,482 (hereafter IMTFE Transcript).

[13] IMTFE Transcripts 36,302.

[14] Apart from unfortunate references to Chinese women as lecherous and deceitful in the lower Yangzi valley, Tojo and his fellow defendants at Tokyo largely seem to have seen Chinese people as falling into three types: enlightened collaborators, elements of easily-

amid his voluminous and often volcanic writings from the period of the Chinese civil war, there are no essays dedicated to the Tokyo Trials. An attack on the Guomindang trial of General Okamura Yasuji, itself laden with references to alleged war crimes carried out under Nationalist auspices, is as close as we come to Maoist concern with the subject.[15] Mao clearly understood that Okamura was a useful counterfoil.[16] The CPC would share little of the muted triumph at Tojo's 23 December 1948 hanging at Sugamo, since in the CPC's strategic vision and public propaganda, the war with Japanese militarism had never really been justly concluded anyway.[17]

The Nationalist trials of Japanese war criminals in postwar Nanjing were, similarly, anathema to the CPC's aims of the Chinese civil war. There could be no acknowledgement of Chiang Kai-shek's ability to extract real vengeance on Japanese perpetrators; if anything, the government which had moved from Chongqing back to Nanjing on 5 May 1946 was pictured as loaded with collaborators (*hanjian*).[18] Mao and his comrades were attempting to mobilize the same kind of popular anger at collaborators as the Nationalists had done during the war, but the trials in Nanjing did not aid Chiang Kai-shek in monopolizing anti-Japanese discourse or the veneer of justice. Yun Xia concluded that the government's anti-*hanjian* campaigns 'exposed the corruption and incompetence of the Nationalist government,' while Shao Dan has similarly concluded that postwar trials

---

whipped-up anti-Japanese mobs and bandits or guerillas who needed to be destroyed. For a eulogy on pro-Japanese collaborators as Manchukuo was coming to an end, see Matsui Tanatsu's testimony at Tokyo. IMTFE Transcript, 20,174.

[15] Mao Zedong, 'On Arresting Okamura and Guomindang Civil War Criminals,' January 1949, in *Selected Works* (Beijing: Foreign Languages Press, 1978), Vol. 4, 327.

[16] Citing Weng Youwei and Zhao Wenyuan (*Jiang Jieshi yu Riben de enen yuanyuan* (Beijing: Publisher, 2008), 296) Kushner notes: 'In March 1950, only several months before the outbreak of the Korean War, US General Douglas MacArthur supposedly warned Okamura that if he were going to go to Taiwan to train men to fight the CCP, such acts were against the law and if discovered the US would prosecute. This declaration proved to be mere rhetoric and occupation authorities never moved forward with any prosecution or investigation.' Barak Kushner, 'Ghosts of the Japanese Imperial Army: The 'White Group' (*Baituan*) and Early Post-war Sino-Japanese Relations.' *Past and Present* (2013), Supplement 8, 123.

[17] On execution methods at Sugamo, see John L. Ginn, *Sugamo Prison* (City: McFarland, 1992).

[18] Adam Cathcart, 'Chinese Nationalism in the Shadow of Japan, 1945–1950,' PhD dissertation, Ohio University, 2005.

of other collaborators in Nanjing only stoked the flames of conspiracy.[19] Communist Party of China critiques of such procedures were more aimed at the Nationalist state at the macro level, connected to underground urban movements of students and intellectuals, not some prelude to a presumably acceptable form of war criminal prosecution led by the CPC.

There was therefore little 'victor's justice' to be accrued specifically to the CPC from the Tokyo Trials. Although war crimes trials were still going on in Japan and around Asia in 1949, these did not appear to spark major controversy among or comment by the CPC.[20] After the formal establishment of the People's Republic of China (PRC) in 1949, the party was flush with captured men from the wrong side of the Chinese civil war, but was not really in possession of a suitable number or type of Japanese defendants for its own proceedings. In one particularly strange case, a Japanese doctor who had worked for Unit 731 was actually working for the CPC in a military hospital in Harbin.[21] For the most part, the party was busy in consolidating its control over the mainland in a wave of local trials or summary tribunals of local collaborators. These prosecutions were enabled by the expansion of alarmingly flexible categories of crimes both conventional and 'counter-revolutionary.'[22] In 1949, the CPC could not move immediately into the space once reserved for the Republic of China in claiming the legitimacy and justice of the Tokyo Trials, or the trials of Tani Hisao and pro-Japanese collaborators in Nanjing in 1946–47. The opportunity for judicial proceedings in which Chinese victims faced Japanese perpetrators had not been lost completely, but it was not a priority for

---

[19] Yun Xia, '"Traitors to the Chinese Race (*Hanjian*)": Political and Cultural Campaigns against Collaborators during the Sino-Japanese War of 1937–1945,' PhD dissertation, University of Oregon, 2010, v; Shao Dan, *Remote Homeland, Recovered Borderland: Manchus, Manchoukuo, and Manchuria, 1907–1985* (Honolulu: University of Hawai'i Press, 2011).

[20] Sandra Wilson, 'War Criminals in the Post-war World: The Case of Katō Tetsutarō,' *War In History*, vol. 22, 1 (January 2015), 87–110; Sandra Wilson, 'After the Trials: Class B and Class C Japanese War Criminals and the Post-War World,' *Japanese Studies*, Vol. 31, 2 (2011), 141–9.

[21] Central Archives, Written Confessions, Vol. 2, Affidavit of Sakakibara Hideo, 234, 299, 323.

[22] Luo Chenxi, 'Construction of Counterrevolutionary Criminals in Suppressing Counterrevolution in Poyang County: An Institutional Path,' paper presented at 'Cold Front: The Chinese Cold War Experience in Comparison,' Chinese University of Hong Kong, 15 September 2014.

the government.²³ All that could be done in the early months of the PRC was to point out, over and over, the flaws in the US occupation of Japan, particularly its failure to prosecute Emperor Hirohito, and its release of men like Kishi Nobusuke who had been released from Sugamo Prison.²⁴

This dynamic changed significantly in late December 1949 when the Soviet Union tried 12 men for crimes that had been overlooked at the Tokyo Trials, focusing on Japan's bacteriological weapons research program led by Ishii Shiro. The Khabarovsk Trials sparked an externally stimulated wave of propaganda about Japanese war crimes which crested in early 1950 and coincided neatly with Mao's time in Moscow.²⁵ Khabarovsk also alerted the Chinese public to the notion that it was possible under the socialist system to try Japanese war criminals for crimes against humanity, and that the concerns exhibited about Japanese militarism at Tokyo could have a judicial life beyond the execution of Tojo and his cohort.²⁶ Within months, the Soviet Union was the source of another gift: In July 1950, it bequeathed about 1000 Japanese prisoners from the Soviet Union, and the former 'Emperor' of Manchukuo, Pu Yi to the CPC. Pu Yi had proven himself to be an exceptionally difficult witness at Tokyo.²⁷ Yet merely possessing him, along with many officials of the puppet state, gave the Communist Party of China an important card that could be played at the appropriate time.

The historiography of the trials that followed was sparked by the release of documents in Beijing in 2005 and 2006. Some of the earliest work from this period drew from the newly opened Ministry of Foreign Affairs (MFA)

---

²³ Barak Kushner, *Devils to Men: Japanese War Crimes and Chinese Justice* (Harvard: Publisher, 2015).
²⁴ Jia Bingbing, in Yuki Tanaka, ed., *Beyond Victor's Justice?*, 208.
²⁵ Valentyna Polunina, 'Soviet War Crimes Policy in the Far East: The Bacteriological Warfare Trial at Khabarovsk, 1949,' in *Historical Origins of International Criminal Law: Volume 2*, Morten Bergsmo, Cheah Wui Ling, and Yi Ping, eds. (Brussels: Torkel Opsahl Academic EPublisher, 2014), 539–62; Adam Cathcart, '"Against Invisible Enemies": Japanese Bacteriological Weapons in China's Cold War, 1949–1952,' *Chinese Historical Review* Vol. 16,1 (Spring 2009), 101–29.
²⁶ *Materials on the Trial of Former Servicemen of the Japanese Army Charged with Manufacturing and Employing of Bacteriological Weapons* (Moscow: Foreign Language Press, 1950), 9.
²⁷ The following exchange with Pu Yi seems to typify the obdurate and unproductive nature of his appearance at Tokyo: 'Q. On what date was Manchukuo established as a country? A. Please don't ask me any more about the question of dates.' He would have no such problems at the Shenyang Trials. IMFTE Transcript, 4,085.

Archive to look at the role of local memories of anti-Japanese sentiment as a backdrop, and then the back story of diplomatic work of Japanese normalization drove events.[28] Jing Chen, a political scientist teaching in the USA, used the PRC MFA documents to show how the Chinese investigation for the trials was in many respects complete in February 1955, but political events necessitated another 15 months of waiting and preparation. Justin Jacobs emphasized how Zhou Enlai's careful timing of the trial was calibrated with respect to Chinese cultural delegations, while Jing's discussion of the Taiwan connection helps to shed light on why the crimes tried at the Shenyang Trials overflowed the conventional periodization of the War of Resistance.[29] As Nash and the present author have pointed out previously, several of the defendants at Shenyang and the parallel procedure at Taiyuan were tried for crimes committed after the nominal surrender of September 1945; including Guomindang-linked warlord and Shanxi strongman Yan Xishan. Jing Chen points out that the incorporation of these crimes and the lenient treatment afforded to the defendants was a clear signal to the Guomindang on Taiwan, writing that 'this administrative measure was aimed at cultivating support in Taiwan for the cause of China's and Taiwan's eventual reunification.'[30] All of these articles tend to agree that the Shenyang Trials were very much colored by China's international political needs at the time. The Ministry of Foreign Affairs Archive materials showed PRC benevolence to the men who had been in custody since 1950, as might be expected for a selective launch at a tenuous time. The documents also revealed the very pragmatic use to which the war criminals were put in the 1950s and how they were essentially pawns in a larger game of international politics. The major expansion of documentary evidence available after 2005 has added much to the understanding of the diplomatic traffic around the trials, and the way in which the party sought to use them as international propaganda. The CPC was very clearly using the trials as a means of bending Japanese public opinion toward a more favorable viewpoint of China, putting the war in the rear view while moving forward toward normalization. Seen in

---

[28] Adam Cathcart and Patricia Nash, 'War Criminals and the Road to Sino–Japanese Normalization: Zhou Enlai and the Shenyang Trials, 1954–1956,' *Twentieth-Century China*, 34, 2 (April), 89–111.
[29] Justin Jacobs, 'Preparing the People for Mass Clemency: The 1956 Japanese War Crimes Trials in Shenyang and Taiyuan,' *China Quarterly* Vol. 205 (March 2011), 152–172.
[30] Jing Chen, 'The Trial of Japanese War Criminals in China: The Paradox of Leniency,' *China Information* Vol. 23, 3 (2009), 451.

a more continuous light of Sino–Japanese propaganda themes, their being raised again in 2014 should be no surprise whatsoever.

But when it comes to international propaganda and the trials, the perception of China as the invariable initiator (or manipulator) does need to come into question. Criticism of the USA for premature release of suspected and convicted war criminals like Shigemitsu Mamoru had been a signal theme of the early 1950s, not least because the Soviet Union had demanded attention to it.[31] The idea that China was not negotiating in depth for their return, and that it was something of a surprise for the foreign affairs bureaucracy, can be seen in an MFA document, which describes the process of transfer from the Soviet Union, and the poor preparation on the PRC side in terms of arranging an appropriate facility for this large number of men.[32] Zhou Enlai had been forced to play for time, and the reception of the war criminals was not made into a public event until late 1954, nearly four years after it had happened. Zhou Enlai and his ministry (indeed, various ministries) had been dealing with questions of Japanese repatriates and prisoners of war rather often in 1950 and beyond.[33] Yet it appears clear that on the issue of repatriating these Japanese war criminals, the CPC was often reactive rather than proactive.

The reactive nature of the CPC toward the issue might also have much to do with questions of state building and capacity in the judicial sector in the years just after the establishment of the People's Republic. Liaoning province, the host for the Shenyang Trials, bordered the very hot Korean War until mid-1953. Communities in eastern Manchuria had

---

[31] MFA Archives, 105-00022-04, *'Yijiuwuyi nian er yue Sulian zhengfu jiu Maikeahse feifa shifang Zhong Guangkui deng Riben zhanfan zhi Meiguo zhengfu zhi zhaohui chaojian,'* (February 1951 Handwritten Note from Soviet Government to US Government Regarding MacArthur's Illegal Release of Zhong Guangkui and other Japanese War Criminals), 15 February 1951; MFA Archives, 105-00022-01, *'Sulian zhengfu jiu zhuRi mengjun tongshuai Maikeahse nishi fang Zhong Guangkui deng zhanfan gei Meiguo zhengfu zhi zhaohui yiwen yi wo waijiaobu dui cizhi yijian,'* (Translated Note from Soviet Government to American Government regarding Supreme Commander for Allied Powers in Japan Douglas MacArthur's Intended Plan to Give Free Rein to Zhong Guangkui and Other Japanese War Criminals and Our Foreign Ministry's Views on this Matter), 12 May to 13 May 1950, 7.

[32] MFA, 118-00151-01, 'Guanyu Sulian yijiao Riben zhanfan de laiwang wendian (Telegram regarding Soviet transfer of Japanese war crimi nals),' 27 June 1951 to 30 November 1951, 1, 5.

[33] MFA Archives, 118-00352-01, *'Guanyu Beijing, Taiyuan deng Riben qiaomin ji Riben zhanfu huguo wenti de chulishi,'* (Regarding the matter of Japanese POWS in Beijing, Taiyuan, etc., Returning to Japan) 1950.

only recently been engaged in mass 'people's courts' or 'accusation meetings' (*kongsuhui*) in order to mete out violence to landlords, Nationalist holdouts, and the politically recalcitrant. The movement to Suppress Counter-revolutionaries, in combination with the Three-Anti, Five-Anti movements placed heavy emphasis on public security organs and policing, without a great deal of concomitant clarity in the courts.[34]

Ultimately, war crimes trials of the Japanese defendants became possible in the PRC, and they were of course useful from an international propaganda standpoint. As Anne Marie Brady has noted, the CPC was keen to manage external perceptions of itself, particularly through people-to-people contacts and visitors (of whatever stripe) who came to the PRC to return home to diffuse the good news of the communist revolution.[35] Starting in 1954, the Japanese inmates became very much part of the CPC's external relations strategy, serving as model convicts with a vastly widened scope of contact with the outside world. In August 1954, China unilaterally repatriated over 400 prisoners to Japan and set the table for negotiations over 1,069 men incarcerated at Fushun.[36] China's Health Minister and representative to the Red Cross Li Dequan announced the names of the inmates in Tokyo in November 1954, and the next spring mail service was introduced. This development resulted in a stream of very carefully crafted letters coming from the Japanese in Fushun to their compatriots back in Japanese cities.[37] These letters were closely read and commented on by Chinese staff not just at the prison but in the Ministry of Foreign Affairs, who sought to use the inmates to burnish China's image in Japan and beyond. Here it might be useful to recall that participants in

---

[34] Luo Chenxi, 'Construction of Counterrevolutionary Criminals in Suppressing Counterrevolution in Poyang County: An Institutional Path,' paper presented at 'Cold Front: The Chinese Cold War Experience in Comparison,' Chinese University of Hong Kong, 15 September, 2014; Julia Strauss, 'Paternalist Terror: The Campaign to Suppress Counterrevolutionaries and Regime Consolidation in the PRC, 1950–1953,' *Comparative Studies in Society and History*, Vol. 44, No. 1 (January 2002), 80–105; Yang Kuisong, 'Reconsidering the Campaign to Suppress Counterrevolutionaries,' *The China Quarterly*, No. 193 (March 2008), 102–121.
[35] Anne-Marie Brady, *Making the Foreign Serve China: Managing Foreigners in the People's Republic* (Oxford: Rowman and Littlefield, 2003).
[36] MFA Archives, 105-00064-01, '*Wo Waijiaobu fayanren jiu Riben zhengfu suowei 'guifan Riben guomin de yaoqiu' fabiao shengming*,' (Our Foreign Ministry spokesperson in response to the Japanese government's published declaration for the so-called 'request to return Japanese citizens') 16 August 1955.
[37] Fushun Center Materials, 80.

non-communist trial proceedings were also highly sensitive to press coverage, occasionally even revealing as much during the trial.[38]

In Yanan, the CPC had used the Japanese turncoats or converts to communism as local propaganda, and their desire to turn the returnees to their advantage was explicitly stated in 1950 with respect to Japanese more sympathetic to the CPC cause. A note within the Chinese Foreign Ministry indicated:

> With regard to Japanese with revolutionary zeal, they should be sent back to their country before or after March of this year to become soldiers of struggle in the Japanese revolution. [...] They can also stimulate Japan's revolutionary movement, improve [...] China's position in the Far East and stimulate the two nation's revolutions. [...] This means that prior to [their] going back, we must continue the satisfying education work so that like those who came back from the Soviet Union, the Japanese who return from China can in their language and actions increase greatly the power of democracy.[39]

Roger Swearingen takes this propagandizing notion back even further, writing: 'Ever since the Siberian expedition [...] Russia had realized the importance of mobilizing anti-militarist elements in Japan to hamper, and, if possible, to contain Japanese expansion on the continent.'[40] The CPC was merely, then, picking up on an earlier strand pioneered by the Soviets.

Zhou Enlai's major speech on the matter considered questions of precedent as well as Soviet aid, saying that one 'possible solution' was to handle the matter 'according to international law organizations and international military courts.' In other words, China had the ability to mount a counterpart prosecution, along the lines of Nuremburg and Tokyo, both of which Zhou referenced, saying that that the latter had tried 'far fewer' defendants than the former. Surprisingly, Zhou cited the Guomindang trial of the Japanese general Yasuji Okamura as being of international import

---

[38] On 31 December 1947, Chief Prosecutor Kennan asked Tojo a question in the form of a statement: 'I want to ask you if this affidavit [...] that you have given through your counsel at the lectern for the preceding three or four day has been intended for the purpose of convincing this Court of your innocence or has been intended to be a continuation of imperialist, militaristic propaganda to the people of Japan.' IMTFE Transcript, 36,535.

[39] MFA Archive, 118-00086-09, 'Riben zhan fu he Riqiao zai Huabei (Japanese prisoners and immigrants in North China),' 1 March 1950.

[40] Roger Swearingen and Paul Fritz Langer, *Red Flag in Japan: International Communism in Action 1919–1951* (Cambridge, MA: Harvard University Press, 1952), 59.

(even though Mao had criticized it severely in 1949), and ultimately concluded that China 'could not go the route of international courts' with the nine hundred-plus defendants transferred by the Soviets.

> Apart from these we have some defendants captured in the War of Liberation (i.e. the Chinese civil war), those men Chiang Kai-shek wanted to use to carry out civil war. Regarding these war criminals, we will use national military courts to try them. At the present time, ten years has already passed, and we have yet to handle the problem. This is because in the past the war criminals had to be moved to the Northeast, and so many of these criminals' files were spread all over China, and investigating them was a very difficult matter. Outside of this problem, China and Japan are still technically in a state of war, having not signed a peace treaty nor reestablished helpful relations. Again, already ten years have passed, we must complete this matter, and now is the time we have decided to handle it. We cannot rely on international courts to handle it, and our preparation of national courts to handle the matter is adequate.[41]

If the propaganda campaign was not entirely new, nor was the notion of conspiracy which was raised with regularity in the Shenyang affidavits. The concept of a voracious, all-encompassing and inevitable imperialism stemming from Japan in the 1930s was mentioned with regularity. In this sense, the Shenyang proceedings held a certain kinship with the conspiracy counts of the prosecution's case at Tokyo, although without the same vocabulary. Referring to imperialism as an indistinct yet unavoidable force allowed the defendants to, in a sense, retreat behind the idea that they were victims of forces beyond their control. It was a strategy which would have been reasonable at the time, certainly conforming to the PRC world view. It would also have been not necessarily so different from the defendants at Tokyo, who at times depicted themselves in the same way. Hideki Tojo tried to avoid being tagged with responsibility for labeling 'the China Incident' when he admitted that it was in fact a war.[42] The discussion of Japanese plots to dominate Manchuria had been a common theme at the Tokyo Trials. But at Shenyang, they were also reinforced by tropes in the

---
[41] Zhou Enlai, '要认真处理好国内外战犯问题,' [Yao renzhen chuli hao guoneiwei zhanfan wenti 'To Genuinely and Correctly Handle the Problem of Chinese and Foreign War Criminals,'] 30 March 1956, *Zhou Enlai Junshi Wenxuan*, Vol. 4 (Beijing: Renmin Chubanshe, 1997), 371–378.
[42] IMTFE Transcript, 36,566 and 36,567.

PRC (presumably borrowed from the Soviet Union) about counterrevolutionary plots, or *fan ge ming yin mou*. When it came to conspiratorial emphasis at Shenyang, the intent was different with regards to defendants who had worked with the Nationalists after 1945 in Shanxi province.

Practical considerations were also pressing in Shenyang: as Sandra Wilson notes in her consideration of Kato, who had been tried in 1949 and released on parole in 1958: 'Cold War considerations had trumped the desire to punish war criminals. US trials of Japanese suspects were winding down, and American prosecutions of suspects in Germany, too, were all but over' in 1949.[43] Certain practical aspects beyond diplomatic needs were also pushing the CPC toward a resolution of the men held at Fushun. Like other countries detaining Japanese for long periods of time, the cost and manpower needed to be accounted for. The Korean War had also caused a need to move the men in late 1950 from Liaoning province, close to the front in North Korea, to Heilongjiang province until the following year. Likewise, at Sugamo Prison in Tokyo the Korean War had resulted in a rapid reduction in the number of staff, requiring a redistribution of tasks and even the explicit consent of the men under guard that they would be more responsible for their own care.[44] Even in prison, the men had hardly been inured to external political and military shocks, and did keep up with the news, although of course filtered through camp guards.[45] In fact, the USA was facing similar pressure from the Japanese with reference to detainees still at Sugamo Prison in Tokyo.[46]

To what extent had the Fushun convicts been inculcated and coached in the Soviet Union already? Judging by the available sources, it had been relatively extensive. Japanese prisoners of war in Siberia and the Soviet Far East had, prior to 1949, already been subject to smaller war crimes trials

---

[43] Wilson, *War and History*, 100–1.
[44] John L. Ginn, *Sugamo Prison, Tokyo. An Account of the Trial and Sentencing of Japanese War Criminals in 1948, by a U.S. Participant* (London: McFarland, 1992), 10–1.
[45] Asked in court if he had been keeping up with Japanese newspapers while imprisoned, Tojo responded 'Yes, of course'; the Fushun convicts were likewise expected to be well read in terms of Xinhua propaganda materials. IMTFE Transcript, 36,599.
[46] Of the 577 men still being held in Allied custody in Sugamo Prison in 1955, 'the largest group is composed of the 210 men sentenced by the United States, of whom 123 are serving life terms. Australia follows with 149 and the Netherlands with 131.' Consulate of Japan in Seattle, 'Japan Report: For Publication and Background Use' 1, 2, 23 August 1955, 4–5 (accessible at University of Washington Library, Seattle).

(smaller than Khabarovsk).[47] The Soviet prosecutor at Tokyo appeared to refer to these directly in 1947 in a session.

What role did the Emperor Hirohito (or rather, his evocation) play at the Shenyang Trials? Because the proceedings were far less wide-ranging and sloppy than the Tokyo Trials, there was far less interest in this question. In the Shenyang Trials, there were few parallels to Tokyo's cross-examination of Tojo which dipped into Hirohito's role, whether it was the type of language used by the monarch or the extent to which he had been involved in crafting an aggressive policy toward China. This was likely because, as Justin Jacobs has noted, the CPC undid its 'uncompromising invectives against Emperor Hirohito, who only a few years earlier had been besmirched in China as a war criminal.' Jacobs continues: 'Now Hirohito's younger brother Prince Takahito was a distinguished guest at [Mei Lanfang's] performances, and rumors that the Emperor himself had watched a performance on television were interpreted as an honor.'[48] The CPC was willing to tone down its anti-emperor rhetoric for the sake of diplomacy, but not entirely.

Rather than try Hirohito in absentia, as had been done more or less at Khabarovsk in December 1949, Pu Yi, being the closest approximation of the Japanese model, testified at the event in Shenyang. The fabled 'last emperor' of the Qing dynasty had been a poor witness at Tokyo from the standpoint of revealing new data. His appearance at Shenyang, while exciting from a visual standpoint, did not reveal much new by way of understanding or unearthing how the state of Manchukuo had functioned or the crimes that had been committed, presumably, in his name. Instead, the emphasis again was unrelenting on how the CPC had been benevolent in the face of his ostensible crimes.[49]

More interesting than Pu Yi's appearance from a factual standpoint is the affidavit by Fujita Shigeru, which goes rather beyond what is

---

[47] Central Intelligence Agency Records Search Tool, National Archives and Records Administration, College Park, MD, CIA-RDP65- 00756R000400030003-2, Kermit G. Stewart, Office of the Chief of Military History, US Army, 'Russian Methods of Indoctrinating Captured Personnel: World War II,' April 1952.

[48] In support of this contention, Jacobs cites Mei Lanfang, 'Dong you ji' ('Journey to the east'), *Xin guancha*, 17 (1 September 1956), 24. See Jacobs, 166.

[49] David Chipp (Reuters special correspondent to Fushun), 'Pu Yi Tells Story of Disappearance: Ex-Puppet Emperor Says He Sinned, but Now Lives as a Human in China Prison,' *New York Times*, 10 August 1956, 4.

emphasized in the Fushun Center materials.[50] Fujita was a striking individual who had cultivated a very large Meiji-style mustache in captivity in the Soviet Union, but he was clean shaven in the photo presumably taken after 1954.[51] In recent press releases about Fujita from the Chinese government, the materials highlight his atrocities from 1938 to 45 in China, and do not mention much beyond these dates. His affidavit, in clearly stating the crimes of which he is guilty, begins with the standard invocation of 'invading Northeast China.' But the second point of guilt moves us immediately into difficult terrain from the standpoint of periodization of the trials themselves. The second point of Fujita's guilt—as he was encouraged to see it—was the crime of collecting intelligence in Jilin in 1913, in order to further the 'invasion plot' of imperialism.[52] Unlike his fellow 'China hand' Matsui Iwane, who was wounded in the conflict, Fujita had been too young to participate in the Russo–Japanese War of 1904–05. His 1913 voyage was his first documented trip to China, where he took an interest in agriculture; work in Tianjin in 1923 followed. The meticulousness with which the investigators worked was both impressive and problematic. If the Japanese were guilty of crimes dating back to the dawn of the twentieth century, is there any evidence that could not be introduced at the trial? By contrast, this makes Tokyo's choice of 1928 as a starting point for the criminal conspiracy leading to crimes against peace look positively disciplined and moderate.

The final crime listed in Fujita's affidavit is extremely curious and suggestive. These are no longer crimes against the Chinese people (as in Shandong in early 1945), but instead crimes against 'the Korean patriotic movement.' Fujita, as it turns out, was apprehended by the Soviet Red Army not in Manchuria, but in Wonsan, northern Korea, on 25 August 1945. Commanded to do so by General Yamada Otozo, he appears to have been attached briefly to Unit 731 as it moved into Korea during flight from the Soviet northern invasion. One section of his affidavit has some additions made to the biological warfare section.[53] When in Korea, the confusion of Japanese settlers who needed protection along with the need to destroy Korean infrastructure (apparently including medicine

---

[50] See also Fushun War Criminals Management Center, eds., *Place of New Life of Japanese War Criminals* (Beijing: China Intercontinental Press, 2005), 41–3.
[51] Central Archives, *Written Confessions*, Vol. 1, 75.
[52] Central Archives, *Written Confessions*, Vol. 1, 179.
[53] Central Archives, *Written Confessions*, Vol. 1, 265 is where Yamada is mentioned as the source of his orders, see also Central Archives, *Written Confessions*, Vol. 1, 165, 257.

factories) kept Fujita rather busy.⁵⁴ Likewise, Suzuki was captured in flight, but his 1954 affidavit also indicated that he was moving with a 'so-called comfort unit' and five Japanese women.⁵⁵ To my knowledge, there was no raising of this last issue at the trial itself.

The Shenyang Trials also took pains to place the CPC at the forefront of resistance, or victimization as the case may be. The Fushun Center materials juxtapose Japanese war crimes with specific martyrs. The point appears to be that sometimes victims had the chance to face perpetrators, but in many cases the victims had already been dead for 15 or more years. Several small handwritten additions to Fujita's affidavit were made, inserting phrases like 'the anti-Japanese people' next to the 'anti-Japanese army.' Such edits served to elide more contemporary concerns about citizen militias into the text, none too subtly projecting backwards a united front between the countryside and the CPC armies.⁵⁶ The entirety of the Taiyuan proceedings, which ran in parallel to Shenyang, emphasized this with far greater explicitness; here the specter of Yan Xishan and nominally Guomindang collaboration with Japanese troops in the postwar was a centerpiece.⁵⁷

Occasionally materials or recollections from the period of detention in the Soviet Union will come through. Fujita, a native of Hiroshima, recalls how he was provided with 'abundant reading materials' in the Soviet Union detention camp which instructed him on how destructive the war had been for his home city of Hiroshima. Although the convict is careful to wedge this into a lesson about the evils of Japanese imperialism, the ability to recollect the Soviet experience is interesting, as is the role and reflection of the bomb itself in the camp experience.⁵⁸ The CPC propagandists played unsubtly upon Fujita's origins when they arranged the rehearsal and performance of a play, 'The Son of the Atom Bomb Explosion' for the convicts. In front of a set depicting the post-explosion wasted milieu of Hiroshima, Fujita watched the performance and was said to weep heavily, saying 'These compatriots, as well as my elder sisters and nephews were personally killed by me and by Mikado—the Emperor of

---

⁵⁴ Central Archives, *Written Confessions*, Vol. 1, 266–269.
⁵⁵ Central Archives, *Written Confessions*, Vol. 1, 32.
⁵⁶ Central Archives, *Written Confessions*, Vol. 1, 209.
⁵⁷ Konrad Lawson, 'Wartime Atrocities and the Politics of Treason in the Ruins of the Japanese Empire, 1937–1953,' PhD dissertation, Harvard University, 2013.
⁵⁸ Central Archives, *Written Confessions*, Vol. 1, 167 on Hiroshima, Vol. 1, 77 on origins.

Japan!'⁵⁹ This theme was also clearly aimed at Japanese public opinion, seeking various outlets to interpret the atomic trauma of the war and its long aftermath.

Sasa Shinosuke was an interesting example of different concerns and approach of the Chinese prosecutors and legal staff at Shenyang. His affidavit, like those of his colleagues, shows a great deal of attention into his class origin and family background. Born in the same year as Mao, from Fukuoka, with a wife considerably younger than he and several children, Sasa had ties to the colonial project beyond Manchuria: his father had tried his hand at farming in Korea for some years just prior to the 1910 annexation, but had lost everything due to floods and come back to Kyushu.⁶⁰ The tendency of the defendants to consistently amplify their own crimes was a certain reversal of the trend at Tokyo. The sequence of importance seems to be: awareness of crimes, then, awareness of imperialism and its evils. In other words, the convicts seemed quickly to realize that visualizing and performing their own consciousness and feelings of guilt over the crimes was in fact the main exhibition, rather than the crimes themselves.

If this was so, then why would the CPC today so heavily emphasize the crimes, and not the more redeeming features of the trials and subsequent repatriation and clemency of the war criminals? The Chinese government clearly feels it has to protect the perceived legacy not just of Tokyo but also the post-Tokyo trials. The 2014 data dump online and propaganda push was however not the first revival of Shenyang Trials. The 2005 anniversary of the end of the Second World War (or War of Resistance, in the PRC parlance) brought a wave of related official interest and publications. In 2006, the opening of the Chinese Foreign Ministry Archive played a central role in allowing historians to access a fraction of the documents around the trial. Today, the explicit reason behind publishing the Shenyang materials is in part to 'stimulate their use by scholars.'⁶¹

Initially, viewers would find the unsubtle and rather gory public relations strategy towards Japan to be predictably grisly, one quite familiar to viewers of Nanking Massacre propaganda. In one of the first 'confessions,' Chinese and global readers were reminded of the awful limits of wartime

---

⁵⁹ Fushun Center Materials, 87.
⁶⁰ Central Archives, *Written Confessions*. Vol. 1, 448.
⁶¹ Xinhua News Agency, '*Guojia dang'anguanju luxu gongbu 45 ming Riben zhanfan qin-Huaxing zigong*' (National Archives Bureau to publish a series of 45 confessions of Japanese war criminals' illegal acts in invading China) *Nanfang Zhoumo* (Southern Weekend), 7 July 2014. http://www.infzm.com/content/102100 (accessed 1 June 2015).

depredation; it included rape, murder, and even chemical weapons. Yet no one seemed terribly concerned that his confession had been gathered after four years of Soviet captivity and then another four years of Chinese indoctrination. Barak Kushner notes that 'after 15 August 1945, Japan faced thousands of war-crimes trials which flipped the former imperial hierarchy of the region in which China now held a legal upper hand.'[62] But having now assumed control of that upper hand, the Communist Party of China seemed to feel insecure of its position.

It was unclear if the bureaucrats in the Central Ministry of Propaganda in Beijing, in combination with their colleagues in archives, expected the re-release of Shenyang Trials propaganda to move hearts and minds in Japan today, serving a pedagogical function for a Japanese public numbed to any collective memory of atrocities in wartime China. If so, it would not be the first time. In the Ministry of Foreign Affairs archives in the mid-1950s the CPC earnestly worked to guide Japanese press coverage of the prisoners, asking them to write letters home, and to anti-Japanese newspapers. Their trials in 1956 in Shenyang were preceded by half a year of public tours and intensive coaching such that they begged for the death penalty and praised the CPC. Today, the party has brought back the war criminals as a retrospective on the violence of the 15-year war. Treating their affidavits as supplementary to the more extensive Tokyo Trials, and understanding some of the less commented on aspects of those documents, may bring some scholarly value to the enterprise, even as state propaganda resurrects them as national humiliation.

---

[62] Barak Kushner, 'Ghosts of the Japanese Imperial Army: The 'White Group' (Baituan) and Early Post-war Sino–Japanese Relations,' *Past and Present* 218 (2013), 119.

Erratum to: From Tokyo to Khabarovsk: Soviet War Crimes Trials in Asia as Cold War Battlefields

Valentyna Polunina

Erratum to:

K. von Lingen (ed.), *War Crimes Trials in the Wake of Decolonization and Cold War in Asia, 1945–1956*,
https://doi.org/10.1007/978-3-319-42987-8_11

The original version of the book was inadvertently published without incorporating the illustrations 1, 2, and 3. The images have been included in this erratum instead.

The updated online version of this chapter can be found at
https://doi.org/10.1007/978-3-319-42987-8_11

© The Author(s) 2018
K. von Lingen (ed.), *War Crimes Trials in the Wake of Decolonization and Cold War in Asia, 1945–1956*,
https://doi.org/10.1007/978-3-319-42987-8_13

1. General Yamada depicted as a 'fascist plague flea,' Izvestiya, 13 December 1949

2. 'The mysterious disappearance of General Ishii,' Izvestiya, 16 January 1950

3. 'Unfulfilled dreams of Samurai,' Ogoniok, 8 January 1950

НЕОСУЩЕСТВЛЕННЫЕ МЕЧТЫ САМУРАЕВ.
Рисунок Бор. Ефимова

Index

A

Abe Shinzo, 262
affidavits, 35, 65, 128, 158, 188, 261, 262, 264, 271n38, 272, 274–8
Aihara, Kazutana, 157n76
Akutsu Toshi, 158
ALFSEA. *See* Allied Land Forces South East Asia (ALFSEA)
ALFSEA Legal Section, 207
Allied Forces Netherlands East Indies (AFNEI), 196n4
Allied Land Forces South East Asia (ALFSEA), 124n12, 124n13, 181, 196, 199, 207, 213
Annam, 167n1, 184
Anslinger, Harry, 44–8, 47n176, 48n183–5, 49n186
Anti-Fascist People's Freedom League (AFPFL), 120, 127
anti-Japanese sentiment, 268
Asia-Pacific region, 6, 102, 145, 148, 149, 156, 221
atomic bomb, 81
Attlee, Clement, 137
Attorney General Netherlands East Indies, 12, 199, 245
Aung San, 14, 120, 129, 130
Australia, 1, 19, 21n35, 54, 73, 102, 118, 120, 133n49, 147n17, 155, 157, 177, 178, 179n65, 203, 212, 221–38, 273n46
Australian National Archive Canberra (NAC), 147, 159
Australian policy for Japan, 227, 229, 237
Australian prosecution of Japanese war criminals, 226
Axis, 20, 67, 79, 81, 117, 171

B

Bajpai, Girja Shankar, 73, 74
Ba Maw, 12, 14, 119–21
Bataan Death March, 159n85
Batavia/Jakarta, 147n17, 196n2–4, 198, 201, 201n28, 205n45

Note: Page numbers with "n" denote notes.

Bates, M.E., 35
B-class cases, 21n35, 93, 108, 145n8, 151, 152n43, 179n64, 180, 187, 192, 221, 222, 223n3
Beijing/Beiping, 93, 98, 103n52, 109, 261, 262, 267, 272n41, 278
Benders J. G. (Captain), 198, 198n13, 198n15
Bernard, Henri, 53, 61n40
Big Three, 144
biological warfare, 241, 246, 247, 252, 254–8, 275
biological weapons, 240, 246, 247, 249, 254, 255
Brereton, George H. (Commander), 149n25
Britain, 11, 21, 26–8, 28n17, 42, 43, 45, 46, 58, 82–6, 102n43, 119, 120, 147n17, 157, 175, 177, 180–2, 197n6, 234
British Military Administration (Burma), 122
Bujinowski, Anthony (Lieutenant), 155
Bunji Kanto, 154n60
Burma, 6, 9, 12–14, 16, 87, 117–42, 170, 173, 211n58, 225
Burma Independence Army (BIA), 120
Burma National Army (BNA), 120

C

Cabadbaran, 156
Cabanatum P.O.W. Camp, 158
Cambodia, 9, 167n1, 173, 183, 186
camp Bilibid Hospital, 153
camp Davao, 153
camp Nichols Field, 153
camp O'Donnell, 153
Campos, Pilar, 164
Canlubang, Laguna, 159

Capas Bridge (Luzon), 158
Carr, Arthur Comyns, 84
Carter (Colonel), 145n6
C-class cases, 94, 108, 145n8, 150, 151, 152n43, 179n64, 180, 187, 192, 221, 222
Cebu (Philippine province), 165
Celebes (Philippine province), 153n50, 211n59, 216n84, 217n84
Chiang Kai-shek, 20, 100, 100n36, 105, 106, 113, 184, 264, 265, 272
China, 2, 25–50, 54, 73, 93–116, 118, 147, 167, 222, 240, 261
Chinese Criminal Code, 108, 109, 112
Chinese Criminal Law for the Armed Forces, 108
Chinese Nationalist Government, 93, 101, 105n58, 108
Chongqing, 20, 56, 103, 105, 119, 122, 265
Cochinchina, 167n1, 186
Cold War, 1–23, 79, 86, 94, 142, 182, 184, 193, 223, 223n3, 225, 226, 236, 239–60, 266n22, 270n34, 273
collaboration, 11, 14, 52, 54, 56, 57, 59, 61, 63, 64, 67, 87, 119, 121, 126, 129, 129n31, 150, 159n86, 176, 177, 178n60, 182, 190, 197, 201n28, 252, 255, 276
colonialism, 2, 15, 23, 25–50, 89, 94, 95n7, 113, 139, 255
comfort station(s), 150, 155
comfort women, 134, 150, 154, 211n58
Commission on Responsibilities, Versailles, 126
Commission on War Criminals, 104, 104n57

common plan, 110n88, 147
conspiracy, 41, 63, 77, 110n88, 147, 206n47, 266, 272, 275
Control Council Law Number 10, 147
Coup d'état March 1945, 60, 167, 178

D

Damen, B. (Mr.), 196
Davao Penal Colony, 158
death penalty, 15, 33, 94, 108, 161, 163, 165, 192, 200, 205, 205n43, 253, 259, 278
decolonization, 1–23, 69–91, 94, 116, 120, 143, 167–93, 195–222, 223, 225, 241
Decoux, Jean, 173, 175
Decoux–Nishimura agreement, 61
Defence of Burma Act and Rules, 132
De Gaulle, Charles, 56, 64, 170n17, 175
Demaso Advincula, 161n98
district officers (Burma), role in investigation, 126, 127
Dorman-Smith, Sir Reginald, 122
drugs, 6, 25–34, 36, 40, 41–50, 112, 113
Dutch East Indies, 154

E

Europe, 1, 3–7, 60, 101–3, 117, 121, 129, 144, 145, 147–9, 168, 173, 195, 240
Executive Order No 68 (Establishment a National War Crimes Office and Prescribing Rules and Regulations Governing the Trial of Accused War Criminals), 161
Ex Parte Vallandigham, 146n16
extraterritoriality, 15, 16, 93–116

F

Far East, 20, 28, 30, 37, 38, 46, 48, 58, 61, 67, 73, 85, 100, 100n34, 103, 104n56, 122, 149, 149n28, 169, 174, 179n64, 193, 221, 231, 240, 246, 248, 255, 257n62, 258, 261, 263, 271, 273
Far East Advisory Committee, 100, 100n34
Far Eastern and Pacific Sub-Commission, 20, 103, 104n54, 104n56, 122
First Indochina War, 173
First Sino-Japanese War, 99, 108
Force 136, 128
forced prostitution, 150, 151, 154–6, 165, 166
France, 2, 11, 12, 21, 28n17, 40, 51–67, 73, 95n8, 98n18, 102n41, 111n93, 118, 157, 167–75, 169n14, 170n17, 171n24, 177–84, 178n60, 179n65, 186, 193, 222, 245
Franco-Thai border, 60, 62
free China, 56, 103
Free France, 56, 57, 62, 64, 177
French Resistance fighters, 170, 174, 177, 188, 189, 193
Fukunaga Kiyozo, 158
Fuller, Stuart, 31–4, 41–9
Fushun (city, PRC), 262, 270, 273, 273n45, 275, 276

G

Gascoigne, Alvary, 84
Geneva Convention on the conduct of warfare, 101
Germany, 4, 11, 53, 56, 59, 60, 99, 100n32, 102, 124, 144n4, 147–50, 149n28, 168, 170, 170n18, 172, 184, 207, 240n5, 247, 249, 250n39, 255, 273

Gledhill, Alan, 16, 16n28, 132, 132n46, 132n47
Golunsky, Sergey, 243
Gorshenin, Konstantin, 249–51
Goto Shimpei, 41
Great Britain, 21, 58, 84, 147n17, 157, 177, 180–2
Grew, Joseph C, 36
Guam, 1, 149, 150, 150n37, 151n38, 158
Guangzhou, 93, 181
Guerrero, Cesar Marie (Bishop), 159n86
Guomindang, 20, 44, 119, 263, 265, 268, 271, 276
Guomindang/Kuomintang, 20, 44, 119, 256, 263, 265, 268, 271, 276
Guomindang trials of collaborators/ hanjian, 20, 119, 263, 265, 268, 271, 276

H

Hague Convention on Respecting the Laws and Customs of War on Land, 109
Haïphong, 60, 62, 64, 174, 174n36
Hajime Ainoda, 163n108
Hankou, 93
Hanoi, 174, 174n36, 185, 190
Haruda, 159n84
Hatta, Mohammad, 211
Hegel, Georg Wilhelm Friedrich, 72, 72n8, 88, 88n68
heiho, 201n26, 211n58, 212n63
Helmick, Milton J., 106
Henson, Maria Rosa, 150n34, 155n69
Hideichi Nakamura, 164n117, 165, 165n122, 165n124
Hideo Tanaka, 161n98, 164n116, 164n118

high commission, 59, 64, 83, 84n50, 176n51, 185
high commission, Saigon, 59, 64, 185
HikotaroTajima (Lieutenant General), 154
Hindu Law, 77, 81, 88
Hirohito, 241, 255, 267, 274
Ho Chi Minh, 168
Homma, Masaharu (Lieutenant General), 153, 153n54, 161, 166n126
Hoo Chi-Tsai (Victor), 33, 45
Hoog Militair Gerechtshof van Nederlands Indië (Supreme Military Court for the Netherlands Indies), 201
Hoshino Naoki, 31, 154n60
Hsipaw (Thibaw), 125
Hukbalahap (the Nation's Army against the Japanese Soldiers, Philippin Communist guerrilla movement), 159n83
Hung Chi Shan Tang, 35

I

Ichikawa Seigi, Major, 133, 134
ICWC (International Research and Documentation Centre War Crimes Trials, Marburg, Germany), 152n43, 155n61, 165, 183, 204
Imamura, Hisamitsu, 154n60
IMTFE. *See* International Military Tribunal for the Far East (IMTFE)
India, 9, 26, 28n17, 40, 54, 69–91, 102, 102n43, 119, 124, 130, 133, 136n60, 139, 177, 179n65, 225, 244, 245
Indian National Army, 84, 130
Indochina, French, 11, 51, 52, 62, 173, 174n36, 175, 185

INDEX   283

Indonesia, 9, 10, 13, 14, 87, 90, 170, 173, 197n8, 210, 211n58, 212n63, 215n75, 217n88, 219, 225
Indonesian independence, 198, 199, 212n63, 216
Indonesian struggle for independence, 195, 199
International Committee of the Red Cross, 101, 132n44, 136n60
International Law Commission, 87, 89
International Military Tribunal for the Far East (IMTFE), 2, 6, 7, 11, 16, 18, 19, 27, 51–67, 69, 74, 80, 93, 113, 134, 168, 179, 221, 231, 240, 241, 241n8, 246, 256, 261, 263, 265n14, 271n38, 273n45
International Military Tribunal for the Far East, Soviet criticism of, 63
International Military Tribunal for the Far East, Soviet delegation, 113, 241
International Military Tribunal (IMT)/ Nuremberg Tribunal, 19, 54, 63, 108, 110, 110n88, 240, 258
International Peace Campaign, 100, 100n36
International Prosecution Section (IPS), 54, 263
internment camps, Burma, 124, 211n28
Ishii Shiro, 19, 254, 256–8, 267
Ivan Zaryanov, 243
Iwasaki Masutaro, 158
Iwataka Kenji, 158

J

Jackson, Robert Houghwout, 149, 149n30
Saintt James's Declaration, 102, 177
Japan, 1, 26, 51, 73, 93–143, 167, 189–90, 195, 221–39, 261
Japanese Surrendered Personnel (JSP), 131, 131n43, 136n60, 214, 214n72, 215n75, 217
Japanese war criminals, Soviet prosecution of, 66, 274
Jaranilla, Delfin, 53
Java, 8, 123, 196n4, 197, 197n6, 197n8, 201, 210, 211n58, 211n59, 212, 212n63, 213, 213n66, 213n70, 214, 214n72, 215n75, 215n77, 216, 216n80, 216n82, 217n84
Jinan, 93, 109
Jiro Mizoguchi, 154n60
Judge Advocate General (JAG), 133, 146, 146n15, 148, 150, 152, 154, 155, 160, 161, 163

K

Kōain (Asia Development Board), 33, 40
Kalagon, 133–5, 137
Kalaw, 124
Katju, Kailash Nath, 85
Katsuyoshi Taninaka, 161n98
Kawane Yoshikata, 159n85
Keenan, Joseph B., 54, 61, 79, 80, 83, 244, 263, 264
Kenichi, Sone, 147
Kenpeitai, 23, 207
Khabarovsk Trials, 240–3, 246–59, 267
Khalkhin-gol River, 244
Kimura Heitarō (General), 134
Kin Ryu Rin, 53
Kiyoshi Nishikawa, 153
Koike, 159n84

Koninkrijk Nederlandsch-Indisch Leger (KNIL) / Royal Netherlands Indies Army, 199, 211n58, 219
Kono, Takeshi (Lieutenant General), 153
Koo, Ji Kyuin/Ku Wei-chiun (Wellington), 44
Korea, 11, 18–20, 22, 31, 36, 41, 42, 79, 87, 118, 206, 222, 225, 230, 234, 235, 237, 238, 258, 273, 275, 277
Korean and Formosan war criminals, Allied legal position on their nationality, 223, 224, 227, 234
Korean and Formosan war criminals, Japanese position on their nationality, 223, 224, 227, 234
Korean and Formosan war criminals, numbers of, 234
Korean government, negotiations with Australian government over war criminals, 227, 234–6, 238
Koreans, 10, 11, 23, 34, 129, 198, 223, 225, 230, 232–4, 236, 238
Korean war, 258, 259, 265n16, 269, 273
Kruglov, Sergei, 249, 250, 250n39, 251
Kudo, Chushiro, 163n111
Kuroda Shigenori, 107n74, 166n126
Kwantung Army, 17, 31, 42, 240, 244, 245, 247, 248

L

Laming, Lt Col. R.C., 133
Lang Són, 62, 63, 65
Laos, 9, 167n1, 173, 174, 183
Lauterpacht, Hersch, 79
laws and usages of war, 202, 202n32
League of Nations Advisory Committee on the Trafficking of Opium and Other Drugs (Opium Advisory Committee or OAC), 26
Commission of Enquiry into Opium between 19, 29–30, 43
Liang Yunli, 102, 103
Lieutenant-Governor General Netherlands East Indies, 198n12, 200
London, 4, 5n10, 73n11, 83, 102, 102n42, 103, 104n53, 133, 140, 141, 144, 147n17, 177, 178, 195n1
London International Assembly (LIA), 5n10, 102, 102n42, 109, 195n1
Lopez, Pedro, 53
Lord Admiral Mountbatten, Louis, 121, 130, 132, 196, 211, 211n59, 212, 214n75
Luzon (Philippine province), 153, 157, 159
Luzon Prisoner Camp No. 1 (Philippines), 157

M

MacArthur, Douglas (General), 48, 57, 58, 85, 86, 122, 148, 148n22, 157, 159n83, 179, 179n65, 197n6, 211, 244, 254, 265n16, 269n31
Maeda Kazuo, 158
Malaya, trials in, 4, 13, 123, 124, 136, 141
Manchukuo, 15, 17, 19, 30–2, 36–8, 40, 40n120, 43, 44, 46, 95, 113, 118, 120, 262, 265n14, 267, 267n27, 274
Mandalay, 124, 136
Manila, 8, 107n72, 133, 143–66
Manila massacre, 131, 133, 135, 144

INDEX 285

Manus Island, 223, 227–9, 233
Mao Zedong, 264, 265n15
Marburg, 152n43, 155n61, 165, 204
Marshall, George Catlett (Major General), 145, 146
Masami Fujimoto, 154n60
Masuoka, Kensichi, 163n114
Matsuoka-Henry agreement, 59, 61
Matsuzaki, Hideichi, 164n118
Maymyo (Pyin U Lwin), 124, 136, 138
McClish, Ernest Edward (Lieutenant Colonel), 156n70
Mei Ru'ao, 264
Mendiola, Nocholasa P., 151n38
Menon, V. K. Krishna, 83, 84
Mexican War, 146n15
Michinori Nakamura, 153n50
MikoTaneichi, 154n60
military brothels, 155
military commission (MC), 106, 144, 145–52, 146n15, 147n19, 148n20, 150n37, 153n54, 154, 156, 157, 161–6
Military Government Courts, 147n19, 170n18
military tribunals, 1, 2, 25, 54, 64, 121, 168, 170, 170n18, 176, 176n47, 182–92, 240, 258
Mindanao (Philippine province), 156
Mitsuji Tanaka, 154
Mongolia, 9, 244
Morimoto Iichiro, 158
Mori Shigeji, 158
Moscow Declaration, 144, 144n4
Moulmein, 124, 124n13, 128, 131, 133, 133n51, 137
Mountbatten, Lord Louis, 121, 130, 132, 196, 211, 211n59, 212, 214n75
Mukden incident, 99, 148
Mullemeister, J. Ph. (Mr.), 196, 196n4, 198n15

Muslims, in Burma, 133, 135
Myitkyina, 124

N

Nanjing, 20, 93, 105n58, 109, 113, 265, 266
Naoki Hamasaki, 154n60
Nationalist Chinese government, negotiations with Australian government over war criminals, 223, 227, 229
natural law, 70, 78–80
Nazi leadership, 19, 81
Nazi war criminals, Soviet prosecution of, 240
Nehru, Jawaharlal, 70, 83, 85, 85n58, 85n59, 86, 90
Netherlands, 2, 5n5, 6, 10, 12, 21, 28n17, 40, 54, 58, 73, 95, 98n18, 102n43, 118, 124, 147n17, 157, 177, 179n65, 195–220, 222, 226, 245, 273n46
Netherlands East Indies (NEI), 195–220
Netherlands East Indies Penal Code, 202n29
Netherlands Forces Intelligence Service (NEFIS), 197, 197n6
Netherlands Indies Civil Administration (NICA) / Allied Military Administration-Civil Affairs Branch (AMACAB), 197, 213n66
Netherlands War Crimes Investigation Team (NWCIT), 198, 198n15
Neutrality Pact, 239n1, 245
Niceto Sanchez, 161n98
Nichols Airfield (Bataan), 158
Nicholson, M.R., 30, 33–5, 45, 46, 46n168
Nimitz, Chester W. (Admiral), 144

Nobusuke, Kishi, 267
Noel-Baker, Philip, 84, 84n55
Noguchi Unit, 206
Nomonhan. *See* Khalkhin-gol River
Nuremberg, 4n5, 4n9, 19, 53, 63, 76n19, 83, 108, 110–12, 148, 148n20, 149n30, 179n65, 209, 240, 241, 241n7, 243, 243n13, 244, 248
Nuremberg Charter, 111, 112, 209
Nurembert Trial. *See* International Military Tribunal

O

OAC. *See* Opium Advisory Committee (OAC)
Occupation of Japan, 226, 227, 230, 263n8, 267
Occupation of Japan, Reverse Course, 226, 227
Okamoto Hitoshi, 158
Okmulgee (Oklahoma, US), 156n70
Okubo Matsuo, 158
Oneto, Robert, 51–67, 186n91
opium
   opium monopoly, 31, 32, 35–7, 43
   opium wars, 26, 96, 112
Opium Advisory Committee (OAC), 26, 28, 28n17, 29, 30, 33, 34, 43, 43n139, 43n141, 44–7, 49
outer islands, 197n8, 201, 201n59, 213n67, 214, 215n75, 216n80

P

Pacific, 1, 6, 8, 20–2, 53, 67, 96, 102, 103, 104n54, 104n56, 118, 122, 123, 145–9, 156, 177, 198, 211, 221–4, 226, 237, 239, 240
Pacific islands, 1, 158
Pacific War, 14, 16–21, 106n66, 173, 202, 202n29, 236, 240

Pal, Radhabinod, 16, 41, 57, 63, 63n47, 70, 72, 74, 75, 75n18, 76, 76n20, 77, 77n23, 78–85, 87n63, 88, 88n64, 88n65, 89, 89n69, 90
Panyushkin, Alexander, 257
Paris Peace Conference's Commission of Responsibilities of the Authors of the War and on Enforcement of Penalties, 203
Patrick, Lord William, 83, 84
Pearl Harbor, 4, 16, 17, 64, 152
Pechkoff, Zinovi, 51, 52, 58, 58n27, 61, 61n37, 66n58, 67, 67n61
pemuda, 213
Peoples Court, 159n86
People's Republic of China, 2, 19, 86, 113, 241, 246, 250, 254, 261, 266
Permanent Military Tribunal Saigon, 64, 167n2, 176n47, 184–5
Pétain, Philippe,
Philippine National Archive, 162
Philippines
   Philippine forces, 144
   Philippine National War Crimes Office, 145
   Philippines Republic, 2, 6, 9, 12–14, 37, 53, 54, 73, 107, 118, 119, 122, 124, 133, 143–66, 175, 179n65, 222, 244
Philippines-Ryukyus Command (PHILRYCOM), 160, 161
Piccigallo, Robert, 156n72, 158, 162n105
Pikit Cotabato (Mindanao), 158
political trial, 239, 242
Potsdam Conference, 144, 180n68, 243
Pound, Roscoe, 106, 106n67
prisoner of war (POW), 123, 124, 132, 133, 145, 152, 153, 159, 200n22, 201, 206, 207, 212, 225n9, 234, 236

propaganda, 9, 12, 17, 35, 40, 60, 97n16, 135, 143, 239, 241–3, 246, 249, 252–9, 261–78
Propaganda, Soviet, 241, 246, 257
Prosecution Division Philippine, 157
Provisional Government of the French Republic, 170, 172
Purge trial. *See* Political trial
Pu Yi, 42, 267, 267n27, 274, 274n49

Q
Q-forms, 128

R
Rangoon (Yangon), 8, 87, 88n64, 120, 124, 124n33, 127n23, 131–3, 133n51, 136–8, 141
Rangoon Jail , 132, 136, 141
Recovery of Allied Prisoners of War and Internees (RAPWI), 213
Regeringsbureau tot Nasporing van Oorlogsmisdrijven (Government Bureau for the Investigation of War Crimes), 198
Release of war criminals, 232n31
Renborg, Bertil A, 36
René Cassin, 170
repatriation, 132n43, 134, 198, 211n58, 212n63, 214n75, 215n75, 224, 228, 229, 233, 234, 236, 238, 277
Repatriation of war criminals to Japan, 53n4, 128, 131n43, 134, 139, 198, 211, 211n58, 212n63, 214n75, 224, 227, 229, 233, 238
Republican legal system, 298
Republic of China, 2, 19, 86, 93–116, 241, 246, 250, 254, 261, 264, 266
Röling, B. V. A., 83, 83n47
Rōmusha, 9, 211n58

Roxas, Manuel (President of the Philippines), 160, 161
Royal Warrant, 118, 118n2, 127n17
Russell, Thomas W (Russell Pasha), 46

S
Sadeo Kaneda, 165
Safonov, Grigori, 249, 250
Saigon, 55n14, 58–60, 64, 155, 167–94
Saigon Military Court, 168, 176, 185, 188, 189, 193
Saito (Major), 153
Sakai Takashi, 110
Samuel T. Shinohara, 144n5, 150, 151n38
San Francisco Peace Treaty, 86, 223, 226, 231
Sangking, 153n50
San Jose (Mindoro), 158
Sawada Shigeru, 62
SEAC. *See* South East Asia Command (SEAC)
Second Sino-Japanese War, 94, 100, 109, 112
Seiichi Onishi, 154n60
Senn, Ernest, 101
Shanghai, 16, 27, 30, 33–5, 42, 93, 96n9, 105n60, 106, 109, 115, 116, 190, 263, 263n8
Shanxi Province (North China), 150, 273
Shenyang, 20, 93, 261–78
Shenyang Trials, 261–78
Shiomi Tasashige, 158
Shizuo Yokoyama (Lieutenant General), 46, 159n84, 161, 163
Show trial. *See* Political trial
Singapore, 125, 126, 128, 137, 141, 173, 179, 181, 190, 196, 198, 198n13, 199, 223n5, 226, 227

Sino-American Commercial Treaty, 106
Sino-American Military Service Agreement, 105
Smirnov, Lev, 247, 247n23, 247n24, 248n29, 249n32, 250, 255n56
Social Welfare Society for Residents of Great Korea, 230
Soemu Toyoda, 147n17
South East Asia Command (SEAC), 7, 11, 121–3, 125, 126, 128–30, 133, 133n48, 136, 140, 195, 210, 211, 211n59, 212, 214, 215
South West Pacific Area (SWPA) Command, 122, 211
Soviet government, negotiations with American government over war criminals, 269n31
Soviet, Policy for Japan, 20, 239, 242, 246n22, 258
Soviet Union, 2, 11, 17, 19–21, 79, 86, 179n65, 239–41, 245, 247, 250, 250n39, 251, 253, 254, 256–8, 262, 267, 269, 271, 273, 275, 276
Soviet, War crimes trials, 239–60
Soviet, War crimes trials policy, 242, 246, 258
Spain, 98n18, 164
Spoor, Simon Hendrik, 197n6, 197n10, 210n56, 216
Staatsblad van Nederlandsch-Indië (Statute Book of the Netherlands Indies), 197, 203n38, 205n43
Stalinist trial. *See* Political trial
Stalin, Josef, 243, 246, 249, 250, 250n39, 253
Standard of 'Civilization', 96, 108
Sturrock, A. M. (Lt Col), 133
subaltern studies, 72
Sugamo Prison (Tokyo), 18, 157n77, 163, 192, 222, 223, 227, 231, 267, 273, 273n46

Sukarno, 14, 211
Sumatra, 121, 196n4, 197, 197n6, 197n8, 201, 201n40, 213
Supreme Commander for the Allied Powers (SCAP), 7, 80, 145, 155, 162, 179n65
suspect lists, Burma, 119, 122, 123, 125–30, 132, 136
Suzuki Keiji, 120

T
Tadashi Yoshida, 154n60
Taipei, 93, 109
Taiwanese, 19, 41, 43, 93, 94n2, 95n6, 129, 227, 229, 230, 232
Taiwan/Formosa, 18, 19, 34–8, 41–3, 94, 118, 198, 206, 221–38, 265n16, 268
Taiwan Youth Cultural Association, 229
Taiyuan, 20, 93, 255n58, 262, 268, 268n29, 269n33, 276
Takao Fujimoto, 165n121
Takasaki Iku, 158
Tanaka Hisakazu, 109, 109n85
Tatsumosuke Ueda, 163n108
Tavoy, 124
TCM. *See* temporary courts martial (TCM)
temporary courts martial (TCM), 196n4, 199–201, 202n32, 202n33, 203, 218, 220
testimony, 33, 35, 62, 67, 122, 126, 136, 245, 265n14
Thailand, 61, 118, 120, 122
Thailand-Burma Railway, 9, 14, 122, 124, 125, 133, 135
Thakins, 120
The International Commission for Penal Reform and Development, 195
Tiger Unit, 153

Tōjō Hideki, 61n41, 62, 62n44, 264, 272
Tokkeitai, 202, 202n33, 206, 206n47, 207, 208, 208n50
Tokyo Trial. *See* International Military Tribunal for the Far East
Tomoyuki Yamashita (General), 133, 134n55, 146, 151, 153, 154n60, 161
Tonkin, 60, 167, 186
Tosimitsu Miyagi, 154n60
tripartite alliance, 59
Truman, Harry S., 244
Tsuneoka Noburo, 164n116, 164n118
Tsuneyoshi Yoshio, 158
Tumalon, Antonie, 161n98

U
Unit 731, 19, 243n12, 252, 266, 275
United Nations War Crimes Commission (UNWCC), 4, 5, 5n10, 7, 20, 53, 96, 101–5, 101n41, 102n42, 102n46, 104n53, 104n56, 109, 110n89, 111, 111n94, 112, 121, 122, 126n20, 127, 129, 130, 144, 145, 147n19, 154n60, 158, 159n86, 170n18, 175, 177–80, 186, 195, 196, 202n29, 202n32, 203, 203n35, 209n51, 210n54
United States, 2, 3, 11–3, 16, 17–19, 21, 22, 25–8, 30, 32, 33, 36, 39, 43–5, 47–50, 52, 54, 56–8, 61, 65, 73, 73n11, 75n18, 79–81, 95, 97, 97n12, 97n14, 98n13, 102n45, 103–7, 105n60, 111n93, 114n108, 118, 143, 144–61, 163–7, 177, 178, 179n65, 180–2, 192, 196, 203, 212, 222, 230, 232, 241, 243–7, 249, 254–5, 260, 268, 269, 273, 273n46
United States Court for China, 106
US Military Commission, 106, 144, 145
USSR. *See* Soviet Union

V
Vichy, 11, 52, 54, 54n8, 56, 56n19, 58, 59n31, 172, 173, 173n33, 173n34, 174n35, 175, 177, 185
Victors' Justice, 7, 7n15, 52n1, 66, 75n19
Viet Minh, 59, 168, 172–4, 176, 176n50, 182, 184, 186, 191, 193
Vietnam, 8–11, 13, 56, 56n17, 56n18, 57n20, 57n21, 122n7, 167n1, 168, 168n4, 168n5, 172, 174, 180n68, 183, 185, 186, 192

W
Wang Chonghui, 103, 103n52, 111, 111n91
war crime, definition for investigation purposes, 7, 10–12, 21, 103–5, 124n12, 124n13, 125n15, 126, 128, 128n27, 131, 133, 145, 148, 149, 159, 175–9, 181–3, 186, 187, 193, 195, 196, 196n4, 197n10, 198, 198n13, 200n22, 202, 204, 225
War Crimes Branch of the Allied Headquarters, 179
War Crimes Investigating Detachment, 145
War Crimes Investigation Teams (WCIT), 125n15, 126, 133, 196n4, 197n10

War Crimes Office (Service Fédéral des Crimes de Guerre), 47, 47n180, 48, 145, 149, 161, 175, 178n59
War Crimes Ordinance of 28 August 1944, 170–2
War Crimes Registry, 181, 196
War Crimes Trials Regulation, 108, 108n76, 114, 115
War of Resistance (Second Sino-Japanese War), 262, 264, 268, 277
War-time Crimes (Exemption) Act, 130, 130n36
Washington Arms Conference, 98
Webb, William, 37, 65, 80, 83, 225, 244
Wedemeyer, Albert Coady (Lieutenant General), 106, 148n21
Wellington Koo, 44, 46, 48, 100, 102, 103, 103n49, 110
Western Allies, 5, 22, 94, 112, 115, 148, 242, 243
West, Major Willis A., 107, 107n71
Wunsz King, 103
WWII (World War Two), 1, 2n1, 4, 5, 7n16, 10, 14, 21n35, 22, 52n1, 76n20, 77, 79, 81, 93, 95n6, 106n64, 107n72, 117, 124n14, 127, 129n31, 131n43, 135n56, 141, 143–66, 169–72, 173n32, 174n35, 174n36, 176n47, 177, 179n65, 182, 188, 193, 195, 211n58, 223, 224, 239, 251, 254, 274n47, 277

X

Xiang Zhejun, 113
Xie Guansheng, 106
Xuzhou, 93, 109

Y

Yalta, 144, 243
Yamada Otozō, 247, 248, 252, 275, 275n53
Yamaguchi, Masakazu, 154n60
Yamawaki Hifumi, 137
Yap, Carmon, 165
Yasuji Okamura, 265, 265n15, 265n16, 271
Yasuo Hiroshi, 154
Yokio Ogo, 154n60
Yokohama trials, 154, 156–8, 159n85, 160, 161, 179

Z

zaibatsu, 245
Zhou Enlai, 268, 268n28, 269, 271, 272n41

The manufacturer's authorised representative in the EU is Springer Nature Customer Service Centre GmbH, Europaplatz 3, 69115 Heidelberg, Germany. If you have any concerns regarding our products, please contact ProductSafety@springernature.com

Printed and bound by CPI Group (UK) Ltd, Croydon, CR0 4YY
23/03/2026
02076735-0013